Psychoanalytic-Marxism

PSYCHOANALYTIC-MARXISM
Groundwork

Eugene Victor Wolfenstein

Free Association Books/London/1993

FAB *'an association in which the free development of
each is the condition of the free development of all'*

THE GUILFORD PRESS
New York   London

Published in Great Britain in 1993 by
Free Association Books
26 Freegrove Road
London N7 9RQ

The right of Eugene Victor Wolfenstein to be identified
as author of this work has been asserted by him in accordance
with the Copyright, Designs and Patents Act 1988.

Printed in the United States in 1993 by
The Guilford Press
A Division of Guilford Publications, Inc.
72 Spring Street
New York, NY 10012

Printed in the United States of America

This book is printed on acid-free paper.

Last digit is print number: 9 8 7 6 5 4 3 2 1

Part of Chapter 4 originally appeared in the *International Review
of Psycho-Analysis* (1990), *17*, 23–45. © Institute of Psycho-Analysis.
Part of Chapter 9 originally appeared in the *International Journal
of Psycho-Analysis* (1985), *66*, 77–94. © Institute of Psycho-Analysis.
The figure on page 129 originally appeared in *Melanie Klein and
Critical Social Theory* by C. F. Alford (1989). © Yale University Press.

A British CIP catalogue record for this book is available from
the British Library.
ISBN 1-85343-192-3

Library of Congress Cataloging-in-Publication Data

Wolfenstein, Eugene Victor.
    Psychoanalytic-Marxism: groundwork / Eugene Victor Wolfenstein.
       p.   cm.
    Includes bibliographical references and index.
    ISBN 0-89862-137-2 (hardcover). — ISBN 0-89862-590-4 (pbk.)
    1. Communism and psychoanalysis. I. Title.
HX550.P77W65 1993
335.43′01′9—dc20   92-44212
                                                               CIP

For Judy

Preface

The present inquiry is a companion volume to *The Victims of Democracy: Malcolm X and the Black Revolution*, although I hope it is intelligible in itself. Both volumes are concerned with the development and articulation of psychoanalytic-marxism. *Victims*, however, is historical, while this is heuristic merely.

The two books are quite different in form. In *Victims* I attempted to represent and conceptualize a social life-world, constellated around the narrative of Malcolm's life. The form reflected the continuity of historical time and the interpenetration of historical events. Here I emphasize the discontinuity of the exposition, and this for three reasons. First, the subject matter of the inquiry is extremely broad. It is not treated exhaustively, if such a thing were possible, but only in outline. Second, I am working with a body of theoretical material characterized in good part by a desire for system and the totalization of concepts. I am partly in sympathy with this desire, partly wary of its tendency to eventuate in dogmatism. Third, the concepts developed in the text stand at a certain remove from empirical reality. Gaps are left in the exposition to acknowledge, in all three regards, its incomplete nature.

Although in writing this book I found myself attempting to sum up a quarter-century of work on the problematics of psychoanalytic-marxism, the result is anything but a last word or definitive statement. It was written at a specific time and in a specific state of mind, with the aim of hewing a psychoanalytic-marxist path between Hegelianism, which has come to stand for the Enlightenment and the totalized rationality of modernity, on the one hand, and the disintegrative trends of postmodernism, on the other. The recurrent concern with the classical antinomy of the One and the Many, also Identity and Difference, reflects this discursive situation.

Speaking of Hegelianism: It should be acknowledged at the outset that Hegel plays a major role in the inquiry, and that his presence creates discursive difficulties. From my perspective, however, these difficulties are unavoidable. For one thing, the project of psychoanalytic-marxism is tied to a dialectical conception of reason, and Hegel is the master teacher of dialectics. For another, his articulation of the problematics of recognition in the fourth chapter of *The Phenomenology of Spirit* has been important in the development of psychoanalytic-marxist theory; and I hope to show that these problematics retain their interpretive significance in our own time.

Yet as the form of the inquiry suggests, there is nothing in this work resembling Hegel's Absolute Spirit or, for that matter, Descartes' *cogito*— no first principle that resolves all skeptical doubts and from which all other certainties proceed. But a simple idea does play a rather important role: Uncertainty generates anxiety; anxiety results in psychic defense and distortions of consciousness. If this were to be a first principle, it would be precisely anti-Hegelian and anti-Cartesian.

*   *   *   *   *

My thanks to Janice Haaken and Robert Young for reading and criticizing the manuscript; to Peter Wissoker and Judith Grauman for editorial guidance; to Michael Landis for computer assistance with the diagrams; and to my students at UCLA, who have done me the great favor of working with me on psychoanalytic-marxist issues for the past twenty-five or more years.

Contents

Psychoanalytic-Marxism

Of All Possible Worlds
We Only Have One . . .

The present project is to construct a groundwork for a psychoanalytic-marxist theory.[1] It arises from an interest in human emancipation. Given the lateness of the hour, linking this theoretical project to this practical interest may seem problematical. There are those, after all, who think that psychoanalysis and Marxism are out of date. Because a psychoanalytic-marxist theory can only be of interest if there is something of value in Marxism and psychoanalysis considered separately, I will begin these introductory remarks by discussing certain of the skeptical doubts that have arisen concerning the historical relevance of the two theories. I will then proceed to discuss the desirability, possibility, and difficulty of a psychoanalytic-marxist theory. Finally, I will outline the course of the inquiry and indicate its limits.

These remarks, I might add, really are just that, remarks. In them I touch lightly upon topics that will be taken up more fully later on. They will have performed their function satisfactorily if they serve to distinguish the road ahead from the ones not taken.

A. Psychoanalysis and Marxism

1.

Here is a way of broaching the issue. One of the characters in Doris Lessing's *The Golden Notebook* writes a short novel in which an Algerian soldier (a member of the F. L. N.) was assigned the task of torturing a French prisoner. The two men—secretly—begin to talk to each other. The

Algerian, a farmer, was persistently aware "that what he felt about life was not what he was expected to feel" by "*them*," whoever they might be (Lessing, 1963, p. 549). The Frenchman, a young intellectual, complained to his torturer that he "was in an intellectual prison-house": "He recognised, had recognised for years, that he never had a thought, or an emotion, that didn't instantly fall into pigeonholes, one marked 'Marx' and one marked 'Freud.'" The Algerian felt he ought to be envious of the Frenchman. The Frenchman was actually envious of the Algerian: "He wished that that just once, just once in his life, he felt or willed something that was his own, spontaneous, undirected, not willed on him by Grandfathers Freud and Marx" (*ibid.*).

The two men were overheard by the commanding officer. He ordered them to be executed. They were "shot together, on the hillside, with the sun rising in their faces, side by side, the next morning" (*ibid.*, p. 550).

What is the moral of the story?

First, there is the attitude of the French intellectual. He finds Marxism and psychoanalysis oppressive. He thinks and feels through them; they constitute an orthodoxy that robs him of spontaneity. He wishes nothing more than to be rid of them. He is a psychoanalytic-marxist *malgré lui* and, we might add, a postmodernist ahead of his time. If he were not about to die in Algeria, he would live to be a deconstructionist in Paris. From his standpoint the project of this book is precisely wrong-headed.

Nor is the attitude of the Algerian any more encouraging. He doesn't envy the prisoner his European sophistication. He appears to live outside all intellectual prison-houses. Yet he is not a free thinker. He only knows himself as other or alien, as what "they" are not. He lacks the categories of self-recognition, and grandfathers Marx and Freud fail to provide them.

It might seem, in other words, that psychoanalysis and Marxism have sunk into either orthodoxy or irrelevancy. Unlike the Nietzschean madman who announces the death of God too early, the psychoanalytic-marxist articulates a vision of human emancipation too late.

2.

Let's start again. Two young men are struggling to know themselves and each other. They are talking freely, as equals. They have momentarily forgotten their assigned roles—forgotten that one of them is there to be the torturer, the other the tortured. Consequently they are executed.

We are here presented with a story within a story. Like a dream within a dream, it may be taken as a representation of reality, or of more than one reality. On the one hand, it represents the agony of war, specifically of the Algerian struggle for national liberation; on the other, it represents a psychical reality, a situation of mental torture. Its narrative impact depends upon the conjuncture, or the fusion, of these two dimensions of human experience.

No theory is needed to reveal the suffering the story signifies. Indeed, social theories can be used to defend us from the immediacy of such experiences, to distance us from them by reducing them to mere instances or examples, by reifying them as concepts and categories. And not just social theories: It is likewise a denial of reality to treat torture as a metaphor, execution as a discourse, death as a text.

Nonetheless, it is necessary to learn from experience, especially when the experience is one of suffering. We must interpret the world in order to change it. The question then becomes, how are we to understand the experience of the two young men in the story? What theory or theories facilitate the interpretation and transformation of situations characterized by human suffering?

The question does not entail a psychoanalytic-marxist answer. It may be that there are better ways of answering it. It might even be the case that psychoanalytic-marxism is not a viable alternative—that, as Lessing implies, it is more the disease than the cure. But whatever doubts there may be about the answer(s), I do not see how it is possible to doubt the importance of the question. In any case, it provides the standard by which I hope the value of the present inquiry will be judged.

3.

Here is another approach to the issue. If we lived in the best of all possible worlds—if nothing further needed to be done or, alternatively, could be done to enlarge the realm of human freedom—then a situationally transformational interest in human emancipation would be nonsensical. I take it as given, however, that we don't live in such a world, that the realm of human freedom can be and ought to be enlarged.

The question then is, are Marxism and psychoanalysis, either singly or in combination, relevant to a practical emancipatory interest? The question can be and has been answered in the negative. First, it has been argued that neither Marxism nor psychoanalysis are or were emancipatory, that both function as instrumentalities of social control or even domination. Second, there are those who argue that the emancipatory impetus of the two is exhausted. Marxism and psychoanalysis interpret a world that no longer exists. New categories and concepts are required if we are to understand and act effectively in our present situation.

These arguments cannot be dismissed out of hand. Let's consider them, briefly, in turn.

The first argument has some empirical validity. We have witnessed Marxism used to justify tyranny and psychoanalysis used as an ideology of conformity and adjustment. These have not, however, been their only uses. Marxism has also functioned as a mediation of emancipatory political practices, and, at least in many instances, clinical psychoanalysis remains true to the aim of enlarging the patient's domain of psychical freedom. It is not unrealistic or unempirical to characterize each of them as an emancipatory praxis. Moreover, I have never seen it convincingly argued that domination is built into—is a necessary or intrinsic feature of—either Marxism or psychoanalysis. It is rather the case that these arguments fail to distinguish between the praxis and the perversion of the praxis. No doubt such perversion is possible, as I have already acknowledged; and it is important to analyze the conditions under which, for example, Marxism becomes Stalinism or psychoanalysis becomes a conformist ego psychology. A physician would not stay in practice very long, however, if s/he failed to distinguish between health and illness.

The second argument is more serious. As the twentieth century draws to a close, we live in a world that differs radically from the one that existed when it began. We would be placing ourselves at a disadvantage if we were to look at twenty-first-century realities through nineteenth-century lenses. Likewise, if we were to treat Marx's and Freud's texts as a canon and confuse social analysis with scriptural exegesis, then we really would be condemning ourselves to irrelevancy. It does not follow, however, that Marxism and psychoanalysis are the private property of antiquarians and hagiographers.

We might think of it this way. In the famous preface to the 1859 *A Critique of Political Economy* Marx argues that at a "certain stage of their development, the material productive forces of society come into conflict with the existing relations of production . . ." (Marx, 1859, p. 4). In the twentieth century we have experienced an unprecedented development of forces of production, a growth in productive capability so great that existing relations of production have indeed become irrational—ecologically irrational. When the century began, the human species could only place finite demands against (what seemed to be) an infinite natural supply. Malthusianism aside, there were no projected limits to economic development. The political question was, who—which social classes, which nations—would benefit from the indefinite expansion of material production? Now, however, the human species places effectively infinite demands upon a demonstrably finite natural supply. From an ecological perspective unlimited growth is the problem, not the solution.

The political question becomes, must material well-being be sacrificed to planetary survival and, if so, whose well-being? Alternatively, will we be able to turn the necessity of ecological rationality to our *mutual* advantage? Finally, will we fail to heed the ecological imperative, bring ourselves to the point of extinction, and (at a minimum) render all pro-gressivist projects obsolete?

Here we have a dialectical inversion, a counterthrust as Hegel would say, and with a vengeance. We are in an historically novel situation. We must learn to think and act in ways that are appropriate to it. This does not mean, however, that we must begin from scratch. Beginning from scratch is, in fact, literally unthinkable. It can't be done. Moreover, the world has not been reborn. In important respects it might even be true that the more things change, the more they stay the same. Even Plato and the Buddha might have something to teach us about living and liv-ing well in the years to come. But let's stay closer to home. The issue in our present undertaking is this: Do Marxism and psychoanalysis still enable us to articulate problems for ourselves that we are interested in solving, and do they help us to solve them?

It is not appropriate to attempt to answer this question in advance. The most that can be said is that if we (1) treat Marxism and psycho-analysis as *problematics* rather than dogmas and (2) remember that our task is to *interpret* reality, not impose our categories upon it, then we may find that these theories improve rather than impair our historical vision.

B. Psychoanalytic-Marxism

Assuming for the moment that Marxism and psychoanalysis are each of value, is it desirable and possible to unify them, and, if they are to be unified, how is this to be done? Should they be joined, can they be joined, and in what way are they to be joined?

1.

What if, for simplicity's sake, we were to define Marxism as a theory of interests rooted in work-activity and economic production, psycho-analysis as a theory of desire rooted in emotional life and human repro-duction (relationships of gender and generation)? Then there would be an evident reason for joining the two theories. Social reality cannot be reduced to either interests/work/economic production or desires/ emotional life/human reproduction. Either perspective is monocular and, to that extent, distortive. A binocular perspective would allow us to see more, and more clearly, than a monocular one. A clearer picture of social reality facilitates rational choices of situationally transformational action. Hence the *desirability* of a psychoanalytic-marxism.

2.

It can be argued, next, that the two theories operate by the same methodological rules. Hence the *possibility* of a psychoanalytic-marxism.

Although Marxism and psychoanalysis have both taken their methodological knocks from positivist critics, their founders firmly identified their projects with the worldview of modern science. What science meant to each of them has been a matter of dispute. But Marx and Freud were self-consciously *antimetaphysical*. In the case of science, says Freud, "there are no sources of knowledge of the universe other than the intellectual working-over of carefully scrutinized observations—in other words, what we call research—and along side of it no knowledge derived from revelation, intuition or divination" (Freud, 1933a, p. 159). In like fashion Marx and Engels claim that in contrast to "German [Hegelian, Young Hegelian] philosophy which descends from heaven to earth," their theory "ascends from earth to heaven" (Marx & Engels, 1845b, p. 154). Its premises are "real individuals, their activities and the material conditions under which they live. . . ." These premises can be "verified in a purely empirical way" (*ibid.*, p. 149).

Marxism and psychoanalysis are this-worldly theories. For each of them, however, there is a distinction to be drawn between the world as it appears and the world as it really is. Appearances, moreover, conceal realities. In each instance the analytical task is to pierce the veil of appearance and bring the concealed reality into view. The synthetical task is to interpret, explain, or determine the play of appearances from the perspective of the revealed reality. If, therefore, we use the term without too many philosophical constraints, we can say that the two theories are *phenomenological*.

Because appearances do not usually announce themselves as such but rather claim to be reality itself, phenomenology is simultaneously *critique*. When, for example, metaphysics is interpreted from the perspective of science, its truth-claims are called into question. They are judged to be false, not merely superficial. More generally, Marxism and psychoanalysis question the truth-claims of ordinary consciousness. They are each theories of false consciousness. And not only of consciousness, that is, of states of mind. Each theory requires and facilitates investigation of falsifying and alienating patterns of activity—of the contradictions inherent in life-worlds as well as in worldviews.

It might be added that phenomenology and criticism are methods of analysis as well as orientations toward reality. Marxism operates through transformational criticism, that is, the critical analysis of subject–object relationships. Psychoanalysis operates through the analysis of defense and, in the clinical instance, the analysis of resistance.

An example might be helpful. For both Marxism and psychoanalysis, or at least for both Marx and Freud, metaphysics converges with theology. Hence each theory contains a critique of religious belief. For Marx religion is an "inverted world consciousness" which reflects with a certain accuracy an "inverted world" (Marx, 1844a, p. 53). In religion, the idea of God, which is actually a product or object of human mentation, is treated as an autonomous subject. Simultaneously the actual human subject is treated as product or object. The Creator is our creation; we mistakenly see ourselves as the creation of the Creator we have created. This inversion of the relationship between subject and object is not, however, a mere error or mental slip. It results from practical relationships of domination, in which people in fact function as objects subjected to alien powers rather than as subjects capable of self-determination. Consequently the critique of religion also must be practical. It requires the elimination of alienating social relationships.

For Freud religion is an illusion, a wish-fulfillment, the "universal obsessional neurosis of humanity" (Freud, 1927a, p. 43). It is a product of human weakness and a defense against the anxiety that results from our vulnerability. The infantile yearning for a strong, protective father is transformed into the belief in an omnipotent, benevolent God the Father. Via projection and displacement the earthly father becomes the heavenly one. But the earthly father is not in fact all that benevolent. His protection is at the same time oedipal domination. God is the transubstantiation not just of the father but of the oedipal father. The celestial relationship of domination mirrors the mundane one. Just as inverted consciousness reflects an inverted world, so religious illusion reflects psychical reality. Psychoanalysis, by revealing the psychological basis of this illusion, tends to dispel it.

It is evident that these two instances of phenomenological criticism differ in content. As form or method, however, they fit together: The analysis of defense mediates transformational criticism. It brings to light the mechanisms or processes through which subject and object are inverted.[2]

Thus far I have contended that Marxism and psychoanalysis are each antimetaphysical, phenomenological, and critical. They also are *not* positivistic. I make this point because, in their own way, positivistic theories—the normal theories of the natural sciences and of the social sciences modeled after them—are antimetaphysical, analytical, and critical. They can be differentiated from Marxism and psychoanalysis, however, on ontological grounds. Positivistic theories are ultimately unidimensional. Reality itself is simply positive, a matter of fact. Facts themselves are unproblematical. They obey the rules of ordinary logic (identity, difference, excluded middle, etc.). For Marxism and psychoanalysis, by contrast, reality is multidimensional, self-contradictory—in a word, *dialectical*.

Dialectics is among the most vexed of the questions that are necessarily attached to an inquiry of the present kind. For one thing, Freud classified psychoanalysis as a positive, not a dialectical, science. For another, Marx himself and many Marxists have tended to identify dialectics with an historical determinism in which the future is treated as the entailed conclusion of a syllogism. Even more open-ended versions of dialectical reasoning might be viewed as imposing a structure and direction upon historical processes that such processes simply do not have. Many postmodernists, who take this critique to its limit, treat dialectics as a kind of intellectual bad faith, in which the fundamental entropy of and gaps in reality are covered over with makeshift totalizations. In their view, the critique of false consciousness, if sufficiently extended, closes a circle: The supposed underlying reality with which the critique ends is indistinguishable from the supposed false consciousness with which it began.

We'll return to the question of dialectical reason presently. For the moment, all I wish to argue is that Marxism and psychoanalysis are united in a conception of reality as inherently self-contradictory and (through the manifestation and overcoming of these contradictions) self-developmental.

Marx contends that dialectical reasoning is inherently "critical and revolutionary" (Marx, 1867, p. 103). We shall see that dialectics may have some darker and more disturbing implications. But psychoanalysis and Marxism, each in its own way, remain loyal to the transformational aims of dialectical reasoning. Each amounts to a *theory and practice, a praxis, of self-emancipation*. Each accepts the imperative of the second thesis on Feuerbach, namely, that the truth of theory must be realized in practice (Marx, 1845, p. 144). And each aims at overcoming the falsification of consciousness and alienation of life-activity that its critical and phenomenological methods reveal.[3]

3.

Theoretical binocularity with its implications for rational choices of action determines the desirability of psychoanalytic-marxism. The methodological commonalities outlined above determine its possibility. And, it might be argued, the desirability and possibility of unification converge in the concept of emancipatory praxis. Emancipatory aims require an orientation toward rational choices of transformational action; rational choices of action are at the least facilitated by and perhaps dependent upon a critical phenomenological methodology and an antimetaphysical, dialectical, and theoretically binocular conception of social reality.

Ultimately the project is to develop and support this position. But not immediately: It would be a fatal error to disregard the fundamental *difficulty* the project involves, namely, that the theories are premised upon diametrically opposed anthropologies, mutually exclusive conceptions of human nature and historical development.

Here is a way of stating the difficulty. Assume we are investigating the phenomenon of white racism. The inquiry might have this form:

Such an investigation begins with the empirical phenomenon of white racism, hence with the representation of the conscious actions and self-consciousness of individuals and collectivities. Through the use of a critical phenomenological method this empirical starting point is dissolved into two conceptual domains. On the one hand, racist beliefs and practices are anchored in the economic and political interests of (let us suppose) a declining petty bourgeoisie. On the other, they reflect the tendencies toward splitting and projection of psychological groups, tendencies which (ontogenetically) originate in repressed oedipal and pre-oedipal desires, that is, in a particular familial constellation.

How, then, are the conceptual domains of production/interests and reproduction/desires related to each other? They are not, to begin with, mutually exclusive. Even in societies where production is centered outside the household, familial and economic relationships are inter-penetrative and mutually conditioning. There are interests attached to relationships of human reproduction and desires attached to those of economic production. And, plainly, work is performed in the household and people have emotional lives while engaged in economic production. Hence there can be a psychoanalytic investigation of the economy and a Marxist investigation of the family. Indeed, an adequate understanding of a phenomenon like white racism depends upon just such inquiries.

In other words, the institutional objects of the inquiry, namely, familial or economic structures, can be analyzed from either a Marxist or a psychoanalytic perspective. Hence they do not constitute the difficulty with which we are concerned, and we may put them aside. We then have Marxism as a theory of interests, of intersubjective relationships of advantage and disadvantage, and psychoanalysis as a theory of desires, of (at root) intrasubjective drives, wishes, fantasies, and intentions. Thus Marx claims that "the human essence is no abstraction inherent in each single individual." It is rather "the ensemble of the social relations" (Marx, 1845, p. 145). For Freud and Freudian psychoanalysts, by contrast, the concrete human essence *is* inherent in each individual, while the ensemble of social relations is the abstraction.

We may push our phenomenological reduction one step further. For Marx interests are a function of work-activity. Desires and emotional life are molded by historically specific forms of the work-mediated relationship of human individuals to each other and nonhuman nature. For Freud manifest desires are a function of sexual and aggressive drives. Work-activity and historically specific economic relationships are sublimations of our basic drives. Productive activity, so far from being a part of our nature, is an externality nonhuman nature imposes upon us.

It thus appears that, at the level of anthropology, the two theories are mutually exclusive. When they are employed in historical and social analysis, they consequently produce dramatically different pictures of reality. Returning to our example of white racism, for an orthodox Marxist the analysis of group psychology is a deflection from economic and class issues, while for an orthodox psychoanalyst economic considerations do not go to the psychological heart of the matter. Any attempt to fuse the two theories would therefore seem to be like a bad marriage, a wedding of incompatibles that is sure to end up in unpleasant wrangling and ultimately divorce. Or, to vary the metaphor, in attempting to join Marxism and psychoanalysis we might find ourselves with theoretical double-vision instead of the hoped-for binocular vision. Alternatively, if we seek to rise above the antagonism or to resolve it dialectically, the result might well be a bland conceptual pudding, an uninteresting set of abstractions resembling Talcott Parson's general theory of action.

What then? As I see it, the theoretical desirability and methodological possibility of a psychoanalytic-marxism make the project worth undertaking. Given the antagonistic anthropologies of the two theories, however, the project can only be realized if we confront head-on the contradictions between them. Only by so doing might we succeed in articulating theoretical first principles that (1) are unifying without being homogenizing; (2) resolve the anthropological contradiction without dulling our interpretive edge; and (3) can serve as a ground for discrete emancipatory practices, that is, for political practice on the one hand and clinical practice on the other.

A question by way of anticipation: How might we develop an anthropological dialectic of work and desire?

C. Limits and Order of Inquiry

1.

The desirability, possibility, and difficulty of developing a psychoanalytic-marxism are the conditions generally defining our project. The present inquiry does not aim at realizing the project, however, but only at constructing a theoretical groundwork for it.

A "groundwork" (*Grundrisse*) is a foundation, as in the instance of the foundation of a building. It is a construction that serves as the basis for further construction.

In the present instance the concept of a groundwork is derived from Marx's discussion of dialectical method in his 1857 *Grundrisse* for a critique of political economy. In a famous passage he raises the question: With what should a political economic theory begin? He explicitly answers: with "simple concepts," the "simplest determinations," the "thinnest of abstractions." Upon closer inspection, however, he implies an additional answer and, along with it, a twofold method of inquiry. There is, on the one hand, the necessity of beginning with a given empirical phenomenon, the "real and concrete," followed by an analytical movement from this starting point to the simple conceptual elements concealed within it. On the other, there is a synthetical movement back from these elements to the real and concrete. Through this process that which is initially a "chaotic conception of the whole" becomes "a rich totality of many determinations and relations" (Marx, 1857, p. 100).

In its full scope I view this conception of method as phenomenological, critical, and constructive.[4] It is phenomenological because it uses abstracting and bracketing procedures to advance from appearances to underlying realities. It is critical because the phenomenological advance involves breaking down existing concepts that are layered between the empirical surface and the theoretical bedrock. Think, for example, of the way Marx reduces the concept of labor as used by Adam Smith and David Ricardo to labor-power (the potential for working) and labor process (actual working). It is constructive because the concepts that result from the analytical process serve as a foundation for a synthetical and concretizing interpretation of the empirical manifold.

A theoretical groundwork, then, is a product of phenomenological advance that serves as a premise (or set of premises) for a "reproduction of the concrete by way of thought" (*ibid.*, p. 101).

The present inquiry is meant to be a groundwork in this sense. It is based upon the tradition of Freudian-Marxist and psychoanalytic-marxist theorizing, as well as upon my own historical and clinical research (Wolfenstein, 1985, 1989, 1990c); and it aims at facilitating further research and theorization. Moreover, its internal structure parallels the larger investigative situation. Chapters 5–7 are the groundwork proper, the most abstract of our concepts and categories. Chapters 2–4 lead into them and Chapters 8–10 lead away from them. As we shall see momentarily, however, the parallel is only a parallel, not a duplication or an instantiation.

2.

Although I have taken the idea of a theoretical groundwork from Marx, I am not sure that he and I would agree on the truth-claims that validly can be attached to such conceptions. Marx sometimes sounds like a this-worldly Hegel, who thinks that dialectical method can secure the identification of the real with the rational. At other times he seems— appropriately in my judgment—to reject any such rationalizing of human experience. For now we may bypass matters of textual interpretation. It will be useful, however, to take a preliminary stab at stating the epistemological limits of dialectical reason.

A convenient entry point is the concept of totality (as in the preceding "totality of many determinations and relations"). Modern social theory inherits from ancient philosophy a set of metatheoretical problems, to wit, what is the relationship between the One and the Many, between whole and parts, or between identity and difference? Hegel claimed to have solved this problem. In his view reality is a self-developing totality in which the parts (moments, determinations) are negatively related to the whole. In the whole there is differentiation, hence difference; the parts are not the whole. Through negative self-relation, however, the whole contains the parts. The difference between part and whole is therefore a "*difference* which is no *difference*, or only a difference of what is *self-same*, and its essence is unity" (Hegel, 1807, p. 99). This conception of totality is then linked to the claim that reason (the knowing of a subject) can be identified with reality (the object to be known). Dialectic in its advance overcomes the opposition of subject and object, transforms it into a difference which is no difference. Consequently reality is, and can be known to be, a totality of determinations. The ontological and epistemological circles are closed simultaneously.

As suggested earlier, the closed circle is a vicious circle. It prevents us from thinking/seeing *sameness* which is no *sameness*, *identity* which is no *identity*.[5] It ontologizes the resolution of dialectical contradictions, denies the possible dissolution of dialectical relationships. If we are to employ a dialectical method, it therefore must be with an epistemological restraint lacking in Hegel.

3.

Restraint: Hegel entered the dialectical heart of darkness and lost himself there. If we follow him, it must be in the role of Marlow, not Kurtz.

4.

Epistemological restraint may be more a matter of character than of principles. Nonetheless we may adopt two rules of thumb for the use of dialectical method.

First, we must resist any temptation to absolutize our theoretical groundwork. We must recognize, with Freud, that our knowledge of the world is always limited to "what is at the moment knowable" (Freud, 1933a, p. 159). Truths grow old and die. Objective truth is not the same as absolute truth. Moreover, at least so far as knowledge of human affairs is concerned, all concepts are inflected with the subjectivity of their originators. They are the product of a phenomenological process, hence also of the real world situation, interests, and desires of the theorist. They never transcend the subjectivity and contingency of the life-world in which they originate. To put it another way, we never progress from interpretations of phenomena (appearances) to revelations of noumena (essential truths). Dialectical method does not permit the transformation of a field of possibilities and impossibilities into psychological or historical inevitabilities.[6]

Second, we must give up on the attempt to totalize social reality, or to patch up the gaps in the structure of the universe. The proper employment of dialectical method does not yield a conceptualized totality, but only a set of concepts that are integrative or totalizing of the phenomena given in experience. This is plainly the case when we interpret an existing situation in the light of alternative projected futures. But even when we are concerned with the past, with an empirical reality that is now fixed and unchangeable, the interpretive situation is indeterminate. As a matter of fact and a matter of interpretation, reality is uncertain and contingent—which doesn't mean we don't try to impose certainty and necessity upon it.

It might be added that, when used with restraint, dialectical method prevents an indulgence of another (anti-Hegelian or inverse-Hegelian) kind, namely, the ontologizing of disintegration, multiplicity, gaps, lacunae, and the like. It resists the detotalization as well as the totalization of social reality. As a matter of method it leaves open the question of the unity or disunity of specific domains of experience. It helps us to determine the conjunctions and disjunctions in the life-worlds we are exploring without, however, determining them in advance. In contrast to both Hegelianism and postmodernism, it does not grant an ontological priority to either the One or the Many. It is constructive, not preconstructive or deconstructive.

5.

So far as psychoanalytic-marxism is concerned, dialectical method is optimally employed in empirical research of one kind or another. Yet such research sometimes facilitates a particular kind of conceptual glissade. We can trick ourselves into thinking that we know what a concept means when we have only established a way in which it can be used, an empirical content of which it is a possible form. Hence the motive for the present inquiry: It seems worthwhile to disentangle the grounding concepts of psychoanalytic-marxism from their empirical integument, so that their structure and interrelationship can be more fully articulated.

It must be admitted that by so doing we face the opposite danger. We might bring out the conceptual relationships too abstractly, without an adequate sensitivity to the resistance they encounter when they enter the real world. After all, the clarity so many seek in the products of social research is more likely to be found in its presuppositions.

6.

The inquiry falls within the tradition of Freudian-Marxist and psychoanalytic-marxist theorizing that originates in the work of Wilhelm Reich. It therefore seems an appropriate act of recognition to begin with this tradition—and, to the extent possible, to let its principals speak for themselves. This is because, in the present discursive context, I think of myself as having one voice among many. I do not wish to drown out the others, but rather to be heard along with them. Consequently the first section of the inquiry amounts to a series of critical encounters but not to an analytical reduction. Put another way the aim in this part is to produce an assemblage of conceptual materials, including the raw materials from which the groundwork proper is constructed.

We begin with a polemical confrontation between Marx and Freud (Chapter 2). Incidentally and to the extent that it is necessary, this will provide psychoanalytic readers with a first impression of Marxism and Marxist readers with a first impression of psychoanalysis. More importantly it will enable us to articulate the differences between the two theoretical and practical positions. The encounter will end in a stalemate.

Next we will turn to the work of the "classical" Freudian-Marxists (Wilhelm Reich, Erich Fromm, and Herbert Marcuse), hence to the initial attempts to overcome the differences between the two positions (Chapter 3). None of these efforts was fully successful; none of them was a complete failure. But taken together, they constitute a problematic, a whole consisting of and partially containing the contradictory relationship of Marxism and psychoanalysis.

After that we will come to the work of a number of theorists who might be viewed as attempting to go beyond the problematics of Freudian-Marxism (Chapter 4). The discourse itself expands, and it becomes less tied to the personalities and conceptual particularities of Marx and Freud. It continues, however, to maintain its connection to the Marxist and psychoanalytic movements. Accordingly we will henceforward characterize it as psychoanalytic-marxism. Moreover, questions of race and gender, by virtue of their own integral social movement, advance from background to foreground. Thus the discourse not only expands, it becomes decidedly polyvocal—in good part because it increasingly intersects with discursive practices originating outside its domain.

One result of the first phase of the inquiry might be anticipated. Almost without exception the Freudian-Marxists and their successors have interpreted psychoanalysis as an individual psychology and Marxism as a theory of social structures. There is unquestionably license for this view in the works of Freud and Marx themselves. The consequence of maintaining it, however, is to condemn the project of a psychoanalytic-marxism to failure. It usually results in superimposing a Marxist conception of history on a psychoanalytic conception of human nature, and then interposing a psychoanalytic individual within a Marxist social theory. Less typically psychoanalytic concepts are subsumed under a Marxist conception of human nature. And either way collective emotional life disappears. I have described elsewhere the experiences that led me to break with this orientation (Wolfenstein, 1990c). For now suffice it to say that adequately joining Marxism and psychoanalysis requires the conceptual integration of work-life and emotional-life at all levels of analysis—from the individual to the collective, from the practical to the anthropological.

7.

As indicated, the unfolding of concepts in Chapters 5–7 constitutes the groundwork proper. Chapter 5 is concerned with metatheory. It is the most abstract point we reach, the one at the greatest remove from social reality. Here we will attempt to establish dialectical reason within the epistemological and ontological limits of praxis. In Chapter 6 we develop an interrelated set of anthropological/historical concepts which, it is hoped, will satisfactorily ground a psychoanalytic-marxist theory. In Chapter 7 we articulate a set of categories that are intended to frame the analysis of historical modes of social production, especially our own.

8.

The last part of the inquiry involves a somewhat more concrete exploration of the capitalist mode of production. In Chapter 8 we focus on class, gender, and race, more particularly on the patterns of domination and fetishistic distortions of recognition characteristic of these relationships in advanced capitalist societies. Chapter 9 is concerned with psychoanalytic practice, partly as a social position from which to analyze pathologies of human development and partly as a praxis of human emancipation at an individual level. Finally, in Chapter 10 a critical analysis of Hegel's theory of the modern state and Marx's conception of proletarian revolution will lead to a consideration of the problematics of transformational political action in our own time.

_____ PART ONE _____

ASSEMBLAGE

CHAPTER 2

Marx Against Freud

Our initial task is to draw out the differences between Marxism and psychoanalysis. This can be done if we stage a polemical confrontation between Marx and Freud, that is, an engagement in which interests are opposed and each party aims at winning. Let's require, however, that the disputants play by the rules: no misrepresentation of the other party's position, no dissimulation of one's own.[1]

For two reasons we will begin with Marx. First, Marx oriented his political project toward human emancipation. He required, consequently, a rigorously historical and social theory. Only such a theory could provide him with a map of the political battlefield. Freud, by contrast, was concerned with intrapsychic, not political, conflict. His work did not require the development of social and historical theory, and he did not in fact develop one. He treats only incidentally the topics that are primary to Marx. Given an orientation toward political transformation, Marx is therefore the better theoretical guide in the first instance. Second, Freud came after Marx, and his social theoretical writings, most notably *Civilization and Its Discontents* (1930), were in part a response to Marxism. Hence the debate will evolve more naturally if we follow the historical path.

A. A World to Win

1.

Marxism originates, historically and conceptually, in the linkage of an epistemology of praxis to the practical interests of the modern working class, the proletariat.

The proletariat, Marx argues in 1844, is a class with *"radical chains,"* a class "which is the dissolution of all classes," in which there is a *"total loss* of humanity and which can only redeem itself by a *total redemption of humanity"* (Marx, 1844a, p. 64). Although the proletariat was merely nascent, in time and as bourgeois society increasingly polarized it would become the numerically largest social class. Its particular class interests would then be simultaneously a universal or human interest. Within bourgeois society proletarian interests are negated, and members of the proletariat are dehumanized. By acting in its own interest, that is, by overthrowing the bourgeoisie, the proletariat negates the negation and realizes the emancipatory interests of humanity.

As Marx views it, the emancipatory interest of the proletariat is both an empirical reality and a concept. Either way it must be realized in practice—"Man must prove the truth, that is, the reality and power, the this-sidedness of his thinking in practice" (Marx, 1845, p. 144). The proletariat can emancipate itself and humanity only by actually transforming the existing situation. Marx's theory of human emancipation is valid only if the proletariat realizes it in practice. There are no a priori or purely theoretical solutions to this-worldly problems.

Theory helps those who help themselves: Marx's role, at once theoretical and practical, is to aid in the development of the class-consciousness of the proletariat. Marxism is the theory and practice of working class struggle.

2.

Marx's debt to Hegel is evident in his conceptualization of class dynamics in terms of negation and negation of negation. The critical component of his approach he owes more to Ludwig Feuerbach, however, than to Hegel. It was Feuerbach who developed the transformational criticism of Hegelian idealism, which Marx then extended into a critique of social relationships.

Feuerbach argued that Hegelian philosophy was a disguised theology and that, like theology, it involved a subject–object inversion. God is an idea, Feuerbach claimed, a human invention, an abstract projection of the human essence. Humanity creates God in its own image; the human is subject, God is object. In religious belief, however, the relationship is inverted: God creates man in his own image. The inversion must be inverted in order to reveal the true nature of the relationship. Likewise the Concept or Idea, which Hegel takes as philosophical and historical premise, must be viewed rather as psychological product.

To Feuerbach goes the credit—or the blame—for materializing the Hegelian dialectic. To Marx goes the responsibility for radicalizing it.

Marx begins his phenomenological journey by accepting the Feuerbachian criticism of religion. Theology, as we have already seen, is the inverted consciousness of an inverted world. In it, as in all ideology, "men and their circumstances appear upside-down as in a *camera obscura*" (Marx & Engels, 1845b, p. 154). But if religion is "*the fantastic realization* of the human being," this is because "the *human being* possesses no true reality" (Marx, 1844a, p. 54).

The transformational criticism of theology and idealist philosophy becomes more concrete in the critique of political reality and ideology:

> Where the political state has attained to its full development, man leads, not only in thought, in consciousness, but in *reality*, in *life*, a double existence—celestial and terrestrial. He lives in the *political community* where he regards himself as a *communal being*, and in *civil society* where he acts simply as a *private individual*, treats other men as means, degrades himself to the role of a mere means, and becomes the plaything of alien powers. (Marx, 1843b, p. 34)

If an individual is the enfranchised citizen of a state, then in his political role he is recognized as human and grants human recognition to others. He is apparently a free and universal being. In actuality, in civil society, in the realm of market transactions, in which he is an economic agent and the owner of private property, he is the creature of his material interests. He serves profit and economic gain the way a religious believer serves God. Members of the proletariat, however, are neither enfranchised citizens nor owners of private property.[2] They constitute a class which is no class, a class with only negative characteristics. They suffer, indeed embody, the inhumanity of society without gaining any of its compensatory material advantages. Hence their interest in overthrowing it.

3.

Programmatically and historically (in Marx's own development), transformational criticism leads from religious ideology to the state, from the state to civil society, and from civil society to political economy. Marx reports that

> my investigation [in 1843/1844] led to the result that legal relations as well as forms of state are to be grasped neither from themselves nor from the so-called general development of the human mind, but rather have their roots in the material conditions of life, the sum total of which Hegel ... combines under the name of "civil society," that, however, the anatomy of civil society is to be sought in political economy. (Marx, 1859, p. 4)

Then, through the transformational criticism of economic production, Marx reached his phenomenological bedrock: the linked concepts of objectification and its perversion, alienation.

It will repay our efforts if we treat in some detail this crucial point in Marx's development. We will gain a more secure footing in the problematics of his theory, and we will avoid the tendency of mistaking Marxist economics for a species of speculative philosophy.

The political economy Marx inherited and criticized was considered to be a science—a social science, we would say. It combined empirical investigation with theoretical analysis. In the classic statement of the theory—Adam Smith's *The Wealth of Nations* (1776)—the analysis turned on a set of central concepts. Briefly stated:

1. Labor is the foundation of all rights of property.
2. Private property is institutionally presupposed.
3. Economic progress results from increasing the productive powers of labor.
4. Increasing the productive powers of labor results from increasing the division of labor.
5. The division of labor originates in the natural human "propensity to truck, barter, and exchange one thing for another" (*ibid.*, p. 17) and is limited by the extent of the market.
6. Money developed to facilitate exchange.
7. Commodities have a use value and an exchange value.
8. The real price or exchange value of commodities is not their money or nominal price, but rather the quantity of labor they embody; labor is the source and measure of the value of commodities.
9. The market price of a commodity, which is determined by the operations of supply and demand, may depart from its real price; but market price tends toward real price, which is also the point at which supply equals demand.
10. The component parts of the price of a commodity—the distributive shares of which it consists—are wages of labor, profit of stock (capital), and rent of land.

Utilizing these concepts in combination with empirical material, Smith argued that capital accumulation and the well-being of a commonwealth are augmented by free trade and diminished by restrictions on trade. To be sure, the individual capitalist does not "intend to promote the public interest"; he "intends only his own gain." But he is "led by an invisible hand [the laws of the unrestricted market] to promote an end which was no part of his intention," to wit, national or public interest (*ibid.*, p. 477). Thus private vice is a public virtue, and unfettered capitalism is the best of all possible worlds.

Marx shared Smith's belief that political economy was a science— but an ideologically encumbered one. In order to separate the ideological chaff from the scientific wheat, he attempted a dispassionate critical analysis of *The Wealth of Nations* and related texts. This critique demonstrated, he claimed, that in a capitalist economy:

> the worker sinks to the level of a commodity and becomes indeed the most wretched of commodities; that the wretchedness of the worker is in inverse proportion to the power and magnitude of his production; that the necessary result of competition is the accumulation of capital in a few hands . . . ; that finally . . . the whole of society must fall apart into two classes—the property-*owners* and the propertyless *workers*. (Marx, 1844b, p. 70)

The premises with which political economy begins are inverted by the time the critique ends. Accordingly Marx is entitled to start again.

He decides to begin, not with "a fictitious primordial condition," a state of nature, natural human propensities, etc., but rather with "an *actual* economic fact" (*ibid.*, p. 71): The more wealth workers create, the poorer they become; the greater the value of the commodities they produce, the less value their commodity (labor) possesses.

With his next step Marx reaches the ground upon which his own critical and dialectical political economy is to be constructed. The "product of labour is labour which has been congealed in an object, which has become material: it is the *objectification* of labour. Labour's realization is its objectification" (*ibid.*, p. 71). Laboring is a process of objectification, in which a subjective potentiality, through the activity of working, is materialized in an object. This is the direct relationship of worker, work, and product. But the "economic fact" epitomizing capitalist production shows that "the object which labour produces—labour's product— confronts it as *something alien*, as a *power independent* of the producer. . . ." In the conditions dealt with by political economy, the realization of labour "appears as a *loss of reality* for the workers; objectification as *loss of the object* and *object-bondage*; appropriation as *estrangement*, as *alienation*" (*ibid.*, pp. 71–72).

Like theology, political economic science is the inverted consciousness of an inverted world. Alienation is an inversion of the objectification process. Workers are subjected to the power of the objects they produce. Their powers of production return to them in the form of a hostile power over them.[3] More concretely, in alienated production the objects which workers create are the possession of the capitalist. They are his private property; transformed into money, they become his capital, his power of commanding labor. Workers must then serve capital and the capitalist the way believers serve not only God but also his high priests. And political economy declares this to be the natural order of things!

4.

We come next to the anthropology Marx attached to the analysis of objectification and alienation.

In the 1844 manuscripts Marx proceeds from the workers' alienation from the product of their labor to their alienation in the process of laboring. He then argues that, taken in combination, these two forms of alienation imply that workers are alienated from their "species being," from their humanity (*ibid.*, p. 75). Alienation is dehumanization.

Marx took the idea of species being from Feuerbach's philosophical anthropology, and doubtless the term retains some of its moral/ethical connotations. But it is also, and (I believe) more importantly, an empirical concept. It is intended to provide an objective answer to the question, what is it that makes us human? What links us to nonhuman species, and what differentiates us from them?

Like the other animals, the human being "lives on inorganic nature" (*ibid.*, p. 70); and like them, s/he is a "*suffering*, conditioned and limited creature" (*ibid.*, p. 115). Human *beings* are finite, sensuous creatures, parts of the natural order. That on the one hand. On the other, *human* beings are defined by the self-consciousness of their life-activity. The nonhuman animal "is immediately identical with its life-activity. . . . It produces one-sidedly. . . . It produces only under the dominion of immediate physical need . . ." (*ibid.*, p. 76). Nonhuman species are merely natural. They satisfy their needs in instinctually determined fashion and through the use of specific, naturally predetermined objects (bees make honey from pollen and only pollen). They are neither free in how they produce nor universal in the scope of their production. But freedom from instinctual limitations and universality vis-à-vis the objects of productive activity are precisely the characteristics of human life-activity. This is because man "makes his life-activity the object of his will and of his consciousness. He has conscious life-activity" (*ibid.*). Or as Marx states the point later in *Capital*, Vol. 1 (hereafter *Capital, 1*):

> A spider conducts operations which resemble those of the weaver, and a bee would put many a human architect to shame by the construction of its honeycomb cells. But what distinguishes the worst architect from the best of bees is that the architect builds the cell in his mind before he constructs it in wax. (Marx, 1867, p. 284)

We see, then, that Marx's anthropology is of a piece with his political economic theory. When he says that we are dehumanized by the alienation of labor, it is because the freedom and universality of production is what makes us human:

> The object of labour is ... the *objectification of man's species life*: for he duplicates himself not only, as in consciousness, intellectually, but also actively, in reality, and therefore he contemplates himself in a world he has created. In tearing away from man the object of his production, therefore, estranged labour tears away from him his *species life*, his real species objectivity, and transforms his advantage over other animals into the disadvantage that his inorganic body, nature, is taken from him.
>
> Similarly, in degrading spontaneous activity, free activity, to a means, estranged labour makes man's species life a means to his physical existence. (Marx, 1844b, pp. 76–77)

When we lose control of what we make and how we make it, we lose the qualities that distinguish us from other species. The alienation of labor is literally the loss of our humanity.

5.

Species being is Marx's conception of human nature. Unlike most such conceptions, however, Marx views human nature as immediately (immanently or definitionally) social and historical.

Marx inherited from Hegel the notion that human subjectivity can only be established intersubjectively, that is, in the process of mutual recognition. Or, to carry the lineage further back, he is radically Aristotelian: "The human being is in the most literal sense a ζωον πολιτιχον [political animal], not merely a gregarious animal, but an animal which can individuate itself only in the midst of society" (Marx, 1857, p. 84). For Marx human nature is *essentially* intersubjective. As we have already noted, he claims that "the human essence is no abstraction inherent in each single individual. In its reality it is the ensemble of the social relations." Hence the alienation of our species being is likewise social: "What applies to a man's relation to his work, to the product of his labour and to himself, also holds for man's relation to the other man, and to the other man's labour and object of labour" (Marx, 1844b, p. 77). This holds in general, as the relation of every man to every man. Social alienation is universal. More particularly it is *class domination*, the domination of capital over wage labor: The alienated "relationship of the worker to labour engenders the relation to it of the capitalist.... *Private property* is thus the product, the necessary consequence, of *alienated labour ...*" (*ibid.*,

p. 79). The private property system, that is, the class relationship of capital and wage labor, originates in and reproduces the alienation of human sociality.

Both our human nature and its alienation are social. Both are likewise historical. Because species being is life-activity, it includes what we collectively make as well as what we collectively are. Because we are self-objectifying, we are in the most literal sense self-productive. Thus in the 1844 manuscripts Marx claims that "the history of industry and the established *objective* existence of industry are the *open* book of *man's essential powers* , the exposure to the senses of human *psychology*. . . . The nature which comes to be in human history—the genesis of human society—is man's *real* nature; hence nature as it comes to be through industry, even though in an *estranged* form, is true *anthropological* nature" (*ibid.*, pp. 89–90). He repeats the claim in *Capital, 1* some twenty years later: Through labor man "acts upon external nature and changes it, and in this way he simultaneously changes his own nature. He develops the potentialities slumbering within nature, and subjects the play of its forces to his own sovereign power" (Marx, 1867, p. 283). History, including the history of alienation, is human nature.

6.

In the 1844 manuscripts Marx claims that "every *category* of political economy can be evolved with the help of . . . [the concepts of alienated labor and private property]," and that each category—capital, money, exchange, etc.—contains a "*definite* and *developed* expression of the first foundations" (Marx, 1844b, p. 80). Broadly speaking this is true, at least of his own theory. From first to last it is structured by the relationship of alienated labor (alienated species being) and private property. In its matured form, however, it also is anchored in the concept of value, more specifically of surplus value.

Marx takes from classical political economy the idea that commodities have a value for use (shoes are to wear) and a value for exchange (shoes have a "natural" price). He argues that a variety of factors determine their use value but that only one factor determines their exchange value: the amount of homogeneous social labor they contain, measured in time. Hence a pair of shoes in which five hours of socially average labor are materialized is worth half as much as jacket in which ten hours of socially average labor are materialized. This does not mean that shoes and jackets will actually exchange in these ratios. Market prices routinely depart from labor prices. But the equilibrium point of supply and demand is determined by labor prices.

Marx's conception of labor value represents a considerable advance in clarity over those of his predecessors (Smith and David Ricardo most notably). The critical point in the theory, however, is the concept of surplus value.

Assume the pair of shoes has an exchange value of ten dollars. The shoe manufacturer has spent five dollars on means of production (depreciation of machinery) and raw material (leather). This represents a labor value that will be re-embodied in the shoes. The additional five dollars represents value added during the labor process.

What, then, is the capitalist to pay the worker who is actually going to make the shoes? If he pays him for the value of his labor (five dollars), then he makes no profit. If he pays him less than the value of his labor, then apparently the law of exchange (that commodities exchange at their values) has been violated. And one cannot create a body of law on the basis of lawbreaking.

Marx sets about to solve this problem of bourgeois political economy. The key question is, what is the commodity that the capitalist purchases from the worker? The classical political economists represented workers as being paid for the value of their labor. This is ideologically attractive: Workers then have no valid reason for objecting to the wage-labor system. But the price the economists pay for this ideological advantage is that their theory is self-contradictory. Marx, by contrast, is not interested in legitimating the system but rather in de-legitimating it. Consequently he is disinclined to take things at face value; and eventually he solves the problem. The worker's commodity is not labor but rather labor-power—the capacity for working, not work itself. The difference between the value of labor-power (the price of reproducing the worker for, say, one day, or one day's wages) and labor (the value added to the shoes during the day's laboring) is a surplus value, a newly created value for which the capitalist does not pay but which he owns.

Using the concept of surplus value as his key, Marx was able to present a compelling and highly integrative conception of capitalist production. In the process he generated new problems and/or reformulated old ones: How are values transformed into market prices? Is there or isn't there a tendency for the rate of profit to fall? Do economic crises result from overproduction or underconsumption? There are those, Marxists among them, who believe that his economic theory cannot solve these problems; and there are those who believe that the labor theory of value is not a useful instrument of economic analysis. We will put these controversies to one side. For now our only task is to represent Marx's theoretical position. Later we will find that Marx's critical analysis of commodity exchange retains its heuristic value, even if it does not determine market values.

7.

Once Marx had established his groundwork, he could proceed to articulate a structural or synchronic conception of social relations. This conception is represented by the following diagram:

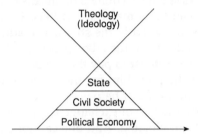

As we have seen, Marx's phenomenological journey took him from theology through the state and civil society to political economy. It created the possibility of interpreting the world from the ground up—of reproducing the concrete by way of thought.

In the diagram the horizontal line represents time and the conceptual structure represents a set of social relations existing synchronously.[4] The foundation (political economy) consists of "relations of production which correspond to a definite stage of development of . . . [human] material productive forces" (Marx, 1859, p. 4). By forces of production Marx means both technologies and the subjective capacities required for their utilization. By relations of production he means the economic institutional framework within which forces of production operate—for example, the household economy of the Greek polis or the market economy of industrial capitalism.

On this foundation there arises both "a legal and political superstructure" and corresponding "forms of social consciousness" (*ibid.*). Private property, for example, is the basic legal relationship in bourgeois society. Classically the private ownership of property makes one a citizen and a member of civil society. The state then functions to protect private property and the rights of citizens. Finally the whole set of relationships, from political economy to the state, is ideologically transformed—inverted—in various ways. Protestant Christianity provides a sanctified reflection and affirmation of bourgeois social relations, liberal political theory provides a secular one.[5]

8.

Marx's synchronic conception of social relationships is set within the dynamic or diachronic frame of a dialectical theory of historical development:

At a certain stage of their development, the material productive forces
of society come in conflict with the existing relations of production, or—what is but a legal expression of the same thing—with the
property relations within which they have been at work hitherto.
From forms of development of the productive forces these notions turn
into their fetters. Then begins an epoch of social revolution. (*ibid.*,
pp. 4–5)

The structural relationships of any society, or at least of those in which
progressive development is possible, are inherently self-contradictory.
Like the shell of a fertilized chicken egg, socioeconomic relationships
make possible the growth of forces that will, in time, shatter them. These
forces are not only objective but also subjective. They consist of both
technologies that cannot be rationally utilized within the existing relations of production and the class or classes of individuals that possess,
at least potentially, the capacity for their rational utilization.

Changes in the foundations of society bring with them corresponding changes in the legal and political "superstructure." The consciousness of political actors does not provide, however, an undistorted reflection of social reality. Even, or perhaps especially, during periods of social
transformation, consciousness retains its ideological character. Hence we
cannot judge "a period of transformation by its own consciousness; on
the contrary, this consciousness must be explained rather from the contradictions of material life . . ." (*ibid.*, p. 5).

There is, evidently, one exception to this rule for the interpretation
of ideology: If political agents are themselves conscious of the contradictions of material life and act rationally to resolve them, then consciousness ceases to be ideological and requires no interpretation. And because
economic transformations "can be determined with the precision of natural science" (*ibid.*, p. 5), such rational self-consciousness is possible, at
least in principle.

9.

So far I have refrained from emphasizing the problematical nature
of Marxist political theory. But now, as we reach the point of transition
to Freud's critique of Marxism, it will be useful to make explicit the
tension within the theory between Marx's epistemology of praxis, on the
one hand, and his conception of historical rationality, on the other.

Whatever else it may or may not be, Marxism is a theory of class
struggle in general and proletarian class struggle in particular. The
opposition of oppressing and oppressed classes is viewed as a structural
feature of all historical societies. This opposition of interests generates
class conflict, and class conflict is the dynamus of historical development.

In the modern (capitalist) era what Mao would later call the "principal contradiction" is the opposition of bourgeoisie and proletariat. The interests of the bourgeoisie are realized and those of the proletariat are negated in capitalist society. Because collective self-interest is the standard of political rationality, it is rational for members of the proletariat to form themselves into a mass movement—a political class—aimed at negating the negation, that is, abolishing the bourgeois private property system. Stating the matter positively, workers have a world to win, a world in which the "free development of each [individual] is a condition for the free development of all" (Marx & Engels, 1848, p. 491).

What, then, is the role of class consciousness in history? If one takes the idea of praxis seriously, then proletarian class consciousness is a necessary condition for the overthrow of capitalism and the construction of communism. A necessary condition—and not a pre-determined one. There can be no a priori guarantees that, when the opportunity for progressive revolutionary action arises, the proletariat will act rationally. Given an epistemology of praxis, no such guarantees are to be sought. Rather, it is accepted as a fact of political life that history contains an irreducible element of subjectivity and contingency. And precisely the subjectivity and contingency of political life determines that Marx must be an involved and passionate polemicist as well as an objective and dispassionate political economist.

To put it another way, an epistemology of praxis means that, if there is such a thing as a science of class struggle, it can only be an inductive, experimental one, a science in which the practitioner makes mistakes, learns from experience, and accepts the uncertainty that attaches to her/his activity.

One can argue that Marx viewed his theoretical and practical activity in more or less the preceding terms. Alternatively, it can be argued that, for Marx, class analysis functioned within a strongly deterministic theory of historical development or rationality. The theory is so strong, indeed, that one can know in advance that the "fall [of the bourgeoisie] and the victory of the proletariat are equally inevitable" (*ibid.*, p. 483).

The claim of historical inevitability closes, totalizes, Marxist theory both epistemologically and practically. Let's loosen it just a bit. There is nothing in Marx's writings to suggest that he was putting forward claims to absolute knowledge. At a minimum his theory recognizes the existence of such historical outliers as a natural catastrophe that could be fatal to human civilization or a technological breakthrough so revolutionary that it would render existing social theories useless. Nor was he, as some contend, a secular prophet, who drew a vision of the future from a book of historical revelations. His predictions were derived from intensive empirical and theoretical analysis. And the high quality of his analysis is demonstrated by the fact that a large number of his key predictions proved to be correct.

Because Marx did not claim absolute historical knowledge and because his work had a markedly empirical–analytical quality, the notion of historical inevitability cannot be taken quite literally. Nor, however, can it be ignored. Marx's analysis of human history was not open-ended. To the contrary, it was mediated by a conception of historical rationality derived from Hegel, one which prestructured or prefigured his interpretive activity. In brief:

> No social order ever perishes before all the productive forces for which there is room in it have developed; and new, higher relations of production never appear before the material conditions of their existence have matured in the womb of the old society itself. Therefore mankind always sets itself only such tasks as it can solve; since, looking at the matter more closely, it will always be found that the task itself arises only when the material conditions for its solution already exist or are at least in the process of formation. (Marx, 1859, p. 5)

History is, if not organic, organic-like. It is analogous to a process of organic growth in which an eggshell doesn't crack until the chicken it contains can and must crack it. Dialectical reason is not just in the eye of the beholder.

One can bring forward historical instances that fit this epistemological bill. The utopian societies in nineteenth century Europe and America appeared before the possibilities of capitalist development had been exhausted. They were historically premature and so they failed. The attempts to build communism in Russia and Eastern Europe appeared before capitalist development was even well underway in those areas. They were historically premature in another sense and so they, too, failed. But one can hardly turn these instances into a law of historical development. The exceptions would surely be the rule—including that most important of exceptions, the persistence of capitalism in the areas of its highest development. If one wishes to stay with organic metaphors, capitalism is an overripe fruit that stubbornly refuses to fall from the historical tree. And the proletariat has been unable and/or unwilling to pluck it.

Marx apparently viewed political praxis and historical rationality as complementary concepts. It seems to me that they are contradictory, but meaningfully so. Taken together they pose the problem of the relationship between what is predetermined, structured, and closed in human experience, and what is open to human agency, to individual and collective self-determination. If, further, one restricts this general question to the instance of human emancipation, one might even view it as *the* fundamental Marxist problematic.

Posing the problem in these terms is, however, polemically premature. Freud, to whom we now turn, operated with a far less refined and problematized view of Marxism.[6]

B. Psychoanalytic Truth, Marxist Illusion

1.

Freud's critique of Marxism is an attempt to draw a line between worldviews. Accordingly we'll begin with his analysis of Marxism in the essay, "A Weltanschauung?" (Freud, 1933a). We will then place the arguments of *Civilization and Its Discontents* within this broader frame.

Freud's general purpose in this essay is (1) to locate psychoanalysis within the worldview of science (positive science) and (2) to defend the scientific worldview against any and all rival claimants to epistemological authority. He provides a particularly sympathetic description of scientific inquiry. He stresses the piecemeal and painstaking nature of scientific work, the laboriousness of the path to and the perpetual incompleteness of scientific knowledge, and the lack of consolation which such knowledge provides. Nonetheless he does hold to the idea of scientific progress: "Our best hope for the future is that intellect—the scientific spirit, reason—may in process of time establish a dictatorship in the mental life of man." Reason by its very nature will "not fail to give man's emotional impulses . . . the position they deserve"; and the "common compulsion exercised by such a dominance of reason will prove to be the strongest uniting bond among men . . ." (Freud, 1933a, p. 171). As he does in *The Future of an Illusion* (1927a), Freud here appears in the double guise of Enlightenment skeptic and optimist.

After dismissing art as harmless and philosophy as pretentious and impotent, Freud turns to the most serious "enemy" of science, religion. His critique follows the lines we considered briefly in Chapter 1 and, once again, is a recognizable incarnation of its Enlightenment forebear. He then briefly treats epistemological relativism, which he views as a kind of intellectually abstract and practically meaningless anarchism. Finally he comes to Marxism.

From the outset Freud characterizes Marxism as a worldview that is "in opposition to the scientific one" (Freud, 1933a, p. 175). There are, first, Marx's "strange" assertions that the "development of forms of society is a process of natural history" and that "changes in social stratification arise from one another in the manner of a dialectical process" (*ibid.*, p. 177). This does not sound like materialism to Freud, but rather like "a precipitate of the obscure Hegelian philosophy in whose school

Marx graduated." He is willing to grant that Marxism gives us "saga-
cious indications of the decisive influence which the economic circumstances of men have upon their intellectual, ethical and artistic attitudes"
(*ibid.*, p. 178). But this "strength has nothing to do with its view of history or prophecies of the future."[7]

Second, although Freud grants that "economic motives" are important, they are not the only ones that influence human behavior. Quite apart
from economic factors, men are dominated by "their self-preservative
instinct, their aggressiveness, their need to be loved, their drive toward
obtaining pleasure and avoiding unpleasure" (*ibid.*). Moreover, tradition
preserved in the super-ego resists economic innovation; and cultural
development, although influenced by economic and other such factors,
"is certainly independent of them in its origins, being comparable to an
organic process. . . ." Marxism errs in excluding these considerations. If,
by contrast, someone could bring them into accord with Marx's economic
analysis, then "he would have supplemented Marxism so that it was made
into a genuine social science" (*ibid.*, p. 179). But as it stands, so Freud
implies, Marxism is only a pseudoscience.

Third, Freud contends that Marxism in practice has come to resemble
the religions it criticizes. It has created ruthless prohibitions of thought,
forbids critical examination of Marx's writings, treats these writings as
sacred texts, directs hostility toward nonbelievers, and promises the true
believers a paradise on earth. Quite unrealistically it "hopes in the course
of a few generations so to alter human nature that people will live
together almost without friction in the new order of society, and that they
will undertake the duties of work without any compulsion" (*ibid.*, p. 180).
Although it may be that Russian Bolshevism is a "message of a better
future," it may also be that economically "the experiment was undertaken
prematurely." And even if scientific progress makes it possible to "put
an end to the material need of the masses" and to "give a hearing to the
cultural demands of the individual," humanity "shall still have to struggle
for an incalculable time with the difficulties which the untameable character of human nature presents to every kind of social community" (*ibid.*,
p. 181). Hence Marxist hopes are false hopes. Like religion and unlike
the sciences, it makes promises it cannot keep.

2.

Freud contends that, as it stands, Marxism is not a science but rather
a pseudoscience, a would-be science, a religion in the guise of a science.
He holds out the possibility that it could be developed into a real social
science, into a "sociology." But sociology, "dealing as it does with the

behaviour of people in society, cannot be anything but applied psychology" (*ibid.*, p. 179). Why? Because "strictly speaking there are only two sciences: psychology, pure and applied, and natural science." And while he does not make the claim in so many words, it seems pretty clear that there is really only one psychology—psychoanalysis. It follows as the night the day—if rather more oddly —that Marxism, if it were to develop into a real social theory, could and would be nothing other than applied psychoanalysis!

3.

The core of Freud's critique in the "Weltanschauung" essay is that Marxism is psychologically untenable. The psychological principles that determine this judgment are given a more substantive treatment in *Civilization and Its Discontents*.

Wilhelm Reich contends that the arguments in *Civilization and Its Discontents* were developed "to refute my maturing work and the 'danger' which was supposed to arise from it" (Reich, 1942, p. 179). Which is to say, Freud was arguing against a "sex–economic" view of neurosis, in which the repression of sexuality is seen as the prime emotional pathogen and capitalism is seen as the prime determinant of sexual repression. Whether or not Freud would agree with Reich's contention, the text seems to bear witness to its validity.

Deductively, Freud's argument rests upon the dual drive theory announced in *Beyond the Pleasure Principle* (1920). Human life is determined in the first and last instances by the play of the *Lebenstrieb* and the *Todestrieb*, the life-drive and the death-drive. The former tends to "preserve living substance and to join it into ever larger units," the latter tends to "dissolve those units and to bring them back to their primaeval, inorganic state" (Freud, 1930, p. 118). Sexuality is a form of the life-drive, aggression is a form of the death-drive.

Given these postulates it follows, first, that sexuality and aggression are built into the human organism. They cannot be eliminated. Second, as drives, they create a pressure, a psychosomatic state of tension, and hence the aim of discharge (tension-reduction). This aim, however, goes against the requirements of civilization. Civilization demands the sublimation of the basic drives, so that their energy becomes available for cultural development. Indeed, "it is impossible to overlook the extent to which civilization is built up upon a renunciation of instinct, how much it presupposes precisely the non-satisfaction (by suppression, repression or some other means?) of powerful instincts" (*ibid.*, p. 97). To be human is to experience "cultural frustration."

Although there are conflicts between Eros (the life-drive/sexuality) and civilization—between self-love and the love of others, between the direct expression of sexuality and its repression and/or sublimation—on the whole Eros favors the development of culture and community. By binding us together it is, so to speak, the life-drive of civilization; and Freud can imagine "an eventual accommodation" of the conflicts it involves (*ibid.*, p. 141).

Not so the conflict between the death-drive and civilization. Human beings are naturally and necessarily inclined to violence:

> As a result, their neighbor is for them not only a potential helper or sexual object, but also someone who tempts them to satisfy their aggressiveness on him, to exploit his capacity for work without compensation, to use him sexually without his consent, to seize his possessions, to humiliate him, to cause him pain, to torture and humiliate him. *Homo homini lupus.* (*ibid.*, p. 11)

Consequently "civilized society is perpetually threatened with disintegration" (*ibid.*, p. 112). It contains this threat by turning the death-drive/aggression back against the self. Routed through the super-ego, it is moralized and becomes anxiety and guilt. In order that others not be destroyed, the forces of destruction are marshaled against the self. At the limit human beings seem to be confronted with a choice between murder and suicide. Short of these extremes we are condemned to an ongoing struggle with aggression, anxiety, and guilt.

How naive, then, are the communists when they "believe they have found the path to deliverance from our evils" (*ibid.*). They think that "the institution of private property has corrupted . . . [man's] nature" and that, if it were abolished, "ill-will and hostility would disappear" (*ibid.*, p. 113). But "aggressiveness was not created by property. It reigned almost without limit in primitive times, when property was still very scanty, and it already shows itself in the nursery almost before property has been given its primal, anal form." Hence the "psychological premises on which the [communist] system is based are an untenable illusion" (*ibid.*).

So much for capitalism and the repression of sexuality as the source of human misery!

Freud's argument has an additional critical implication. Work and property are sublimates of the basic drives. With respect to human nature, they are epiphenomenal. It would be a mistake, moreover, to rest hopes for human happiness on a restructuring of economic life. To be sure, work attaches the individual to reality and gives him a place in the human community. It also involves the displacement (hence utilization) of the basic drives. And when professional work is "freely chosen," it may be a "source of special satisfaction." And yet

> as a path to happiness, work is not highly prized by men. They do not
> strive after it as they do after other possibilities of satisfaction. The great
> majority of people only work under the stress of necessity, and this
> natu ral human aversion to work raises most difficult social problems.
> (*ibid.*, p. 80)

If there is a "natural human aversion to work," then all labor is alienated labor. Changes in property relationships and economic life might
alleviate some of our suffering, but they would not transform the
human condition.

In sum: Marx has placed his bet on the wrong horse in a race that can't
be won. Marxism is an illusion, and one with a very dubious future.

4.

It is an understatement to say that Freud's polemic against Marx has
its problems. Moreover, *Civilization and Its Discontents* is quite extraordinarily phallocentric, even by Freud's standards. It begins with a rejection of the religious significance of the oceanic feeling (interpreted as the
fusion of mother and infant) and ends with the slaying of the primal
father as the *fons et origo* of civilization. In between women are viewed
as enemies of public life and are reduced to the status of objects of male
desire. And, as will be argued below, Freud's treatment of the origins of
the state is best interpreted as either ideology or fantasy.

It is therefore somewhat puzzling that the text is held in such high
regard. Puzzling, that is, if we consider it simply on its anthropological
and historical merits; for it seems to me that its reputation is derived
from Freud's clinical authority. Because he can claim that his speculations about human civilization are the product of clinical inquiry, they
gain a kind of communicative legitimacy. It is not clear that these
notions have such a secure clinical foundation; nor is the transition from
the clinical consulting room to the field of historical inquiry as unproblematical as Freud's authorial practices would make it appear. Be that as
it may, the polemical and speculative aspects of Freud's theorizing must
be seen against the backdrop of his clinical theory and practice. Accordingly we will delay our Marxist critique of his cultural theory until after
we have given some attention to the clinical foundations of his theorizing, and to the theory he built upon these foundations.

5.

Just as Marx's political economic research gives his work a scientific warrant, so Freud's clinical inquiries give psychoanalysis a claim to
scientific interest.

Although in recent years the epistemological status of psychoanalysis has been intensely debated, we have seen that Freud placed it within the worldview of the positive sciences.[8] He does differentiate between the natural and the social sciences, in a way that is reminiscent of the classical German distinction between *Naturwissenschaften* and *Geisteswissenschaften*. But in contrast to the neo-Kantian interpretation of this categorical distinction, for Freud the social sciences are not epistemologically distinguishable from the natural ones. So far as valid human knowledge is concerned, there is only one game in town.

We might think of it this way. Biographically, Freud's path led from Ernst Brücke's physical physiological laboratories to the clinical practice of neurology, and from there to the invention of psychoanalysis. One might see in this a parallel to Marx's advance from Hegelianism to critical political economy, that is, an advance that results in overturning not only the theoretical but also the epistemological premises with which the inquiry began. But in Freud's mind the invention of psychoanalysis left his epistemological frame unchanged. To be sure, clinical psychoanalysis rendered much of clinical neurology obsolete. It also required placing a theory of mental function between the brain and behavior. Nonetheless all valid knowledge continued to be viewed as the product of scientific inquiry. The clinical practice of psychoanalysis had the same relationship to psychoanalytic theory as experimental physiology had to physical physiological theory. There was also a clinical art—psychoanalytic technique —that mediated the psychological science. It did not have, however, a separate epistemological warrant. If, therefore, one wants to see Freud breaking not only with neurology but also with science, one does so without his permission.

Clinical psychoanalysis, then, resembles an experimental situation in which knowledge is generated and tested. The analysis takes place within a methodologically controlled setting. The time, place, and fee for the treatment, once established, function as givens. The analyst always sits in the same place, out of sight of the patient; the patient always reclines on the couch. The analyst abstains from personal involvement with the patient and maintains an attitude of impartiality and neutrality with respect to her/his communications. The frame of the interaction being thus invariant, the variable becomes the patient's behavior and communications. S/he reacts to the analyst and the analytic situation differently depending upon her/his state of mind. The analyst interprets the reaction, that is, offers a hypothesis about its intrapsychic cause. The patient's response to the interpretation will tend to validate or invalidate it, and so the process continues.

6.

If on the one hand clinical psychoanalysis resembles a laboratory experiment, on the other it is akin to a medical practice in which a dis-

ease is treated. The course of the analytic inquiry brings into consciousness (1) determinants of behavior that were unconscious hitherto; (2) the
fears and prohibitions that forced them into unconsciousness; and (3) the
mechanisms or intrapsychic processes that rendered them unconscious.
Once the unconscious becomes conscious, it loses its pathogenic quality.
The patient is relatively freed from the neurotic distortion of consciousness and life-activity.

The analytic process, to put it another way, elucidates what has been
repressed, why it has been repressed, and how it was repressed. It proceeds in a prescribed manner. Take the example of dreams. The patient
is encouraged to free associate to an element in the manifest (consciously
remembered) dream, that is, to say whatever comes to mind about it, no
matter how repugnant or seemingly irrelevant. Various determinants of
the dream element emerge. At some point free associations stop. Nothing more comes to mind. The patient has encountered a resistance. The
resistance signifies a conflict. It points toward a conjuncture of repressed
wish and the reason for its repression. The analyst, who has allowed her/
his attention to float freely alongside the patient's, offers an interpretation about the meaning of the resistance. This may engender resistance
in turn. It may also result in insight for the patient about the meaning of
the dream.

As a clinical art psychoanalysis began with the interpretation of
dreams and neurotic symptoms. In time Freud adapted the technique to
a wider range of neurotic disturbances. He also came to recognize that
the patient's most important reactions to the analysis and the analyst were
transferences—wishes, fears, and modes of relating that originated elsewhere, most importantly in the relationships of the patient's natal family. From one perspective he viewed these transferences as a resistance,
as a defense against knowledge of the unconscious, and as an interfer-
ence with the therapeutic aims of the analysis. At the same time he saw
them as emanating from the unconscious, as a movement of the repressed
wishes of the patient toward consciousness. Most of all he eventually
accepted that the transference relationship of patient and analyst constituted the field of psychoanalytic inquiry: the "struggle between the
doctor and the patient, between intellect and instinctual life, between
understanding and seeking to act, is played out almost exclusively in the
phenomena of the transference. It is on that field that the victory must
be won—the victory whose expression is the permanent cure of the
neurosis" (Freud, 1912, p. 108).

Not all neuroses can be cured. But in favorable cases the patient can
be restored to mental health. S/he begins with "a torn mind, divided by
resistances." As the analysis progresses and the resistances are removed,
"it grows together; the greater unity which we call ... [the patient's] ego
fits into itself all the instinctual impulses which before had been split

off and held apart from it" (Freud, 1919, p. 161). Analysis permits self-unification.

The cure of a neurosis must not be mistaken, however, for a transcendence of the human condition. From early on Freud resisted any temptation to play the role of therapeutic messiah. If a patient were to complain that, by Freud's own account, the illness originates in unchangeable life circumstances, he would respond:

> "No doubt fate would find it easier than I do to relieve you of your illness. But you will be able to convince yourself that much will be gained if we succeed in transforming your hysterical misery into common unhappiness. With a mental life that has been restored to health you will be better armed against that unhappiness." (Breuer & Freud, 1895, p. 305)

Psychoanalysis does not give the patient a passport to a better world.

7.

Clinical psychoanalysis is part experimental research, part therapeutic practice. Although the research and therapeutic aims may clash, they are realized through the same technical modalities: the patient's free associations, the analyst's freely floating attention, the interpretation of resistance and transference. Taken in combination these aims and methods of inquiry result in a model of the mind that may be represented in the following manner:

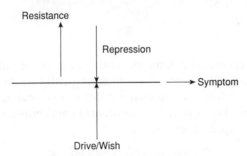

Consciousness; Secondary Process; Reality Principle

Resistance

Repression

Symptom

Drive/Wish

The Unconscious; Primary Process; Pleasure Principle

At one extreme the individual is a conscious being capable of attention, judgment, reasoning, and choices of action (psychical secondary process). S/he takes cognizance of reality and is able to delay and/or vary behavior in response to objective possibilities. That is, her/his action is regulated by the reality principle. At the other extreme mental functioning is unconscious and inaccessible to consciousness. It is obedient to the pleasure principle; that is, it aims at immediate discharge, immediate relief from unpleasurable tension. Unconstrained by reality and rationality, it operates through a psychical primary process of displacements, condensations, fusions, and defusions of emotional valences and meanings.

Between consciousness and the unconscious is psychic conflict. In the unconscious the basic drives hold sway. They place a pressure on the psyche for gratification, a pressure that takes form as a wish, or a set of (perhaps contradictory) wishes. In the course of development some of these wishes, most importantly the ones that violate parental regulations, laws, and taboos, are repudiated. They are repressed, forcibly maintained in a state of unconsciousness. (In the diagram, the horizontal line represents this repressive division of the psyche and the downward arrow the continuing force of repression.) They continue to press toward discharge (the upward arrow). If the pressure they exert becomes too great, symptomatic behaviors may result, compromise formations combining a wish with its repudiation. An hysterical paralysis of the arm, for example, might express both the wish to masturbate and a prohibition against it. (The lateral arrow represents the production of symptoms as compromise formations.)

When an individual enters analysis, s/he consciously intends to cooperate with the treatment. But s/he and the analyst soon encounter her/his characteristic resistances. These resistances (represented by the other upward arrow) are the other face of repression, the face it presents to the world even when symptoms are absent. They manifest themselves in the transference relationship, where they can be analyzed and dissolved. Concomitantly repression is lessened, the division of the self is reduced, and symptomatic behavior becomes less necessary.

8.

Sometimes Freud articulated psychoanalytic theory in terms of a set of interrelated higher-order (phenomenologically more abstract) concepts.[9] He characterized the discourse at this level as metapsychological.[10] Its relationship to the clinical derivation and employment of psychoanalytic concepts is represented below:

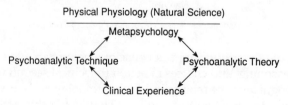

Physical Physiology (Natural Science)

Metapsychology

Psychoanalytic Technique   Psychoanalytic Theory

Clinical Experience

Freud constructed psychoanalysis from the bottom up and from the top down. On the one hand, the field of clinical experience determined and was determined by psychoanalytic technique and theory, which were themselves interpenetrative and mutually determining. On the other, Freud started from settled and unshakeable positive scientific convictions. One implication of his epistemological position was that the body had ontological priority over the mind. Moreover, mental processes were just as determined (constrained, causally explicable) as physical ones.

The metapsychology was intended to unite these two theoretical domains, or at least to state the problem of joining them. Thus it, too, can be approached from the bottom and the top. In the former regard we might look again at the diagram on page 39. Metapsychologically it represents the mind *topographically* (as a functionally divided psychical space) and *dynamically* (as a field of intrapsychic conflict). Over time Freud developed the topography into a *structural* model of the psyche (id, ego, super-ego), while the dynamic dimension of the theory was elaborated into a rich conceptualization of defensive mechanisms and processes (reaction-formation, projection, introjection, etc.). And because Freud located the etiology of the neuroses in infantile sexual fantasies and experience, the theory involved a vital *ontogenetic* dimension. Although Freud did not give the genetic perspective metapsychological status, his followers subsequently conferred this honor upon it.

The preceding dimensions of the metapsychology are readily derived from clinical experience. They usefully perform a synthetical function. The final metapsychological dimension, the *economic*, is more problematical. Freud united under this rubric concepts depicting the production, circulation, distribution, and consumption of a hypothetical psychical energy, more specifically libido (the psychical emanation of the physiological sexual drive). These concepts were derived from the neurological theory Freud learned in Brücke's laboratory. They amount to a set of analogies, conceptions of mind stated in neurological language. Not surprisingly, therefore, they look suspiciously like metaphors disguised as concepts. Although they do provide a means of articulating (1) the mind–body relationship and (2) quantitative aspects of clinical experience (for example, the intensity of an emotion), they are supernumerary—they duplicate the phenomena they purportedly explain. They emanate from the nervous system the way Platonic *eide* (Forms) emanate from the Good. The one transcendental explanation is as good as the other.

Later on we will have to rethink the metapsychology and bring it into accord with an equally rethought Marxist anthropology. But we will leave neurology to the neurologists, and thank them to repay the courtesy when it comes to the mind.

9.

Among other things, the metapsychology is a statement of the mind/body problem. Our immediate interest, however, is in the mind/history problem. This interest will be advanced if we focus upon the concepts that link psychoanalysis most directly to social theory: anxiety, guilt, and the oedipal configuration.

A four-year-old boy has discovered and become fascinated by his penis. He is excited by seeing it erect, by making it erect, and by the feeling of its being erect. His experience with his penis stimulates his curiosity about his mother and father's nocturnal relationship. On the borderline of his consciousness it stirs up fantasies about their sexual interaction and, fatefully, the desire to take his father's place in that interaction. But his father is bigger and more powerful than he is; and he has a bigger, more powerful, and more desirable penis. Consequently the boy's exciting and excitable penis causes him anxiety: To use it is to lose it. His father will punish him for his rivalrous impulses by cutting them off at the root.

In his hour of need the boy finds a way out of the dilemma. He obeys the father in his head, the emergent God the Father, and represses his sexual desires. He continues to wage a rearguard action against the temptation to masturbate, but he has no awareness of the desire to take his father's place with his mother. Yet he is not happy. His sexual drive has not been extinguished, his oedipal ambitions live on in his unconscious. The father in his head knows all, sees all, condemns all. And unconsciously the boy knows he is guilty as charged.

That is not the worst of it. In his competition with his father the boy is driven by aggression as well as sexuality. The death-drive fuels his ambitions, transforms his feeling of rivalry into a dread-filled hatred: God the Father takes possession of the boy's hostility, moralizes it, turns it back upon him. Cruelty to the self becomes the order of the day. Guilt is intensified to the point of disease.

The boy is father to the man; man is the neurotic animal—so goes the story of civilization, a story in which women are an afterthought and a subplot.

10.

Because the oedipal configuration is his interpretive paradigm, Freud's depiction of civilization is admirable in its simplicity and coherence. Whether it has anything to do with actual human history is doubtful. But we will put aside our doubts for just a moment longer.

Freud's interpretation of history begins with the primal father and the primal horde—the primal oedipal situation. The horde consisted of a powerful male, his sons, and a number of females. By dint of strength of body and will, the father ruled over the horde despotically. He alone had sexual access to the females; his sons were forced into either sexual abstinence or exile. In time they united into a brother-band, killed and devoured their father, and so freed themselves from his domination. But after they had killed him, their love for him resulted in feelings of remorse. Moreover, their ingestion of his flesh was accompanied by the introjection or internalization of his image. Remorse became guilt, and the "dead father became stronger than the living one had been" (Freud, 1913, p. 143). The sons obeyed him posthumously. They transformed him into a totem animal they were forbidden to kill, and sexual relations with mothers and sisters became taboo. In the course of time totemism evolved into religion, the totem animal became the living God, and the incest taboo became the law of laws.

The brother-band is the prototypical political organization. After the death of the father it becomes a "totemic community," in which all of the brothers have equal rights and equal obligations (Freud, 1921, p. 135). Here we have primitive justice and the emergence of the rule of law. But the primal oedipal pattern reasserts itself. Individuals and/or groups of individuals make themselves into political rulers. The "justice of the community then becomes an expression of the unequal degrees of power obtaining within it; the laws are made by and for the ruling members and find little room for the rights of those in subjection" (Freud, 1933b, p. 206). The rule of law is more or less disguised, more or less open, domination.

More closely considered, justice is itself domination, loss of freedom. For the "liberty of the individual is no gift of civilization" (Freud, 1930, p. 95). Rather the individual at the beginning of history, like Faust at the beginning of the tragedy, has "Renounce, renounce shalt thou, thou shalt renounce!" dinned everlastingly into his ears (Goethe, 1832, p. 56).

11.

In his occasional ventures into history and social theory Freud does not ignore technological and economic factors. He notes their importance for cultural development; he links them to war and domination; and he observes that economic and technical gains do not necessarily make people happy. Hence one might be tempted to write off his misrepresentation of Marxism as the product of circumstance and ignorance, and to interpret him as a Marxist *malgré lui*. To do so would be a definite mistake.

For Marx work is the fundamental human activity. It is the expression and development of one's human nature. Individually and collectively human nature is human self-production. For Freud human nature is an instinctual essence that evolves, if at all, only in long, slow, involutional waves—as an extremely gradual loss of instinctual intensity, a kind of instinctual entropy, twilight of the life-drive, triumph of the death-drive (Freud, 1933b, p. 214). For practical purposes, however, the drives may be taken as a constant, and human nature as a given. And as for work, it is epiphenomenal. The capacity for work results from renunciation—from the inhibition and sublimation of sexual and aggressive drives. Work has unhappiness built into it and, fundamentally, it changes nothing. Hence, and as we have seen, Freud views Marx's project of human emancipation through economic transformation as an illusion.

12.

It is not too much to say that renunciation is the fundamental premise of Freud's practical *weltanschauung*. Renunciation of instinctual happiness is a requisite for cultural survival. In theory and practice Freud offers us only amelioration of and consolation for the pain of being human—only the chance to be ordinarily unhappy.

Freud does not quite foreclose the future. He maintains a tenuous hold on the Enlightenment project of human community and universal peace. It might be possible to link emotional identifications more closely to economic and political interests than has been the case hitherto. It may be that a strengthening of intellect comes along with the involution of the basic drives. And perhaps one could educate a "community of men who had subordinated their instinctual life to the dictatorship of reason," an "upper stratum of men with independent minds, not open to intimidation and eager in the pursuit of truth, whose business it would be to give direction to the dependent masses" (*ibid.*, pp. 212–213). Here we have the return of Plato's philosopher-kings.

Such hopes, if hopes they are to be called, are "utopian," as Freud himself hastens to acknowledge. In his more characteristic guise of realist he is more pessimistic. "Men," he observes, "have gained control over the forces of nature to such an extent that with their help they would have no difficulty in exterminating each other to the last man" (Freud, 1930, p. 145). The forces of production are the legions of the God of Death. It may be that "eternal Eros" will be able to restrain his "equally immortal adversary." Maybe not.

In the preface to *Capital, 1,* for example, Marx acknowledges that he does not paint the capitalist in rosy colors. He goes on to say:

> But individuals are dealt with here only in so far as they are the personifications of economic categories, the bearers of particular class-relations and interests. My standpoint, from which the development of the economic formation of society is viewed as a process of natural history, can less than any other make the individual responsible for relations whose creature he remains, socially speaking, however much he may subjectively raise himself above them. (Marx, 1867, p. 92)

Motives, including economic motives, exist, but they are fundamentally determined by, rather than determining of, social structural relationships.

Marx's position is no doubt contestable, and Freud might seem just the one to contest it, but he fails to do so. Having reduced all valid knowledge to either natural science or psychology, all he can find in Marxism are the motives that Marx himself views as epiphenomenal. He cannot even pose the question of how objective determinants of human action interact with subjective ones, how (more narrowly) interests interact with motives. He has begged it by methodological fiat.

Later on we will raise precisely this question. When we do, we will take very seriously the passage from Marx cited above. Accordingly we will not ask Marx to provide us with a theory of motives. Nor will we deny that he has something to tell us about individuals. Individuals, he claims in this text, are agents with objectively determined interests. These interests, we might add, are in part constitutive of the subjectivity of individuals. Hence we will not allow Freud's imperialistic claim to possession of the individual. Conversely, we will not grant Marx a monopoly in the realm of sociological interpretation.

5.

Individuals work, as both Freud and Marx emphasize. All meaningful work involves disciplined effort, as both would acknowledge. But there is all the difference in the world between creative work and alienated labor. Marx's theory is structured by the recognition of this difference; Freud's is disfigured by his unwillingness to recognize it.

As we have seen, Freud claimed that there is a "natural human aversion" to work, and that the "great majority of people only work under the stress of necessity." This seems odd to him, given (1) that work performs useful emotional as well as instrumental functions and (2) that it is a "source of special satisfaction" when it is "freely chosen."

Why not try to resolve the apparent contradiction? If free choice is a necessary condition for finding satisfaction in one's work, one might try to ascertain who does and who does not have such choices. One might also surmise that, if given a chance, individuals would tend to make such choices in the light of their own constitutional (innate or developed) make-up, and that absence of choice would correlate with an absence of regard for such constitutional factors. The hypothesis then would be that those who have free choice would value their work positively, those who lack free choice would value it negatively. Next one would observe that the "great majority of people" do not choose their work, but are rather forced to work—that, as Marx emphasizes, they are alienated in their laboring and from the products of their labor. Hence their aversion is not to work as such, but rather to alienated labor. Hence also a remedy for at least one of the discontents of civilization: Replace, to the extent possible, alienated labor with self-realizing work.

6.

Needless to say, Freud would not accept this way out of his conceptual dilemma. From first to last his theory is marked by an almost Platonic contempt for the Many or, as he calls them, the "dependent masses."

At the one (presumably historical) extreme we find the relationship of the primal father to the members of the horde. The members are no different from modern group members, who are libidinally bound to each other through their common libidinal bondage to the group leader, and who are notable for their intense affectivity, low level of intellectuality, and lack of individuality. The primal father is the prototypical group leader: He, "at the beginning of history, was the 'superman' whom Nietzsche only expected from the future," a man of "masterful nature, absolutely narcissistic, self-confident and independent" (Freud, 1921, pp. 123–124). At the other extreme we have the utopian vision of the "upper stratum of men" who subordinate their instincts to the "dictatorship of reason" and give direction to the masses.

In short, Freud ontologizes both elitism and individualism. Anything that hints at human equality, at dethroning "the individual" and granting individuality to ordinary people, is condemned as unrealistic ... or—worse—as "American" (Freud, 1930, p. 116).

7.

From a Marxist standpoint Freud's anthropological and historical ideas cannot be taken literally. They are quite obviously inverted or false forms of consciousness. Freud has various psychological notions that he projects onto a blank historical screen. Then he treats these products of his subjectivity as if they were objectivities, historical actualities. He hides this transposition in a language of methodological restraint. He grants that the primal horde might be viewed as a "Just-So Story" (Freud, 1921, p. 122) and that his ideas about social evolution are conjectural. But he clearly believes in the veracity of these notions, in much the same way as the faithful believe in their various deities.

In form, then, Freud's interpretation of history is yet another instance of an "inverted world consciousness." So far as content is concerned, it can be interpreted two ways. First, it amounts to liberal ideology with a premodern twist. Like the liberals, Freud begins with a state of nature and evolves political society out of this condition via compact. Unlike the liberals and like conservative social theorists, Freud conceptualizes natural conditions as familial and patriarchal. He ontologizes not only a Hobbesian conception of man as wolf to man, but also patriarchal domination as the human condition. Second, we might treat Freud's historical notions as fantasies—but not just his. The primal horde, for example, provides us with an image of unconscious emotional trends in certain familial and societal relationships. If we recognize it as a fantasy, it has a significant interpretive value. If it is treated as history, it must itself be interpreted.

Either way, Freud's interpretation of history is a more or less covert mythology. It is oddly reminiscent of Hegelianism. In it we find cosmic forces of life and death that materialize themselves in particular social and historical phenomena. World historical individuals attempt to subordinate these forces to their will. Ultimately, however, they and we are the playthings of "Heavenly Powers" (Freud, 1930, p. 133). It is but a short step from these formulations to the notions we find in the introduction to Hegel's *The Philosophy of History* (1956). A cunning of reason determines our destinies for Hegel, a cunning of unreason determines them for Freud; two sides of the same coin.

8.

For the most part Freud comes to grief when he leaves the clinical consulting room. His story of civilization may be good psychology but it is bad history, and his critique of Marxism is largely without force. Not entirely, however: Freud is properly skeptical of the messianic tendency he perceives in Marxism, the bold claim that human nature is so malleable that a new kind of human being can be formed from this raw material. Can be and will be: When the idea of human perfectibility is combined with the idea of historical inevitability, Marxist true believers can be promised a heaven on earth. This cunning of reason is no more credible than Freud's cunning of unreason.

What then? We are left with the core notions of the two theories, and with the problems that result from their juxtaposition. These are now our problems. Let's summarize them before we turn to the Freudian-Marxist attempts at their solution.

D. Contradictions

1.

Marx and Freud agree on the epistemological primacy of science, but their agreement is less substantial than it might at first appear. When Marx advanced from philosophical critique to scientific inquiry, he brought dialectical reasoning with him. It enabled him, so he believed, to solve problems that the classical political economists either did not recognize or could not resolve. Freud, by contrast, sees in dialectics only the obscurities of Hegelian philosophy. His own conception of science is (broadly speaking) empiricist and positivist. We might wish to reconceptualize psychoanalysis in dialectical terms, but this is not Freud's position.

2.

For Marx human nature is intersubjective or relational, an ensemble of social practices. For Freud it is an essence, that is, the fundamental attributes of the individual as individual.

3.

For Marx human nature is an historical process. The species is both malleable and self-productive. For Freud human nature is an evolutionary given. It changes, if at all, very slowly, and not as the self-determination of the species.

4.

For Marx to be human is to be self-expressive, to actualize that which we are potentially. For Freud to be human is to be self-repressive, to inhibit the expression of the basic drives.

5.

For Marx the way we work is what makes us human and what makes us historical—what differentiates us from the rest of nature. For Freud work is a sublimation of the basic drives. History is an attempt to master or tame these drives. The drives make us what we are.

6.

At all levels of analysis, from the anthropological to the practical, Marx conceptualizes the economic dimension of human experience. He observes aspects of emotional life, but only observes them. They are left in a pretheoretical condition and are treated as dependent variables. Conversely, Freud conceptualizes the emotional dimension of human existence. He observes aspects of economic life, but he leaves them in a pretheoretical condition and treats them as dependent variables.

7.

For Marx forces and relations of production constitute the fundamental social institutions. The family, insofar as it is not itself the fundamental productive unit, is to be interpreted from the perspective of economic production. For Freud the family is the primary social institution. Economic relationships are not brought into a determinate relationship to familial ones.

8.

For Marx history consists of class struggles, of the battle between those who are objectively the oppressors and those who are objectively the oppressed. For Freud history is primarily a playing out of familial dramas, most notably of the oedipal relationship. It is a psychodrama with objective consequences.

9.

For Marx hostility between collectivities is primarily a function of interests, which in turn derive from historically variable modes of production. It is possible to envision a mode of social production that mutualizes interests and radically reduces collective hostilities. For Freud hostility at any level is primarily a function of the death-drive, of innate human aggressiveness. No change in the social order can alter this fact of human life.

10.

Arguably Marxism and psychoanalysis both fall into the epistemological category of praxis. For each of them the truth is not given a priori but only a posteriori; and it must be created as well as discovered. But Marxism is a praxis of human emancipation, psychoanalysis is a praxis of individual emancipation. The one is public and political, the other is private and (in important respects) extrapolitical. Although this does not necessarily place them in opposition, it renders problematical any attempt to bring them into a practical relationship to each other.

*   *   *   *   *

We may put the conflicts generated by the more ideological tendencies in each theory behind us; the conflicts generated by their core concepts mark the path that lies ahead. But we cannot advance by jumping over these contradictions. We cannot simply join the two sides of the dispute with an "and," as if we were dealing with complementary notions. Nor can we arbitrarily decide in favor of the one or the other. We can, however, put ourselves in a better position to resolve the conflicts if we detach the substantive notions of each theory from the claims to ontological priority which their originators assigned to them.

As a shorthand notation let's term Marxism an objective theory, psychoanalysis a subjective one. The terms themselves have a complicated history. Here they refer merely to the opposing sets of propositions enumerated above. The point, then, is that Marx claims ontological priority for the objective dimension of human experience while Freud claims ontological priority for the subjective dimension. We need not, however, accept either claim. Instead, we may take the relationship between the objective and subjective determinants of human activity as problematical, that is, as something to be investigated rather than something to be presupposed. By so doing we open up an area of inquiry that is otherwise hedged round with dogmatic assurances.

CHAPTER 3

Freudian-Marxism

1.

Anxiety is where opposites interpenetrate.

2.

Classical Freudian-Marxism is primarily the work of three men: Wilhelm Reich, Erich Fromm, and Herbert Marcuse. They were not the only ones interested in linking the two theories. A number of the early psychoanalysts (Siegfried Bernfeld and Otto Fenichel most notably) were both quite radical in their political orientation and interested in critical applications of psychoanalytic theory (Jacoby, 1983). Marcuse's colleagues T. W. Adorno and Max Horkheimer also explored certain of the possible relationships between psychoanalysis and critical theory (Jay, 1973, pp. 86–112). But our purposes will be adequately served if we focus our critical attention on the paradigmatic efforts of the principal contributors.

As we shall see, there are major differences in the approaches taken by these three men to the task of joining Marxism and psychoanalysis. But they shared a certain cultural and generational experience. They were all born at the turn of the twentieth century (Reich in 1897, Marcuse in 1898, and Fromm in 1900); they were assimilated middle European Jews; and they experienced the failure of working class movements and the rise of fascism in western and middle Europe during the interwar years.

Not surprisingly, therefore, we find certain commonalities in their definitions of the problem. Practically they were critics of capitalism and identified themselves with the project of going beyond it. Theoretically they were concerned with the question of consciousness, more specifically of false consciousness. The phenomenon of working class authoritarianism was the

53

most dramatic case in point. But they also were acutely sensitive to the conformist tendencies in capitalist culture and consciousness more generally, tendencies which they viewed as destructive to both critical thought and transformational action. Orthodox Marxism, they believed, did not sufficiently explain these phenomena. They looked to psychoanalysis, viewed as (1) a theory of human nature and (2) a depth psychology of the individual, for alternative and supplementary explanations.

A. Wilhelm Reich: The Gates of Eden

1.

There is no need to retrace the strange path that led Reich from the problematics of Freudian-Marxism through sex–economic theory to the discovery of the orgone, and from the discovery of the orgone to imprisonment, insanity, and death (I. O. Reich, 1969); but we may take note of its beginning. When Reich wrote "Dialectical Materialism and Psychoanalysis" in 1929, he was a politically active Marxist and a practicing psychoanalyst. Between 1929 and 1933 he attempted to unite these two practices. He worked within the Austrian Social Democratic Party and then the German Communist Party to develop a sex–political movement, in which working class individuals were offered both psychotherapeutic services and political education. Although the movement had considerable popular success, he was rewarded for his efforts by expulsion from first the Communist Party and then the International Psychoanalytic Association.

Reich was a prickly, dogmatic, uncompromising, and undiplomatic character. It is hard to imagine any organization, other than one he himself led, that could contain him. Nonetheless his fate is a sobering reminder that psychoanalysis and Marxism are not only theories, but also mutually hostile social institutions, organized entities that are replete with bureaucratic and authoritarian tendencies. Also, just because they are mutually opposed, they severely limit the possibilities for establishing a practical common ground. Perhaps things are changing. We seem to be entering an altogether more fluid political situation. Time will tell if it is also more hospitable to the Reichian project.

2.

In "Dialectical Materialism and Psychoanalysis" Reich begins by raising the question of "whether, and to what extent, Freudian psychoanalysis is compatible with the historical materialism of Marx and Engels" (Reich, 1929, p. 5). "Compatible" is the key word here, for Reich denied from the outset the possibility that psychoanalysis and Marxist "sociology" could be merged theoretically. On the one hand, he argued, psychoanalysis cannot "replace a sociological doctrine, nor can a sociological doctrine develop out of it"; on the other, "Marxism cannot illuminate neurotic phenomena, disturbances in man's working capacity or sexual performance" (*ibid.*, p. 8). It cannot explain "psychological facts," by which Reich meant "individual phenomena" or such things as can be explained through psychology's "experience of the individual." Hence "only insofar as social facts are to be examined in psychological life or, conversely, psychological facts in the life of society, can the two act mutually as auxiliary sciences to one another." They cannot be reduced, the one to the other. Methodologically, by contrast, "psychoanalysis can only correspond to Marxism [that is, to dialectical materialism] or contradict it" (*ibid.*).

Reich's position is one method, two theories. Ultimately this is not satisfactory. Marxism and psychoanalysis each make claims at the anthropological level, and these claims are mutually exclusive. Unless the controversy is resolved, one theory or the other must be taken as noumenal, the other as phenomenal. In the Reichian instance a version of psychoanalytic theory is granted ontological priority and a Marxist conception of history is loosely attached to it. As we shall see momentarily, the ideological tendencies in psychoanalysis are thereby given free rein, and Reich finds himself pulled along a political road quite the opposite from the one he had intended to follow.

Nonetheless Reich's position has two distinct advantages. First, it leads into an exploration of the dialectical nature of psychoanalytic knowledge. Although Reich inclines toward a diamat version of dialectics, he argues plausibly for a dialectical interpretation of neurotic symptoms and related phenomena. Second, his insistence upon the relative autonomy of Marxist and psychoanalytic theories makes it difficult to slide into either psychological reductionism or economic determinism. His view is intended to be binocular, not monocular. Instead of giving us a one-dimensional interpretation of political reality, he forces us to think through the problematical relationship between the "sociological" and psychological dimensions of our experience.

3.

Reich does not manage fully to maximize these two advantages of his position. In the first place, and as I have argued elsewhere (Wolfenstein, 1990c), he sets up the sociopsychological problematic in such a way as to preclude a solution. He places a psychoanalytic individual at one end of a theoretical continuum, a Marxist society at the other. By methodological fiat he precludes thinking in Marxist terms about the individual or in psychoanalytic terms about society. Moreover, by setting up the problem this way, Reich inadvertently re-establishes the category of "the individual," that is, an individual who exists outside of and in an a priori relationship to society.[1] And because work relationships are theoretically determined only at the level of collective structures, this individual is purely psychoanalytic. Economic life, and history along with it, becomes epiphenomenal, a mere forming or deforming of a pregiven and fundamentally unchangeable human nature.[2] Hence the binocularity of the theory tends to, although it never completely does, collapse.

In the second place, Reich partially undermines his dialectical interpretation of psychological functioning. Dialectical reasoning depends upon identifying immanent negativity—internal contradiction along with the drive to resolve the contradiction—in the object of the analysis. Reich, however, tends to externalize the contradictions of emotional life. He contends that "sexual energy is *the* essentially constructive, positive and productive force in the psyche" (Reich, 1929, p. 16). The self-preservative instinct, which might be interpreted as a work-drive, plays "no direct role" in "building up the psychical apparatus" (*ibid.*). Work can never be more than a product or sublimate of sexual energy and development. Consequently there is no opening for a genuine dialectic of work and desire. Further, Reich rejects Freud's idea of a death-drive which, whatever its problems, insures that we view ourselves as self-contradictory. He argues instead that "the destructive instinct is psychologically a reaction against the failure of an instinct to be satisfied . . ." (*ibid.*, p. 18). There is considerable validity to this contention. But like all versions of frustration-aggression theory, it has the misleading implication that failure and frustration are merely accidental rather than intrinsic features of human experience, so that in principle hatred and destructiveness could be eliminated. Finally, and perhaps most fatally, Reich interprets sexuality in largely (1) unproblematic and (2) physiological terms. He treats it as a drive of the organism which, if not inhibited or distorted from without, results in pleasurable experience. It is but a short step from this conception to the equation of mental health with orgastic potency and the replacement of psychoanalytic treatment by direct physical interventions of one kind or another. Mind is very nearly reduced to body, and we are left with a not-very-dialectical dialectics of nature.

4.

Although Reich's conception of both psychical reality and the relationship between psyche and society is not satisfactory, the space for a binocular and dialectical analysis of politics and false consciousness is not entirely eliminated. He is able, for example, to provide a psychoanalytic mediation of Marx's position that the "ideas of the ruling class are in every epoch the ruling ideas" (Marx & Engels, 1845b, p. 172) while simultaneously historicizing the psychoanalytic conception of the reality principle. To put it another way, he provides an answer for a question that Marx fails to address: How do ideas reflecting particular class interests and an historically contingent structure of social practices become identified with reality as such—even or especially by those individuals whose interests and everyday life experience would seem to form a basis for recognizing ruling class ideas as, simply, ruling class ideas?

Reich's response to this question is elegant in its simplicity. He takes from Freud the notion that instinctual life is regulated by the pleasure principle but is "given form by the social existence of the individual" (Reich, 1929, p. 19). The forming and limitation of instinctual satisfaction takes place under the aegis of the reality principle—the individual is forced to seek pleasure in ways that are realistic. This is true in any society whatsoever. But, Reich continues, "the definition of the reality principle remains formalistic unless it makes full allowance for the fact that the reality principle as it exists today is only the principle of *our* society." Moreover, "the ruling class has a reality principle which serves the perpetuation of its power." If, therefore, "the proletariat is brought up to accept this reality principle—if it is presented to him as absolutely valid, e.g., in the name of culture—this means an affirmation of the proletarian's exploitation and of capitalist society as a whole" (*ibid.*, p. 20).

Here we have a psychoanalytic version of the ancient idea that character is formed via internalization. Character structure reflects class structure. Reich's articulation of the concept, however, leaves something to be desired. He does not bring out clearly enough that the reality principle operates *unconsciously*. He tends to conflate the manifest content and the latent meanings of social practices. Consequently he does not bring into focus the series of mediations and contradictions that link the primal roots of the experience of reality to political practices. Moreover, his presentation is peculiarly undynamic. Reality appears to be a mere external stimulus to which the individual responds. Indeed, Reich gives us a moralized subject–object split: A good (pleasure-oriented) subject has its functioning distorted by a bad (pleasure-limiting) reality. Once again we have Natural Man, an inherently healthy animal who somehow seems to have fallen in with unhealthy historical companions.

5.

One of the strengths of Reich's approach to social theory is his focus upon familial relations. Although in later theorists we will encounter a tendency to discount the role of the family in the formation of the modern self, Reich takes it as axiomatic that character is initially formed in the family. Here he is standing on good psychoanalytic ground. And not only psychoanalytic ground: Marx himself had acknowledged that the family is a basic social institution (Marx & Engels, 1845b, pp. 156–157) and Engels had developed an historical interpretation of the family in *The Origin of the Family, Private Property, and the State* (Engels, 1884). For better and (as we shall see) for worse, Reich availed himself of Engels' analysis. But there is no psychology of the family in the orthodox Marxist canon. Reich made good the omission.

Reich states his position in this "simple formula": "The economic structure of society—through many intermediary links such as the class association of the parents, the economic conditions of the family, its ideology, the parents' relationship to one another, etc.—enters into a reciprocal relation with the instincts, or ego, of the newborn" (Reich, 1929, p. 37). Through the mediation of the family the child internalizes social ideology and so becomes a "realistic" member of society. This is true universally. In capitalist society, however, or in any society featuring the patriarchal family and monogamous marriage, character is fashioned into a self-denying structure which, in turn, functions to distort and repress sexuality. Internalized social morality is then conservative: The "exploited person affirms the economic order which guarantees his exploitation; the sexually repressed person affirms even the sexual order which restricts his gratification and makes him ill, and he wards off any system that might correspond to his needs" (Reich, 1932, p. 245). Conservative, or worse: In the early 1930s, with fascism on the rise, Reich came to see the family as "the authoritarian state in miniature" (Reich, 1933, p. 30).

One might protest that Reich's portrait of family pathology is overdrawn. The more basic challenge, however, would be the contention that he is depicting not an historically specific form of the family, but the family as such. This might be Freud's rejoinder. Family life begins in the patriarchal horde and, after a detour through the totemic community of brothers, resumes its patriarchal form. Particular families, or family life in particular societies, might be more or less authoritarian. But the family is *eo ipso* patriarchal and repressive.

In "The Imposition of Sexual Morality" (1932) Reich attempts to meet the patriarchal challenge head on. Basing himself upon Malinowski's researches among the Trobriand islanders as well as upon Engels' work (which in turn was based upon that of Lewis Morgan), Reich argues that, historically, matriarchy preceded patriarchy, communal property preceded private property, and uninhibited, healthy sexuality preceded repressed, neurotic sexuality. He contends that the institution of the marriage dowry, in which the wife's brother pays an annual tribute to the husband, was the mechanism by which the one form of social organization evolved into the other.[3] Hence patriarchal domination and the repression of sexuality, which Freud identified with civilization itself, is historically contingent. One can therefore envision a postpatriarchal as well as postcapitalistic society without taking a leap, conceptual or practical, into a postcivilized abyss.

It cannot be said that Reich's counterattack is altogether successful. His portrayal of matriarchy is as overdrawn in its blessedness as his portrayal of patriarchy is overdrawn in its miserableness. Moreover, the data establishing the existence of the matriarchy is questionable at best. And his depiction of the matriarchy provides no internal basis for the evolution of the marriage dowry which brought it to an end. Once again we seem to be encountering a split, this time between an all-good and pleasurable matriarchy and an all-bad and painful patriarchy. Idealized pre-oedipal relationships are opposed to radically devalued oedipal ones.

It would be a mistake, however, to throw out the baby with the bathwater. Reich successfully establishes the family as a fundamental and historically variable social institution, within which character is formed and/or deformed. Henceforward the analysis of economic production must be complemented by the analysis of human reproduction. We will have to contend with the fact that economic agents were and are family members, likewise that families are economic units. And we will not neglect one other implication of Reich's analysis: All social relationships are gendered and intergenerational.

6.

Reich uses the anthropological, historical, and institutional dimensions of his theory to frame an analysis of the rationality or irrationality of individual and collective choices of action. Here the practical basis of his theoretical efforts is most in evidence.

Reich defines "rational" broadly as "having meaning and purpose," "irrational" as lacking in meaning or purposefulness (Reich, 1929, p. 43). In his actual usage, however, he operates with an interest-based conception of reason: Actions that tend to realize an interest are rational. The category of "interest" includes not only economic advantage at both the individual and social class levels, but also (and most notably) sexual knowledge, gratification, and health. These primary categories of interest are not reducible to each other. They are independent although also socially interdependent.

For our present purposes, the crucial point is Reich's analysis of the relationship between rational and irrational forces in the determination, and hence explanation, of social action. He argues, first, that actions that are rational from the standpoint of economic or sexual interest cannot be reduced to irrational tendencies. Thus he is critical of analysts who "fail to appreciate sufficiently the rational character of work," who "see in the products of human activity nothing but projections and satisfactions of instincts" (*ibid.*, p. 43).[4] Nonetheless meanings that are irrational from the standpoint of need satisfaction may be attached to work activity: The "cultivation of the earth with tools and the sowing of seed serves, socially and individually, the purposes of producing food. But it also has the symbolic meaning of incest with the mother (Mother Earth)" (*ibid.*). Cultivation of the earth is not literally, and in that sense realistically, incest with the mother. The symbolic meaning is unrealistic and therefore irrational. It may also be irrelevant, as when there is no feature of the activity of cultivation that cannot be explained in terms of economic rationality. In any case it is intelligible. Because in both sexual intercourse and agricultural cultivation there is penetration of the giver of life with a "tool" in order to plant a seed, the one activity can symbolize the other. And if cultivation is accompanied by magic rituals and artificial phalluses are placed in fields as fertility charms, then explanation of cultivation practices require investigation of the economically irrational meanings.

One can distill from Reich's example and from his analysis in general a methodology of social inquiry:

1. Determine the interests (economic, sexual, or other) that are actually or objectively relevant to a choice of action.
2. Ascertain whether choices made and actions taken tend to realize these interests. If they do, the analysis need go no further.
3. If choices made and actions taken are not adequately explained in terms of manifest interests and/or are counterproductive from the standpoint of those interests, then psychoanalytic exploration and explanation is appropriate.

We have here the methodological framework for a psychoanalytic theory of political choice. It gives interests (individual or class) and consciousness of these interests their due, while also permitting investigation and explanation of irrational actions and false consciousness. It also has certain limitations. It presupposes the objectivity and also the simplicity of social interests. And it presupposes the ability, on the part of the actor or the interpreter of the action, to differentiate between efficacious and inefficacious means to the given ends. In fact, however, social interests are problematical and complex, and the boundary between efficacious and inefficacious practices is not always clearly discernible.

Let's assume a political situation in which working class activity has not eventuated in revolutionary movement. The Reichian analyst begins with an assessment of the objective reality of the situation. He then judges that members of the working class are acting irrationally given this presumably objective reality, and so has recourse to a psychoanalytic exploration of their economically irrational motivations. But what if the initial assessment is incorrect or incomplete, and what if the analyst mistakes his interpretation of the situation for the situation itself? Then the false consciousness is in the eye of the analyst, and it is the analyst who requires analysis.

Or take the converse instance. There is a strike or a political uprising. Given the analyst's conception of the interests involved, he might view the event as psychologically unproblematical. He might well be right. The analysis should then stop at the second step. A psychoanalytic investigation of unconscious and irrational motivation would be unparsimonious, supernumerary, or even ideologically distortive. Yet a closer analysis of the matter might reveal politically significant irrationalities. What if, for example, there is a latent meaning of oedipal rebellion in the workers' actions? They might then resemble Nietzsche's pale criminal, who "was equal to his deed when he did it" but who "could not bear its image after it was done" (Nietzsche, 1883–1885, p. 150). The strike is defeated or the uprising is put down. Psychoanalytic investigation might reveal that an unconscious sense of guilt resulted in self-defeating choices of action. But the analyst, having already eliminated psychoanalytic considerations, has no choice but to attribute the outcome to the superior power of the enemy or perhaps to tactical errors. He has used his method of inquiry as a defense against the recognition that the workers fell victim to a causality of oedipal fate.

At this juncture one might be tempted to opt for the position that political reality is a night in which all cows are black . . . all is projection and satisfaction of instinct. But if anything is irrational, it is just such a flight from reality. Interests and conflicts of interest are real. There is simply no way around that. They are also inherently problematical and infiltrated by irrationalizing tendencies. There is equally no way around that. It's not easy to know what is rational and what is not. So it goes.

7.

Whatever the complications that attend the analysis of social interests, we might grant Reich that individuals are unconsciously anchored in the social practices of existing realities, and that this may limit or even irrationalize the making of political choices. Members of an oppressed class may unconsciously identify with the interests of their oppressors. What is to be done?

From a Marxist perspective the question of political transformation has two aspects: Where are we going, and how do we get there? In each respect Reich adds a sexual dimension to orthodox Marxist economic positions. Sexual drives are repressed and distorted—negated—in bourgeois society. But the negation can be negated. Especially in young people repressed sexual drives are an internal contradiction. Sexual repression, the negation of healthy sexuality, produces sexual rebellion, the negation of the negation. If the energy of sexual rebellion is linked to the class struggle, a society embodying healthful sex–economic principles can be brought into being. To realize this potentiality, however, one must reject the hyperrationality of those Marxists who live in a theoretical house without windows, who try to deduce the strategy and tactics of mass movement from the a priori principles of their theories, and who model political communication on textual exegesis. Instead one must begin with the actual experience, including the personal and sexual experience, of ordinary working people. What follows? *"Everything that contradicts the bourgeois order, everything that contains a germ of rebellion, can be regarded as an element of class consciousness . . ."* (Reich, 1934, p. 295). To use the classical terms: First comes spontaneity, then comes consciousness.

Reich accepts, as many revolutionaries do not, the necessity of building revolutionary movement from the ground up—of basing revolutionary politics upon the everyday experience and spontaneous rebellion of ordinary people. He also avoids the narrow economism of those orthodox Marxists who insist on defining the class struggle in one-dimensional terms. By including sexual issues in revolutionary politics he opens the door to racial and cultural issues as well.

Reich also makes promises that he can't keep. He shares with Marx the view that proletarian revolution is the determinate negation of the existing social order or, more generally, that history is dialectically rational. Although he stops short of explicit claims that a sex–economic (sexually healthy and economically rational) society is the inevitable outcome of historical development, he clearly holds to the idea that there is an inherent and progressive rationality to historical processes. Perhaps it would be most accurate to say that he has a kind of medical model of history, in which unhealthy deviations (for example, fascism) are possible but in which healthy development is the norm. Would that it were so!

Finally, Reich has an Edenic conception of postcapitalist society. This comes through most clearly in "The Imposition of Sexual Morality," which, taken as a whole, reads like a sex–economic theodicy. Humankind once lived in the garden of communal property and sexual bliss. There were no neuroses and no perversions, not even anxiety worth mentioning, but only a full, satisfying, and healthy sexuality. Then the snake—the marriage dowry, patriarchy, and private property—entered the garden and paradise was lost. Thankfully there is redemption from sin, not through God's grace but through sex–political struggle and socialist revolution: The "abolition of the commodity economy necessarily brings about the elimination of sexual morality and replaces it on a scientifically higher and technically more secure level with sex–economic regulation and support for sexual activity" (Reich, 1932, p. 242). With the elimination of capitalism, monogamous marriage, and antisexual morality, we will find ourselves in a society where "neurosis, perversion, antisocial sexual behavior and disturbances in the capacity to work" are unknown. No more greed, no more envy, no more human nature as we know it. Amen.

Reich attempted to storm the gates of Eden. He paid the price: isolation, imprisonment, insanity. We who have turned away from Edenic pursuits can experience the pathos in his fight and in his fate. But our skepticism of his messianic hopes need not deter us from accepting his contribution to our own struggle: the beginnings of a dialectical and materialist conception of psychoanalytic-marxist method; a binocular social theory emphasizing familial relationships, providing a partial explanation of false consciousness, and focused upon choices of political action; and an orientation toward the practical realization of the theory.

B. Erich Fromm: Displacement Upward

1.

Reich was interested in maintaining the autonomy of psychoanalysis and Marxist sociology. Fromm aims at their integration. Hence he views as erroneous Reich's thesis that "psychology only deals with the individual while sociology only deals with 'society'" (Fromm, 1932a, p. 142).[5] To the contrary: "Just as psychology always deals with a socialized individual, so sociology always deals with a group of individuals whose psychic structure and mechanisms must be taken into account" (*ibid.*).

Fromm thus attempts to give us a highly integrative social theory. Let's see how well he does at it.

2.

In his social psychological essays of the early 1930s, Fromm presents himself as an instinct theorist: The "*active and passive adaptation of the biological apparatus, the instincts, to social reality* is the key conception of psychoanalysis" (*ibid.*, p. 141). The task of analytic social psychology is then to understand the "*instinctual apparatus of a group, its libidinous and largely unconscious behavior, in terms of socio-economic structure*" (*ibid.*, p. 144). Although he gives more emphasis than Freud to the plasticity of the sexual drives, he is here standing on orthdox psychoanalytic ground. And despite the methodological dispute between them, he and Reich have largely similar substantive orientations.

Within a few years there is a fundamental shift in Fromm's position. In *Escape from Freedom*, his major contribution to the discourse of Freudian-Marxism, he states that "contrary to Freud's viewpoint, the analysis offered in this book is based on the assumption that the key problem of psychology is that of the specific kind of relatedness of the individual toward the world and not of the satisfaction or frustration of this or that instinctual need *per se*" (Fromm, 1941, p. 12). Instincts do not disappear from the theory, but they cease to play a leading or even an active role. They are replaced by the emotional conflicts that accompany processes of individuation—more specifically, the anxiety of moral aloneness, the characteristically modern sense of disconnection from communal relationships.

We can be more precise. For Reich, as for Freud, the drives have a substance or content. They involve a specific demand for satisfaction, however diverse the objects, modalities, or distortions through which satisfaction is obtained. They constitute the noumenon beneath the manifold of phenomena, hence also the point of view from which interpretations are made. Fromm inverts these ontological claims and the associated interpretive perspective. An individual might, for example, have "oral" character traits. But "the oral sensation [in infantile feeding situations] is not the cause of this attitude; it is the expression of an attitude toward the world in the language of the body" (*ibid.*, p. 292). Character is the product of intersubjective experience. The body may express meanings, but it does not originate them. Hence one interprets from relationship to psyche, and then from psyche to soma.

Although for Fromm there is no biologically fixed human nature, there are "qualities inherent in man that need to be satisfied and that result in certain reactions if they are frustrated" (*ibid.*, p. 287). These include "a tendency to grow, to develop and realize potentialities which man has developed in the course of history—as, for instance, the faculty of creative and critical thinking and of having differentiated emotional and sensuous experience" (*ibid.*, p. 288).

We now know where we are. Fromm has attempted to bring Marx's conception of the human essence as the ensemble of social relations down to the level of the individual. The human essence is a drive toward self-development that becomes a particular character structure through the internalization of social relationships.

3.

Character is the nexus of Fromm's social psychology. He was not the first to give this ancient notion psychoanalytic employment. Freud wrote about character types, as did Reich. Indeed, Reich was primarily responsible for shifting the focus of clinical psychoanalysis from the interpretation of symptoms to the interpretation of psychic structure. He also used the idea of character structure in his sociohistorical work. In the latter context his aim was to demonstrate how varying historical circumstances produce different forms of character, which in turn react upon and help to determine the course of events.

Fromm builds on this Reichian foundation; and like Reich, he sees the family as the social institution within which character is formed. But where Reich attempted to interpret character from the inside out as well as from the outside in, Fromm's analysis is securely anchored in social relationships: Character leads the individual to act according to social necessity and to gain satisfaction from so doing (*ibid.*, p. 283). *Social character*, in turn, comprises the personality traits common to members of a specific group, be it the members of society as a whole or of a social class or stratum (*ibid.*, p. 277).

4.

Not just character, then, but social character is Fromm's choice for mediating the relationship between socioeconomic structure and ideology. Social character is to provide the psychological dimension missing in classical Marxist theory without creating the dualism of individual and society that is found in Reich's approach. Yet it might appear that Fromm offers us nothing more than a Marxist conception of the individual: Different historical modes of production and different social classes engender different types of individuals, who then act in historically and socially appropriate fashion. Surely we don't need psychoanalysis to reach this banal conclusion. But Fromm is a psychoanalyst, and he generates a knowledge of historical reality one cannot find in orthodox Marxism.

As a species and individually, Fromm argues, human beings begin in a state of fusion with their environment—with nature in the one case, the mother in the other. The two processes of development, phylogeny and ontogeny, then run a parallel course. Development in each instance involves differentiation, individuation, and freedom from the limitations of merely natural and instinctive existence. But the freedom to develop as an autonomous being is simultaneously freedom from a world of security and reassurance. Optimally, a new world of relatedness can be created. If, for example, a child is able to develop inner strength as well as the capacity for love and productive work, then these may become the basis for a spontaneous solidarity with others. But the course of development rarely runs so smooth. Separateness may result "in an isolation that has the quality of desolation and creates intense anxiety and insecurity" (*ibid.*, p. 31). If this trend is predominant, then the surrender of individuality and submission to authority may function as escapes from the emotional burdens of freedom.

Fromm's depiction of development is actually more dialectical than the preceding summary suggests. This is especially evident at the phylogenetic level. Evolving "man" is first of all a part of nature and a creature of instinct. But specifically human existence "begins when the lack of fixation of action by instinct exceeds a certain point; [and] when the adaptation to nature loses its coercive character . . ." (*ibid.*, p. 32). To be human is to be free from natural necessity. It is also to be more vulnerable and dependent than other creatures. Human beings are born weak, require parental attention for a prolonged period, and cannot rely on instincts to guide their actions. "Yet this very helplessness of man is the basis from which human development springs: *man's biological weakness is the condition of human culture*" (*ibid.*, p. 33).

Human beings are creatures of culture, self-created through cultural activity—creatures also with the freedom and necessity of making conscious choices. The human individual must think, otherwise it won't be. Hence the distinctively human quality of self-preservative activity. Man "invents tools and, while thus mastering nature, he separates himself from it more and more" (*ibid.*, p. 33). He becomes aware of his lack of identity with nature; and, tragically, he comes to recognize the finitude of his own existence.

Early on, human beings are united by "primary ties," the organic bonds of community. The community lessens the burden of "negative" freedom (freedom from natural necessity), mitigates the sorrows and thousand natural shocks the human individual is heir to. These ties are broken in the course of historical development, however, and the individual is ever more alone. S/he is progressively freed from submission to the primary community, but there is a gap or a lag between freedom from communal bondage and freedom to be a self-governing and creative individual. This gap or lag is the negative moment in the dialectic of human freedom, the moment of isolation, insecurity, and doubt, of lack of connection and lack of meaning. To escape from it, individuals and groups of individuals may try to restore the primary ties they have gone beyond. But there is no turning back. The attempt to negate the negative moment in freedom results in self-destructive submission to alien authority. Hence the imperative of actualizing freedom rather than escaping from it.

Thus Fromm offers us a theory of history cut from Marxist cloth but interwoven with psychoanalytic threads. And, by focusing upon the contingencies of individual and collective emotional development, he reopens the dialectic of human freedom that Marxist claims to the rationality and inevitability of historical processes tend to close off.

5.

Fromm deploys his conception of the dialectic of freedom both diachronically and synchronically. With regard to the diachronic dimension he preserves and builds upon Marx's depiction of the development, economic alienation, and class antagonisms of capitalism. He attempts to demonstrate how capitalism at its origin gave birth to the morally alone individual. He depicts Lutheranism and Calvinism as authoritarian responses to moral aloneness, and as forerunners of fascism:

> Luther and Calvin psychologically prepared man for the role which he had to assume in modern society: of feeling his own self to be insignificant and of being ready to subordinate his life exclusively for purposes which were not his own. Once man was ready to become nothing but the means for the glory of a God who represented neither justice nor love, he was sufficiently prepared to accept the role of a servant to the economic machine—and eventually a "Führer." (*ibid.*, p. 111)

The object of Fromm's analysis is somewhat indefinite. At first glance he seems to be describing "modern man" or "modern Protestant man" in this passage. As is evident, however, he is especially concerned with German social character. Even more specifically he views authoritarian trends as characteristic of the lower middle class. Taken in the latter sense he is contending that the historically engendered social character of lower middle class Germans predisposed them to accept submission to Hitler as an escape from freedom.

The synchronic or structural dimension of Fromm's argument extends this line of analysis. He contends that the German lower middle class was most vulnerable to the dislocations of the 1920s and 1930s. Already deformed in its social character by authoritarian predispositions, its status was being undermined by the crises and social alignments of monopology capitalism. "Its anxiety and thereby its hatred were aroused; it moved into a state of panic and was filled with a craving for submission to [authority] as well as for domination over those who were powerless" (*ibid.*, p. 220).

Fromm would have a good deal of trouble justifying his psychohistory of fascist social character at an historiographical or social scientific tribunal.[6] He fares better, however, if we interpret his concepts as Weberian ideal-types.[7] By so doing we shift the emphasis from empirical accuracy to heuristic value. This is a step back on the road to knowledge of social reality; it is also a retreat to a more defensible position.

6.

Fromm presents us in seriatim fashion with three "mechanisms of escape" from freedom, namely, authoritarianism, destructiveness, and automaton conformity. By so doing he emphasizes that any one of these might be constitutive of a type of social character. Thus fascism is an expression of an authoritarian character structure, while automaton conformity may underlie the consciousness of individuals who view themselves as free and self-determining citizens of democracies. But as suggested above, Fromm does not adequately demonstrate the class and societal distribution of these character types. Moreover, the three mechanisms of escape are not mutually exclusive. Taken together they might constitute a defensively layered type of social character, in which more primitive modalities can be found beneath more sophisticated ones. Let's assume, with Fromm, that the modern individual unavoidably experiences powerlessness and aloneness, a personal insecurity so great that it can lead not only to anxiety but even to panic. A social character structure of the following type might provide refuge from this experience:

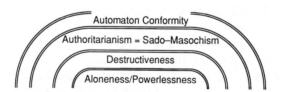

Here character is pictured as a structure of defensive barriers to the experience of moral aloneness. The most basic and most desperate defensive response to isolation and powerlessness is destructiveness. The individual wishes to destroy the world that threatens to overpower him, or, as a last resort, to destroy himself in order not to be overpowered. Such destructiveness is not instinctual. It is rather the outcome of unlived life:

> Life has an inner dynamism of its own; it tends to grow, to be expressed, to be lived. It seems that if this tendency is thwarted the energy directed toward life undergoes a process of decomposition and changes into energies directed toward destruction. (*ibid.*, p. 184)

The drive for life and for destruction are thus in a relationship of "reversed interdependence." The individual who cannot live bends his will toward destruction.

As indicated, Fromm treats authoritarianism as an independent response to isolation and powerlessness. His argument is stronger if it is seen as a defense against and expression of destructiveness as well as of isolation and powerlessness. This is because, in his construction of it, authoritarianism combines two trends: merger of the self into a group identity (symbiosis) in order to escape aloneness, and sadomasochistic emotional dynamics to compensate for an experienced impotency. But the dynamics of domination and submission are not comprehensible unless we recognize in them a destructive craving for revenge. We are then in a position to understand the passion to dominate and be dominated.

Authoritarianism is a more structured and viable response to aloneness and powerlessness than raw destructiveness. It may form the basis for quite stable ideological positions, although the destructive tendency in it is never far from the surface. In automaton conformity, by contrast, these hostile trends may drop from sight:

> [The] individual ceases to be himself; he adopts entirely the kind of personality offered to him by cultural patterns; and he thereby becomes exactly as all others are and as they expect him to be. The discrepancy between "I" and the world disappears and with it the conscious fear of aloneness and powerlessness. (*ibid.*, pp. 185–186)

The individual has escaped from isolation at the price of authenticity. S/he has developed what D. W. Winnicott later termed a "false self" (1960). The capacity for autonomous thinking, feeling, and willing has been sacrificed to the security of being like all the others. At the same time, we would add, the individual is defended against more primitive desires to dominate, to submit, and to destroy.[8]

7.

Fromm thus offers us a striking conception of alienated selfhood and falsified consciousness, and he has a standard of authentic selfhood and true consciousness against which to judge these escapes from freedom. Character deformed by defenses against moral aloneness is constrained and compulsive. It lacks the spontaneity and expressiveness of the free individual. By contrast *"positive freedom consists in the spontaneous activity of the total, integrated personality"* (Fromm, 1941, p. 258).

In spontaneous activity, Fromm continues, the individual "unites himself anew with the world," preserving the self while affirming the selfhood of others. The primary modalities of (what Hegel would term) mutual recognition are love and work. Through them, and through spontaneous activity more generally, the individual "recognizes that *there is only one meaning of life: the act of living itself*" (*ibid.*, p. 263). And precisely this affirmation of life permits the risking of it for self-chosen aims. But death "is never sweet, not even if it is suffered for the highest ideal" (*ibid.*, p. 268). The tragic moment is preserved, not canceled, in the dialectic of positive freedom.

8.

The spontaneity of positive freedom is not constitutive of the social character of our time. Hence to realize positive freedom social character must be transformed. Fromm offers us no strategy for its transformation, but he indicates the political road he believes we must follow, namely, the road to democratic socialism. The individualism that came into prominence with the Renaissance must be universalized and the fundamental values of democracy must be preserved. Unregulated economies must be replaced by planned ones and the rule of the few must be replaced by the rule of the many. To combine these latter imperatives a way must be found to unite centralization with decentralization. For unless planning is blended with active participation and "the stream of social life continuously flows from below upwards, a planned economy will lead to renewed manipulation of the people" (*ibid.*, p. 275). And for there to be active participation in the social process individuals must be imbued with "faith in life and in truth, and in freedom as the active and spontaneous realization of the individual self" (*ibid.*, p. 276).

Once again, amen.

9.

We began this section with Fromm's objections to Reich's program of one method, two theories, and with his aim of integrating sociology and psychology. Both points are expressed in the claim that "just as psychology always deals with a socialized individual, so sociology always deals with a group of individuals whose psychic structure and mechanisms must be taken into account."

Let's begin again with this position, which is simple in appearance, complex and problematical in substance. For one thing, "sociology" as such is a purely formal category. It would reduce to social psychology if it lacked a content of its own. We would be back at Freud's claim that there are only two valid forms of knowledge, natural science and psychology—back at precisely the position Reich is intent upon undermining. Fromm, however, follows Reich in granting sociology a content of its own, namely, relations of production and social class. For "sociology" we may therefore substitute Marxist political economy.

We may then represent the methodological situation this way:

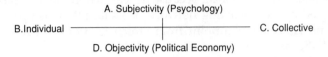

In this diagram we undo the conflation of subjectivity with individuality. The horizontal axis represents a gradient of social relationships extending from single individuals to larger and larger collectivities, ultimately to the human species. The vertical axis represents a gradient between relationships that are exclusively objective (based in work and production) at one extreme, exclusively subjective (based in desire and emotional life) at the other, with various admixtures of objectivity and subjectivity in between. Taken as a whole, the diagram permits us to analyze the interplay of objective and subjective factors anywhere along the continuum from specific individuals to the species.

We might read Fromm as criticizing Reich for conflating subjectivity with individuality and collective life with objectivity. By contrast, he wishes to analyze the subjectivity of collective experience. And he objects to placing the individual outside of social relationships. Well and good. But, first, if his insistence on human sociality isn't to degenerate into sociological idealism, then his theory must include the recognition that human individuals are natural (biological, sensuous, psychophysiological) beings. And this recognition must be conceptual as well as observational. Fromm must grant Reich that human individuals are embodied; and he must derive the social implications of this fact. Second, if he wishes to extend psychology to the study of collectivities, then he must also extend political economy to the study of individuals. Otherwise the analysis becomes psychologistic. Indeed, he can only avoid psychologism if he considers the objectivity of human experience at the theoretical level of anthropology. Third, if he is serious in his desire to undo the conflation of individual and psychology, then he must be able to articulate a genuinely social psychology, that is, not just a social extension of individual psycholgy but rather an integral theory of collective emotional experience. Failing the development of such a psychology, his departure from Reich in this regard would be largely nominal.

10.

It is evident, I think, that Fromm has not satisfied the first of these evaluative criteria. As Marcuse contends in his well-known critique of neo-Freudian revisionism (1962), Fromm empties Freud's theory of its vital core. By shifting the center of the theory from biology to society, from instincts to relationships, he creates an image of the individual as a cipher of social circumstance. Because he leaves nothing *in* the individual that is *outside* of the existing network of social relationships, he leaves himself no Archimedean point from which to protest against domination and alienation.

Here is another way of stating the criticism. In any subject–object relationship there are at least three moments or interpretive perspectives: the substance of the subject; the substance of the object; and the two-fold process of interaction between subject and object, that is, the movement from subject to object and from object to subject. Fromm empties the first moment of meaning. Relatedness then can only be determined from the position of the social object. The weight of the object then falls upon and into the subject, which can offer no resistance.[9]

Weakness from one perspective is strength from another. Fromm is exceptional among psychoanalysts for his genuine appreciation of Marx's conception of human species life. Indeed, the historical framework of *Escape from Freedom* is very nearly isomorphic with that of *The German Ideology*. Hence he comes close to satisfying our second criterion. He takes productive activity seriously, even at the level of the individual. But in comparison to Marx's rigorous analysis of work and production, Fromm's position is indefinite and humanistic. And because he has systematically removed the vital principles from psychoanalysis, the determinate and mutually contradictory ontologies of the two theories never confront each other. A vague *Lebensphilosophie* covers over the clash of *Weltanschauungen*.

As for the third criterion, it might appear that the concept of social character constitutes the basic building block of an adequately social psychology. Despite the name, however, social character does not carry us much beyond the territory staked out by Reich. Reich, too, depicts historically and socially determined patterns and distributions of character types. To that extent he is not a methodological individualist. But he is a psychological individualist: In his theorizing, social psychology is nothing other than aggregated individual psychology. Likewise Fromm. Although his individual is relational rather than biological, his reasoning limits social psychology to the sum and substance of its individual parts.

We might think of it this way. When Marx conceptualizes the commodity as the "elementary form" of the capitalist mode of production, he appears to be functioning as a social atomist (Marx, 1867, p. 125). But in fact he arrives at the commodity by a process of abstraction from a totality of social relations. The totality is the actuality from which the commodity is abstracted. The capitalist mode of production is not reached by adding up commodities. Or again, when Marx conceptualizes a social class, he is not adding up the attributes of its members or simply describing an attribute of each individual that is the same for all. Rather the social class, that is, a structure, web, or pattern of practices, is the unit of analysis.

I trust the point is clear. The concept of character structure is a plausible candidate for the role of the "elementary form" of a social psychological theory. The concept of social character acknowledges that there are structural constraints on and therefore commonalities in character formation. Fromm has not given us, however, a genuinely social psychology, but only an aggregative individual psychology. He is a social atomist in actuality, not merely in appearance.

It is tempting but perhaps not quite fair to say that Fromm is relational where he should be individualist (the first criticism) and individualist where he should be relational (the third). In any case his reach exceeds his grasp. His identification with Marx's historical ontology expresses his desire to unify Marxism and psychoanalysis, as does his relational conception of selfhood. But the relational self signifies the sacrifice of psychoanalysis at the Marxist altar, while at the same time his psychological individualism reflects his unwillingness or inability to complete the act.

11.

One implication of the preceding argument is that Fromm has more in common with Reich than it might at first appear. They are, so to speak, the Romulus and Remus of Freudian-Marxism. The quarrel between them is a family affair.

For example, Reich tends to reduce selfhood to sexuality; Fromm tends to remove sexuality from selfhood. Their positions are opposed. Yet from their opposed positions they arrive at parallel conceptions of human destructiveness. Reich contends that "a man's readiness to hate and his guilt feelings are dependent . . . upon the state of his libido economy," and that "sexual dissatisfaction increases aggression while gratification reduces it" (Reich, 1929, p. 18). Fromm views destructiveness as, most fundamentally, the result of unlived life, or as the decomposition of the drive toward life. More concretely, he thinks it results from powerlessness and aloneness. At either level, for Fromm as for Reich, hostility is relegated to the status of contingency and consequence. Each of them falls victim to what is, in Freud's opinion, the illusion that destructiveness is not an integral part of the human condition. From his perspective their quarrel is at the same time an agreement not to look at why they are quarreling.

12.

One of the strengths of Freud's theory is that he never strays far from the problematical boundary between psyche and soma. The drives, both sexual and destructive, operate along this borderline. Because they serve the pleasure principle, and because the reality principle limits the possibilities of satisfaction, they are sources of conflict. The experience of anxiety signifies and makes manifest this boundary dispute. At the same time Freud problematizes the relationship between internal and external reality. Here, too, we find conflict and anxiety.

Neither Reich nor Fromm manages to maintain this doubly problematical conception of human individuality. The tendency in Reich is to reduce mind to body. The embodied but merely embodied individual then confronts and is in conflict with social reality. Fromm displaces the locus of conflict upward and outward. A disembodied individual then experiences the anxieties of connection and disconnection. In neither case do we find selfhood determined from below as well as from above, from inside as well as from outside. Both theorists escape from . . . anxiety.

Thus Reich and Fromm develop opposed conceptions of the self. Moreover, their conceptions of selfhood move with equal and opposite force away from the crucial loci of selfhood, away from the points where opposites interpenetrate and anxiety is generated. Their theories are defensively decentered.

13.

We will find as we proceed that theories, at least the interesting ones, are complex structures built around the simultaneous engagement with and retreat from loci of conflict. One of these loci is political choice. Reich, in his early theorizing, was never far from questions concerning the choice of action. His conception of political rationality—of assessments of rationality in terms of interests—is the unmistakable bearer of this concern within his theory. Fromm, by contrast, relatively devalues and marginalizes both interests and reason. Questions about the truth or falsity of consciousness are replaced with questions about its authenticity. Actions are to be judged by their spontaneity, not by the interests they serve. Although this is a useful corrective to the hyperrationalism, albeit dialectical hyperrationalism, of some Marxists, it moves Fromm away from concrete situations in which decisions must be made. It tends to displace rather than to complement the analysis of interests and rational choices.

This displacement of politics has two aspects. First, in Fromm's usage authenticity and spontaneity are extremely indefinite concepts. It is even more difficult to judge the authenticity and spontaneity of an action than it is the interests and reasons behind it. From the standpoint of political practice, therefore, these concerns may well function as a smokescreen. Second, Fromm's focus on authenticity and spontaneity enables him to execute a glissade from psychology to ethics, and from the imperatives of political action to the formalism of the categorical imperative. The articulation of humanistic values takes the place of the analysis of psychopolitical realities. Thus there is a concealed gap between the falsity of the world that exists and the veracity of the world that (merely) ought to exist.

We might take the point one step further. What if Fromm's values are precisely not spontaneous, but rather the uncritically maintained repressive values of the Enlightenment? Then the articulation of humanistic values is itself a repressive act, part and parcel of maintaining the moral structure within which the ugliness of reality is concealed and by which it is justified. This is Marcuse's position. He contends that Fromm and the other neo-Freudian revisionists fail to recognize the ideological loading of humanistic values. In using them as a standard for judging modern society they may appear to be critical and political. They are actually conformist and moralistic. Hence the tone of their writings "frequently comes close to that of the sermon" (Marcuse, 1962, p. 237).

Perhaps it is time to stop saying "amen."

C. Herbert Marcuse: Death, Where Is Thy Sting?

1.

If one holds up spontaneity as a criterion of authentic selfhood, then one might try in compulsive and forced fashion to conform to it. Marcuse is surely correct in pointing out the repressive potential of such humanistic values. But any value can function repressively. Take the classical instance. Kant's categorical imperative—"So act that the maxim of your will could always hold at the same time as a principle establishing universal law"—was intended as an articulation of moral autonomy, as a principle proceeding from the free will (Kant, 1788, p. 30). But as has often been pointed out, it is hard to imagine a position of greater moral heteronomy than the self-imposed duty of submission to a formal law detached from one's own interests and passions.

That is not quite right. Rather, it is in the nature of values to function both expressively and repressively. Nothing, especially not values, escapes the inherence of contradiction.

Marcuse identifies himself with the power of negative thinking. His criticism of Fromm is aimed at, among other things, his positivism—his failure to carry the dialectical critique of domination through to its end. We may fairly bring this standard to bear upon Marcuse's own theorizing. Does he fully engage the contradictions of human alienation? What if they cannot be fully engaged? And what if the dialectical critique of domination is itself a value, hence itself in part its opposite, an instrument of domination? Is there a way out, other than an escape from contradiction?[10]

2.

Reich construed psychoanalysis as an individual psychology; Fromm attempted to reconstruct it as a social psychology. Marcuse has yet a third position. Although it may appear that Freud has given us only an individual psychology, in fact this "individual psychology is in its very essence social psychology" (Marcuse, 1962, p. 15). Freud "discovered the mechanisms of social and political control in the depth dimension of instinctual drives and satisfactions." Hence psychoanalytic categories "do not have to be 'related' to social and political conditions—they are themselves social and political categories" (Marcuse, 1970, p. 44). Indeed, psychoanalysis "reveals not only the secret of the individual but also that of civilization" (Marcuse, 1962, p. 15).

Marcuse wants to have it both ways. With Reich, he insists that there is an essential human nature; with Fromm, he insists that human nature is inherently historical. There is a common psycho-logic running through the history of both the individual and civilization.

But this means that he also has it neither way. He offers us a purely (albeit reinterpreted) psychoanalytic conception of human nature, with respect to which the social world revealed in Marxist theory remains entirely external. Thus he flies into precisely the psychological reductionism Reich sought to avoid by asserting the relative autonomy of Marxism and psychoanalysis. And he secures the unity of individual and society through a bold and extremely questionable employment of Freud's metaphor/concept of psychic energy. The problematics of psychosocial relationship, of intersubjectivity, are displaced onto libidinal ebbs and flows. Consequently he loses the focus on intersubjective linkage that is the great advantage of Fromm's social psychology.

3.

Like Hegel and Marx before him, Marcuse proceeds on the assumption that there is a concealed negativity in the positive and a latent positivity in the negative. He likewise gives to dialectical reason its full ontological signification. The negativity of the positive and the positivity of the negative are seen as inhering in reality and not just in reasoning about reality. Unlike Marx, however, he is a philosophical critic of science rather than a scientific critic of philosophy.

Here we have another glissade, one that completes, or at least threatens to complete, a circle—a circle with an empty political center. Marx's break with Hegel was at once epistemological and political. He advanced from philosophy to science in the interest of practical efficacy. To be scientific meant, among other things, to be capable of producing effects in the real world. And, fortuitously or necessarily, an emancipatory political science was possible. There existed a subject capable of practicing it. The proletariat, by thinking and acting rationally, could/would change the world. It was the immanent negativity in the positivity of capitalist reality.

By the time we reach Reich, confidence in the immanence of proletarian revolution was waning, while dialectical reason was sliding toward formalism and dogmatism. Reich remains true, however, to Marx's scientific and practical orientation, both of which are identified with the revolutionary project. Fromm, writing *Escape from Freedom* as the horror of Nazism was unfolding, detaches Freudian-Marxism from revolutionary politics. Theory moves away from being the political science of social transformation and toward the role of being the dialectical conscience of an untransformed society.

Finally, with Marcuse dialectical reason regains its subtlety and its critical cutting edge. It is now employed not *as* science, but rather *against* science. Science is viewed as a practical and ideological instrument of domination. It is used by the powers-that-be against any potential force of opposition. An emancipatory political science has become a contradiction in terms, and the postulated practitioner of the science no longer exists. The proletariat has been absorbed into the structure of domination. As Hegel contended, "the whole is the truth"—and as Hegel was determined to deny, "the whole is false" (Marcuse, 1960,

p. xiv). Social reality is a one-dimensional negative totality. There seems to be no choice, therefore, but critically to interpret a world one is powerless to change.

And yet Marcuse never stopped trying to change it.

4.

Marcuse's turn toward Freud was a movement within the circle of a bad totality. The threatened closure of the circle was determined by the lack of a collective agent of social transformation. Marcuse attempted to keep it open by finding a hidden emancipatory trend in psychoanalytic theory.[11]

Freudian theory, he contends, is at once "the most unshakeable defense" and the "most irrefutable indictment" of Western civilization (Marcuse, 1962, p. 11). Civilization is necessary for human survival; civilization requires the renunciation of instinctual satisfaction. Human beings are the civilized and therefore unhappy animals.

This contention depends upon Marcuse's interpretation of the relationship between the pleasure principle and the reality principle. He identifies the aims or values of immediate satisfaction, pleasure, joy, play, receptiveness, and absence of repression with the former; delayed satisfaction, restraint of pleasure, toil, work, productiveness, and security with the latter (*ibid.*, p. 12). Ontogenetically and phylogenetically, civilization requires the transition from the one state of being to the other. The transition does not abolish the domain of the pleasure principle, however, but rather represses it. The demand for gratification is preserved in and as unconscious fantasy. In this way the genetic process establishes a structural relationship—of domination. From the beginning civilization—rationality, utility, the values of social order—is domination. And from the beginning it is continually threatened by a return of the repressed, by the "drive for integral gratification" that is preserved in the unconscious.

Marcuse acknowledges that we cannot return to a pre-civilized condition. Yet he does not accept present-day reality as the ultimate or only possible order of things. The past, which lives on in memory, "generates the wish that the paradise [lost] be recreated on the basis of the achievements of civilization." Hence the psychoanalytic "orientation on the past tends toward an orientation on the future. The *recherche du temps perdu* becomes the vehicle of future liberation" (*ibid.*, p. 18). . . . In the end as in the beginning.

Here we have yet another version of the greatest story ever told. To be sure, this version is simultaneously individual and social. But it has the familiar three beats to the measure. An initial natural condition gives way to a history of alienation, that is, to an inverse or self-negating development of the original potentiality. One can at least imagine, however, a negation of the negation, a return to the natural through the social, a naturalization of the social that is also a socialization of the natural.

Or perhaps one can at most imagine it.

5.

The promise and the problem of Marcuse's historical vision originate in his interpretation of Freud's instinct theory. He contends that Freud, in venturing beyond the pleasure principle, resecured it. He grants Freud the manifold of the death-drive: (1) the ontological primacy of the Nirvana principle, namely, the fundamental instinctual aim of eliminating all stimulation or reducing it to the lowest possible level; (2) the conservative nature of the instincts (their tendency to restore an earlier state of things); and therefore (3) death or inorganicity, equated with the absolute absence of stimulation, as the ultimate point of return or regression. He also accepts the view that destructiveness derives from the death-drive. He goes on to observe, however, that because Freud equates pleasure with the absence of stimulation, in this view of things *death and pleasure converge* (*ibid.*, p. 24). If the human organism is driven toward its death, this is because it is driven away from the pain of life. Destructiveness, too, is then a protest against suffering:

> If the "regression-compulsion" in all organic life is striving for integral quiescence, if the Nirvana principle is the ground of the pleasure principle, then the necessity of death appears in an entirely new light. The death instinct is destructiveness not for its own sake, but for the relief from tension. The descent toward death is an unconscious flight from pain and want. It is an expression of the eternal struggle against suffering and repression. (*ibid.*, p. 27)

The *recherche du temps perdu* is the quest for integral quiescence, integral gratification, absence of pain, pleasure/death. "The memory of gratification is at the origin of all thinking, and the impulse to recapture past gratification is the hidden driving power behind the process of thought" (*ibid.*, p. 29). And not only thought: Phylogenetically and ontogenetically, we seek in the end what we remember of the beginning.

We see, then, that Marcuse robs the death-drive of its sting. It aims not at destruction but rather at deliverance.

6.

Marcuse has license from Freud for his interpretation of instinct theory. There is precisely the same ambiguity concerning the relationship of memory, pleasure, and death in the one as we find in the other. Marcuse is only quite rigorously following the logic of Freud's speculative theorizing—following it beyond the world of human experience. They are both Platonists, whether or not they wish to be.

First, they each suppose some registration of an inorganic state in the organic human being, a memory (or some equivalent to memory) of the death that preceded life. Unless the death-drive is to be devoid of psychological consequences, they require for their position something resembling Plato's arguments in the first part of the *Phaedo*, that is, that everything comes from its opposite, so that the soul that is living now must have been dead at an earlier time (in Rouse, 1956, pp. 473–475). This is a begged question. The existence of the soul is presupposed, and life and death are reduced to the status of alternative predicates of the existent subject. Likewise for Freud and Marcuse. They necessarily assume an experience of the human organism prior to the empirical existence of the organism, the human being's memory of its own not-being.

Second, they establish the identity of "pleasure" and "death" through the middle term, "absence of pain," and by the additional identification of pain with stimulation. But because to be alive is always to experience some stimulation, pleasure in this sense cannot be a human experience. Hence it cannot meaningfully be differentiated from the pleasure sought by the Platonic philosopher, that is, the pleasure of the soul apart from the body—and this despite Marcuse's desire to re-embody Fromm's disembodied psyche.

A third point results from joining the first two. If life is never free from pain, then memory is necessarily (in part) painful. We not only seek to recapture the pleasure of the past but long to escape from its pain. Yet we may misremember and create in fantasy a paradisiacal past that never existed. Past then becomes future, and we set sail for the gates of Eden.

So much for knowledge as recollection, infancy as bliss, and intimations of immortality. If in reality there is a place where life and death interpenetrate, it contains an abysmal dread along with the *promesse de bonheur*.

Or: Marcuse interprets Freud's instinct theory as the promise of happiness, history as the breaking of the promise. But what if the promise was made to be broken? What if, as Freud (1930) contends, "the purpose of life is simply the programme of the pleasure principle . . . and yet its programme is at loggerheads with the whole world, with the macrocosm as much as with the microcosm" (p. 76)? Then Marcuse is making promises that he can't keep.

Yet, so it seems to me, Marcuse is onto something. What if the drive to experience pleasure and (stated negatively) not to experience pain is at the center of human experience? And what if—again recalling Plato —pleasure and pain are "hung together . . . by their heads to the same thing, and therefore whenever you get one, the other follows after" (in Rouse, 1956, p. 463)? Then the Nirvana principle and the death-drive are worthy of their names: As Marcuse emphasizes, they express the desire to escape from life itself, from the fearful pain of human existence.

7.

Reading Hegel and depending on mood and predisposition, one is either beguiled or infuriated by his simultaneous engagement with and disengagement from reality, by the way he slides away from contradictions in the process of grasping them—and grasps them in the process of sliding away from them. So, too, in reading Marcuse. In contrast to Hegel, however, Marcuse is self-conscious about the ambiguity of his position. He works very much in the manner of a surrealist like René Magritte, who aims at producing a sudden opening into a concealed world of terror and beauty, a redemptive moment of illumination, the experience of an aesthetic as well as an epistemological break with established reality. When we criticize Marcuse for being unrealistic, we should be aware that we are also paying him a compliment. And in paying him this compliment we are nonetheless criticizing him.

Consider his treatment of repression and the reality principle. Although he is intent upon staking out a territory beyond their limits, he does not wish to deny either their existence or their necessity. He accepts the orthodox Marxist position that material scarcity imposes upon humankind the necessity of laboring; and he accepts the orthodox Freudian position that the energy required for labor must be produced through the repression and sublimation of the instincts. Civilization—human reality in the broadest sense—necessitates repression. But the "basic (phylogenetic) restrictions of the instincts" that humanize the human animal, the "power to restrain and guide instinctual drives, to make biological necessities into individual needs and desires," increase rather than reduce gratification (Marcuse, 1962, p. 35). The reality principle mediates without contradicting the pleasure principle.

Basic repression, to put it another way, engenders the specifically human form of instinctual freedom. But repression does not stop at the level needed for civilized life as such. Rather, as Reich argued earlier, in substance the reality principle is an historical variable, not a constant. The level of repression it requires is likewise variable. Thus the higher the level of material scarcity, the more demanding the reality principle, and the greater the degree of necessary repression. Conversely, the higher the level of abundance, the more the reality principle approximates to the pleasure principle, and (potentially) the greater the degree of socially functional instinctual freedom.

Historically, however, there has been a limit to the range of variation in the reality principle and the level of repression it entails. Because advances in civilized life are the product of overcoming material scarcities, and because the distribution of scarcity is uneven and hierarchical, the history of the species is the history of domination. Whatever its specific content, the reality that is psychologically encoded by the reality principle is a reality of domination. Repression is raised to the level required by social domination and acts so as to perpetuate domination. Not necessary repression, but surplus repression, is the foundation of actual civilized life.[12]

The reality principle that enforces surplus repression Marcuse terms the "performance principle." The performance principle entails (1) the diversion of libido from pleasurable experience to socially useful performances and (2) the desexualization of the body, so that "libido becomes concentrated in one part of the body, leaving the rest free for use as the instrument of labour" (*ibid.*, p. 44). The performance principle transforms the individual into a vehicle for producing labor values and for reproducing the condition of domination.

We may note that Marcuse's argument depends upon Freud's conceptualization of psychical energies, specifically upon the idea that work-energy is created through the repression and sublimation of sex-energy. It is charitable to call this idea dubious. But its employment permits Marcuse to honor the "realism" in Freud's interpretation of civilization while simultaneously challenging it. For if an historically specific version of the reality principle is more restrictive than the level of material scarcity requires, then it is self-contradictory. It designates as unreal precisely that which is realizable. It defines as necessary a degree of repression that is in fact excessive. Hence in this instance to be unrealistic is to grasp the actual emancipatory potentialities that the existing reality principle denies. It is possible to conceive of a reality beyond the reality principle, and to use this projected reality as the standard for judging the rationality or irrationality of the existing social order.

It might appear that Marcuse is engaging—within Freudian limits— the historical reality of repression. Like Freud he identifies civilization with repression. He grants that we cannot have the one without the other, and he is not arguing for an impossible recapturing of the prerepressed, prehuman past. But by shifting the primary meaning of repression he simultaneously slips away from the point of engagement. He contends that basic repression is a humanizing "power to restrain and guide instinctual drives, to make biological necessities into individual needs and desires." It increases rather than decreases gratification. This is at least a half truth. Even "primitive" forms of gratification, such as nursing at the breast, involve some restraint or guidance of instinct. But the other half of the truth is equally important. Restraint of instinct is inherently painful. Repression, which involves a major restraint of instinct, is proportionally more painful. Hence for Freud repression is always a self-laceration. It is both painful in itself and an accommodation to the pain of animate/human existence. To be civilized requires a loss of gratification.

In other words, Marcuse's shifting of the meaning of repression deprives pain of its ontological significance. The glissade is especially striking in light of his recognition that the death-drive is a response to pain. But he treats his own conception as a Medusa's head and protects himself from its reality with the philosopher's shield of Athena.

Marcuse thus follows Hegel in denying the reality of the reality he reveals. Our critique does not, however, invalidate his historicization of repression. In this regard his appropriation of Freud parallels Marx's appropriation of Hegel. In the 1844 manuscripts Marx distinguishes between objectification and alienation. The latter, as we have seen, he treats as a perversion of the former. Hegel, on the other hand, identifies objectification and alienation: From the standpoint of the absolute subject, any objectification is a loss. Hegel ontologizes what, at the level of social reality, Marx treats as an historical variable. Similarly Marcuse distinguishes between repression as such and the surplus repression that accompanies social domination. Just as Marx relativizes alienation, he relativizes repression. And, by placing repression and alienation within the same theoretical frame, he helps us to see more clearly the relationship between them.

8.

There is a kind of dialectical beauty in Marcuse's transition from ontogeny to phylogeny. Following Freud he claims that the individual in modern society "is in archaic identity with the species" (*ibid.,* p. 51). Each individual is the inheritor of the history, or prehistory, of the species. The whole is embodied and recapitulated in the part. "Individual psychology is thus *in itself* group psychology . . ." (*ibid.*).

This much is straight Freud, albeit framed as a dialectical unity of opposites. But Marcuse uses the Freudian identification of ontogeny with phylogeny to "undermine one of the strongest ideological fortifications of modern culture—namely, the notion of the autonomous individual" (*ibid.*, p. 52). Psychoanalysis "reveals the power of the universal in and over the individuals." It dissolves the autonomy of the individual and shows that it is actually "the *frozen* manifestation of the general repression of mankind" (*ibid.*).

One might protest that the individual's incarnation of the archaic heritage of the species is a highly questionable proposition. Marcuse would not be troubled by the protest. In an often-quoted passage he claims that the "truth of psychoanalysis lies in its loyalty to its most provocative hypotheses" (Marcuse, 1970, p. 61). By "truth" he means something quite different from "factual" or "empirically verifiable." The truth contradicts (phenomenal) reality. It is concealed within or beyond accumulated facts and operationalized concepts. One seeks it by attacking the epistemological forces that repress it.

Once the walls of facticity have been breached in this fashion, there is no need to distinguish between anthropological just-so stories and plausible historical narratives. Marcuse is free to make social critical use of Freud's phylogenetic mythology. This is better than discarding it. Freudian myths are revelatory of psychological reality when they are subjected to transformational criticism. Throw out the myth and you throw out the conscious manifestation of important unconscious fantasies. But Marcuse, to his ultimate disadvantage, bypasses the critical process through which we learn to distinguish between fact and fantasy. Although he admits that Freud's phylogeny may forever be "beyond the realm of anthropological verification" and that its value is only symbolic of historical processes of domination (Marcuse, 1962, pp. 54–55), he nonetheless collapses history into its symbolic representation. We are left with an historical just-so story.

In the beginning is the primal horde, and the life of the horde is domination. The sons rebel against the system of domination, that is, against their father. Freedom is born in this rebellious action. Matriarchy and the gratification of hitherto suppressed sexual desires replaces paternal tyranny. The patricidal sons are overcome by guilt, however, and they surrender their hard-won freedom. The rule of the father, or at least of the fathers, is re-established. The revolution is defeated and the sons are guilty a second time. The first time they betrayed their father, this time they betray themselves. Domination, rebellion, domination— the great wheel of history begins to turn.

From this point of origin Marcuse traces out a dialectic of civilization which consists primarily of a play of instinctual forces and secondarily of objective constraints upon and transmutations of these forces. The upshot of the process is two-fold. On the one hand, there is an escalating discrepancy between potential liberation and actual repression. The rationality of progressive domination becomes increasingly irrational. On the other, there is the "technological abolition of the individual" (*ibid.*,

p. 87) and the obsolescence of the Freudian conception of man. The role of the father and the family in the shaping of character is taken over by society itself. The ego shrinks, the ego ideal is collectivized, the individual becomes just one of the masses, instincts are regressively defused and desublimated (Marcuse, 1970, pp. 56–59). In a world without fathers freedom becomes domination, a domination that is all the more hateful and hate-filled, the more unnecessary it becomes.

This historical vision cannot be taken literally. It is held together by instinctual energies that really are just in the theorist's mind; it hovers uneasily between a critique of and a nostalgia for the autonomous individual and patriarchal domination (yesterday's oedipal curse is today's lost oedipal blessing); and it overstates the case for the historical obsolescence of the psychoanalytic conception of the self. Marcuse's dialectics of civilization are not the dialectics of history. In the end we are left with the task of transforming his psychophilosophical speculations into politically usable empirical interpretations. Nonetheless we have something to gain by following Marcuse's own methodological example and permitting ourselves a metaphysical moment.

First, just as Marx interprets political economy from the perspective of the proletariat, Marcuse interprets Freud from the perspective of the rebellious sons. He meets Freud on his own phylogenetic ground and inverts it. The Freudian myth, beneath its veneer of political neutrality, is patriarchal. The Marcusean myth, which is avowedly political, is patricidal. It counters the morality of domination with the morality of liberation. There is guilt in the revolution betrayed as well as the revolution made. When it is properly used as fantasy and metaphor, it doubles the possibilities for psychohistorical interpretation.

Second, the concept of regressive yet still (politically) repressive desublimation enables us to advance beyond Reich's conception of sexual liberation. Marcuse sees, as Reich does not, that an attenuation of intrapsychic conflict may result in a flattening out of emotional life. Sexual freedom may be nothing more than bread and circuses for the one dimensionalized masses. And because Marcuse grants that destructiveness is an instinctual derivative, the concept of repressive desublimation also focuses our attention on the dangers that can attend the destructuring of existing social and psychological structures.

9.

Hegel claimed that "what is rational is actual and what is actual is rational" (Hegel, 1821, p. 10). Marx perceived a different actuality but concurred in the judgment of its rationality. That very difference, of course, renders the judgment doubtful. So, too, does the problematical history of the attempt to realize the Marxist revolutionary project. Hence the epistemic sutures of the Hegelian position split apart, and the surpassed/repressed moment of epistemological questioning returns.

Marcuse joins Reich in linking epistemological issues to political and psychological ones. Reich's solutions, however, are his problems. Reich treats dialectics as materialist science; Marcuse treats it as critique of materialist science. Reich identifies rationality with choices of action that are (1) instrumentally efficacious and (2) aimed at the realization of objective interests. Marcuse seeks to free reason from precisely these instrumental limitations.

As noted earlier, these points of difference have an historical foundation. Marcuse (1964) observes:

> The critical theory of society was, at the time of its origin, confronted with the presence of real forces (objective and subjective) *in* the established society which moved (or could be guided to move) toward more rational and freer institutions by abolishing the existing ones which had become obstacles to progress. These were the empirical grounds on which the theory was erected, and from these empirical grounds derived the idea of the liberation of *inherent* possibilities—the development, otherwise blocked and distorted, of material and intellectual productivity, faculties, and needs. (p. 254)

Although the temporal referent in this passage is vague, it presumably includes the 1920s and 1930s, when German intellectuals like Reich and Marcuse were (or could easily be) engaged in proletarian class struggle, and when material progress could still be viewed as an emancipatory tendency. By the 1950s and 1960s, however, and especially with American society in mind, Marcuse concludes that "'liberation of inherent possibilities' no longer expresses the historical alternative" (*ibid.*, p. 255). The instrumentalities of productivity and progress now function to sustain rather than to undermine social domination, and the members of the working class, who operate these instrumentalities, have been transformed into a mass formation, integrated into and likewise sustaining of the existing system. Rationality—at least scientific, instrumental, Enlightenment rationality—is the logic of domination. "Contrasted with the fantastic and insane aspects of . . . [this] rationality, the realm of the irrational becomes the home of the really rational . . ." (*ibid.*, p. 247).

From a slightly different angle Marcuse's contention is that the Reichian moment has passed. The interest in human emancipation can no longer be empirically identified with the political and sexual interests of the working class. The working class has been integrated into the system of domination, and the emancipatory interest, lacking this historically immanent foundation, has become transcendental. It exists outside the reality and rationality of the social system.

Here is a third way of looking at it. Hegel claimed that speculative dialectics demonstrated the identity of subjective certainty and objective truth and that, by so doing, dissolved (surpassed, sublated) the epistemological or phenomenological moment. Marx politicized and radicalized this position. The self-objectification of the proletariat, by which it overcomes its alienation, secures the identification of emancipatory reason and social reality. The proletariat realizes itself and the truth of Marx's theory in practice. Consequently epistemological questioning becomes an academic concern. But, Marcuse contends, the proletarian moment has come and gone. The class struggle is over and we have lost. In its aftermath the objective reality of domination repels and represses the possibility of an emancipatory subjectivity. The latter can only exist outside the system. Critical reason once again stands in an external or merely phenomenological relationship to the object it seeks to know and transform. It necessarily regresses from ontology to epistemology, from science to philosophy. Only by taking this step backward does it preserve the possibility of once again going forward.

We see, then, that the critical theorist occupies a no-man's land between the bad totality of the present and a purely utopian future. Suspended above an historical abyss, s/he can do no more than "remain loyal to those who, without hope, have given and give up their life to the Great Refusal" (Marcuse, 1964, p. 257).

10.

Between the present and the future: the abyss, the dream, the fantasy, the aesthetic moment.

11.

The third of the three great Kantian critiques attempts to mediate the relationship of cognition (natural science, pure reason) and desire (science of morals, practical reason) with the feeling of pleasure and pain, with aesthetics broadly conceived (Kant, 1790). Albeit with numerous critical modifications, Marcuse follows Kant. The domain of pure reason coincides with the technological or instrumental rationality of the natural sciences. The domain of practical reason coincides with the emancipatory political orientation of critical theory. Ambiguously, between these extremes, we find the aesthetic dimension.

In my judgment the ambiguity is three-fold. First, as Marcuse himself points out, the original Kantian position "merges the original meaning of *aesthetic* (pertaining to the senses) with . . . [a] new connotation (pertaining to beauty, especially in art)" (Marcuse, 1962, p. 159). Marcuse preserves this double meaning, which permits him to fuse psychoanalytic categories (aesthetics in the first sense) with artistic valuations (aesthetics in the second sense), to identify the erotic and the beautiful.

Second, the aesthetic dimension of critical theory interpenetrates or perhaps slides into the domain of cultural critique, so that the concept of culture has the double meaning of "artistic" and "everyday life." In the latter regard Marcuse (along with Adorno, Benjamin, and Horkheimer) is notable for his sensitivity to the political meanings embedded in cultural practices. One might even say that, in Kantian fashion, the critique of culture mediates the critiques of instrumental reason and political domination. At the same time a romantic conception of the aesthetic experience is used to devalue popular culture—aesthetic revenge of the obsolescent individual.

Third, aesthetic judgments can be political ones. Politics is aestheticized and aesthetics is politicized. Beauty and ugliness become political categories. Indeed they sometimes seem to replace political categories, so that we are led into an aesthetic as well as a philosophical retreat from political reality. The power of negative thinking is then . . . imaginary.

If we combine the second and third ambiguities we have a variant and augmented Platonism, in which the rebellious philosopher-artist says "no" to the culture of the masses. A variant Platonism: Marcuse wants to save Plato from himself, to liberate philosophy from the performance principle and the repressive employment of reason, and in the process to end the ancient war between philosophers and poets. An augmented Platonism: Plato appears in his historically developed form of German idealist philosopher. But Platonism nonetheless: With stubborn persistence the individual stands in judgment of the corruption of the polity.

Marcuse's aesthetics are, additionally and fatally, infiltrated by the Platonic conflation of liberation and death. When, via the first ambiguity, his reading of Freud is joined to his interpretation of the philosophy of aesthetic experience, the imagination is placed under the aegis of the Nirvana principle. On the one hand, aesthetic experience is placed outside of time: If "the 'aesthetic state' is really to be the state of freedom, then it must ultimately defeat the destructive course of time" (*ibid.*, p. 175). On the other, it is identified with the "Great Refusal," with the aim of the "ultimate form of freedom—'to live without anxiety'" (*ibid.*, p. 136). But one cannot in fact defeat time or live without anxiety. The Great Task (so to speak) is to live in time and with anxiety.

Here is another way of thinking about it. The aesthetic transcendence of temporality and anxiety is a real and meaningful human experience. But aesthetic experience can be oriented toward transformation as well as transcendence. The folksinger Woody Guthrie printed "this machine kills fascists" on his guitar. We might do the same. Yet Marcuse's aesthetics gives us no license to sing songs of freedom.

12.

What, then, about the question that began this section? How does Marcuse fare when judged by the standards of a critical dialectical reason?

As I hope is now evident, this question cannot be answered univocally. Rather, from beginning to end Marcuse's version of Freudian-Marxism involves a delicate dialectical glissade. Each "moment" of his theorizing is simultaneously an engagement with and a disengagement from social reality. His concepts are at once vitalizing and devitalizing; they are both expressions of and defenses against the contradictions of the life-world, or the life-and-death world.

Let's consider once more the central issue, that is, the project of human emancipation. Marcuse, we must remind ourselves, experienced the catastrophic failure of the European workers' movement, its displacement by fascism, the Second World War, then (in exile) the Cold War, McCarthyism, and the pervasive apathy and absence of critical consciousness that was the United States in the 1950s. The chasm separating the late capitalist system from a possible socialist one was not a fantasy. It existed, and still does. It is to Marcuse's great credit that he remained committed to the emancipatory project in theory despite the stasis of the emancipatory movement and that, when the opportunity arose, he seized the opportunity of joining theory to practice.

Yet his representation of the historical abyss is also a misrepresentation, a failure of dialectical reasoning masking as dialectical reasoning. Instead of grasping the contradictory tendencies in the world as it is and accepting the contradictions that are necessarily part of any possible world that might be, he split the manifold of historical experience into the bad totality of the existing world and the good totality of a utopian future. The interest-based problematics of political choice, in which possible gains must be weighed against possible losses, disappear. They fall victim to philosophical repression.

Here, I think, is how the process of repression operates. Marcuse begins with and in situations of political choice. His philosophy is consistently *engagé*. But the engagement de-realizes the self-same situation of choice. The bad/good world with its ambiguities and anxieties is split into the either/or of an all-bad present and an all-good future. At the same time fantasies, be they promises or memories, are put in the place of criss-crossing interests and contradictory emotions. Political reality is displaced by political imagination. Consequently there is only an imaginary bridge between present and future. Finally, because the imagination is brought under the aegis of the Nirvana principle, the death-drive—interpreted as a desire for integral quiescence and gratification—takes its position as the ultimate determinant of human experience.

Idealism by any other name. . . .

D. Conclusion

So much for the critical appropriation of classical Freudian-Marxism. We have seen that the three theorists who most contributed to it have a manifold and complex relationship to each other. Hence they contribute in various ways to our own perspective. But at a minimum and most simply, they convert the contradictions that separate Marxism from psychoanalysis into contradictions within their theorizing. We need not judge at this point whether any or all of these contradictions have been resolved. Nor would it be appropriate to attempt to synthesize their positions. By way of summary, however, we may briefly review their approaches to the problematic of "the individual" and society.

More than anyone else, Reich is responsible for defining the Freudian-Marxist project. His position is one method (dialectical materialism), two theories. He conceives of psychoanalysis as a theory of the individual, Marxism as a theory of society, and intends to give them autonomous and equal status. Taken in the immediate sense, however, the two theories are incompatible. Hence their juxtaposition proves unstable and Reich lapses into a kind of sexual individualism.

Fromm attempts to resolve the contradiction by a thorough-going socialization of the individual. He effectively counters Reich's sexual reductionism by focusing upon the historically variable quality of human relatedness. Yet he, too, fails to advance from individual to social psychology. The concept of social character marks the limit of his theorizing.

Reich and Fromm present us with mirror images of social reality. Reich flees from the problematics of social life into sexual romanticism and a reduction of mind to body. But in his early work he maintains a grip on the harsh reality of choices of political action. Fromm, by contrast, engages the problematics of social life. He also hides within them. He retreats from body into mind, from sexuality into issues of relatedness, from the political "is" into the moral "ought." Reich is fixated on genital functioning; Fromm displaces the issue upward. Neither of them, it seems, can tolerate the anxiety we find at the point where opposites interpenetrate.

Like Fromm, Marcuse aims at theoretical integration, and like Fromm, he rejects Reich's sexual reductionism. But in contrast to Fromm he views the socialized individual as the problem, not the solution. He finds in the late "metaphysical" Freudian conception of the individual a last bastion of revolutionary protest against the encroaching power of one-dimensionalizing social domination. But unlike Freud he slides away from the intractability of psychic pain. He, too, escapes from the anxiety that accompanies all meaningful human action.

At the end of Freudian-Marxism we apparently find ourselves where we were at the beginning, namely, with opposed theories of the individual and society. Or even further back: The issue of individual and society is now raised only within the limits of both theoretical and methodological individualism. The shell of contradiction limiting the integral development of psychoanalytic-marxism is not cracked by the Freudian-Marxists; if anything, it is thickened. But whatever the limitations of the interpretive framework, psychoanalysis and Marxism have been joined.

CHAPTER 4

Beyond Freudian-Marxism?

1.

In this chapter we are concerned with (1) the attempts of various theorists to go beyond the paradigm of classical Freudian-Marxism and (2) the impact of women and Third World peoples upon the Freudian-Marxist discourse.[1] The narrative line roughly follows the rise and fall of the liberation movements of the 1960s and early 1970s. The underlying theme is the oscillation and tension between the tendency toward unification and the countertendency toward pluralization in the theories generated by these movements.

2.

Zeno: See, Parmenides, they still haven't solved the problem of the One and the Many.

Parmenides: Neither, Zeno, have we.

Empedocles (to himself): How is it that these two fail to perceive the double process through which these opposites interpenetrate. For all things mortal "never cease their continuous exchange, sometimes uniting under the influence of Love, so that all become One, at other times again each moving apart through the hostile force of Hate" (Freeman, 1978, p. 53).

3.

The One and the Many is a problem on many levels. At least for now, our concern is with these two: the political and the psychological.

The political problem has various forms. The Many are hoi polloi (the masses) and are viewed as morally inferior by the One, the aristocrat, intellectual, or philosopher. Or reverse the perspective: The Many are the masses, the people, the wretched of the earth who view the One—the ruling class, the State—as their oppressor. Alternatively the masses are absorbed into the State, leaving the individual who would speak for them isolated, without constituency, outside the effective unity of the One and the Many. Yet again, the masses come to constitute a political movement, of which radical intellectuals are an organic part. If successful, it shatters the existing social order and reforms the One as the common interest and life of the Many.

The history of Freudian-Marxism may be presented in these terms.

Marxism originated in the European political struggles of the 1840s; psychoanalysis developed outside or, at best, on the periphery of the political struggles of *fin de siècle* Vienna. The former speaks the imperatives of mass movement, the latter speaks against them.

Classical Freudian-Marxism reflects three distinct historical moments. First, Reich's earliest work testifies to the vitality of working class struggle in the late 1920s. Just as Marx, in analogous circumstances, sought to transform political economy into a revolutionary science, so Reich sought to develop a revolutionary role for psychoanalysis.

Second, working class struggle is displaced by fascist mass movement. The psychoanalytic and/or critical individual is now affirmed against the swelling tide of collective barbarism.

Third, the tide recedes. According to Fromm and Marcuse we find ourselves in a mass society of automaton conformity and one-dimensionality. As in the second instance, the Many are called to judgment by the One or the Few.

By the 1960s collective struggle was again the order of the day. Was it a class struggle? Perhaps. It was unquestionably a racial, sexual, and generational struggle, and a movement toward human liberation.

Marcuse, the most vigorous of the classical Freudian-Marxists, sought to join his critical theory to the practices of the liberation movement. More generally the interest in joining psychoanalysis and Marxism was revitalized as a tendency within the movement. Emancipatory hopes, wishes, and fantasies flourished—briefly. The movement failed to remake the world. It shattered—it was shattered—and those interested in uniting Marxism and psychoanalysis were once again placed in the self-contradictory position of being antisocial socially emancipatory individuals. The time had come for the solitary rereading of *One-Dimensional Man*: "It is only for the sake of those without hope that hope is given to us" (Marcuse, 1964, p. 257).

Carried along by the shifting currents of the emancipatory project, Marxism loses the highly defined character Marx gave to it. His historical vision is challenged; questions are raised about his epistemological leanings and about the priority of such categories as economic production and social class. Marxism itself is pluralized. Nonetheless Marx's name continues to signify, better than any other, the struggle for human emancipation.

An analogy: When Malcolm X returned from his pilgrimage to Mecca in 1964, he was entitled to the name El-Hajj Malik El-Shabazz. He did not, however, discard the "X": "I'll continue to use Malcolm X," he said, "as long as the situation that produced it exists" (in Wolfenstein, 1990c, p. 310). For a similar reason we retain the name "Marxism." When joining Marxism to psychoanalysis, however, we will use a lowercase "m." This choice indicates our unwillingness to be members of any personality cults.

4.

The same reasoning suggests replacing "Freudian" with "freudian." Because over time the theory has lost its exclusively Freudian stamp, however, it seems warranted to characterize it as psychoanalytic.

Let's briefly review the pluralization of psychoanalysis.

At its origin psychoanalysis was a theory of sexuality and the unconscious repressed. By the 1920s Freud complicated the theory in three ways. He focused on the ego as the locus of repression. He began the analysis of the processes through which external objects (mother, father, etc.) become internal object relationships. And he introduced the death-drive as the complement and opposite to sexuality/the life-drive.

In the history of psychoanalysis, as in Freud's anthropological mythology, patriarchy is followed by matriarchy, in this case matriarchal rivalry. The mantle of orthodoxy fell on Freud's daughter, Anna, who placed the ego at the center of psychoanalytic theorizing. The rival claimant to the throne was Melanie Klein, who placed internal object relations at the theoretical center. Both Anna Freud and Klein retained something of Freud's later drive theory, but Klein more than Freud emphasized the destructive emotional tendencies associated with the death-drive.

From one theory to two, and from two to many. Neo-Freudian revisionists like Erich Fromm and Karen Horney were object-relational without being drive theorists. In Great Britain an independent version of object relations theory was developed by W. R. D. Fairbairn; and a middle position between Klein and Freud was developed by the Balints, D. W. Winnicott, and others. In the United States Anna Freud's ego psychology was for many years the orthodox position, eventually to be rivaled by the self psychology of Heinz Kohut. And in France Sartre and others

developed an existential form of psychoanalytic theory, while Jacques
Lacan and his followers gave a linguistic and Hegelian turn to a presumably classical version of the theory.

The works we are now to consider reflect this pluralization of psychoanalytic theory. Accordingly it seems inappropriate to characterize
them as Freudian-Marxist. Indeed, even classical Freudian-Marxism is not
straightforwardly Freudian. Fromm was an object relations theorist in
advance of the advent of object relations theory; and both Reich and
Marcuse are more heterodox than they might be willing to acknowledge.
Nonetheless the conventional designation of Freudian-Marxism serves
to identify a discourse with definable features. At this juncture, however,
it becomes positively misleading—hence the designation, psychoanalytic-
marxism.

Yet it would be a mistake to interpose anything resembling an epistemological break between Freudian-Marxism and psychoanalytic-marxism.
We observe, rather, changes within a discourse, a discourse that retains
a recognizable definition and that turns upon many of the same, unsolved
problems. It is already evident, for example, that we must continue to
analyze a tension between essentialist (intrasubjectively based) and relational (intersubjectively based) trends in psychoanalysis, as well as one
between totalizing and pluralizing trends within the discourse itself.

5.

First, we will review the existential approach to joining psychoanalysis and Marxism in the works of Jean-Paul Sartre and Frantz Fanon. Here
the historical context is the de-Stalinization of Marxism in Western
Europe and de-colonization, especially in Africa.

Next, we will consider two characteristic works that reflect the
German New Left experience: Jürgen Habermas' *Knowledge and Human
Interests* (1971) and Michael Schneider's *Neurosis and Civilization* (1975).[2]

Third, we will come to *Anti-Oedipus* (1972) by Gilles Deleuze and
Félix Guattari. This may be read as a reflection of the French New Left
experience. We will contrast it with a later "anti-oedipal" analysis, C. Fred
Alford's *Melanie Klein and Critical Social Theory* (1989), which is of interest both for its own sake and for its articulation of Kleinian theory.

Fourth, we will come to the feminist challenge to the prevailing discourses of Marxism and psychoanalysis. Although we will focus on three
texts—Gayle Rubin's "The Traffic in Women: Notes on the 'Political
Economy' of Sex" (1975); Nancy Hartsock's *Money, Sex, and Power* (1985);
and Jessica Benjamin's "The Bonds of Love: Rational Violence and Erotic
Domination" (1980)—we will refer to a number of others, in order to

demonstrate the feminist imperative of fundamentally rethinking Freudian-Marxist categories.

Fifth, we will take up opposed reactions to the limitations of the
New Left movement: Joel Kovel's *The Age of Desire* (1981) and Richard
Lichtman's *The Production of Desire* (1982). Where the former works reflect in various ways the vitality of an emancipatory social movement,
these latter reflect the political void left by its demise.

6.

It is a Marxist commonplace that all social communication is ideologically inflected, a psychoanalytic one that all conscious communication is in part unconsciously determined. A development as well as a
critique of these positions is Foucault's claim that any discourse is
a power–knowledge relationship: "Truth isn't the reward of free spirits,
a child of protracted solitude, nor the privilege of those who have
succeeded in liberating themselves. Truth is a thing of this world: it is
produced only by virtue of multiple forms of constraint. And it induces
regular effects of power" (Foucault, 1980, p. 131). Thus all public speech
in the present historical situation is constrained by the conjoined hegemonic discourses of instrumental and bureaucratic reason. Orthodox
Marxism and psychoanalysis are merely local instances of this discursive generality.

As the rappers in the group "Public Enemy" say, it is possible to
"fight the power." At least in intention, the Freudian-Marxists and psychoanalytic-marxists are waging such a battle. But their discourse, too, is
a power–knowledge relationship. The question then becomes, who is
empowered by it?

A text such as the present one is likewise a power–knowledge relationship. In the previous chapter, for example, only the voices of Reich,
Fromm, and Marcuse were heard. All other positions were subjected to
authorial exclusion. The exclusionary act is justified by an interest in
contributions to psychoanalytic-marxism at the paradigmatic level. But
all exclusions can be justified and they remain exclusions nonetheless.

Thematization is another version of textual power–knowledge relationships. Thematizing a discourse is itself a way of totalizing it, even if
the totalization is in the name of thematic disjunction. The theme bespeaks
the author. Fair enough, when the author speaks only for or of her/him-
self. Not so fair when the text purports to represent a discourse, and
especially one consisting of many voices and points of view.

The reader will no doubt have recognized the preceding paragraphs
as my apologia for the exclusions and thematizations that follow.

A. De-Stalinization and De-Colonization

1.

The postwar period was the Ice Age of the free spirit, or the would-be free spirit. Marxism was barely distinguishable from Stalinism; psychoanalysis could scarcely be disentangled from the bureaucracy and orthodoxy of the psychoanalytic associations, which in turn were comfortably integrated into the established patterns of domination. No one wanted to be reminded that "human fact is irreducible to knowing, that it must *be lived and produced*" (Sartre, 1968, p. 14).

"The white man is sealed in his whiteness. The black man in his blackness" (Fanon, 1952, p. 9). There are vicious circles of more than one kind.

"The colonial world is a world divided into compartments. . . . The zone where the natives live is not complementary to the zone inhabited by the settlers. The two zones are opposed, but not in the service of a higher unity. Obedient to the rules of pure Aristotelian logic, they both follow the principle of reciprocal exclusivity" (Fanon, 1961, p. 31).
When the European and Anglo-American ice floes began to break up, it was because the Manichean colonial world was breaking down.

For our purposes the link between de-Stalinization and de-colonization can be signified by the relationship between Jean-Paul Sartre and Frantz Fanon. Three texts: *Search for a Method* (1968) at the one extreme, *Black Skins, White Masks* (1952) at the other, *The Wretched of the Earth* (1961) where the opposites interpenetrate.

2.

In *Search for a Method* Sartre attempts a rapprochement between Marxism and existentialism. In the hands of the Communist (Stalinist) parties Marxism has become a lifeless orthodoxy. The analysis of concrete events has been replaced by the imposition of "unchangeable, fetishized 'synthetic notions.'" The "open concepts of Marxism have closed in. They are no longer *keys*, interpretive schemata; they are posited for themselves as an already totalized knowledge" (Sartre, 1968, p. 27). Yet Marxism is "the one philosophy of our time which we cannot go beyond" (*ibid.*, p. xxxv). It alone is realistic, revolutionary, and capable of being "simultaneously a totalization of knowledge, a method, a regulative Idea, an offensive weapon, and a community of language," in short, a "vision of the world" (*ibid.*, p. 6).

Existentialism by contrast seeks "man . . . *where he is*, at his work, in his home, in the street" (*ibid.*, p. 28). It is alive and analytical where Marxism is dead and synthetical. It cannot replace Marxism as a vision of the world, but it can provide the needed revivification.

We might add that Sartre is well aware that any concept or conceptual set can be fetishized and reified. He resists the name "existentialism" because "it is in the nature of an intellectual quest to be undefined." To name it is to be finished with it (*ibid.*, p. xxxiii). He does his best to develop concepts that are inherently open and unfinished—concepts which, if they are fetishized, become immanently self-contradictory.

3.

Marxism must be opened if it is to be open. It must be brought back to the plane of lived experience. Hence the importance of psychoanalysis. Psychoanalysis is "the one privileged mediation which permits. . . [dialectical materialism] to pass from general and abstract determinations to particular traits of the single individual" (*ibid.*, p. 61). It alone "enables us to study the process by which a child, groping in the dark, is going to attempt to play, without understanding it, the social role which adults impose upon him" (*ibid.*). Psychoanalysis is to function as the methodology of Marxist psychobiography.

But only as a method: "Psychoanalysis has no principles, it has no theoretical foundation . . ." (*ibid.*). It provides access to the territory of familial relationships and the child within the adult and, by so doing, concretizes Marxism concepts; but its concepts are useless.

On the one hand, we do not need Sartre to tell us that psychoanalysis can function as a vehicle for psychobiography; on the other, there is no need to limit the social theoretical function of psychoanalysis to this alone. And having come this far we need not accept a Marxist-cum-existential disavowal of psychoanalytic theory. But something more is at stake in this question of mediation.

4.

For example: Watts, the black ghetto of Los Angeles, explodes into violent acts against property in the aftermath of an incident of police brutality in the summer of 1965. From some black leaders come statements of regret. They are countered by the language of the streets—"burn, baby, burn."

Officially speaking, this is a race riot. The "official speaking," *we* might say, is an attempt to contain, constrain, and derealize the event. But what if we also say that the mass action is an instance of class struggle and oedipal rebellion? By what right do we transform the actual event into these categories? Are we even conscious of the transformation?

In other words, if we take some version of psychoanalytic-marxism as our theoretical generality, we then require a method that will discourage the disguised or open imposition of this generality upon the lives of individuals and collectivities, or the reduction of Reality to psychoanalytic-marxist Reason. We require a method that remains heuristic, that can teach us something—that returns us to everyday experience from preformulated conceptualizations of it, before it once again aims at the conceptualization of this experience.

Sartre characterizes this as the "progressive–regressive method." The terms "progressive" and "regressive" roughly parallel the terms "synthetical" and "analytical." "Marxist method is progressive because it is the result—in the work of Marx himself—of long analyses" (*ibid.*, p. 133). The task is to recover the analytical moment and process in the face of Marxist presyntheses and pretotalizations.

It might appear, therefore, that Sartre's approach anticipates deconstructionism. There are, indeed, resemblances. Like Derrida and his followers, Sartre seeks to break down theoretical constructions, to prevent the immediate identification of concepts with events, and to deny the finality of any inquiry. He is also acutely sensitive to the ruptures and breaks in the objects of historical inquiry. But even leaving aside the deconstructionist obsession with textuality and the written word, there is a fundamental difference in orientation. Sartre is concerned with choices and the meaning of actions. He recognizes that, within situational constraints and perhaps blindly, people try to do and change things. The term "progressive" has a meaning in practice as well as in method: Individuals attempt to synthesize, integrate, and totalize their lives. The displacements celebrated by deconstructionism are interpreted by Sartre in relation (so to speak) to placements, that is, to the project.

5.

For Sartre "man is characterized above all by his going beyond a situation, and by what he succeeds in making of what he has been made ..." (*ibid.*, p. 91). Hence human action is projective: "The most rudimentary behavior must be determined both in relation to the real and present factors which condition it and in relation to a certain object, still to come, which it is trying to bring into being." The project in turn involves, concretely, a "double simultaneous relationship":

In relation to the given, the *praxis* is negativity; but what is always involved is the negation of a negation. In relation to the object aimed at,
praxis is positivity, but this positivity opens onto the "non-existent," to
what *has not yet* been. (*ibid.*, p. 92)

Knowing is a moment of this praxis. By that very fact it is never absolute. It "remains the captive of the action which it clarifies and disappears
along with it." Theoretically and practically we totalize without ever,
except (if then) retrospectively, being totalized.

Sartre's conceptualization of the project, and of praxis in terms of
the project, involves a radical departure from the determinism of both
orthodox Marxism and orthodox psychoanalysis. Perhaps he goes too far
in the opposite direction. One could argue that he replaces the predeter-
minism of structural constraints and past history with the indeterminacy
of his "going beyond a situation." Or it may be that the project is a
vehicle for an escape from the inertia of the present. And, at a minimum,
we must be sure not to limit the conception of a project to the instance
of individual choices of action. But whatever questions might be raised
about project and praxis as methodological principles, they have the great
advantage of rooting theoretization in situations of constrained practical
choice.

6.

Sartre situates his theorizing within the problematics of Marxism.
Consequently he is oriented toward the analysis of alienation and dehumanization. "Every man," he claims, "is defined negatively by the sum
total of possibles which are impossible for him; that is, by a future more
or less blocked off" (*ibid.*, p. 95).

The claim is in the form of a universal. Yet it does not apply equally
to oppressor and oppressed. We seem to have a loss of particularity that
flies in the face of Sartre's own methodological resolve.

Case in point. White people are the oppressors, black people are the
oppressed. Sartre, a white man, puts forward a universal claim about
oppression. Fanon, a black man, might recognize himself in it. But what
does it mean when a black man's vehicle for self-recognition is a white
man's conception of his situation? Whose game is being played, whose
language is being spoken, whose identity is being recognized or not recognized . . . and by whom?

We can be more specific. *Black Skins, White Masks* is a record of
Fanon's struggle with the pressing personal and collective issue of racial
identity. He perceives in black people an inferiority complex that is
the outcome of a double process: "primarily, economic; subsequently,

the internalization—or, better, the epidermalization—of this inferiority" (Fanon, 1952, p. 11). Whiteness and blackness become signifiers of a relationship of domination. White people congratulate themselves on their superiority. Black people, accepting the reality of the relationship and their inferiority within it, aspire to be white. Thus "the juxtaposition of the white and black races has created a massive psychoexistential complex." Fanon "hopes by analyzing it to destroy it" (*ibid.*, p. 12).

Fanon represents the phenomena of racial self-falsification in the mode of psychoanalytic or psychoexistential critique. There are, first, the pathologies of language. Black people talk up to white people and try to sound white; white people talk down to black people in an un-self-conscious caricature of black linguistic idioms. Then there are the two crucial relationships of misrecognition: the black woman who seeks to find herself in a relationship with a white man, the black man who seeks to find himself in a relationship with a white woman. Here we have a masquerade. Black women and men seek whiteness in sexual encounters with white men and women seeking blackness: I will pretend you are black if you will pretend I am white; I will pretend you are white if you will pretend I am black. But the pretense is imbalanced. White people want only to pretend, black people want to be transformed.

Not everyone is caught up in the masquerade. Fanon depicts his struggle to come to terms with his blackness, to affirm his blackness as such, as absolute, not as a would-be or want-to-be anything else. He nonetheless seeks himself in the universals of European philosophy, ultimately in Sartre's philosophy. He reads in *Orphée Noir* that "negritude is the minor term of a dialectical progression," that it is "a transition and not a conclusion, a means and not an ultimate end." This is the unkindest cut. Fanon turns to Sartre as a friend and finds his identity relativized: "For once that born Hegelian had forgotten that consciousness has to lose itself in the night of the absolute . . . [and] that this negativity draws its worth from an almost substantive absoluteness" (*ibid.*, pp. 133–134). There is no recognition forthcoming from the philosopher of recognition.

How, then, is Fanon to achieve self-recognition, if he cannot see himself in the mirror Sartre holds up to him? The answer would seem to be, by holding up a mirror to himself. But he cannot see himself, at least not all of himself, in the mirror of negritude, of blackness and only blackness. The universalization of black particularity is not an adequate response to the particularization of black universality. To be affirmatively black is to be neither just a particularity nor just a self-enclosed universal. In a black and white world racial self-recognition must be interracial mutual recognition. The black self must meet the white self on a plane of equality; each must then find a way to grant recognition to the other.

Fanon, adapting Hegelian categories to the specific situation of black people, sees the need for mutual recognition. But in reality, the interracial relationship approximates to the classical Hegelian paradigm of one-sided recognition, that is, the relationship of master (lord) and slave (bondsman). And even Sartre, his white counterpart, remains trapped in the dialectic of misrecognition. Maybe Fanon should have heeded the warning of the invisible man: "beware of those who speak of the *spiral* of history; they are preparing a boomerang. Keep a steel helmet handy" (Ellison, 1947, p. 6).

Speaking of spirals and boomerangs: What if Fanon is betrayed not only by his friends but also by his categories? What if the mere use of dialectical reason involves putting on a white mask? Can one think black thoughts with white concepts? Or is there, perhaps, a universal language we could all learn to speak?

Or would such a language still be a power–knowledge relationship, specifically, the language of universalized domination?

7.

Black Skins, White Masks is primarily a psychoexistential critique, secondarily an analysis of objective conditions of domination. *The Wretched of the Earth* reverses the relationship. Problems of self-recognition become a middle term in the logic of colonialism and de-colonization. Fittingly, the tension in Fanon's relationship with Sartre is at least partially overcome. Fanon asks Sartre to write the preface for *The Wretched of the Earth*, Sartre writes it. They are on the same side of the Algerian struggle for national liberation. They speak, more or less, as one.

Fanon's depiction of the colonial situation is recognizably Marxist. But there is a twist or two:

> When you examine at close quarters the colonial context, it is evident that what parcels out the world is to begin with the fact of belonging to or not belonging to a given race, a given species. In the colonies the economic substructure is also a superstructure. The cause is the consequence; you are rich because you are white, you are white because you are rich. This is why Marxist analysis should always be slightly stretched every time we have to do with the colonial problem. (1961, p. 32)

Existentially, historically, the relationship of settler and native is simultaneously racial and economic. Accordingly the political dissection of colonialism and de-colonization requires a class–racial analysis. No theoretical priority can be given to the categories of political economy.

The analysis begins with the fact that colonialism is institutionalized violence—institutionalized, and internalized: It engenders a self-destructive counterviolence in the colonized individual. Black people attack black people. The self-hatred analyzed in *Black Skins, White Masks* emerges as the enactment of intraracial violence in *The Wretched of the Earth*.

The first, spontaneous step toward de-colonization is the negation of this self-negation, the recovery of selfhood in the violent rejection of the master–slave relationship. In the context of de-colonization the struggle for recognition takes the very concrete form of violent insurrectionary action.

The violent act of rebellion is a necessary but not sufficient condition for national liberation. Violent action is pathologizing even if, in the colonial context, it is also humanizing.[3] Spontaneous rebellion must evolve into organized mass movement and spontaneous anger must be transformed into critical consciousness if the energies released in the violent action are not to be dissipated.

8.

The better part of *The Wretched of the Earth* is devoted to a sophisticated if problematical analysis of the interaction between class–racial tendencies and alignments in the African liberation movements and in the nascent postcolonial regimes. Our present concern, however, is with Fanon's and Sartre's existential recasting of both psychoanalysis and Marxism.

For Fanon, black liberation was a project. It was problematical both in itself and in relation to the project of human liberation, to which he was also committed. The project was concretized in Algeria, in and as the praxis of the national liberation movement. At the level of theory, the project was mediated through Fanon's existential approach to social analysis, which resulted in a subtle and evocative phenomenology of both racial recognition and de-colonization. Hence, in reading Fanon, one cannot make racial issues invisible, and one cannot forget the human fact must be "lived and produced."

Although Fanon joins Marxism and psychoanalysis practically, the contradictions between their anthropological presuppositions are bypassed. Theoretical depth is replaced by existential narrative, as if Marxist and psychoanalytic concepts were merely metaphysical and not articulations (however flawed) of practical problems. We recover lived reality, but only by conceptual default.

With Michael Schneider and Jürgen Habermas, by contrast, we regain the concepts and lose the lived experience.

B. Revising Critical Theory

1.

The New Left was pulled by opposing tendencies toward unification and pluralization. On the one hand, there was the perception of a common enemy, variously termed global capitalism, the Establishment, the international power structure. On the other, there were specific liberation movements, with specific agendas. Empedocles would have been right at home.

The conceptual circle we are now entering is characterized by abstract—Kantian and Hegelian—versions of these same tendencies. In *Knowledge and Human Interests* Habermas aims at the pluralization of critical theory; in *Neurosis and Civilization* Michael Schneider aims at its unification.

2.

Knowledge and Human Interests is an argument against both scientism and Hegelianism. It also can be read as a critique of orthodox Marxism, hence as an attempt at epistemological de-Stalinization. And it introduces a dramatic shift in the discourse of psychoanalytic-marxism. Where for the Freudian-Marxists psychoanalysis is to provide Marxism with a missing psychological or subjective theoretical dimension, for Habermas psychoanalysis is important as the singular example of a praxis of self-emancipation through self-reflection. Psychoanalysis has a claim to our political interest far more as therapy than as theory.

First the critique of Marxism. Habermas (1971) sees Marx's theorizing as a combination of two fundamental notions: "*self-generation through productive activity*" and "*self-formation through critical-revolutionary activity*" (p. 55). Epistemologically, however, Marx tended to collapse self-consciousness into self-production. When he accepted Hegelian dialectics, he also accepted Hegel's epistemological monism, the unification of pure and practical reason within one theory of knowledge. Contra Hegel he anchored his epistemology in the concepts and methods of natural rather than philosophical science, and so brought dialectical reason into the real world. But by taking labor and production as the paradigmatic human activities he unavoidably granted the technological rationality of the natural sciences a privileged epistemic position. Technological rationality became identified with reason as such, subjectivity and human freedom lost their epistemological warrant, and the realm of freedom was collapsed into the realm of necessity.

Here is another way of stating the argument. In Habermas' opinion self-reflection is essential to both Hegelian and Marxist theory. But in each instance the theorist's methodological self-reflection denies that self-reflection plays this essential role. Hegel's *The Phenomenology of Spirit* (1807; hereafter *The Phenomenology*) turns upon the disjunction between the knowing subject and the object to be known. But the phenomenological enterprise culminates in absolute knowledge, in which the disjunctive or reflective moment vanishes. Similarly, a self-reflective process is integral to Marx's development of his theory as well as to the formation of the emancipatory self-consciousness of any historical agent. Marx, however, identifies dialectical method with positive science and so obscures the critical role played by self-reflection. Epistemology, in which there is a problematical subject–object relationship, is collapsed into ontology, in which there is an unproblematical subject–object identification. The critical and self-reflective subject who lives in the theory dies in the articulated or manifest method. The power of negative thinking paradoxically establishes the positivity of all human knowledge.

Habermas is thus one of those readers of Marx who see two trends in Marx's thinking. He is an inverse Althusserian. In *For Marx* (1970) Louis Althusser attempts to save Marx the scientist from Marx the philosopher. Habermas wants to protect Marx the philosopher from Marx the scientist. Dueling dualisms, so to speak.

Let's assume, however, that Habermas' critique of Marx is politically strategic, that he wishes to preserve the moment of subjective freedom, of political self-consciousness, from a one-dimensionalizing objectivism. Then his strategy fails. By his own account it is precisely Marx's self-reflection that obscures the self-reflective element in his theory. And if Marx's self-reflection is self-deception, then so is Habermas'.

Being self-reflective about self-reflection accomplishes nothing, or very little. The real problem is the anxiety that accompanies political choice. The solution to the problem is accepting that there is no solution to the problem. To make rational choices one must be able to tolerate the anxiety they involve.

3.

In his effort to avoid scientistic reductionism and preserve an epistemological grounding for emancipatory struggle, Habermas retreats to a pre-Hegelian—neo-Kantian, neo-Fichtean—position. He takes as a given the Kantian distinction between pure and practical reason. He attempts to provide these two categories with the content denied to them by Kant, and to attach each of them to a knowledge-constituting interest. Pure reason, which seeks to answer the question "What can I know?," is attached to work—to "possible technical control over objectified processes of nature"—and has assigned to it the content and empirical–analytic methods of natural science (Habermas, 1971, p. 191). Practical reason, which answers to the question "What ought I do?," is rooted in communicative interaction and language. As expressed through hermeneutic methods of inquiry it "maintains the intersubjectivity of possible action orienting mutual understanding . . ." (*ibid.*).

We will leave aside for the moment any doubts we might have about the adequacy of these categorical relationships. Insofar as they are adequately established, they serve to open up the epistemological door barred by positivistic conceptions of knowledge. Thus far, however, Habermas finds himself with a new version of the original Kantian antithesis between pure reason (here the content and methods of natural science) and practical reason (the content and methods of the cultural sciences and communicative interaction). He tries to resolve it by joining an emancipatory interest with the power and process of self-reflection, that is, with a specific conception of emancipatory praxis.

An interest in emancipation, Habermas contends, can be expressed in the question "What may I hope?" This question "is both practical and theoretical at the same time" (*ibid.*, p. 203). It unites and transforms interactional and instrumental interests. It is neither adequately posed nor satisfactorily answered in the Kantian system. By contrast, J. G. Fichte, in *The Science of Knowledge* (1794), provides it with an epistemological locus. The "development of the concept of the interest of reason from Kant to Fichte leads from the concept of an interest in actions of a free will, dictated by practical reason, to the concept of an interest in the independence of the ego, operative in reason itself" (Habermas, 1971, (p. 209). Further, it "is in accomplishing self-reflection that reason grasps itself as interested" (*ibid.*, p. 212). This interest is emancipatory when the "act of self-reflection . . . 'changes a life'. . ." (*ibid.*). It cannot, Habermas cautions, be realized in isolation: "The emancipatory interest itself is dependent on the interests in possible intersubjective action-orientation and in possible technical control" (*ibid.*, p. 211). But the interest that attaches to these modalities of knowing comes to consciousness through self-reflection. Accordingly self-reflection is constitutive of the parts as well as the whole.

4.

Fichte thus occupies a particularly strategic position in the development of Habermas' argument, just as he does in the history of post-Kantian philosophy. It will be useful to take a brief detour through this historical territory.[4]

In the *Critique of Pure Reason* (1781) Kant granted the empiricist claim that "all our knowledge begins with experience"; but he argued that "it does not follow that it all arises out of experience" (p. 41). It is rather the case that all human knowledge depends upon certain a priori conditions, features of the human mind without which knowing and knowledge would not be possible. These include the sensuous intuition of time and space, the synthetical unity of apperception (the unity of the "I," along with its capacity to combine the discrete data of experience into a manifold), and various categories of judgment and the understanding (for example, cause and effect). Thus Kant reconstituted the Cartesian *cogito*, which had disintegrated into a bundle of associations in the philosophies of Locke and Hume, as a kind of container of mental experience. The reflective and self-reflective "I" or ego of critical theory began to emerge.

One of Kant's aims was to rescue certain or absolute knowledge— truth in the metaphysical sense—from Humean skepticism. He sought to realize this aim in various ways, most notably by rigorously distinguishing between noumena (things-in-themselves) and phenomena (things as they appear for-us). Because objects are known to us only in or through the instrumentalities of human understanding, that is, within the space of our mental apparatus, we can have no valid knowledge of them in-themselves. But within the limits of the understanding, he contended, our knowledge is certain.

We may safely leave to one side the arguments by which Kant sought to demonstrate this position. It is evident, however, that in his efforts to rescue true knowledge he severely limited its scope. Indeed, he created the basic problem German idealist philosophy then attempted to solve, namely, the disjunction or split between subjectivity and objectivity. In this instance Kantian truth lacks objectivity. The objective world gets swallowed up by the concept of things-in-themselves. Knowledge is consequently merely subjective. The subject who knows and the object to be known are placed on opposite sides of an unbridgeable epistemic chasm.

This subject–object split in the sphere of pure reason was replicated in the sphere of practical reason. In the *Critique of Practical Reason* (1788) Kant opposed the "ought" of formal moral laws to the "is" of substantive interests and passions. Here, too, truth was merely subjective.

Additionally, Kant's critical inquiries left a split between the spheres of pure and practical reason. Pure reason, which signified the domain of natural science, seemed to follow different rules from those governing practical reason, which signified the domain of "spiritual" (that is, cultural) life and action. Even if one granted Kant the arguments by which he established the necessity that attaches to laws of nature on the one hand and the freedom that attaches to the moral law on the other, it was not clear how the two realms of knowledge could be united into one epistemic kingdom.

Kant himself attempted the unification in the *Critique of Judgment* (1790). The categories of judgment were to mediate between those of pure and practical reason. Thus feelings of pleasure and pain were meant to join the cognitive faculties and the faculties of desire, and the principle of purposiveness was to join conformity to law in nature with final purpose in spiritual life. But Kant's most notable successors—including Fichte and Hegel—tended to find his arguments unpersuasive. Hence each of them attempted to produce a unified system or science of knowledge that resolved the subject–object split.

In *The Science of Knowledge* Fichte, with whom Habermas identifies himself, claimed that his "system . . . [was] nothing other than the Kantian" (Fichte, 1794, p. 4). But he also claimed that his method was independent of Kant's. In his attempt to unify pure and practical reason, he reverted to an analysis of the ego—the absolute or transcendental, not the empirical, ego—as the locus of all knowing. That is, he was not concerned with your ego or my ego, with the self of specific, concrete individuals. Rather his interest was in the formal or conceptual relationship of the existential and the thinking self, the "I = I" of the Cartesian *cogito* and the Kantian synthetical unity of apperception. He viewed the self in this sense as initially unconditioned: "The self exists because it has posited itself" and equally "the self posits itself simply because it exists" (*ibid.*, p. 98). He then derived the relationship of self (subject) and not-self (object) from this first principle, but as a difference internal to the absolute self. Identity and difference in the self thus became the starting points for all further knowing. And because the categories of identity and difference in the self were constituted through reflection, the science of knowledge unfolds within and as self-reflection.

5.

Here, then, is the epistemological position to which Habermas wishes to retreat, that is, to autonomy or subjective freedom constituted through self-reflection. To be sure, he intends to reconstitute it as an emancipatory praxis. But whatever its adequacy in that regard, it is inadequate as epistemology. On the one hand, self-reflection is not precluded as a formal aspect of natural scientific and hermeneutic inquiries. As a formal procedure, as self-*reflection*, it therefore fails to establish epistemological boundaries. On the other, as *self*-reflection, it merely poses the problem of how selfhood is constituted. And it does so in a way that may preclude a solution. Fichtean subjectivity is self-enclosed, abstract. The real world of objects is external to it. As Hegel demonstrated against Fichte, however, selfhood can only be established by the dialectical interpenetration of subject and object. Hence if Habermas is serious in his·turn toward Fichte, he is stuck with a reflective ego that can have no real intercourse with the world around it.

What then? We are left with a plausible and useful distinction between the interests of the natural and the cultural sciences, and with the idea of emancipatory praxis. But the epistemological categories have no determinate relationship to each other and, thus far, emancipatory praxis is an empty set.

6.

I imagine an intelligent reader of Foucault biting her/his lip in frustration. Interests of whatever kind, s/he is thinking, proceed from real world power relationships. They are quite concrete advantages and disadvantages. Thus when a crime is committed, we ask, who benefits? But Habermas doesn't raise this question, which brings us back to our senses. Instead he places interests beyond the reach of practical relationships of power.

Who benefits from this displacement, the reader asks?

7.

Psychoanalysis appears on the scene as an example, indeed as "the only tangible example," of a Fichtean science, that is, a science that is both emancipatory and methodologically self-reflective (Habermas, 1971, p. 214). Habermas' discussion of it is restricted to Freud's work and, as in the case of his analysis of Marxism, it is both an interpretation and a critique.

Habermas contends that the basic and most valuable elements of psychoanalytic theory emerge from the therapeutic process. By contrast, he sees Freud as attempting to derive the fundamental principles of the theory not from practice, but rather from an energy-distribution model of the mind. By so doing Freud shifts the epistemological locus of psychoanalysis from the category of self-reflection, with its associated practical and emancipatory interests, to that of natural science, with its interest in instrumental action. Freud even admits the possibility that psychoanalysis might one day be replaced by pharmacology. Habermas' critique of this shift follows along the same lines as his prior critique of Marx and Hegel. It is succinctly expressed in the claim that there can be no substitute for self-reflection, no technical solution to the problems of subjectivity, "unless technology is to serve to unburden the subject of its own achievements" (*ibid.*, p. 248).

There is something useful in this critique of Freud's scientism. But—as Marcuse would hasten to point out—Habermas throws out the baby with the bathwater. In rejecting Freud's metapsychology he follows Fromm in displacing the locus of psychoanalysis upward—away from sensuousness, sexuality, and aggressivity. Habermasian individuals lack both drives and passions. They are creatures of intellect and language; would-be, if not actual, rationalists. Hence, when in later chapters we pick up the thread of his argument concerning emancipatory praxis in general and clinical psychoanalysis in particular, we will be careful to populate the theory with bodies as well as minds.

8.

Habermas' intellectualism shows up in his depiction of therapy as well as in his critique of theory. The psychoanalytic theory of neurosis and its treatment, he argues, can (in part) be viewed from the perspective of communication and symbolic interaction:

> The analyst instructs the patient in reading his own texts, which he himself has mutilated and distorted, and in translating symbols from a mode of expression deformed as a private language into the mode of expression of public communication. This translation reveals the genetically important phases of life history to a memory that was previously blocked, and brings to consciousness the person's own self-formative process. . . . [T]he act of understanding to which it leads is self-reflection. (*ibid.*, p. 228)

In his critique of metapsychology Habermas argues that Freud fell victim to a scientisitic misunderstanding of his own theory and practice. Habermas here falls victim to a textualist misunderstanding of his own category of emancipatory praxis. Nothing could be more disastrous in practice than treating analytic interactions as an exercise in textual criticism, except perhaps treating them as the testing of natural scientific hypotheses. This is not to deny that there are analogies between psychoanalytic inquiry, on the one hand, and natural scientific and hermeneutic inquiry, on the other. There are even ways in which scientific and hermeneutic methods are modified for psychoanalytic employment. But to characterize psychoanalysis as either an hermeneutic or scientific process is to erect epistemological defenses against the painful and anxiety-filled reality of actual psychoanalytic experience.

Despite the abstract and/or defensive aspect of his approach to clinical practice, Habermas is able to adduce three "peculiarities" of the psychoanalytic process that link analytic knowledge to emancipatory self-reflection. First, the patient must possess or come to possess a "passion for critique": "analytic knowledge is impelled onward against motivational resistances by the interest in self-knowledge" (*ibid.*, p. 235). Second, the patient "must be brought to regard the phenomena of his illness as part of his self": "the ego of the patient [must] recognize itself in its other, represented by its illness, as in its own alienated self and identify with it" (*ibid.*, pp. 235–236). And third, the analyst "is required to undergo analysis in the role of patient in order to free himself from the very illnesses that he is to treat as analyst." Habermas observes that such a training analysis does not eliminate the possibility of interpretive error, that is, of falsifying countertransference responses to the patient on the part of the analyst. Nonetheless the analyst makes himself the "instrument of knowledge" not "by bracketing his subjectivity, but precisely by its controlled employment" (*ibid.*, p. 237).

At his best, then, Habermas interprets psychoanalysis as an intersubjective process in which both parties struggle to uncover and master alienated dimensions of the patient's selfhood. Viewed this way the process contains its own standard of verification. Psychoanalytic truth, he argues, does not inhere in the theory itself, nor in the patient's acceptance or rejection of a particular interpretation. Only the "successful continuation of a self-formative process" counts as verification of psychoanalytic interpretations. Here we hear an echo of Sartre's conception of project and praxis: Human truth must be produced, not deduced.

Thus Habermas grasps—as Marcuse does not—the emancipatory nature and heuristic implications of psychoanalytic practice. He does not really work out these implications for political practice. There is, after all, a fundamental difference between a struggle framed by the opposed objective interests of social classes and one framed by the mutual subjective interest of analyst and patient. Failing an analysis of this difference he cannot satisfactorily link his interpretation of psychoanalysis to Marxist praxis. Nonetheless, by shifting the focus of critical interest from psychoanalytic theory to clinical practice, he indicates a way of going beyond the philosophical limitations of his Frankfurt School forebears.

9.

In *Knowledge and Human Interests* Habermas is, at most, marginally Marxist. He is a pluralist in more senses than one. Schneider by contrast develops a conception of psychoanalysis within strict Marxist limits. *Neurosis and Civilization* has the unity that Habermas' text lacks. But in dramatic contrast to Habermas, Schneider's "Marxist/Freudian synthesis" reveals little understanding of or interest in the reality of psychoanalytic experience. He gains the theoretical unity of Marxism and psychoanalysis at the expense of psychoanalysis.

Schneider structures his investigation in a promising fashion. He first argues for Freud against "vulgar Marxism," then for Marx against the bourgeois ideological aspects of psychoanalysis. This gives the impression of a mutual critique of ideological tendencies. But the critique of Marxism is half-hearted. Only the most vulgar of Marxist misunderstandings of psychoanalysis come under scrutiny, and Marx's own positions are never challenged. By contrast he reduces psychoanalytic theory to the "science of the pseudo-nature of the bourgeois individual" (Schneider, 1975, p. 60) and psychoanalytic therapy to a dependency-inducing relationship of solidarity for the "individualized individual" of bourgeois society (*ibid.*, p. 112). All the interesting questions that psychoanalysis poses for Marxist praxis are thus eliminated by ideological fiat.

10.

Despite this formidable case of ideological myopia, Schneider sees a possibility for the development of psychoanalytic-marxism that had been overlooked by his otherwise more discerning predecessors and contemporaries:

> What matters . . . , on the one hand, is to pick up the beginnings, the seeds, of a materialist psychology and psychopathology that are strewn throughout Marx's *Capital* and to develop them further; and, on the other hand, to derive Freud's magnificent structural description of the bourgeois soul, especially as a theory of illness and neurosis, from the laws of economic movement of bourgeois society itself. (*ibid.*, p. 118)

This may give the appearance of another genuflection to Marx. There is a way in which, however, *Capital* invites a psychoanalytic reading. Marx there depicts a dialectic of alienated social relationships, in which subjectivity adheres to objects (commodities) while simultaneously human individuals serve simply to mediate the relationships of these subjectified objects. Fundamental to this dialectic is the confinement of use values and the sensuous properties of objects within the exchange value relationship, that is, within the boundaries of abstract labor value. Thus the commodity itself is a relationship of domination—of abstract or exchange value over sensuous, useful values. And thus a psychoanalytic question is apposite: What happens intrapsychically to individuals who have become mere mediators of commodity sociality?

Schneider provides two kinds of answers to this question. First, and more conventionally, he argues that participation in capitalist production and consumption is pathologizing. He views normal adjustment to social reality as routinized pathology. Here he is following the lead of the classical Freudian-Marxists, all of whom view ordinary consciousness as systematically falsified. He also tries, with varying degrees of success, to demonstrate that capitalism engenders specific forms of mental illness and that types of mental illness are class-specific. Finally in this regard, he contends that mental illness is a protest against as well as a symptom of the objective pathologies of capitalism. This line of analysis, made famous most of all by R. D. Laing, is in good part romantic. But it contains at least a grain of truth. An outbreak of neurotic illness can signify an unconscious protest against emotional alienation. Hence there may be a sort of rationality in its apparent irrationality, while the apparent rationality of adjustment may be substantively irrational.

It is in his other, and more fundamental, answer to the question posed above that Schneider opens up a new line of analysis. His central thesis is that

> the structure of social instincts and needs becomes, with the historical development of the structure of the commodity and money, just as *abstract* as the latter. The "abstraction" of use values and of those useful needs and satisfactions which correspond to them and which lie at the root of the commodity and money form is in a certain sense to be regarded as the germinal political–economic cell of those processes of psychical "abstraction" which Freud described with his concept of "instinctual repression." Freud's theory of repression, regarded in this light, is the psychological complement of Marx's theory of commodities and money. (*ibid.*, p. 122)

At the very center of Marxist theory, in the analysis of the "elementary form" of social wealth, Schneider finds a conceptual isomorphism with the psychoanalytic theory of the "elementary form" of the self.

Here is a way of picturing his contention:

Commodity Structure:		Character Structure:
Exchange/Abstract Value		Consciousness
——————————	(Alienation = Repression)	——————————
Use Values/Sensuousness		Desires/Sensuousness

The diagram represents two relationships of repressive abstraction. Commodities are produced via the alienation of sensuousness and use values. Character is produced via the repression of sensuousness and desires. The one process yields exchange values, the other pathological forms of consciousnsss.

Schneider is much too quick to turn this conceptual isomorphism into a causal relationship, to wit, commodity structure determines character structure. Let's take a step back. If we reduce the two units of analysis to a common "elementary form," we have a relationship of self-negation or negative self-relation, in which sensuousness is the negated dimension. We then find two instances of this relationship, one in the realm of economic production and one in the realm of emotional production. Perhaps if we work out the implications of this two-fold embodiment of *negated sensuousness and selfhood* we might regain something of the unity and concreteness that was lost in Habermas' pluralism and abstraction.

C. Exploding Freudian-Marxism

1.

So far our postclassical discourse has rested upon the assumptions that orthodox Marxism and orthodox psychoanalysis each tells us something important about reality. Each, if I may revert to an old-fashioned expression, is presumed to be part of the solution as well as part of the problem.

Exit Marx and Freud. Enter Deleuze, Guattari, and Foucault.[5] Also Nietzsche: "I am no man, I am dynamite" (Nietzsche, 1888, p. 326).

First we will blow things apart. Then, with C. Fred Alford's assistance, we will attempt to put them back together.

2.

In his preface to *Anti-Oedipus* Foucault (with an apparent lack of irony) characterizes the book as an *"Introduction to the Non-Fascist Life"* (Deleuze & Guattari, 1972, p. xiii). By fascism he means not just or even primarily the totalitarian practices of a Hitler or Mussolini. The enemy is rather "the fascism in us all, in our heads and in our everyday behavior, the fascism that causes us to love power, to desire the very thing that dominates and exploits us" (*ibid.*).

Woody Guthrie, we noted earlier, had the words "this machine kills fascists" printed on his guitar. Deleuze and Guattari offer us a different machine. According to Foucault it has seven moving parts:

- Free political action from all unitary and totalizing paranoia.
- Develop action, thought and desires by proliferation, juxtaposition, and disjunction, and not by subdivision and pyramidal hierarchization.
- Withdraw allegiance from the old categories of the Negative (law, castration, lack, lacuna), which Western thought has so long held

sacred as a form of power and an access to reality. Prefer what is positive and multiple, difference over uniformity, flows over unities, mobile arrangements over systems. Believe that what is productive is not sedentary but nomadic.

- Do not think that one has to be sad in order to be militant, even though the thing one is fighting is abominable. It is the connection of desire to reality (and not its retreat into the forms of representation) that possesses revolutionary force.
- Do not use thought to ground a political practice in Truth; nor political action to discredit, as mere speculation, a line of thought. Use political practice as an intensifier of thought, and analysis as a multiplier of the forms and domains for the intervention of political action.
- Do not demand of politics that it restore the "rights" of the individual, as philosophy has defined them. The individual is the product of power. What is needed is to "de-individualize" by means of multiplication and displacement, diverse combinations. The group must not be the organic bond uniting hierarchized individuals, but a constant generator of de-individualization.
- Do not become enamored of power.[6] (*ibid.*, pp. xiii–xiv)

Anti-Oedipus thus comes into the world equipped with both an ethics and a method. With admirable brevity Foucault states the intention of going beyond the horizon of the Enlightenment; beyond dialectical reason; beyond, in sum, the problematics of modernity, including those of Marx and Freud.

Foucault's statement presupposes the reading of the text. Let's therefore turn to *Anti-Oedipus* before returning to the commandments in which it is presumed to eventuate.

3.

The subtitle of *Anti-Oedipus* is *Capitalism and Schizophrenia*. It might seem, therefore, that Deleuze and Guattari are interested in joining some version of Marxist or objective analysis with some version of (if not psychoanalytic) psychological or subjective analysis. But the "and" is misleading. Their aim is to eliminate the notion that there is any combining to be done. We are only "engaging in an enjoyable pastime" when we are "content to establish a perfect parallel between money, gold, capital, and the capitalist triangle on the one hand, and the libido, the anus, the phallus, and the family triangle on the other . . ." (*ibid.*, p. 28). It is rather the case that *"social production is purely and simply desiring-production itself under determinate conditions. . . . There is only desire and the social, and nothing else"* (*ibid.*, p. 29).

Deleuze and Guattari are truly anti-Cartesian as well as anti-Oedipean. They evidently abhor geometry, and perhaps with good reason: In this instance at least, they get the parallels and the triangles wrong. But let's allow the mathematical details to pass. The substantive point is that Deleuze and Guattari treat the distinction between Marxism and psychoanalysis as a Gordian knot. They cut it and, by so doing, fuse desire with production. There are then only historically variable forms of desiring-production.

Another act of forgiveness: We will ignore the hyphen and assume at least the *conceptual* existence of an entity or process that can be described as desiring-production. What is it?

4.

Anti-Oedipus does not contain anything so prosaic as a definition of desiring-production. The meaning of production, however, is tolerably clear. Production is actual doing and making—concrete, material activity that yields results. It may be contrasted with exchange, as in the classical Marxist distinction between the realm of production and the realm of exchange.

The meaning of desire is more complex and more elliptical. The concept, moreover, is not native to either Marxism or psychoanalysis. It first emerged as a crucial theoretical category through Kojève's quite Marxist reading (1969) of Chapter 4 of Hegel's *The Phenomenology*. Subsequently it was given a position of prominence in psychoanalytic discourse by Lacan, from whence it found its way into *Anti-Oedipus*. It figures as well in the work of Fanon, the feminists, Lichtman, and Kovel. Given the ubiquity and importance of the concept, it therefore is worth while to do a bit of etymological backtracking.

In the first chapters of *The Phenomenology* Consciousness aims at gaining knowledge of an object outside itself. It identifies truth with knowledge of the object as such, that is, of the object without any contamination by the act of knowing or by the subjectivity of Consciousness. The aim is not realized. Consciousness recurrently finds itself in the object. By so doing it discovers itself. It becomes self-conscious, or Self-Consciousness. Self-knowledge arises as the object of the inquiry.

Initially Consciousness existed in a deadened, reified world of would-be objectivity, a world lacking in or abstracted from subjectivity. As Marcuse (1960, p. 112) points out, that world resembles the fetishized realm of commodities and money analyzed by Marx in *Capital*. When it falls away, we find ourselves in a life-world. Emergent Self-Consciousness is now characterized by *Begierde* (appetite), which Kojève translates as *désir* (an emotional or spiritual hunger). Taken in combination the two words come close to Hegel's meaning. The object of his analysis is an intense, greedy appetite or lust that cannot be satisfied sensuously.

Self-Consciousness first seeks to give itself substance and completeness as a living being by incorporating objects—by eating them. This proves, by dialectical inversion, its dependence upon these objects. It cannot gain self-certainty through them, yet this is what it wishes. A gap or disjunction becomes apparent, between sensuous experience and the subjective impulse that initiates it. The concept of desire signifies the disjunction.

From this point the Hegelian tale becomes intersubjective. A proto-self seeks confirmation of its selfhood from an other proto-self. We have entered upon the dialectic of recognition. For Hegel this means that we have surpassed, gone beyond, desire as the internally contradictory linkage of subject and object. Nonetheless the life and death battle for recognition as well as the subsequent relationship of master and slave are suffused with desire, and this in two ways. First, (at its best) the Hegelian dialectic always winds its way along the boundary of the sensuous and the supersensuous in human experience, along the line of conjunction and disjunction between body and mind. But this is to say that we cannot escape a dialectic of desire. Second, until its very end *The Phenomenology* is concerned with the nonidentity of subject and object. If this nonidentity matters, if it concerns something of importance to a subject or self, then it is experienced as both pain and promise, as present lack and future gratification. Hence desire cannot be surpassed. Indeed, the proclaimed identity of subject and object with which Hegel (en)closes *The Phenomenology* might be interpreted as a last-gasp defense against the perpetual overreaching and shortfall of desire—its irremediable lack of completion.

Enter, briefly, Lacan. Among other things, Lacan reads Freud through Kojève's Hegel. Hence he finds *désir* in Freud's *Wunsch* (wish). Because Freud does not rigidly differentiate *Wunsch* from *Begierde* or *Lust*, there is some etymological justification for this interpretation. In any case Lacan interprets the theory of wish-fulfillment as a theory of desire. The emotionally intense experience of a lack, along with the fantasies to which it gives rise, is placed at the center of psychoanalytic experience.

What, then, does desire mean to Deleuze and Guattari? Negatively, it is not socially superstructural, primarily intrapsychic, merely subjective, or the mental representation of a bodily impulse or condition. Positively, it has Hegelian and Lacanian resonances, although without Lacan's insistence on lack or shortfall, and without his differentiation of desire from biological need and intersubjective demand. Hence it is an appetite, at once sensuous and supersensuous, sexual and aggressive, as well as the activity of the appetite: breathing, eating, digesting, defecating, vomiting, fucking, and being fucked.

If on the one hand desire has a phenomenological meaning, on the other it has a "scientific" one. It is purported to be a material process or flow, akin to a flow of energy or a flow of information. Deleuze and Guattari depict it in a kind of hydraulic or volcanic language resembling Freud's narrative of the libido. Indeed, they are only too happy to use the concept of libido, which they interpret as the abstract form of desire matching Marx's concept of abstract labor:

> Just as Ricardo founds political or social economy by discovering quantitative labour as the principle of every representable value, Freud founds desiring-economy by discovering the quantitative libido as the principle of every representation of the objects and aims of desire. (1972, p. 299)

Here we have conception without production. It is at least arguable that the labor theory of value has an empirical foundation and application; the same cannot be said for the libido theory of psychical values. In the one case people work for defined periods of time and at ascertainable levels of productivity. The socially average productivity of labor can be calculated, and the value of products correlated with the amount of socially average labor they contain. This is not to say the theory is unproblematical; but it does have a claim to scientific interest.

In the other case we have a concept/force that is unmeasurable and measures nothing. Lacking a demonstrable content or presence, its use is supernumerary and obscurantist—scientistic, as Habermas correctly observes. It is a metaphor masking as a Helmholtzian or Fechnerian concept, a bit of Freud's fantasy life articulated in the language of neurology. Using it to materialize psychoanalytic theory is about as useful as building a bridge out of daydreams.

Anti-Oedipus overflows with the language of the material sciences. In this regard the use of libido theory is paradigmatic: The language of materialism masks a lack of an empirical referent. Its use signifies an encompassing metaphysical miasma. If we dispel it, we are left with desire in the former sense: a primitive appetite, the activity of the appetite—also the fantasies accompanying it, and especially its frustration.

5.

Desiring-production is the activity of machines. So-called individuals are machines, parts of individuals are machines, and, importantly, individuals are parts of machines. Society is a machine consisting of machines, machines coupling and uncoupling, working and breaking down. And the social machine comes first, comes before individuals, including families of individuals, in the same sense that the body comes before parts of the body.

Without, I hope, too much distortion, Deleuze and Guattari may be seen as offering us the three-fold identity, society = desiring-production = machine(s). (There is also the "body without organs," but it can wait.) The concept of a social machine of desiring-production seemingly undermines the parallel (paralyzed) triangulations of Marxism and psychoanalysis. It is at once a critique and a construction, or a deconstruction and a reconstruction.

We might picture it this way:

Marxism:	**Psychoanalysis:**
$(M - C - M + \Delta M)$	(Father–Mother–Child)

Social Machine(s) of Desiring-Production

In this representation I have attempted to help Deleuze and Guattari with their geometry. Marxism is characterized by the general formula of capital, psychoanalysis by the oedipal triangle. Arguably these are parallel constructions. Money (M) passes through the production of commodities (C) to yield capital, money with the added substance of surplus value $(M + \Delta M)$. The phallus passes into and through the feminine orifice, yielding the child.[7] Viewed from below, however, these two constructions are a splitting-apart of desiring-production. Just as, for Hegel, the Understanding (nondialectical, nonspeculative thinking) splits apart the flow of subject into object and object into subject, so for Deleuze and Guattari psychoanalysis and Marxism, in themselves and in their fixed opposition to each other, split and reify the flows of desiring-production.[8] And just as Hegel thinks that the Understanding itself is the problem it purports to solve, so Deleuze and Guattari think Marxism and psychoanalysis are problems claiming to be solutions.

6.

One can read in the pages of *Anti-Oedipus* the political controversies and alliances that lie behind it. It is implicitly critical of orthodox Marxism, but explicitly Marx is honored.[9] It is profoundly critical of psychoanalysis, including Lacanian psychoanalysis, but the critique of Lacan is directed, quite disingenuously, at his followers. In both these respects Deleuze and Guattari resemble Hegel, who claimed that the critique of identity in *The Phenomenology* was aimed at the followers of Schelling but not Schelling himself—a ruse of reason that fooled nobody, least of all Schelling.

Be that as it may, the critique of Freud and orthodox psychoanalysis is forceful and direct. Desire is not, in the first instance, familial and oedipal. It is social and an-oedipal. It only becomes familialized and oedipalized in specific historical instances. Psychoanalysis mistakes this deformation of desire for desire itself. Just as the political economists ontologized the private appropriation of labor and its products, so psychoanalysis ontologizes the privatization of desire. One must remove Oedipus from the picture altogether if one wishes to see the reality of desiring-production. Hence Deleuze and Guattari vote for Artaud instead of Freud (*ibid.*, p. 14):

> *I don't believe in father*
> > *in mother*
> > *got no*
> > *papamummy*

For desire itself there is no father–mother–child. The oedipal triangle is rather the straitjacket of desire.

Let's take a step back, so this last statement will not be mistaken for a metaphor.

For Freud the human animal is essentially neurotic. When the neuroses are analyzed they reveal, as the nucleus of human selfhood, the repression of oedipal desires. Moreover, the family is the basic building block of civilization. Political relationships are external and theoretically subsequent to familial ones. Freud's theory is at once patriarchal, phallocentric, and privatizing.

For Deleuze and Guattari the human animal is fundamentally psychotic, that is, schizophrenic. Schizophrenia in this sense must be distinguished from the clinical entity, which results from repression. The schizophrenic flow is not bound up in or directed at papa–mummy–me. As schizophrenic delirium reveals, it is inherently social and historical. It cuts across the social field, breaks it and rejoins it, rearranges it in endless multiplicity. Oedipalization is the constraining and distorting of this schizophrenic flow of desire, its intrapsychic psychiatric institutionalization, a confinement on the inside that is of quite the same nature as psychiatric confinement on the outside. The schizo in each of us and the schizo in mental hospitals rebels against Oedipus—Oedipus who persecutes us, Oedipus who makes us paranoid, Oedipus the fascist. When we break down from Oedipus, we are dangerously close to breaking with and through Oedipus.

7.

You are in a movie theater watching and listening to a bizarre film in which machines, some of which are people or parts of people, are noisily breathing, eating, defecating, copulating, forming, and dissolving—not as a continuous, stable representation, but as a flow marked by breaks and disjunctions. Then you are in the movie, or the movie is around/in you. Your body becomes the disjoined flow of desiring-machines, painfully localized, and painfully lacking in location. You cannot determine where or when this is happening.

The desiring-machines are too much with you, on you, in you. You are becoming unbearably anxious and disoriented. You—if we can speak of "you"—become or retreat to the "body without organs":

> In order to resist organ-machines, the body without organs presents its smooth, slippery, opaque, taut surface as a barrier. In order to resist linked, connected, and interrupted flows, it sets up a counterflow of amorphous, undifferentiated fluid. (*ibid.*, p. 9)

You are now experiencing the "*repulsion* of desiring machines by the body without organs." They, in paranoid fashion, recurrently break into and persecute the body without organs. It, in schizoid fashion, recurrently repels them.[10] "The forces of attraction and repulsion, of soaring ascents and plunging falls, produce a series of intensive states based on the intensity = 0 that designates the body without organs . . ." (*ibid.*, p. 21). There you . . . and you and you and you . . . are/are not.

If you could stabilize your response to the experience you might say it was one of terror, or of sublimity. Later you might refer to it as a bad trip.

Just so.

8.

Like Foucault and the R. D. Laing of *The Politics of Experience* (1967b), Deleuze and Guattari are aligned with the antipsychiatry movement. They view standards and theories of mental health (including psychoanalysis) as instrumentalities of oppression and, conversely, insanity as approximating an experience of liberation. They also join Foucault in opposing totalizing and rationalizing theories of history. In both regards they aim at a break with prevailing or hegemonic concepts of Reason. Yet, so it seems to me, they remain bound to those conceptions. They resemble Platonists on an acid trip, Hegelian materialists on a schizophrenic voyage.

9.

Again, these statements are something more than metaphors. Recall the ontology Plato offers us in *The Republic* (in Rouse, 1956). A line extends from the Good, true Being, down through the forms, mathematical objects, and visible things, to mere images of visible things. An analogous line extends from Callipolis and the true philosopher to tyranny and the tyrannical individual. The latter, a creature of unconstrained, unnecessary, and illicit desire, is frankly paranoid, although not quite insane. There is some of her/him in all of us. In our dreams this beast

> skips about and, throwing off sleep, tries to go and fulfil its own instincts.
> You know there is nothing it will not dare to do, thus freed and rid of all
> shame and reason; it shrinks not from attempting in fancy to lie with a
> mother, or with any other man or god or beast, shrinks from no blood-
> shed. . . . (p. 370)

The tyrant is Oedipus run amok. He lives out the paranoid, and oedipal, nightmare.

We may combine the two lines. At the top is the Good, along with rational and ethical conduct shaped through participation in the Good. At the bottom is immorality and mental abnormality, an oedipal phantasmagoria.

Deleuze and Guattari preserve this image of the world virtually intact. They introduce only two modifications. First, in a familiar Nietzschean fashion, they construct the line from the bottom up, so that reason and morality are viewed as perversions of desire, rather than desire being viewed as the perversion of reason and morality. Second, they add one rung to the ladder, a bottom rung of schizophrenia. Consequently even, or especially, the paranoid/oedipal level is viewed as repressive. And because we are to locate ourselves within this an-oedipal and anti-oedipal field, we experience the familiar Platonic images in unfamiliar ways. The polarities of polis and psyche is collapsed into each other, justice in the realm of words (one word, one meaning) is abandoned, bizarre objects copulate in unrestrained frenzy around and through us.

10.

From *The Republic* down to and through *Anti-Oedipus*, critical reason retains its formal identity. One way or another, the Apparent is forced or persuaded to give way to the Real. The Real changes over time. It is progressively, or at least successively, materialized. Hegelian philosophy is the great breaking and linking point in this process. For the reader of Hegel, the Real reaches back toward the Platonic Good and/or forward to the existential project. In whichever direction it is taken, however, with Hegel the principle or Concept of critical reason has at last been articulated: It is negation that not only reveals error but creates truth.

Marx, Freud, and the Freudian-Marxists are, or can be interpreted as being, Hegelian materialists. They either claim to demonstrate or take as axiomatic three propositions. First, the Real is natural, sensuous, and historical (evolutionary, developmental). Second, specifically human development necessarily involves a simultaneously liberating and alienating break with the simply natural. Both sides of this development are contained in the Rational. To say that something is rational is to say that it is both liberating and alienating. But—here we come to the critical side of the position—the double nature of human rationality is not recognized; it is denied. Bourgeois political economy covers over the alienation of labor, ordinary consciousness covers over the repression of desire. The apparently rational is importantly, maybe even primarily, the rationalization of domination. Third, and in the final instance, the critique of domination leads to a reconciliation of the Rational and the Real, in which the meaning of each term changes in the sublation of their mutual estrangement. We then have, classically, the moment of Marx's and Marxist ecstasy, when "communism, as fully developed naturalism, equals humanism, and as fully developed humanism equals naturalism"—communism which is "the riddle of history solved, and . . . knows itself to be this solution" (Marx, 1844b, p. 84).

For all of their protests against triangular reasoning Deleuze and Guattari belong to this Hegelian materialist lineage. They simply substitute desiring-production for Hegel's Absolute Spirit or Marx's species being. Or we could say, desiring-machine/body without organs is their version of the subject/object of history. The names of the parts have been changed, but the machine continues to run, if somewhat more crazily.

11.

Assume for a moment that Nietzsche's insanity was an instance of schizophrenia. There is then a Nietzsche before and after a schizophrenic break.

Nietzsche sane: There are good reasons for including Nietzsche in the discourse of psychoanalytic-marxism. The analysis of guilt in *On the Genealogy of Morals*, for example, goes beyond anything we can find in Freud. Nor are the will to power and the idea of eternal return "merely" philosophical notions, suitable to be interpre*ted* but not to be interpre*tive*.

Nietzsche insane: His mental health had always been precarious. In the latter part of 1888 his self-control weakened. With this loss of restraint came a torrent of words and thoughts, parallel in so many ways to those wonderful and tormented/tormenting late paintings of van Gogh. Then

Nietzsche substantially disappeared. He broke down and wrote no more. Perhaps a remnant remained: He could be led to the piano in his mother's house, where he would improvise a music of some kind. A sad image, an insane counterpoint to his own earlier image of the music-practicing Socrates.

Deleuze and Guattari, schizoanalyzing Nietzsche: "There is no Nietzsche-the-self, professor of philology, who suddenly loses his mind and supposedly identifies with all sorts of strange people; rather, there is the Nietzschean subject who passes through a series of states, and who identifies these states with the names of history: '*every name in history is I. . . .*' The subject spreads itself out along the entire circumference of the circle, the center of which has been abandoned by the ego" (Deleuze & Guattari, 1972, p. 21).

The reference here is to a line in a letter Nietzsche wrote as he was breaking down. It signifies a spreading, malignant undermining of emotional capacity, a diminishing ability to maintain (as it were) the synthetical unity of apperception. Nietzsche responds to this erosion, to the experience of his self fragmenting and disappearing, in an anxious, manic fashion. Deleuze and Guattari, by contrast, offer us a neatly philosophical depiction of that experience—and not, I think, an honest one. Nietzsche was losing himself; they are constructing themselves. *Their* decentered subjectivity is a concept, a perfectly intelligible notion propounded by two coherent and cohering selves. Unlike Nietzsche after the fall, they are not insane. They are pseudomadmen who wish to use their fantasies of insanity as a critical perspective. If they were genuine madmen, they would not have been able to write *Anti-Oedipus* but only (at the very most) something like Daniel Paul Schreber's *Memoirs of My Nervous Illness* (in Macalpine & Hunter, 1955). If they were concerned with actual schizophrenic experience, then *Anti-Oedipus* might have been compassionate rather than celebratory. As it is, we are treated to schizophrenia-as-spectacle, an enjoyable pastime for those who relish cruelty.[11]

We are a step closer to being able to interpret Foucault's claim that *Anti-Oedipus* is an "*Introduction to the Non-Fascist Life.*"

12.

A strength of *Anti-Oedipus*, as of postmodern discourse more generally, is its challenge to philosophies of identity. But as the merely pseudoschizophrenic nature of the text suggests, breaking with the philosophy of identity is more difficult than it might seem.

Let's go back to the beginning. Empedocles proclaimed that all things mortal "never cease their continuous exchange, sometimes uniting under the influence of Love, so that all become One, at other times again each moving apart through the hostile force of Hate." The One and the Many, likewise identity and difference, seem to constitute a flow, at once continuous and (in the negative moment) disrupted. But the flow, as the medium, maintains its identity amidst the changes. Hence we have a philosophy of identity, despite the appearance of difference and multiplicity. So, too, with Deleuze and Guattari. The pseudoschizophrenic flow, for all its breaks and disruptions, remains self-same, a universal, albeit a colorful one.

To be sure, as Hegel demonstrated in his explorations of perception (thing and properties) and understanding (the play of forces) in *The Phenomenology*, the argument can be reversed. Then self-sameness or the One is the appearance, multiplicity or the Many is the reality. Deleuze and Guattari come into their own. All things move away from the center. But the reversal can in turn be reversed and the totality restored. And so on to infinity.

The significance of this exercise in dialectics will be more evident if we shift from logic to psychologic. Empedocles already articulates what Freud was later to designate as the life-drive and the death-drive. The life-drive is erotic. It joins selves and the self together. The death-drive, less visible in itself, can be tracked in the disintegrating and fragmenting effects of hatred.

We may leave to one side all the possible criticisms of the death-drive. Within this Empedoclean/Freudian frame two states of mind (be they individual or collective) may be pictured. In one of them life, love, and the drive toward unity predominate over death, hatred, and the drive toward fragmentation. In the other death, hatred, and the drive toward fragmentation predominate.

These abstract portraits are drawn from everyday experience. The first is a sketch of sanity, the second of insanity. Note that neither is a pure state. But sanity involves the capacity to contain the forces of self-negation, while insanity is marked by the loss of that capacity. If, therefore, we take the One, self-sameness, and identity in a psychologically meaningful sense, it is literally insane to try to go beyond them. Hence Deleuze and Guattari remain bound to the psychology they attack. As implied above, their ability to write a book like *Anti-Oedipus* depends upon it.

And this being so, one might even ask: What if the domain of self-sameness—of the capacity for negative self-relation—is enlarged rather than narrowed by working through oedipal thematics?

13.

These last remarks shed a certain light on Foucault's seven theses. If we read *Anti-Oedipus* as a protest against the hegemonic combine of orthodox Marxism, orthodox psychoanalysis, psychiatric institutions, penal institutions, and the state—a phantasmal combine but not an entirely unreal one—it has a degree of emancipatory force. It takes the Marcusean critique of one-dimensionality a dramatic step further. It makes his affirmation of polymorphous perversity seem tame and all too sane. It out-Marxs Marx in its radical critique of everything that exists.

But if capitalism and its associated orthodoxies constitute the totalizing disease, who would really chose to take the proliferating cure? Are we ready, for example, to follow Deleuze and Guattari into Reich's orgone box? For in their judgment the "simultaneously schizophrenic and paranoiac nature" of Reich's late theory is more to be applauded than decried: "We admit that any comparison of sexuality with cosmic phenomena such as 'electrical storms,' 'the blue color of the sky and the blue-gray of atmospheric haze,' the blue of the orgone, 'St. Elmo's fire, and the bluish formations [of] sunspot activity,' fluids and flows, matter and particles, in the end appear more adequate to us than the reduction of sexuality to the pitiful little familialist secret" (1972, p. 292).

In this passage Deleuze and Guattari attempt to hedge their bets. They are not announcing themselves as Reichians, but only as favoring the secretions of the orgone to the secrets of Oedipus. A bet is a bet nonetheless and—if they mean to be revolutionaries—they lose. For, like Reich, they mistake regression into the world of bizarre objects and processes for a journey into the ur-reality of human experience. Psychotic experience is not, however, human nature, but rather a malignant deformation of our nature. Melanie Klein to the contrary notwithstanding, we do not come into the world as little paranoid schizophrenics, who only gradually become less psychotic. Unless we are biologically damaged, we come into the world as sensuous/supersensuous organisms with the capacity for the life-sustaining ingestion and digestion of experience. If we become desiring-machines, it is through a catastrophic failure of the metabolic process.

Yet Deleuze and Guattari would base social life on desiring-production. What kind of life would it be, if it were founded on schizophrenic and paranoiac flows?[12] It would be saved from fascism only by its inability to preserve itself, or it would generate fascism, absolute and totalizing power, in order to preserve itself.

Think back to Fromm's analysis of fascism in *Escape from Freedom*. He contended that the destructiveness, sadomasochism, and authoritarianism of fascism were psychological escapes from moral aloneness and powerlessness. We wondered if moral aloneness and powerlessness really got to the heart of the matter. But what if we substitute the persecutory desiring-machines and catatonic body without organs for moral aloneness? Then we would understand fascism as both expressing and containing the terror of madness.

Taken seriously, *Anti-Oedipus* would be an *Introduction to Fascist Living*. What, then, are we to make of Foucault's theses?

14.

If Freudian-Marxism is the initial position, then *Anti-Oedipus* is in the position of negation. It proves to be self-negating.

On one reading its authors don't take insanity seriously. In this case we have a provocative and stimulating array of metaphors, an anti-Hegelian but still Hegelian metaphysics, a parlor game for radicals who find that politics is much too slow a boring of hard boards. Passing through *Anti-Oedipus* is then like a trip to Milliways, the restaurant at the end of the universe (Adams, 1980). There you can watch the universe come to an end, see it dissolve with terrifying splendor into the great void, finish your dinner, and go back to from where and when you came. Three cheers for the cataclysm!

Alternatively, Deleuze and Guattari are seriously proposing a theory and practice of schizophrenia, in which case their project would be realized only if humanity succeeds in blowing itself to bits—no restaurant, just the end of the human universe. Or, if we draw back from the brink, we would find ourselves in a world of waking nightmares.

Yet the negation of the negation neither restores the original position nor closes the dialogue. The idea of desiring-production interpenetrated with social production introduces a significant break with the equation, psychology = individual (or family member). And we also must grant to *Anti-Oedipus* what its authors grant to Oedipus. They concede that oedipal thematics are not the invention of psychoanalysis. But they criticize psychoanalysis for reinforcing oedipal bonds rather than contributing to their dissolution. In parallel fashion we must acknowledge that the realm of desiring-production (sometimes chaotic, sometimes organized into a bipolar oscillation between desiring-machines and the body without organs) is not the creation of Deleuze and Guattari. To the contrary, they articulate in a particularly compelling way psychodynamic processes that are widespread and politically explosive. But like the psychoanalysts whom they criticize, they, too, mistake the problem for the solution.

15.

Deleuze and Guattari are not alone in their opposition to Freudian orthodoxy. C. Fred Alford also wishes to dethrone the primal psychoanalytic father. But in *Melanie Klein and Critical Social Theory* he mounts his attack from another direction, with another ultimate aim, and with considerably more restraint. We will find, indeed, that his position is the dialectical inversion of theirs.

Alford's aim may be stated in the form of the question, "what would a Kleinian version of Herbert Marcuse's *Eros and Civilization* look like?" (Alford, 1989, p. 1). What happens to critical theory if one replaces Freud with Klein?

In fairness, we should note the limited scope of the enterprise. Alford is not committing himself to Klein, nor is he attempting a thorough-going revision of critical theory. He is intent upon following a hypothetical line of argument to the end. We will try to be mindful of these limits, but also of our own interests in his project.

Alford's argument has two basic presuppositions. First, he distinguishes between psychologies that explain emotional life from the outside in and those that explain it from the inside out. Freud and Klein fall into the latter category, non-Kleinian object relations theorists like Harry Guntrip or Erich Fromm fall into the former. Alford stands with Freud and Klein.

Second, Alford distinguishes between a psychoanalysis of drives and a psychoanalysis of passions. Drives aim at tension reduction through discharge; the object or other is, in the first instance, a vehicle for the realization of this aim. Passions (paradigmatically love and hate) are, by contrast, constitutive of and constituted by object relations from the outset. Freud, he contends, is fundamentally a theorist of the drives, Klein of the passions. He stands with Klein, or this interpretation of Klein, against Freud.

There are evident advantages for a critical theory of society in such a psychology. Like classical Freudianism it provides a substantive conception of human nature; unlike classical Freudianism it is social or relational from the outset. There is no inner world beyond object relationships nor an outer one beyond the passions.

There are corresponding disadvantages. Kleinian psychoanalysis, even more than Freudian, tends to disavow or at least devalue objective reality. The external world is dimly perceived and scarcely understood.[13] Alford recognizes this limitation of the Kleinian position, and he unquestionably perceives the importance of the objective factors she disregards. But true to Klein, he leaves them in a state of conceptual underdevelopment. Although this lack may be an artifact of his self-imposed investigative limitations, the result is a one-sided view of social reality. To put it simply, Klein is brought to bear upon critical theory; critical theory is not brought to bear upon Klein.

If on the one hand Alford is overly Kleinian, on the other he is not Kleinian enough. He identifies himself with an interpretation of Klein that emphasizes the verbs rather than the adjectives or nouns—processes rather than things and forces (*ibid.*, p. 7). At the same time he draws a line between drives and passions, and another between mind and body. In the process the nouns (drives and the body) are deprived of theoretical import. Kleinianism is reduced to a psychodynamic theory of love and hate.

Whatever the problems with Freud's theory of drives, it articulates a link between mind and body and gives due recognition to the forces that hit the mind from below. Klein preserves this dimension of Freudian theory, even if and as she (1) links drives to objects and (2) builds up a complex theory of emotional life on this basis. Consequently, whatever the problems with her position, it is extraordinarily rich in content. So far as the inner world is concerned, Klein stops at nothing. Alford pulls up short.

16.

In *Anti-Oedipus,* paranoid and schizoid phenomena are richly evoked and overflow, but the structure of emotional life is obliterated—blown away. *Melanie Klein and Critical Social Theory* provides the missing form or structure, but the paranoid and schizoid content of emotional life is either minimized or presupposed. Hence the insanity of the former and the sanity of the latter. But sanity at what cost?

Here is how Alford pictures Klein's conception of the intrapsychic situation (p. 39):

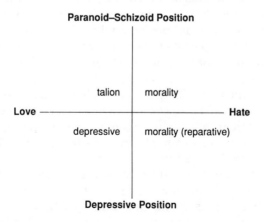

For Klein each position is a distinctive constellation of drives, aims, objects, and defenses. Alford narrows the focus to the management of the passions of love and hate characteristic of each, as well as to the opposed moralities they involve.

The paranoid–schizoid position is earlier ontogenetically and more primitive emotionally. It is followed developmentally by the depressive position but it does not disappear. It remains as a structuring element of the self. Adult emotional life involves an oscillation between these two modalities.

The paranoid–schizoid position is a "normally occurring psychotic state" in which splitting and projective identification are used to cope with intense anxiety "that stems from the operation of the death instinct" (*ibid.*, p. 29). The infant fears disintegration and annihilation as a consequence of its own hatred. It projects its hostility and a bit of its own ego into the outer world, paradigmatically into the mother's breast, which is then experienced in fantasy as a bad or persecutory object. The object is partial rather than complete, a breast and not the person of the mother. Loving impulses are also projected outward and create, in corresponding fashion, the good or life-sustaining object.

At the paranoid–schizoid level of development the "infant's foremost anxiety . . . is that his persecutors will destroy him and his good object. The primary defense is not so much projection (already used to create good and bad objects and externalize them) but splitting and idealization . . ." (*ibid.*, p. 32). The objects are held rigidly apart and the good object is endowed with omnipotence and invulnerability. The defensive structure is unstable, however, not least because the infant is envious of the goodness of the good object. This is, after all, a world of doubles. There is a good infant attached through love to a good object, a bad infant attached through hate to a bad object. The bad infant/object feels deprived by and is envious of the good infant/object. It therefore seeks to spoil, degrade, and destroy a goodness it cannot hope to possess.

In the paranoid–schizoid position, which Klein and Alford view as the foundation of selfhood, there is no concern for the consequences of actions, and certainly not for their effects on others. At most there is the operation of a talion morality, a cold exchange of goods and evils.

And what if the foundation, the paranoid–schizoid position, cracks, fragments, or dissolves? Then we have a world of . . . schizophrenic fluxes and flows, of persecutory desiring-machines and bodies without organs, in short, the real world of phantasms and horrors that Deleuze and Guattari idealize in *Anti-Oedipus*.

The depressive position is developmentally more advanced than the paranoid–schizoid position. It involves the child's emerging recognition that the mother is a person and not just a function, and that she has passions of her own. Importantly "he" begins to understand that "the bad mother who frustrates him, and whom he has destroyed in phantasy a thousand times, is also the good mother who tenderly meets his needs" (*ibid.*, p. 33). He fears that his hate-filled, envious attacks have "destroyed all that is good in the world . . . ," and he "attempts to recreate the other. . . [he] has destroyed, first by phantasies of omnipotent reparation, later by healing and affectionate gestures toward real others" (*ibid.*, p. 35). These reparative gestures certainly have a component of self-interest, but they fundamentally express a gratitude toward the object for its goodness. Hence Alford argues that "depressive love is *caritas*, accompanied by anxiety that we are not strong enough to protect and repair those we love. Love and guilt are linked, but *caritas* stems primarily from gratitude" (*ibid.*, p. 39).

If we bracket the issue of drives and the body, we have here an unusually clear representation of these two fundamental Kleinian concepts. But again we must confront a pair of problems—a way in which Alford is at once too Kleinian and not Kleinian enough.

Alford's falling away from Klein parallels his shift from embodied drives to disembodied emotions. Klein's articulation of the paranoid–schizoid and depressive positions is intensively interwoven with oral, anal, and oedipal themes. This is problematical, insofar as Klein collapses all three sets of issues into the first six months of neonatal life. Because the paranoid–schizoid and depressive positions are not merely or even primarily developmental stages, however, but constellations of emotional life in general, it is possible to spread out her narrative over a longer time period without loss of analytical potency. In Alford's narrative, by contrast, orality and anality have been reduced (along with the body) to the level of metaphors or modalities of emotional expression, and Oedipus has all but disappeared. This is unfortunate for at least two reasons. First, the oedipal triad is a real and vital constituent of emotional life. One cannot make psychoanalytic sense of psychological phenomena without it. Second, a problematized Oedipus is of critical importance for a feminist psychoanalysis. That is, it is the conjuncture of the preoedipal (mother–child) and oedipal (father–mother–child) configurations that provides one of the basic situations in which we are—for better and worse—engendered. By displacing Oedipus, Alford simultaneously marginalizes sexuality and gender.

On the other side, Alford accepts the characteristically Freudian—I am tempted to say postmodern—defect in Klein's account of the origins of emotional life. Freud consistently argued that our sexual life begins in pieces and is only gradually made whole under the aegis of genitality. Similarly Klein pictures us as initially disintegrated by the death-drive, hate, and immaturity, and only subsequently integrative of self, passions, and objects. Both accounts are inherently implausible: It is as difficult to produce wholes out of parts as it is to produce something out of nothing. It is far more plausible that, for example, the infant experiences nursing at the breast within or as a psychophysiological manifold or gestalt, and that the gestalt expands and becomes more internally differentiated over time. No doubt, the manifold is just that, a manifold, and not a oneness. And just as certainly it can fragment under the pressures of frustration, rage, and panic. Then the infant's experience has certain resemblances to psychotic states. But ontologizing the experience of disintegration is as theoretically incoherent in Klein and Alford as it is in Deleuze and Guattari.

To put it another way, the Kleinian version of the paranoid–schizoid position pathologizes human nature. In it the metabolic process of emotional life is reduced to catabolism. The most that one can then hope to do is repair the damage done. By contrast, if we accept the necessary interpenetration of anabolic and catabolic processes for healthy development, we understand Klein's version of the paranoid–schizoid position as a pathological formation, and one that plays a life-historically and social-historically variable role. We then ask, what can be done to avoid the damage in the first instance?

17.

This is not Alford's question. True to Klein in yet another regard, he believes salvation lies in reparation, not prevention. Hence he wishes to frame critical theory with "the four Rs":

> (1) to make *reparation* for millions (no, billions) of human lives shattered by greed, aggression, and fear; (2) to *remember* and memorialize the suffering of those who cannot be made whole again; (3) to *reform reason*, in order to make it less instrumental and domineering; and (4) to *reconcile* with nature in recompense for its domination by men and women. (*ibid.*, p. 9)

So far, so good. But note the absence of the fifth R: *revolution*.

18.

Whatever the limits or limitations of Alford's analysis, we have something to learn from his skilled interpretive and critical use of the paranoid–schizoid and depressive positions.

Alford takes up four major topics, each of which is important to a critical social theory: the psychology of large groups, the uses and abuses of reason, aesthetic experience, and civilized individuality. He argues that large groups tend toward the paranoid–schizoid rather than the depressive position. Hence the destructiveness they legitimate and facilitate. There is, moreover, a kind of fit between the pathologies of the large group and instrumental reason. Instrumental reason proceeds in a paranoid–schizoid fashion. In theory and practice it tears apart the object, compartmentalizes it with the pure and applied logic of either/or, and uses it up without regard for its inherent value or properties.

And what content goes with this conceptual form? What results from large groups operating through and in the social field of instrumental reason? At the limit, we would say, the fascist life: desiring-production, desiring-machines, paranoid terror, schizoid retreat to the body without organs.

In contrast to the paranoid–schizoid features of large groups and instrumental reason, aesthetic experience can (although it doesn't always) permit the working through of destructiveness. Alford argues quite persuasively that it can permit us to experience the damage done along with the desire to repair it. His aesthetics are much more of this world than Marcuse's, although they remain at the political margin. Analogously— and perhaps more practically—he contends that a reparative conception of reason might help us to undo some of the damage that has resulted from a paranoid–schizoid relationship to each other and the natural world.

Alford links his reparative conception of reason not just to individuality but to individualism. Concomitantly he transforms the large group into what Kleinians term a "bad object." Or, to put it another way, he tends to collapse existential collectivities into psychological groups. Moreover, he bypasses the question of the interests (objective advantages and disadvantages) that are attached to collectivities. Because, however, a practical employment of reparative reason necessarily must be grounded in social interests and expressed through collective action, this tends to condemn us to an Hegelian painting of grey on grey, that is, to reflection and not political transformation.

Still and all, Alford helps us to confront, within the framework of critical theory, the paranoid–schizoid and depressive dimensions of our emotional lives. Hence we may claim for him what Foucault claimed for Deleuze and Guattari. He enables us take a step toward nonfascist living.

D. Doubling the Discourse

1.

Question: What wasn't new about the New Left?

Answer: Masculinity. Whether men are in positions of state power or engaged in presumably emancipatory praxis, they find it difficult to listen to women, to look at the world from a woman's perspective, or to relinquish to women any of their power and prerogatives.

Think of Freud with his many women patients. What did he learn from them? Although psychology "is unable to solve the riddle of femininity" (Freud, 1933a, p. 116), it nonetheless has figured out that women are castrated men, who are psychologically defined by their lack of a penis. Women, it teaches, blame their mothers for this humiliating deficiency, are alienated from her and from themselves.

Not so, say Deleuze and Guattari in *Anti-Oedipus*. In the unconscious there is a "microscopic transsexuality, resulting in the woman containing as many men as the man, and the man as many women, all capable of entering—men with women, women with men—into relations of production of desire that overturn the statistical order of the sexes. Making love is not just becoming as one, or even two, but becoming as a hundred thousand" (Deleuze & Guattari, 1972, pp. 295–296).

What are we to make of this? In the one case women play the part of sphinx to oedipal conquerors, in the other the oedipal drama is covered over by endlessly multiplied entities. In neither case are women recognized as selves and as women. These exclusions at the level of theory merely replicate exclusions at the level of practice. Only when feminists finally forced their way into the "discourse of modernity" was its phallocentrism seriously challenged.

So far as psychoanalytic-marxism is concerned, taking feminism seriously requires a fundamental alteration in the terms of debate. "Man" must be replaced by "women and men." The discourse must be doubled.

2.

If we don't limit ourselves to the conjuncture of Marxism and psychoanalysis, it would be more accurate to say that the discourse *has been* doubled. In recent times we have witnessed an extraordinary flowering of feminist theorizing, parallel in its own way to the development of racial and ethnic (broadly, anticolonial) discourse during the 1950s and 1960s. The parallel is not incidental. In each case oppressed collectivities developed social movements aimed at ending their oppression. In the process they challenged the hegemonic discourses of those who oppressed them.

The theories generated in these movements cannot be contained within the discourse of psychoanalytic-marxism. But neither can psychoanalytic-marxism be contained by either or both of them. Rather they are on different analytical levels. Psychoanalytic-marxism is a theory of human emancipation. In itself, however, human emancipation is an empty universal. By contrast, emancipatory struggles are particular and concrete. They generate theories and practices that are attuned to the interests and desires of specific collectivities. Psychoanalytic-marxism cannot replace these theories, and it is not, in itself, a practical movement. Its aim is to contribute something to these more concrete struggles, in the hope that by so doing it simultaneously facilitates the realization of the more general emancipatory project.

3.

There is a postmodern tendency to valorize the abstract category of difference and to devalue the category of sameness. In my view this is to fetishize them. Metatheoretical or metadiscursive categories like the One and the Many, or Sameness and Difference, do pose certain interesting logical and linguistic problems. Paradoxes of quantity emerge from the analysis of the former, paradoxes of quality from the latter. But when it comes to both everyday experience and social theory, it is not the categories themselves that are at issue. If, for example, you and I are alike in the enjoyment of human freedom, or if we are united through friendship, then sameness is a good. If the difference between us is that I have power over you which, additionally, I abuse, then difference is a bad. The categories themselves are value-neutral. We grant them a power they do not have when we valorize them in-themselves.

Let's be a bit more concrete. In the classical version of Marxist theory the basic difference is between the class that owns and controls means of production and the class that doesn't. Difference in this instance means domination and alienation. The Marxist aim is to overcome class differences, that is, to eliminate classes altogether and thus to realize a fundamental human identity. Human identity includes difference, the non-antagonistic differences between unique human individuals. But as barriers to self-expression and self-realization these are "differences which are no differences."

Differences between social classes are historically variable. We can imagine societies without them. Indeed, there were societies before them. But there have not been, nor can we imagine, human societies without sexual differences. Within the manifold of historical variation, the biological distinction between women and men will remain. Indeed, as social theoretical categories go, sexuality is one of the most reliable: All societies have sex/gender systems oriented around differences between two sexes. Hence we may ask, does difference mean domination (the dominion of men over women), or does it mean liberation (the willingness and ability of women to live their lives for themselves, in uniquely feminine fashion)? Or are there both differences and identities that we have not yet lived, or perhaps even spoken?

Once we've started down the path of difference it is difficult to know where to stop. Feminists properly protest against a discursive sameness that makes it impossible for women, as women, to be heard. But the category of "women" can also function hegemonically. Its use may signify that the interests of some women are being ideologically disguised as the interests of all women. bell hooks points out that, when white feminists analogize the experiences of women to those of black people, they "unwittingly suggest that to them the term 'women' is synonymous with 'white women' and the term 'blacks' synonymous with 'black men'" (hooks, 1981, p. 8). Black women become invisible (see also Barrett, 1988, pp. v–vi; Flax, 1990, pp. 175–178).[14]

Yet can we really make do without the category of "women"? Don't women themselves, in the most varied of circumstances and in a multiplicity of ways, recognize themselves in it?

4.

A proper treatment of psychoanalytic-marxism and the problem of gender would be a considerable undertaking. We would begin phenomenologically with the complex and multiple life-worlds of women and men. We then would consider how these worlds have been or can be interpreted when feminism is joined to Marxism *or* psychoanalysis. Finally we would see if we could work through the contradictions between these two approaches and thus arrive at the desired version of feminism.

Such a project goes well beyond our present limits. We will, however, briefly discuss its two sides (feminism and Marxism, feminism and psychoanalysis). Then we will consider how these positions might be combined. For this purpose we will give primary attention to texts by Gayle Rubin, Nancy Hartsock, and Jessica Benjamin.

Rubin's essay "The Traffic in Women: Notes on the 'Political Economy' of Sex" (1975) occupies a special position in any psychoanalytic-marxist discussion of sex and gender. It is simultaneously Marxist and psychoanalytic, and it is quite remarkably synoptic. It even might be characterized as a groundwork for a psychoanalytic-marxist theory of sex/gender systems. There is, to the best of my knowledge, nothing else quite like it.

Because they are not paradigmatically psychoanalytic-marxist, the other choices are less strictly determined. They do, however, raise questions we would like to answer. In *Money, Sex, and Power* (1985), Hartsock both criticizes and extends Rubin's argument, and she focuses upon important epistemological issues. In "The Bonds of Love: Rational Violence and Erotic Domination" (1980), Benjamin takes the problem of recognition into the deepest reaches of sexuality and gender and, by so doing, forces a rethinking of its terms.

We will find as we proceed that the production of gender is a vital concern. Consequently we will weave certain arguments from Dorothy Dinnerstein's *The Mermaid and the Minotaur* (1976) and Nancy Chodorow's *The Reproduction of Mothering* (1978) into the discussion of Rubin, Hartsock, and Benjamin.

5.

From its beginnings Marxism contained a space for the analysis of sexual relations. In *The German Ideology*, just after arguing that human history begins with production aimed at the satisfaction of needs and of the new needs that production itself creates, Marx goes on to contend that the "third circumstance which, from the very outset, enters into historical development, is that men, who daily remake their own life, begin to make other men, to propagate their kind: the relation between man and woman, parents and children, the *family*" (Marx & Engels, 1845b, p. 156). The institutions of economic production and human reproduction and, it is evident, the interaction between them, are fundamental to the structure of society—fundamental diachronically, with respect to social evolution; fundamental synchronically, with respect to the structure of existing societies.

In his published writings Marx did little more than define the family and reproduction as an area of possible inquiry. Engels, however, basing himself primarily upon the research of Henry Morgan, developed a complex theory of the "origin of the family, private property, and the state." He divided human history, in familiar dialectical fashion, into three phases. There is first a period of mother right, sexual freedom, and sexual equality. Then comes the "overthrow of mother right," the "*world-historic defeat of the female sex*" (Engels, 1884, p. 217), which ushered in the long period during which private property, the patriarchal monogamous family, and the subordination of women developed. Finally there is the period yet to come, when the egalitarianism of primitive society will be revived, in a higher, historically more developed form.

It is easy to criticize Engels' account, both in general and at the level of the data used to support the generality; yet his approach has several enduring advantages. In it the family and sexual roles have a history. Because that history is linked to the history of economic production, it is intelligible or determinate. Male domination/female subordination loses its grounding in nature. The natural law of male supremacy can be recognized as ideology. And because the hierarchical ordering of sexual roles is historical, a theory and practice of women's liberation is possible and rational.

Here, then, we have the basis of what was later to emerge as socialist or Marxist feminism, in which the critique of patriarchy is linked to that of capitalism, and women's liberation is linked to socialist revolution. Thus the title of Zillah Eisenstein's important collection of essays, *Capitalist Patriarchy and the Case for Socialist Feminism* (1979).

Socialist feminism has its own history—its internal debates and its controversial relations with other versions of feminism.[15] Like Marxism, it has the great advantage of focusing on concrete issues. These include wages, job discrimination, and the devaluation of "women's work." Hence it leads to rigorous empirical and historical research, and it has functioned as a vehicle for organizing and developing self-consciousness in political struggle. It has even been argued quite persuasively that, at the practical level, socialist feminists, or feminists with socialist leanings, have reinvented Marxism—in their own image, and in their own interests (Hartsock, 1979). Nonetheless, as Michèle Barrett observes about her own work, the "confident combination of 'Marxist Feminist' [in the 1970s] . . . uncomfortably reminds us of an attempt to bring together two worldviews that have continued to go their separate ways in spite of our efforts at marriage guidance" (Barrett, 1988, p. v).

There are various reasons why the union of Marxism and feminism has been unstable. I will mention only three. First, the Marxist critique of capitalism makes it quite clear that women cannot be free if private property and social classes are not eliminated. So long as capitalism remains, most women will be oppressed. Hence there can be an ideologically inspired flight from Marxism, a retreat to liberal feminist positions or from the political battlefields altogether. Second, and conversely, there is a battle women have waged against Marxist dogmatism within emancipatory movements. Marxists, be they men or women, often insist upon the priority of the orthodox categories and issues. The emancipation of women is viewed as a secondary, superstructural, or essentially ideological issue. In this case women cannot find or recognize themselves in the theories and practices of the Left (Campioni & Grosz, 1991).[16]

The first two points also could be stated this way: Transforming capitalism into some version of socialism is a necessary but not sufficient condition for the emancipation of all women. The retreat from Marxism may involve a denial of that necessity, or a weariness with struggling against those who deny its insufficiency.

Third, even when Marxism is used with sophistication and subtlety, it cannot adequately illuminate the psychological experience of sex and gender.

Reenter psychoanalysis.

6.

From the standpoint of socialist feminism, psychoanalysis appears first in the guise—as Kate Millett puts it—of counterrevolution (Millett, 1970, p. 176 ff.). In the myth of the primal horde, Freud identifies patriarchy with civilization. Paternal might becomes paternal right, the law of the father is the law of laws. Moreover, at the ontogenetic level the little girl necessarily experiences herself as anatomically inferior to boys. As noted above, she wishes for and is envious of the penis. She blames her mother for her deficiency and turns to her father to fill in the gap: The wish to have his child is the wish to possess his penis. Her stance toward her father is passive, receptive, and masochistic. In later life she marries a man, the successor to her father, who can give her a penis— temporarily, in sexual intercourse, and symbolically, in the form of (especially) a male child. Thus, as the Lacanians in particular emphasize, the male genital is the signifier of patriarchal law. But in this, its symbolic role, it is transformed: The biological organ, with its ups and downs, becomes the phallus, perpetually erect and invincible. Nietzsche was only half right. Man is not only the neurotic but also the phallocentric animal.

One might think that women, at least women who are not held captive by patriarchal ideology, would turn their backs on this phallocentric depiction of the human condition. But on the one hand, psychoanalysis is the one psychology with the possibility of illuminating the preconscious and unconscious roots of gender identity. On the other, the patriarchal and phallocentric distortions of the theory are not without interest. They do tell us something about ourselves, if not about human nature. Thus Juliet Mitchell, in her now classic *Psychoanalysis and Feminism* (1975), refuses to treat Freud's depiction of female sexuality as mere ideology. Instead she uses it the way Marx used the works of the classical political economists. The political economists accurately, if partially, depicted the operations of capitalism. Their fundamental error was to ontologize or naturalize economic laws that were historically relative. In similar fashion Freud accurately depicts the psychology of patriarchy. Like the political economists he ultimately ontologizes (biologizes) this psychology. The ideological framework of the argument is properly subject to criticism. But, Mitchell contends, patriarchy is the historically dominant form of male-female relationships. Freud, far more than his critics, provides us with a theoretical mirror in which we can see our engendered selves.

Mitchell attempted to tie her critical appropriation of Freud to both a Marxist analysis of capitalism and a Lacanian version of psychoanalytic theory. By and large, later psychoanalytically oriented feminists have not followed her lead in taking Marxism seriously. They have, however, followed her example in showing a marked preference for Lacanian versions of psychoanalytic theory. From the standpoint of ideology critique this makes good sense. Lacan is far and away the most phallocentric and narcissistic of psychoanalytic theorists. One must defeat him in order to win the struggle for psychoanalysis. But this is not the whole story, not even, perhaps, its principal narrative line. Why, especially outside France, all the attention to the narcissistic Lacan? Why the emulation of his language and style? Why the willing acceptance of his terms for the debate about gender? Is this critique, or is it compliance?[17]

Here is a related point. Over the past several years there has been a tendency in feminist theorizing to replace Marxism with postmodernism. The tenuous connection between Marxism, psychoanalysis, and feminism that we find in Mitchell's book is dissolved. At the same time the economic, social, and political oppression of women fades from view, and a concern with writing, texts, language games, and the symbolic order takes its place.[18]

Feminists rightly protest against class essentialism (as in the reduction of all emancipatory struggle to class struggle) when feminism and Marxism are conjoined. It hardly seems an improvement to displace feminist struggle into the domain of language and to redefine it as a battle over discursive practices. Consequently we might experience a dialectical counterthrust: The more psychoanalysis is used as a vehicle for the textualization of sexuality and gender, the more an interest in the emancipation of women pushes us back toward the problematics of socialist feminism.

7.

Marxist feminism pushes us toward psychoanalytic feminism, which pushes us back toward Marxist feminism. Thus the debate between Marxist feminism and psychoanalytic feminism replicates the split between Marxism and psychoanalysis with which we began. Need it be added that this is not the only way of seeing the relationship of Marxism, psychoanalysis, and feminism?

8.

There have been two principal objects in the feminist critique of ideology: "phallocentrism" and "patriarchy." These terms have multiple usages and points of reference. It might prove helpful to simplify their meaning. We could link phallocentrism to male dominance in the domain of fantasy life, whether individual or collective. Correspondingly we could attach patriarchy to male dominance in the history of production, human reproduction, and social practices.[19] The critique of ideology would then have to be approached from both directions.

Viewed this way we have the characteristic psychoanalytic-marxist problem of working through a subject–object relationship. At the same time we have erected a barrier against collapsing the objective world into the subjective one or the subjective world into the objective one. Instead the object of our critical analysis becomes *patriarchy/phallocentrism*.

9.

In "The Traffic in Women" Rubin's focus is on what she terms the "sex/gender system," that is, "the set of arrangements by which a society transforms biological sexuality into products of human activity, and in which these transformed sexual needs are satisfied" (Rubin, 1975, p. 159). Gender, the social role of female and male, is to be distinguished from sexuality, the biological distinction between men and women. The latter is a given; the former is historically contingent and variable.

Rubin begins with Marx, but critically: "In Marx's map of the social world, human beings are workers, peasants, or capitalists; that they are also men and women is not seen as very significant" (*ibid.*, p. 160). She acknowledges the explanatory power of Marxist theory, and that one might, within its limits, explore the nature of the work that women perform. But gender cannot be completely analyzed through the optic of a theory of production, not even one expanded to include the sexual reproduction of the species.[20]

From another angle we could say that Rubin retains Marx's method while replacing or perhaps duplicating his object of analysis. In his various depictions of capitalism Marx differentiates between the production and exchange of commodities. These extremes are, in part, mediated by the division of social labor. The division of labor in production eventuates in and requires the exchange of products among producers. Hence if one's analytical starting point is exchange, one may advance from it through the division of labor to the foundation of economic life, the domain of production.

This, roughly speaking, is how Rubin proceeds.[21]

10.

One of the problems with Marxist or Engelian analyses is that the focus upon capitalist relations of production obscures the social structures and practices within which most of humanity has functioned most of the time, namely, kinship systems. In precapitalist and, even more, prestate societies, "kinship is the idiom of social interaction, organizing economic, political, and ceremonial, as well as sexual, activity" (*ibid.*, p. 169).

Wilhelm Reich, basing himself upon the Trobriand Island researches of Malinowski, had focused upon the marriage gift, the dowry, in the establishment of patriarchy and economic inequality. He viewed male economic interests as the prime determinant of such transactions (Reich, 1932). Rubin, basing herself upon the work of Lévi-Strauss, radicalizes Reich's analysis: The gift is the woman herself. The exchange of women establishes the linkages of the kinship system. The incest taboo insures that these linkages will be established. And if

> women are the gifts, then it is the men who are the exchange partners. And it is the partners, not the presents, upon whom reciprocal exchange confers its quasi-mystical power of social linkage. The relations of such a system are such that women are in no position to realize the benefits of their own circulation. As long as the relations specify that men exchange women, it is men who are the beneficiaries of the product of such exchanges. (Rubin, 1975, p. 174)

Reich was far too economistic in his analysis, as well as gender-blind in his economism. He saw the dowry exchange but not the traffic in women. He failed to recognize that, whatever the play of economic interests, the marital exchange empowers men vis-à-vis women. The man gains subjectivity at the woman's expense. His subjectivity results from the alienation of hers. She functions like money in a commodity exchange, as a means of circulation or even a measure of (male) value. But she does not possess as her own the social values she transmits.

In developed societies women are no longer exchanged in this fashion, although, as Rubin observes, in many marriage ceremonies it is still the father who "gives away" the bride. And, it should be stressed, even when women are exchanged they retain a subjectivity of their own, expressed primarily in interactions with other women.[22] Nonetheless this elementary structure of gender has not been historically superseded. The manifest freedom in women's lives tends to conceal the latent meaning, woman = gift.

11.

Still basing herself upon Lévi-Strauss, Rubin advances from the traffic in women to the sexual division of labor. She argues that biological necessity has relatively little to do with the extent and sharpness of gender distinctions. Rather the "division of labor by sex can . . . be seen as a 'taboo': a taboo against the sameness of men and women, a taboo dividing the sexes into two mutually exclusive categories, a taboo which exacerbates the biological differences between the sexes and thereby *creates* gender" (*ibid.*, p. 178). The taboo has a purpose. By exaggerating the differences between men and women it makes men and women dependent upon each other. It thereby helps to insure that the smallest viable economic unit will contain at least one man and one woman.

A consequence of the rigid sexual division of labor is that gender is heterosexualized. Same-sex sexuality is at odds with the requirement that social units consist of both men and women. Manifest homosexuality and the homosexual component of human bisexuality become taboo. Human sexuality is generally impoverished.

12.

With the sexual division of labor we come to a version of the question of sameness and difference. Are women and men fundamentally the same or fundamentally different? To state it in extreme terms, are there two human natures or one?

Rubin presupposes a basic human androgyny. Human sameness is exaggerated into gender difference. Exaggerated gender difference legitimates heterosexuality and functions to repress homosexuality. But many radical and Lacanian feminists emphasize the differences Rubin seeks to minimize (Jagger, 1983, p. 83 ff; Gallop, 1982). In their view sameness translates into maleness: To say men and women are the same is to say that women resemble men. Maleness remains the standard by which women are to be judged. Not surprisingly women fail to measure up. Moreover, the language and discursive practices of gender relationships are phallocentric. Language, one might say (or one is forbidden to say), contains the concealed symbolic equation, penis = tongue. Lacking the one, women are deprived of the other. The phallus totalizes discourse in its own image. It is therefore pointless for women to attempt to speak to or through male discourse. Where the phallus is the only organ of sensibility, women must necessarily remain insensible. Accordingly what must be recognized is the sameness of women and their difference from men. The bonds between women, including sexual bonds, are secured by rejecting identification with both men and maleness.[23]

It is evident that the two sides in this dispute have a common enemy, namely, a hierarchical sexual division of labor that renders women dependent upon and socially inferior to men, and that functions to repress both the homosexual component in human personality in general and homosexual relationships in particular. A patriarchal division of labor redirects love, erotic connection, from women toward men. Women are to love men, not women—not, therefore, themselves!

13.

Rubin's argument is historically relativistic. Biological sexuality is a gift of nature, but the sexual division of labor is culturally engendered. Historical existence does not entail ontological essence.

But is the sexual division of labor as historically relative as all that? How well do such deontological or antifoundational arguments accommodate three of the signal conditions of human existence: (1) heterosexual relationships are necessary for the biological reproduction of the species; (2) only women bear children; and, (3) biologically, only women can nurse them. One would expect these facts to have social and psychological implications. If so, then the problem is to sort out in what ways men and women are the same, in what ways they are different—and to do so in such a way that the critique of male domination is strengthened.

We may take the question one step further. Dorothy Dinnerstein (1976) claims that, anthropologically, women have been placed in a paradoxical position. Men and women have in common the large brain, competent hands, and upright posture that make human beings historical and cultural creatures. To a remarkable extent humans create their own nature, women no less than men. But accompanying the human ascent to bipedalism is our prolonged infantile dependency. Hence compared to the females of all other species, human females spend the most time involved with the care of the young—and, just because they are human, they are the least suited to this limitation:

> It has been in a biological sense "natural," then, for the overt activity of women to remain relatively restricted, and equally "natural" for them to use their human nervous systems (which are as organic as their reproductive systems) to transcend this restriction. But what is most "natural" of all, humanly, is precisely this internal stress and inconsistency. (*ibid.*, p. 21)

Dinnerstein is very far from arguing that anatomy is destiny. She contends, rather, that under modern conditions the historical justification for the sexual division of labor is all but undermined. Very little of a woman's adult life need be spent in bearing and nursing children. There is no Darwinian imperative limiting women to or excluding men from the care of children. Indeed, she views a change in parenting practices— namely, shared parenting—as vital to human survival. More to the present point, however, is her articulation of the paradoxical nature of women's role in the sexual division of labor, to wit, that women both are and are not destined for motherhood.

Speaking of paradoxes: Could we say that human bisexuality means that we both are and are not destined for heterosexuality?

14.

Anatomy may not be destiny, but in all historically existing social systems it has cultural meaning—and, from the perspective of women, "de-meanings." Women are demeaned and deprived of meaning. Rubin utilizes the Lacanian variant of psychoanalytic theory to elucidate the production of these de-meanings. In this way we advance from the sexual division of labor to the production of gender.

Prior to the ontogenetic advent of Oedipus, Rubin contends, human beings are bisexual creatures. "Each child contains all of the sexual possibilities available to human expression" (Rubin, 1975, p. 189). The Oedipus complex, however, is "an apparatus for the production of sexual personality . . . a machine which fashions the appropriate forms of sexual individuals" (*ibid.*). It creates two sexes: the one possessing the penis/ phallus, the one lacking the penis/phallus. The "lack" is itself an artifact of phallocentrism, and in the language of phallocentrism, it can have only one meaning: castration—which is to say, the absence of meaning.

The Oedipus complex thus creates two unequal sexes. The phallus "carries the meaning of the dominance of men over women." Moreover, "as long as men have rights in women which women do not have in themselves, the phallus also carries the meaning of the difference between 'exchanger' and 'exchanged,' gift and giver" (*ibid.*, p. 191). At the heart of the exchange relationship "the phallus passes through the medium of women from one man to another—from father to son, from mother's brother to sister's son, and so forth" (*ibid.*, p. 192). In this way women mediate the phallic linkages of kinship structures. But the woman never gets the phallus herself. It is never hers to give away. Rather, by accepting her castration, her lack, she gains only the consolation prize of a child, the symbolic penis, as a gift from men. But even this gift is not truly hers, for the power of disposition remains in the hands of the men. No wonder, then, that there is envy of the penis, when the penis signifies the "act of psychic brutality" that engenders women, that makes them female (*ibid.*, p. 197).

Here we have a body language for social relations of domination, a body language which, by covering over a deeper, unconscious level of symbolization—the level of breast, vagina, and womb—is itself an instrument of domination.

15.

If we compare Rubin's emergent psychoanalytic-marxist theory of sex/gender systems with the versions of Freudian-Marxism and psychoanalytic-marxism previously considered, we observe a fundamental shift in the nature of the discourse. Rubin (1) brings kinship and gender out of the theoretical shadows, and (2) does so through a highly integrative use of both Marxist and psychoanalytic theory. In both regards she helps us to see our situation more clearly.

Yet her argument, like all arguments, is not without its limitations. These are brought out forcefully and usefully by Nancy Hartsock.

Hartsock contends that Rubin's analysis never really leaves the realm of exchange, that is, that both the division of labor and the production of gender are analyzed from the standpoint of exchange and circulation. By relying upon Lévi-Strauss (and, we would add, Lacan), Rubin "gives pride of place to the abstract instead of the concrete and devalues material life activity in favor of the production of symbols" (Hartsock, 1985, p. 294).

Hartsock's argument can be clarified by reference to Marx. In *Capital, 1* Marx begins with commodities as objects with values for use and values for exchange. He proceeds to investigate the relationship between these forms of value at the theoretical/empirical level of the market or process of circulation. As we shall see in Chapter 8, he deciphers the language that commodities and money speak to each other. But the analysis of exchange does not reveal how surplus value (capitalist profit) is possible. Hence it becomes necessary to advance from exchange to production, from the market to the factory, in order to see how workers are forced to produce surplus value for the capitalists. The secrets of class domination are revealed only through the examination of the production process itself. If, conversely, one stays at the level of the market, the realities of capitalist production remain hidden from view.

Rubin, Hartsock contends, borrows her analytical instruments from theorists who look at the world through the abstract optic of exchange. Her analysis is similarly abstract, therefore, even when she intends to talk about concrete social relationships and practices. Moreover, because a focus on exchange rather than production obscures the practical interaction of human individuals with the nonhuman environment, Rubin's theoretical orientation forces her into splitting nature (sex) and culture (gender).

Although I agree with Hartsock that Rubin's argument is displaced upward, I don't think she gives adequate recognition to Rubin's accomplishment, to wit, a stunning interpretation of gender and exchange. And she bypasses the polemical context of Rubin's essay. Rubin is arguing against the immediate identification of biological sexuality with gender, an identification that has been a mainstay of patriarchal and phallocentric arguments. She is also seeking to loosen the hold of an oppressive normative heterosexuality in gender roles. Hence what Hartsock views as a weakness Rubin might claim as a strength.

Beyond that, the relationship between biology and culture is more complex than either Rubin or Hartsock—or, for that matter, Marx—seems inclined to acknowledge. It is easy enough to proclaim the separation of the one from the other, or to judge the proclaimed separation as a split. It is a good deal more difficult to determine what the actual relationship(s) are or might be.

To put it another way: We can use a binary logic to split ourselves off from the natural world or a dialectical logic to place ourselves inside it. We might even contend that a dialectical view of nature and human history contains the binary opposition of the two as a surpassed moment. But beneath the level of these epistemological debates, closer to the ground of the everyday experience of sex and gender, the boundaries between our natural and our historical being are importantly problematical. The formulation "sex/gender," with its slash, its ambiguous mark of connection and disconnection, places the problem properly before us.

16.

As Hartsock emphasizes, grounding our knowledge of sex/gender systems means that we must investigate and conceptualize the actual social practices through which gender is produced and reproduced. This in turn means asking the right questions, the ones that cut beneath male-dominant discourse and help us to reorient our thinking. Hence the importance of Nancy Chodorow's *The Reproduction of Mothering* (1978), which did us the service of turning a fact into a problem: Why do women and, normatively, only women do the mothering, and what are the consequences of this fact for gender development?

Almost nothing seems so evident to us as the fact that women do the mothering. It comes naturally, we think, even instinctively. But when we think of it this way, Chodorow contends, we repress the problematical and historically contingent relationship between the two terms. And once women's mothering is ontologized, its consequences for gender formation are deproblematized.

As the title of her book so concisely indicates, Chodorow views mothering as a socially and psychologically inculcated pattern of orientations and actions. These patterns are intergenerationally reproductive:

> Women, as mothers, produce daughters with mothering capacities and
> the desire to mother. These capacities and needs are built into and grow
> out of the mother–daughter relationship itself. By contrast, women as
> mothers (and men as not-mothers) produce sons whose nurturant

capacities and needs have been systematically curtailed and repressed. This prepares men for their less affective later family role, and for primary participation in the impersonal extra-familial world of work and public life. (Chodorow, 1978, p. 7)

Women's mothering reproduces both the sexual division of labor and the split between the public and private realms. A change toward shared parenting practices is required if these twin pillars of male dominance are to be overturned.

Chodorow's argument can be challenged from various quarters. In my opinion it suffers from the same weaknesses that we find in Fromm's *Escape from Freedom*. Fromm rejects the biological dimension of psychoanalytic theory and considerably weakens the orientation toward class struggle in Marxism. In parallel fashion Chodorow is psychologically object-relational (in the non-Kleinian sense) and sociologically abstract. Her analysis is free from the disturbing influence of both drives and class/racial antagonisms.

17.

Whatever its limitations, Chodorow's work gave a name to a problem, brought it into collective consciousness, and thus facilitated a process of feminine self-recognition. But if women's mothering is the problem, what is the solution? As we would expect, Chodorow follows Dinnerstein in opting for shared parental responsibilities, so that children will no longer learn to nurture and to be autonomous from different parents—so that, in turn, nurturance and autonomy will not be distributed between separate sexes.[24]

Let's grant that rigid gender differentiation is pathological and that shared parenting would be curative. We may also put to one side the ways in which shared parenting can function as male domination, as an imperialistic extension of male power and prerogatives. Even so, there remain aspects of the experience of mothering that are out of the reach of men, hence also things that only women can know. Just as workers see the world from a different angle than their bosses, women see it from a different angle than men.

This difference, it can be argued, has epistemological implications.

18.

According to Marx, and later to Georg Lukács (1971), the class standpoint of the proletariat grants it an epistemological privilege vis-à-vis the bourgeoisie, one that it can turn to its practical advantage. The bourgeoisie looks at the world from the perspective of exchange, the proletariat sees it from the perspective of production. The latter perspective is deeper and more encompassing than the former.

Hartsock (1985) accepts this argument, and restates it with admirable concreteness:

1. Material life (class position in Marxist theory) not only structures but sets limits on the understanding of social relations.
2. If material life is structured in fundamentally opposing ways for two different groups, one can expect both that the vision of each will represent an inversion of the other and the vision of the ruling class will be partial and perverse.
3. The vision of the ruling class structures the material relations in which all parties are forced to participate, and therefore cannot be dismissed as simply false.
4. In consequence, the vision available to the oppressed group must be struggled for and represents an achievement that requires both science to see beneath the surface of the social relations in which all are forced to participate, and the education that can only grow with political struggle.
5. Because the understanding of the oppressed is an engaged vision, the adoption of a standpoint exposes the real relations among human beings as inhuman, points beyond the present, and carries a historical and liberatory role. (p. 118)

Hence the epistemological privilege of the proletariat.

This line of argument extends back to Hegel, who contended that, in the relationship of lordship and bondage, the bondsman's position is epistemologically superior to the lord's. In Hegel's case as in Hartsock's, this view is not without a basis in reason and experience. At a minimum it is true that workers who are engaged in the actual process of production learn important lessons from this experience, and that women who are engaged in the actual process of human reproduction learn from theirs. But as the history of both capitalism and Marxism demonstrates, it is striking how much the masters can learn from the experience of the slaves, especially when it comes to maintaining their own advantage. Conversely, it's not so clear that oppressed people, or those who theorize in the interest of oppressed people, see reality more clearly and encompassingly than their oppressors. They see it differently to be sure, often with a sharp critical eye for existing abuses of power, and sometimes with a willingness to work for a better world; but as Mannheim argues in *Ideology and Utopia* (1936), the standpoint of the oppressed has its characteristic illusions and falsifications of consciousness. Sociologically and historically, it is difficult to legitimate epistemological prerogatives.

19.

If, on the one hand, Hartsock argues that the oppressed are episte-mologically privileged vis-à-vis the oppressor, on the other she argues that femininity is epistemologically privileged vis-à-vis masculinity. The feminist standpoint, Hartsock argues, is "deeper-going" than even pro-letarian class consciousness. The sexual division of labor gives women access to domains of experience that are not truly open to men:

> Women's experience in reproduction represents a unity with nature that goes beyond the proletarian experience of interchange with nature. . . . In addition, in the process of producing human beings, relations with others may take a variety of forms with deeper signifi-cance than simple cooperation with others for common goals—forms that range from a deep unity with another through the many-leveled and changing connections mothers experience with growing children. Finally, women's experience in bearing and rearing children involves a unity of mind and body more profound than is possible in the worker's instrumental activity. (Hartsock, 1985, p. 234)

Thus feminist consciousness, which is based on the cycle of human re-production (mothering), gets beneath the level of class consciousness, which is based upon the cycle of economic production.

Surely we would acknowledge that there are experiences open only to women and with respect to which their knowledge cannot be equaled. Further, women engage in productive activity along with men but men cannot bear children along with women. And, we might add, caring for human beings within the cycle of human reproduction has an ethical value not rightfully attributable to economic production. Economic pro-duction ought to be a means toward human reproductive ends, and not the other way around. This does not mean, however, that human repro-duction is epistemologically privileged vis-à-vis economic production. Moreover, even if we limit ourselves to the analysis of human reproduc-tion, the argument is problematical. For if Hartsock wishes to grant epis-temological significance to the fact that men cannot be mothers, she must grant a like significance to the fact that women cannot be fathers. And then who is left to mediate between the epistemologies of mother-hood and fatherhood?[25]

There is, however, another way of reading Hartsock's text: In a dis-cursive situation of male dominance, there is something to be said for reversing the epistemological priorities.[26] Or as Malcolm X said, looking at his situation from an African-American standpoint: "What is logical to the oppressor isn't logical to the oppressed. And what is reason to the oppressor isn't reason to the oppressed" (in Epps, 1968, p. 133).

20.

Hartsock's approach is Marxist-feminist, not psychoanalytic-marxist. But it does contain a psychoanalytic moment. Basing herself primarily on Robert Stoller's research into perversity and sexual excitement (1975, 1979), Susan Griffin's *Pornography and Silence* (1981), and Georges Bataille's *Death and Sensuality* (1977), she argues that masculinity in our culture derives from men's fears of ceasing to exist as separate beings. These fears are expressed most clearly in sexual fantasies and the fetishistic dehumanizations of pornography, where the "body, constituting a reminder of loathsome mortality, must be denied and repressed. The whole man is reduced to the phallus; bodily feelings are projected onto the woman, who is reduced to a body without a will of her own. And in the sexual fantasy and philosophy about sexual fantasy, creativity and generation take the form of a fascination with death" (Hartsock, 1985, p. 252).

Hartsock is, I think, essentially correct in both this interpretation of phallocentrism and her judgment that phallocentrism is our culturally normative form of masculinity. Masculinity = erotized domination. Let us note before passing on, however, that phallocentrism is not only an encoding of erotic domination, but also an extremely primitive encoding of the erotic. The phallus, the fantasized self-sustaining and omnipotent penis, is what the Kleinians term a part-object, an isolated and reified part of the psyche/soma. It signifies a domain of paranoid experience, one in which intersubjectivity has not yet been achieved.

And how, practically speaking, is masculine power expressed? Ultimately, Hartsock contends, it takes the form of a "trial by death," that is, a life and death struggle for recognition (*ibid.*, p. 240).

21.

In Fanon's articulation of the dialectics of racism we have already encountered the problematics of recognition. According to Jessica Benjamin (1980, 1988), the dialectics of gender production must also be framed in these terms. Biological individuals become selves—male and female selves—through failures of mutual recognition.

Benjamin contends that early versions of psychoanalytic theory located the origins of selfhood in processes of recognition. The infant becomes a self by differentiating itself from its mother/the other. The theory "placed the mutual functions of recognizing the other and establishing one's own autonomous identity in opposition" (Benjamin, 1980, p. 147). Observation of mother–infant interaction demonstrates, she argues, that this is not the whole story. But it is an important chapter. It reflects in theory the male repudiation of the mother in reality. The male child establishes his maleness defensively, against his identification with his mother: I (male) ≠ Her (female). Women by contrast become female through identification with their mothers: I (female) = Her (female). No wonder, then, "that most theories of psychological development have been largely unable to maintain (even in thought) the tension of simultaneous sameness and difference" (*ibid.*, p. 147).

Male ≠ Female, Male = Not-Female; also, Male > Female, Male over Female, Male is greater than Female. The "repudiation of the mother by men . . . [also means] that she is not recognized as an independent person, another subject, but as something Other: as nature, as an instrument or object [of need gratification], as less-than-human" (*ibid.*, p. 147). He is to be recognized; she is to recognize him. "She becomes all too able to recognize the other's subjectivity, but—like mother—does not expect to be treated as an independent subject. . . . She becomes in her own mind object, instrument, Earth Mother. Thus she serves men as their Other, their counterpart, the side of themselves they repress" (*ibid.*, p. 148).

The hierarchical division of the sexes has, Benjamin continues, an implication for the critical theory of society.[27] She accepts the Frankfurt School position that rationality in the Western world is equated with instrumental efficacy and the one-sided objectivism of the natural sciences. She argues that this narrowed idea of rationality reflects the male experience of gender formation. Maleness is founded on breaking the link with the mother, on eliminating the ambiguities and ambivalences of sexual identity, on establishing a categorical distinction between the male as subject and the female as object. Western rationality transforms this experience into epistemology. The either/or of gender formation becomes a logic of domination: Male > Female; Difference > Sameness; Rationality > Irrationality.

Unlike those theorists who fetishize "difference," Benjamin offers us an altogether more subtle appreciation of the role of sameness and difference in gender formation. Yet it seems to me that she does not bring out clearly enough the logic that is implicit in and vital to her argument. The impossibility of maintaining the interpenetration of sameness and difference, the pathology of one gender based on sameness and another based on difference, depends upon the logic of either/or, that is, upon positive or nondialectical logic. The logic of either/or breaks the link between opposites and, by so doing, precludes relation. It expresses, in abstract form, the *act* (both mental and physical) by which the boy rejects his identification with his mother. It creates the empty space between the sexes that is denied by the interposition of the phallus. The phallus is then a pseudolink, an absence of connection claiming to be a connection.

The phallus signifies the self-contradiction of a relationship of domination, that is, a relationship between a self and a negated self. Within this logic the vagina signifies the empty space, the feminine lack. Decoded, it means rather the *emptied* space, a devoured and violated fullness.

22.

Within the generality of the engendered failure of mutual recognition Benjamin develops an exquisite analysis of erotic domination. She uses for this purpose *The Story of O*, which she views as "an exceedingly self-conscious attempt to represent the themes of erotic domination—the tension between separation and recognition, rationality and violence, transcendence and negation of self, the active phallus and the passive orifice" (*ibid.*, p. 155).

Benjamin's analysis turns on the psychoanalytic explication of one passage from the story. O has been taken to Roissy castle, which is "organized by men for the ritual violation and subjugation of women" (*ibid.*, p. 156). The ideology of Roissy castle is explained to her this way:

> You are here to serve your masters. . . . Your hands are not your own, nor are your breasts, nor most especially, any of your orifices, which we may explore and penetrate at will. . . . you have lost all right to privacy or concealment. . . . you must never look any of us in the face. If the costume we wear . . . leaves our sex exposed, it is not for the sake of convenience . . . but for the sake of insolence, so that your eyes will be directed there upon it and nowhere else so that you may learn that there resides your master. . . . it is perfectly all right for you to grow accustomed to being whipped. . . . this is less for our pleasure than your enlightenment . . . [so that you learn] through this suffering, that you are not free but fettered, and teach you that you are totally dedicated to something outside yourself. (cited pp. 156–157; slightly abbreviated)

Benjamin brings out several related aspects of this scene. O is to surrender all subjectivity, all self-control. She is to exist in order to be violated. This relationship of objectification and violation is signified by the penis, which at the same time embodies the separate subjectivity of the men. Their subjectivity is also expressed more generally in the rationality of their control over and violation of her. Like Dolmance in de Sade's *Philosophy in the Bedroom* (1795), they are agents of enlightenment, teachers of the logic of domination.

Within the framework of rational violation, the dialectic of misrecognition must be played out with a certain delicacy. Because the subject becomes the object it consumes, the object must never be completely deprived of subjectivity. Hence for the story to continue, the objectification of O must remain incomplete. The men "must be careful never to wholly consume her as *will-less* object, but rather to command and consume her *will*" (Benjamin, 1980, p. 157). They must eat her alive and she must consent to be eaten; which is to say, she must will the violation, she must be self-negating as well as self-negated. She must be radically self-abnegating. Her surrender of selfhood is, however, simultaneously a transcendence (albeit a perverse one) of selfhood. O is devoted to a god, her lover. To lose her self is to become one with him. For her, freedom means only difference, distance, aloneness. In her suffering she escapes from freedom.

If Benjamin had so chosen, she could have framed the story of O's quest for self-transcendence along the lines of Hegel's depiction of the Unhappy Consciousness—the consciousness that finds in its selfhood only sinfulness and separation from the ultimate Being, that strives to negate itself in order to merge with the infinite Other. But where Hegel finds a way out of the dilemma through the experience of mediation (the process through which the extremes interpenetrate), in the dialectic of erotic domination no such solution is possible. The position of mediation, which implies the relative autonomy of each self in the relationship, is ruled out in advance. The masters must consume the slave until she is emptied of life and they are once again alone and unrecognized; the slave must be consumed until she is reduced to thinghood or literally destroyed. The dialectical regression comes to a dead-end.

23.

Benjamin's argument can be strengthened, I believe, if we combine it with a line of analysis developed most forcefully by Dinnerstein. As we know, Dinnerstein focuses on the fact that neonatal parenting has been almost exclusively a feminine role. At the outset parenting is mothering. This means that mothers are the world within which we all experience the most profound dependency and the most primitive emotions. Consequently

> *Woman, who introduced us to the human situation and who at the beginning seemed to us responsible for every drawback of that situation, carries for all of us a pre-rational onus of culpable responsibility forever after.*
> (Dinnerstein, 1976, p. 234)

Vengeance is mine, saith the child in each of us, vengeance for the pain of being human. Psychosexually, however, the drama of revenge has two roles. Men emerge as the avengers, whose aim it is to inflict the pain they formerly suffered, to humiliate the woman whose power they experienced as humiliating. Women are there to be the objects of male vengeance, and to suffer the humiliation that confirms his superiority.

No wonder that Dinnerstein and Chodorow believe a change in parenting practices is necessary if we are ever to escape engendered relationships of lordship and bondage!

E. The Mourning After

1.

Feminism in the 1960s and early 1970s developed alongside of and in (often conflictual) interaction with the racial, generational, and class movements of that period. For all its complexity, cross-currents, and contradictions, this set of collective practices constituted a political and cultural matrix from which theory could develop and to which theory could respond. By the mid-1970s, however, the emancipatory moment had passed. Postmodernism, including postmodern feminism, reflects this passage.

In mood and substance Joel Kovel's *The Age of Desire* and Richard Lichtman's *The Production of Desire* also reflect the absence of collective emancipatory praxis. They are the work of radical intellectuals cut off from radical movements. They are also notable attempts to engage Marxism and psychoanalysis directly, and at a paradigmatic level. Kovel and Lichtman are in the tradition of Reich, Fromm, and Marcuse, for whom psychoanalysis and Marxism occupied a privileged theoretical position. And like the earlier thinkers they attempt to develop first principles for the interpretation of human nature and history. Whether in so doing they solve problems left unresolved by their theoretical forefathers we shall see in due course.

Although Kovel and Lichtman are both writing in the aftermath of mass movement, they provide us with mirror images of social reality. Lichtman rules out in advance the project of theoretical synthesis. He argues that "the systems of Marx and Freud are incompatible and that, consequently, a choice must be made for one and against the other" (Lichtman, 1982, p. ix). Marxism, he continues, although imperfect, can be corrected; Freud's theory is "fundamentally unsound." Hence his aim is to incorporate Freud's understanding of the repressed unconscious into an expanded Marxist theory.

Kovel, by contrast, is a "Marxist psychoanalyst." Like Lichtman he believes that Marxism "remains the principal alternative open to humanity and the one philosophy around which history will turn" (Kovel, 1981, p. xii). But on the one hand, he is willing to tolerate the contradictions between Marxism and psychoanalysis in order not to lose the purchase on reality that each one provides. And on the other, he is willing to work in the direction of theoretical synthesis. In both these ways he evinces a respect for Freud and the Freudian project quite absent in Lichtman's work.

I should note in advance that I am not going to attempt to mediate the opposition between Lichtman and Kovel, despite the fact that in certain respects my own approach bridges the distance (or falls) between them. To his credit Lichtman forces a choice, although perhaps not the one he intended. In his view we are for Freud and against Marx or for Marx and against Freud. At one level I agree. Freud's social theorizing falls within the liberal bourgeois worldview. One cannot hold to it and Marxism at the same time. Hence the political choice is clear. If one is a Marxist, one cannot be a political Freudian. But psychoanalytic theory should not be reduced to Freud's political worldview, nor is it necessarily properly located within it. And as a psychology, as a theory of (especially) emotional life, it is not so easily subsumed within even an expanded Marxist theory. Hence the importance of developing a psychoanalytic-marxist political theory. Hence also the necessity of rejecting Lichtman's either/or.

These comments are, however, premature.[28]

2.

Lichtman entitles his first chapter "Marxist Despondency and the Turn to Freud." This despondency or pessimism results from the enduring and dehumanizing power of capitalism. Because capitalism has endured, the "apparent stasis of the dialectic and the failure of revolution is the one fundamental problem that Western Marxists face in the twentieth century" (Lichtman, 1982, p. 2). And because dehumanization is social reality, *"people come to want what is destructive of their need"* (*ibid.*, p. 3). The latter statement at least in part explains the former. And it leads to the question of how, psychologically speaking, people come to want what is destructive of their need. Lichtman turns to Freud in his search for an answer to this question.

He does not, however, turn away from Marx. The distinguishing feature of Lichtman's analysis is his single-minded and clear-headed adherence to Marx's conception of human nature. He attributes to Marx the idea that to be human "is to be required, by the very absence of a fixed, instinctual disposition, to create one's own nature" (*ibid.*, p. 61).

Human beings are by their very nature self-creative: *"our distinguishing characteristic as human beings is our capacity to give ourselves specific determinations in social time"* (*ibid.*, p. 69). Our self-creation, moreover, is social. The "smallest intelligible unit of social explanation is human beings in specific social relations transforming the natural environment through historically determinate technology." And our sociality is dialectical. Each term of the social relationship "derives its meaning from its place in the totality; each term fills out the meaning of the others" (*ibid.*, p. 64).

Objections can be offered to Lichtman's formulations from within Marxism. He reduces dialectics to the idea of interpenetration or reciprocal determination. He seems to have forgotten that dialectical determination is negation, that the dialectical totality is constituted through negative self-relation. He omits from his "smallest intelligible unit" the biological reproduction of human beings, which Marx himself views as foundational for social analysis. But he is surely correct in viewing Marx's conception of human nature as social, dialectical, and historical.

3.

Given this conception, what becomes of psychoanalysis? It is neither more nor less than a psychology of alienated sociality. Stripped of the claim that it reveals something about human nature, it tells us only how a repressed unconscious is created and functions when social relationships are repressive.

There are really two points here. Lichtman is in the tradition of those theorists who see Freud's thinking as infiltrated by bourgeois political categories, including the ontologizing of these categories. But he takes the critique one step further. He rejects the idea that, at the level of ontology or anthropology, there is a Freudian wheat that can be separated from the Freudian chaff. Insofar as Freud claims to speak about human nature, Lichtman treats him as a bourgeois ideologist pure and simple.

Yet he does allow—and this is the second point—Freud's claim that there is "a repressed unconscious governed by irrational, peremptory, insatiable demands which act beyond our understanding and behind our conscious choice," that is, that psychoanalysis rightfully identifies a domain of alienated subjectivity (*ibid.*, p. 185). Freud is descriptively correct. Bourgeois individuals are divided selves. The divisions and the dividing, however, are social. Hence the basic formula through which Lichtman attempts the Marxist appropriation of psychoanalysis:

*An aspect of mental life becomes a defense to the extent that the inclination
it is employed to structure is defined as socially prohibitory. And an originally amorphous inclination becomes a determinate unconscious motive, drive,
or "instinct" to the extent that it is defined as "censorable" and so forced
away from the self-consciousness of the self and into the literally alien prov-
ince of the id-unconscious.* (ibid., p. 192)

Here we have a Reichian conception of character structure without
Reichian innate sexuality, hence also without Reichian notions of internalization. We do not track a movement from outside in or inside out.
We rather observe the psychological structuring of alienation, a process
within a field of interaction. The theory operates on one plane, and within
the horizon of Marx's anthropology.

4.

Lichtman develops a conception of psychoanalytic therapy that is
of a piece with his conception of psychoanalytic theory. He does not deny
that therapy can effectively ameliorate psychic pain. But

the Freudian ideal of freeing the individual from the crippling domination of the past for the sake of a new capacity to determine one's
own nature simply ignores the enormous pervasive influence of social
domination and ideology in determining both the form and content of
current choice. . . . The more we are freed from past terrors and
archaic fantasies, the more we become susceptible to the subordination which obtains beneath the façade of liberal "self-determination."
The growing dominance of the "rational" ego permits the increased
intrusion of irrational social reality. (ibid., p. 274)

Psychotherapy can do no more than enable one to act in accordance with
the rules of an irrational society that masks as rational. Through it one
trades one psychopathology for another. Yet in the process, or for those
who observe the process from a Marxist perspective, psychotherapy does
reveal an "underside of existence" that is covered over by ordinary,
"healthy" consciousness. To this extent it functions or could function as
a critique of false consciousness.

5.

In passing, and in contrasting himself explicitly with Reich, Fromm,
and Marcuse, Lichtman comments that "few writers deeply exposed to

the literature and practice of psychoanalysis have ever emerged from it unscathed" (*ibid.*, p. 253). Exposure to psychoanalysis can be dangerous to your political health. It results in a watering down of Marxism and/ or theoretical incoherence.

Lichtman, I will grant, comes away from his encounter with psychoanalysis unscathed. But like Schneider, he also comes away without what is most vital and problematical in psychoanalysis. He introduces a psychoanalytic element into Marxist anthropology and social theory, but only by reducing psychoanalysis to a theory of psychical process, that is, by emptying it of all substance.

We might think of it this way. A patient arrives late to a psychoanalytic session. He is not sure why. I, his analyst, feel mildly annoyed and disinterested in the interaction. The patient remarks that he had the fleeting thought that I don't want him to be himself. I ask him, what comes to mind about that? Between us we arrive at memories of his being forced to sit in darkened rooms with his drunken, abusive, and economically defeated father. His father resented his academic and other successes. He would belittle them, and ridicule his son for taking them seriously. As these memories emerged, my patient and I mutually understand why he was late: He did not want to enter that darkened room again. I, additionally, understand my mood as the hour began, as a countertransferential identification with his mood.

What would Lichtman take away from this interaction for theoretical employment? He would note the social determination of the initial familial situation and the process by which it is replicated in the character structure of my patient. He would point out that the analytic interaction, although therapeutic, leaves presently existing equivalents of the pathogenic social situation unchallenged and unchanged. Clinical psychoanalysis provides no cure for Marxist despondency.

Quite right. But what about the emotional dimension of the interaction? Is it adequately explained as the joint product of social pathology and originally "amorphous inclinations"? And if what psychoanalysts call human nature is reduced to these formless inclinations and emotional reality is thereby marginalized, is psychoanalysis of any real interest to Marxists? They might be gratified to hear, if they hadn't already heard it from the Freudian-Marxists or from Schneider, that psychological alienation parallels social alienation. But what would they learn that would be of practical value, or even that would answer theoretical questions they are concerned to raise?

Paradoxically, Lichtman's work might be of greater value and interest from a psychoanalytic perspective. His analysis ends where clinical psychoanalytic inquiry begins. Psychoanalysts, looking outward from their consulting rooms, might be able to use his conception of the social structuring and division of the self. But they would not be willing to leave behind the knowledge gained through clinical experience, when they walked out into the world of alienated sociality.

6.

The Age of Desire is in almost all respects the mirror image of *The Production of Desire*. It is a highly personal and partly fictionalized meditation upon the practice of psychoanalysis. Beginning with clinical experience (presented through a series of composite case studies) Kovel works his way outward through the domains of the family, the psychoanalytic and psychiatric establishments, and the more general contradictions of capitalism, to a point of intersection between history and what he terms the transhistorical. This outer limit reflects his experience of the inner world revealed through psychoanalytic practice. He proves Lichtman's point that one rarely escapes from the clinical consulting room unscathed.

Kovel is walking home after a session with a patient he calls Jane (Kovel, 1981, p. 66). Jane was a successful lawyer who intermittently would lose herself in eating binges. These were most likely to occur when she had reason to feel good about herself.

The session seemingly had gone well. Jane had been appreciative of Kovel's integrity and analytic understanding; Kovel had been accepting of her gratitude. But as he walked along he was "seized by a kind of mad feeling," a voracious, devouring otherness, a "blind, unreasoning frenzy, a distillate of pure hate" (*ibid.*, p. 67). When the feeling subsided he recognized that he had experienced the equivalent of one of Jane's eating binges, and that the session with her had somehow induced the attack.

Here we have desire in both its intrasubjective and intersubjective dimensions—Jane's unreasoning appetite and Kovel's countertransferential identification with her appetite. The clinical situation permits its emergence. But what is it? According to Kovel, desire is a "striving toward an object that cannot yet be named in the languages of history" (*ibid.*, p. 70). Desire designates our ontogenetically earliest states of mind and the sensuous immediacy out of which selfhood develops. It is who we were and who we continue to be outside of the historical specificity of nation, class, race, gender, and language. Or again, desire is "the movement of life as it becomes mental and names the objects for its existence": "It always stands outside history insofar as it contains nameless striving; yet desire is also always part of history insofar as it is carried out in a world of real, already named objects" (*ibid.*, p. 80).

The Jane who felt good about her performance as a lawyer and the Joel Kovel who felt good about himself as an analyst are historical beings, within whom there is preserved/repressed a transhistorical dimension. Because it has been repressed, alienated from the historical self, it is experienced as an otherness, or as the Other of the Self. It (the It, the id) hates the restraints placed upon it. The more it is restrained, the more implacable becomes its hatred, and the more it-like it becomes.

But what does "it" desire? Assuming a subject, what are the objects of desire? Or to make the question more concrete, what was the object of Jane's desire? It was precisely the dissolution of the gap between subject and object. Kovel states that "what I could not let myself realize until it broke on me was the rage that was brewing in Jane over the recapturing of her desire for an absolute union with me, and my frustration of this wish" (*ibid.*, p. 73). During the session they had colluded to cover over the disjunction between them, to replace Jane's frustrated desire for fusion with a false experience of fusion. They fobbed each other off and Kovel, at least, paid the price.

Can a desire, specifically the desire for a fusion at once sensuous and supersensuous, even be gratified? Yes and no:

> Although desire can never be absolutely fulfilled, there is a point of relative gratification that is experienced as a state of goodness, and below this, one of relative ungratification, experienced as badness. Under conditions of goodness, the restlessness accruing as a result of the lack of desire's realization is transferred onto the child's exploratory activity. The objects that the child constructs in the course of his/ her activity are themselves invested with desire. Here desire takes on the shape of Eros, or love, and unifies the self with object in ever-widening totalities. In the state of badness, on the other hand, lack of gratification is experienced as a danger to the self. Objects are shunned or attacked, while consciousness is suffused with hatred of one degree or another. (*ibid.*, p. 74)

Here we have an ambiguity and a point of entry into history. Or rather two points of entry, one of goodness and creativity, one of badness and destructiveness. Kovel would no doubt grant that in practice the two openings cannot be so neatly separated, that they are indeed dialectically interpenetrated. Even so the question remains: Does a dialectic of good and bad adequately acknowledge that "desire can never be absolutely fulfilled"?

We cannot answer this question, which arose also with respect to Marcuse's distinction between necessary and surplus repression, at present. It is to Kovel's credit, however, that it arises. Moreover, by evoking the clinical experience of desire, he gives psychoanalytic substance to Habermas' category of emancipatory praxis and to Lichtman's depiction of mental process.

7.

Yet it could be argued that Kovel falls victim to desire in the course of analyzing it, that is, that the concept of the transhistorical is the product of desire and not the source of it.

What is human, Kovel contends, emerges out of the tension between the historical and the transhistorical. The transhistorical is the dialectical opposite or negation of history. It is what history is not. The human body, for example, "is not clay to be molded by history. . . . It is neither above history nor below it, but somehow pressed into history and transformed by it . . ." (*ibid.*, p. 63). Extending this line of reasoning, the transhistorical "may roughly be defined as nature" (*ibid.*, p. 64). From another angle it is the past, because the past "is what is transformed by historical activity." Hence there is a convergence between nature and the past, which is captured in Freud's notion of the conservative or regressive quality of the instincts. Conversely the "utopian impulse, of which Marxism is the most important current embodiment, is based upon the forward projection of a past, i.e., 'natural' bliss and a critique of existing civilization on this basis" (*ibid.*, p. 65).

Thus it is evident that desire and the transhistorical overlap Freud's conceptualization of the drives and human nature. Kovel rejects the notion of instinct as such and, along with it, Freud's biologistic tendency. But he argues that "the concept of instinct cannot be dismissed as mere biologization, because in it Freud also theorized his abiding insight that we are not automatically civilized, that civilization does not take all of us, but that beneath its influence there is a wordless, 'thinglike' stratum" (*ibid.*, p. 232). What Freud termed instincts Kovel prefers to conceptualize as "configurations of desire"; but desires move in instinct-like patterns. In the clinical situation,

> Once desire is freed from the constraints of ordinary discourse, it reveals an unmistakable tendency to repeat itself in very elementary patterns that have an "organic" feel to them, much as the rhythms of hunger or sexual arousal. It is for this reason—a compelling one for somebody who has spent a long time listening to people in a psychoanalytic way—that the Freudian notion of instinct as a "borderline concept between the mind and body" is not to be dismissed. (*ibid.*)

Although Kovel tries to hedge his bets, he is working with a basically Freudian distinction between nature and history, or between a primary human nature and a secondary (historical) one. He falls into the trap that Lichtman is intent upon avoiding.

Kovel's version of this trap is psychoanalytically manufactured, but there are a number of other available models. Think back to German idealism. In Kantian philosophy an epistemological line separates the natural world from the moral one. The former is a realm of necessity, of the determinism of cause and effect. The latter is a realm of freedom, of the self-legislation of the free will. In the Romantic reaction to Kant (which in this respect includes both Nietzsche and Freud), nature is identified with freedom in the form of passion and lack of inhibition, while morality is identified with necessity and alienation—duty as autocastration. Nature functions as a "beyond," paradise lost (and perhaps to be regained).

The same opposition can be carried over into conceptualizations of history. Then history is alternately the realm in which the human species frees itself from natural necessity and/or the realm of domination, while nature is the prehistorical reality that the species transcends and/ or the repository of sensuous potentiality that history represses.

Various dialectical resolutions of the opposition of freedom and necessity are possible. Hegelians, Marxists, and Freudian-Marxists are old hands at constructing them. But to a remarkable extent the underlying "either nature or history" remains a structural feature of the reasoning. This results from identifying history with specifically human transformations of the extrahuman environment—as if nature does not have a history because we have not created it or human history is not natural because we have. Here we have a species of narcissistic idealism or, rather, the species' narcissistic idealism.

It might seem that I am attempting to catch Kovel in a trap of my own, and a merely verbal one at that. He states quite clearly that he is not proposing the kind of dualism of nature and civilization we find in Freud, and he adds for good measure that "if pressed to the wall to define 'human nature,' I would have to say it is that part of nature that transforms itself; i.e., it is in human nature to make history" (*ibid.*, p. 65). Thus it might appear that he and Lichtman are standing on the same historically firm Marxist ground. Such is not, however, the case. Kovel, like Marcuse, wants to preserve an unhistoricized nature as a reservoir of hope. He finds in the unbound timelessness of the Freudian unconscious the desire to go beyond the multiform master–slave relationships of history. *This* desire he does not analyze. Perhaps he is afraid one must murder to dissect—that analysis would destroy desire and that he, too, might then fall into Marxist despondency.

8.

Kovel locates desire on the horizon of the historical/transhistorical. Lichtman would argue, correctly, that desire must be located within rather than at the horizon of history. And he would point out that Kovel's failure in this regard is characteristically psychoanalytic: Essentialist theories of human nature, no matter how sophisticated, function as defenses against the unremitting historicity of human existence.

But what if the problem is too little psychoanalysis, not too much? Then we might need to take one step further in the analysis of desire.

Because Kovel is a psychoanalyst, let's pose the question clinically. What is required of a psychoanalyst, if s/he is to be a vehicle for the emergence of the patient's desire? W. R. Bion contends that genuine psychoanalytic experience requires of the analyst a "disciplined denial of memory and desire" (Bion, 1970, p. 41). S/he must not be concerned with what has happened in the patient's past, or in past sessions, and s/he must not burden the present moment with hopes, fears, or fantasies about the future. S/he must be an empty container into which the patient's memories and desires can be poured.

Judging from his clinical reporting Kovel accepts some version of Bion's standard. When his own desire to be a good analyst intruded upon Jane's analysis, he recognized it. He then did the self-analytical work required to reopen the space within which Jane's desire could be experienced. To vary Bion's notion, he appropriately engaged in the disciplined analysis of memory and desire.

Assume for the moment that social analysis, like psychoanalysis, requires a disciplined denial of memory and desire but that, in the extra-clinical context, we are both patient and analyst. Then our situation is inherently self-contradictory. As patient—as interested parties to historical conflicts—we are creatures of desire; as analyst we are charged with the dissolution of desire. Not surprisingly, then, our political self-analysis may encounter a resistance we can't overcome. Our political desires may escape from analysis. And when the analyst is sophisticated, the escape, too, will be sophisticated—for example, subtly placing a dialectical boundary between history and the transhistorical.

From such a perspective, the transhistoricization of desire constitutes a resistance to or defense against the analysis of desire. What, then, is the motive for the defense? Surely it is the fear that freedom is a fantasy, hope an illusion—that the emancipatory impulse is the product of desire, and that desire must necessarily shatter on the visible and invisible reefs of the historical flow. Transhistoricizing desire, as implied above, is a defense against political despair.

We have not taken the analysis far enough. For hopelessness and despair are themselves defenses against hope—not the illusory hopefulness of desire but the problematical hopefulness of emancipatory praxis. But this hopefulness, because it involves a confrontation with the unknown in which everything is at stake, is perhaps the most frightening thing of all. Marxist desire and Marxist despondency are equal and opposite defenses against it. Marcuse was wrong: It is to the hopeful that hopelessness is given.

9.

Although it may be that Kovel uses a transcendental notion of desire as a defense against historical uncertainty, he does not shy away from historical analysis. One of the notable features of *The Age of Desire* is its sociological complexity and concreteness. For the most part Kovel looks at his world from the inside—from inside the experience of his patients and his own experience as both psychoanalyst and psychiatrist. And his vision is not monocular, not just psychoanalytic and subjective. It accords objective reality its due.

Kovel adopts the term "totality" to designate the interpenetrating determinacies of objectivities and subjectivities in social reality. He does not, however, totalize his conception of totality. He resists theoretical as well as narrative closure. The stories he tells—an unhappy bank executive suffocating in an objectified and institutionally monetized anality; a rich girl who receives therapeutic nonassistance but struggles to keep hope alive; an out-of-work man who becomes paranoid and falls victim to the psychiatry industry, who becomes the raw material for its production of the psychotic-as-commodity; the psychoanalyst who feels the pain produced by but has lost the will to struggle against the psychiatry industry—have beginnings but not endings. Kovel's totality is an episodic web, tattered at the edges. It looks and feels uncomfortably familiar. It reinstates at the level of the concrete the uncertainty and anxiety it defends against in the abstract.

10.

It might be said that Lichtman is an epistemologically more sophisticated successor to Fromm, while Kovel is a psychoanalytically more sophisticated successor to Marcuse. Just as Lichtman's rigorously Marxist delineation of mental process goes beyond the conglomerative quality of Fromm's conception of social character, so Kovel's thoroughly psychoanalytic portrayal of desire advances us beyond Marcuse's Hegelian intepretation of Freud's metapsychology.

Kovel takes an additonal step beyond Marcuse's self-imposed philosophical limitations. He establishes praxis as the dialectical complement to desire, thus according it a structural or foundational position in his theory.

For Marx praxis is the dialectical unity of theory and practice. It includes but is not limited to material production. For Kovel praxis includes but is not limited to Marx's conception of it. He defines praxis as "the creation of new objects out of old," be the objects material or ideational (Kovel, 1981, p. 235). Praxis, like desire, is transhistorical. Indeed, it denotes the "reality-making side to people of which desire is the negation." Thus "desire and praxis negate each other but also define each other. Desire is the claim of the nature that is, so to speak, left behind by the object making of praxis, while praxis is an activity shaped by an imagination whose hidden term is desire" (*ibid.*, p. 236).

If one must have a concept like the transhistorical, it is vital to preserve in it a version of Marx's notion of species-being. Species-being includes the idea that human subjectivity is constituted in and as a process of objectification. Kovel retains this meaning (as does Lichtman) and so takes a step beyond psychoanalytic reductionism in his view of human nature. But only one. By identifying praxis with objectification, he simultaneously identifies it with conscious or even self-conscious activity. This leaves the territory of the preconscious and unconscious securely in the possession of desire, hence also of psychoanalysis. And because the unconscious is more deeply transhistorical than consciousness, we are necessarily left with a fundamentally psychoanalytic conception of human nature.

Here, again, Kovel mirrors Lichtman. Lichtman secures the integration of psychoanalysis into a Marxist anthropology at the expense of psychoanalysis; Kovel secures the anthropological unity of psychoanalysis and Marxism at the expense of Marxism.

There is an additional problem with the pairing of praxis and desire. If on the one hand Kovel's version of praxis does not extend deeply enough into human nature to weigh effectively against desire, on the other it extends so broadly that it approximates an empty universal. For Kovel, virtually any consciously purposeful action is an instance of praxis. What, then, is in the name that goes beyond or gives conceptual meaning to the activities named? Why not just call a conscious action a conscious action?

To put it another way, Kovel surrenders a Marxist concept with specific and importantly problematical meanings for a highly generalized and unproblematical notion. Marx poses for us the problem of the relationship between the objectification process and a praxis that includes a theory of the objectification process. Moreover, in his theory the objectification process has a determined although not necessarily reductive relationship to work activity. Kovel, by contrast, fuses praxis with objectification, loosens the connection between objectification and work, and uncouples praxis from theory. Consequently history must repeat itself. We are forced to distinguish objectification from both conscious activity and praxis; reconnect objectification to work and production; distinguish between conscious activity in general and praxis in particular; and reestablish the theoretical moment in praxis. Only then are we in a position to work out the relationship between work, desire, conscious activity, and praxis.

It is not my intention, however, to gainsay Kovel's accomplishment. Unlike Habermas, he does not cordon off praxis from production. Unlike both Habermas and Lichtman, he does not present us with a psychoanalysis emptied of desire. Unlike Deleuze and Guattari, he does not fuse and confuse production and desire. Rather his dialectical unification of praxis and desire makes it possible to see ourselves as self-productive creatures who are shadowed by desire and creatures of desire who are forced to produce themselves.

F. Psychoanalytic-Marxism

1.

We have concluded the third and final stage of our critical propadeutic. It is time to look backward before going forward.

In Chapter 2 we began with Marxism and psychoanalysis as two separate theories, each of which had a definite structure (ordering of concepts) and agenda. The relationship between them was external and polemical although—given an interest in theoretical unification—it could be stated as a set of problems.

In Chapter 3 the distance between the theories was narrowed. One might even claim that they had become internally related or, at least, that a set of problematical conceptual relationships had been generated. Although one might observe some loss of the theoretical definiteness of Marxism and psychoanalysis considered singly, classical Freudian-Marxism also had a definite identity of its own. Reich, Fromm, and Marcuse talked to each other. They addressed the same issues in the same language. They shared an interest in human emancipation and they thought Marxism and psychoanalysis were relevant to that interest. They defined Marxism as a theory of objective and collective relationships, psychoanalysis as a theory of subjective and individual ones. Within this discursive context they raised the question: How are the two theories to be joined? And they concurred in the judgment that the answer to this question would take the form of anthropological/historical theory having the triadic form of a dialectical process—more or less open-ended, more or less Marxist, more or less Hegelian.

It cannot be said that the writers we have been considering in this chapter have overthrown, dismembered, sublated, or otherwise consigned classical Freudian-Marxism to a museum of antiquities. Marx and Freud— as well as Reich, Fromm, and Marcuse—continue to animate their discourse. But the terms of the discourse have been both refined and loosened. We now have more variegated visions of social reality. On the one hand, these theoretical developments are a consequence of changed historical circumstances, in which new problems have come to the fore. On the other, they have a discursive dimension. They reflect individuals thinking with and against each other as they try to work out solutions to intellectual problems.

2.

It would serve no good purpose to attempt a totalization of the discourse of psychoanalytic-marxism, and even less of one to set it up in opposition to Freudian-Marxism. We may, however, briefly note several promising ways in which the conceptual manifold has been refined and/ or enlarged:

• *Praxis and dialectical reason.* Emergent psychoanalytic-marxism aims at putting scientism behind it. Dialectical reason retains a position of methodological or epistemological prominence, but the regressive (analytical or even deconstructive) dimension of dialectical method is given greater recognition. In parallel fashion history (as field of inquiry and action) is relatively destructured. Dialectical reason is also decisively linked to praxis and the emancipatory project.[29] Some loss of conceptual determinateness is necessarily involved in this reorientation, as well as (not so necessarily or desirably) a loss of conceptual clarity.

• *Individual ≠ psychology.* Although the anti-oedipal critique of psychoanalysis resembles a demolition derby, it does challenge the identification of the psychological with the individual. Whether or not we wish to maintain the concept of desiring-production as a social universal, we are free and/or forced to think about a social psychology that is something other than an aggregating of individual characteristics.

• *Desire and the passions.* At the theoretical level there is a turn from conceptions of drives (in the orthodox psychoanalytic sense) and relationships (in the Frommian sense) to desire, with its rich Hegelian resonances. There is also an opening created for a Kleinian analysis of emotional life. This does not mean, however, that these earlier psychoanalytic concepts have been replaced. Moreover, the task of establishing the position of desire in a psychoanalytic-marxist anthropology and theory of history remains.

• *Insanity/ in sanity.* From the beginning Marxist, psychoanalytic, and Freudian-Marxist theories have been concerned with the issue of rationality and irrationality. The turn toward Kleinian theory deepens and sharpens the issue. It gives new meaning to the question of an insanity within sanity; and it permits a more sophisticated analysis of psychotic-like dimensions of individual and collective activity.

• *A critical theory of gender and race.* Classical Freudian-Marxism focused on individuals and families at one extreme, political-economic structures at the other. The pluralization of emancipatory politics problematized other interests and generated other theoretical categories, most notably those of race and gender. Henceforward psychoanalytic-marxism must also be a critical theory of patriarchy/phallocentrism and racism.

• *The problem of recognition.* A second turn toward Hegel is found in the appropriation of the category of recognition for psychoanalytic-marxist theory. This development is a consequence of the pluralization of emancipatory politics. Classical Marxism, as a theory of class warfare, can bypass the issue. The aim is to eliminate opposed classes, not to generate mutual recognition between them. Indeed, mutual recognition between classes could only be a form of false consciousness. But the world we seek to win cannot be all female, all male, all black, all white, all African, all Asian, all European, etc. At the existential level some particularity is not only unavoidable but vital and vitalizing. Hence the importance of the problematics of recognition.

• *Ecological sanity.* De-Stalinization and de-colonization led, directly and indirectly, to the pluralization of emancipatory struggle. Advanced capitalism, bureaucratic domination inside and outside of capitalist societies, unlimited application of technological rationality in the search for unlimited wealth, and exponential growth in life-destructive capability led and lead in the opposite direction. They have, albeit negatively, united us globally as never before. Whether or not we wish it, the Many of us are One. Hence, as Alford argues, any critical social theory must be reparative. It must reflect the imperatives of ecological sanity.[30]

It remains to be seen whether or not, or to what extent, we can lay the groundwork for a theory adequate to these issues and to the larger complex of problems our preliminary inquiry has brought to light. Perhaps we have come some way, however, toward justifying the assertion in Chapter 1 that Marxism and psychoanalysis, singly and together, continue to raise questions we wish to answer. If so, then we can proceed with the confidence that even our failures and limitations may be of some heuristic value.

PART TWO

GROUNDWORK

CHAPTER 5

Dialectics and Method

I n the first part of this inquiry we proceeded by means of critical analysis to develop some of the conceptual raw materials needed for the construction of a theoretical groundwork. We now begin again, this time with questions of method. Why with questions of method? This question is itself methodological.

Generally speaking, a method is a way or mode of doing something. The term has, however, two more particular social theoretical meanings. *Technically* (or instrumentally), a method is a procedure for theorizing, as in the instance of a procedure for developing empirical or historical material into concepts, or for reworking existing conceptual materials into new ones. The technical method joins theory to object and must necessarily coexist with the inquiry itself. It is immanent in and integral to any kind of research.

One may also analyze the relationship between theory and object, including the methodological relationship of theory and object. This is method or methodology in the *reflective* or metatheoretical sense. Method as reflection, or as theoretical self-consciousness, includes questions about the logical, epistemological, and ontological status of propositions and arguments.

A distinguishing feature of the Frankfurt school of critical theory is its protest against collapsing reflective into technical reason, especially in the instance where technical reason has in its turn been collapsed into the methods or a semblance of the methods of the natural sciences. The Frankfurters also object to identifying metatheory with the philosophy of science. They seek to preserve the philosophical reflexivity of reason, the capacity of the theorist to turn back upon him/herself and investigate the subjective as well as objective conditions under which theorizing takes place. As we have seen, in *Knowledge and Human Interests* Habermas even went so far as to claim that self-reflection is the sine qua non for the emancipatory employment of reason. For our part we had reason to challenge this position. But we would do well, I think, to identify ourselves with the insistence upon the double—technical and reflective—role of methodology.

The present chapter is methodological in the reflective sense. It has two purposes: to articulate the metatheoretical foundations of psychoanalytic-marxist theory in general, and to effect a transition between the first and subsequent phases of our work. Hence its position here, at the turning point in our investigation.

We will first reformulate the idea of praxis and, in the process, establish the epistemological limits of the inquiry. Then, through a critique of the Hegelian dialectics of being, thinking, and acting, we will attempt to give this conception of praxis a dialectical content.

A. Epistemology: Rethinking Praxis

1.

It will prove useful to begin again with Marx's depiction of method in *Grundrisse*.[1]

Marx, we will remember, distinguished between two theoretical processes: one in which an empirical manifold is dissolved into a set of abstract determinants; another through which the "abstract determinations lead toward a reproduction of the concrete by way of thought." Thus:

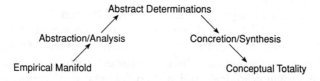

The first process is analytic or regressive; the second is synthetic or progressive. Breaking down the empirical manifold makes it possible to build up the conceptual one.

2.

So far as the first phase is concerned, it must be emphasized that Marx was not a naive empiricist or realist. He recognized that empirical data came intermingled with concepts and interpretations. The analysis of data, abstraction from a given "chaotic conception of the whole" (Marx, 1857, p. 100), necessarily involved a critical working through of existing conceptualizations. It is both analytical and critical work that yields those "simple concepts" from which the concretizing or synthesizing process begins.

3.

Terms like "abstraction" and "concretion" can give rise to intellectualist misunderstandings. One might imagine a process of abstraction, for example, in which an empirical manifold is systematically reduced to a set of categories, which in turn are systematically reduced to a few simple notions. In like fashion one would then picture a process of concretion advancing straightforwardly from these categories to the reproduced totality.

Think, by contrast, of the actual processes through which Marx himself arrived at such abstract concepts as species being and alienated labor. At a minimum three dimensions of experience were involved. First, in 1842–1844 Marx was immersed in a complex political situation, partly by choice and partly by necessity. He was developing rapidly from liberal to radical to revolutionary intellectual identified with the interests of the working class. Second, he was attached to Hegelian and Feuerbachian categories, including the methodological ones (dialectic, transformational criticism). Third, he read political economy in the light of his political interests and through the optic of these theoretical and methodological categories. The result was to see workers as alienated from their species being, and to see species being as creative work. Thus he arrived at alienated labor as the first principle for a critical political economy.

Subsequently, when Marx had more thoroughly immersed himself in economic research and the literature of political economy, his categories became more refined. But as we see in reading *Grundrisse*, the key concepts of (1) the commodity as the elementary unit of economic analysis, (2) the distinction between labor and labor-power, and (3) the surplus value of commodities as dependent upon that distinction emerged quite unsystematically. Moreover, we find him continuing the work of abstraction as he was attempting to concretize and totalize his research.

In short, the process of abstraction is never quite so abstract as all that, nor the process of concretion quite so concrete. And the distinction between them is itself in part an artifact of abstraction.

4.

There is a parallel to but not a duplication of Marx's method in our own investigation. We began, not with empirical materials, but rather with theories. We represented them, or aspects of them, and in so doing abstracted from them. But we did not attempt anything like the reduction of this manifold of concepts to a few simple abstractions. To the contrary: We aimed at the multiplication of problems and possible solutions, although within the limits of the psychoanalytic-marxist project. Hence the analogy to the economic process of working up raw material from natural resources, rather than to the analysis of chemical compounds.

Despite rather than because of its postmodernist associations, and as noted at the outset, we might think of this as a conceptual assemblage.

In the second phase of the inquiry we will advance from more to less abstract concepts. But as noted at the outset, our work will fall short of a reproduction of the concrete in conceptual form.

5.

Although our inquiry is structured in a fashion that mirrors Marx's method, we also must stress again the important difference between Marx's position and our own.[2] Marx draws an epistemological boundary line between abstraction and concretion. Although he recognizes that the concept as concept, as thought, is a product and not an empirical premise, and so distinguishes his method from Hegel's, he nonetheless considers that concretion or synthesis is "obviously the scientifically correct method" (Marx, 1867, p. 101). He consigns the analytical processes through which the basic concepts arise to the mere history of a science.

This distinction between the history of a science and science proper is related to the distinction between inquiry and presentation we find in the postface to *Capital, 1*. There Marx defends himself from accusations of Hegelianism by stressing how in the phase of inquiry one has "to appropriate the material in detail, to analyse its different forms of development and to track down their inner connection." Once this is done successfully, then the "real movement," the "life of the subject matter," can be "reflected back in ideas" where, however, it may appear to be an "*a priori* construction" (*ibid.*, p. 102). Indeed! Realism in this strong sense is hardly distinguishable from absolute or objective idealism. Hence Marx's self-defense is not totally successful.

Let's think of it the other way around. If one does not divorce the path of inquiry from that of demonstration, then one recognizes that the interests and contingencies of the former are more or less carried over into the latter. No doubt, one can attempt to guard against this eventuality, that is, to erect a methodological barrier between the subjectivity of the theorist and the objectivity of the theory. Such attempts are not doomed to absolute failure, nor are they to be abandoned. But along with attempts at safeguarding the objectivity of inquiry, we would do well to accept and be self-conscious about the necessary interpenetration of the subject who knows and the object that is to be known.

I might add this note. Other interpretations of Marx's position are possible, including ones that stress his awareness of the unfinished and contingent quality of social theoretical research. Be that as it may, the main point is that the interpenetration of abstraction and concretion means that theoretical first principles and the syntheses built upon them necessarily retain a problematical quality. Platonists ancient and modern are wrong: It is not possible for an argument to "push its way up to the region free of assumptions and reach the beginning of all, and grasp it, clinging again and again to whatever clings to this" (Plato, *The Republic*, in Rouse, 1956, p. 311).

6.

It is equally important not to go too far in the other direction. Practical and theoretical problems do sometimes get solved; social research is not or need not be a mere reproduction of the researcher's subjectivity. As Freud correctly argued against what he termed philosophical anarchism, "it sounds wonderfully superior so long as it relates to opinions about abstract things: it breaks down with its first step into practical life." If we were seriously nihilistic about human knowledge, "we might build bridges just as well out of cardboard as out of stone, we might inject our patients with a decagram of morphine instead of a centigram, and might use tear-gas as a narcotic instead of ether" (1933a, p. 176).

7.

Taken together, the preceding points amount to an elimination of the extreme epistemological positions. Absolutist and nihilistic knowledge-claims are equally uninteresting. In between lie various theoretical and practical problems, more or less solved, more or less soluble, with various kinds of technical methods available for their solution.

In like fashion we eliminate either the reduction of knowledge to or the divorce of knowledge from the projects and problematics in which it originates. What we know is both a product and a transformation of our interests and desires.

8.

We pass through a kind of methodological defile when we advance from abstraction to concretion, or perhaps in this context I should say from discovery to demonstration. In the first phase we let a thousand flowers bloom. We give full reign to our subjectivity—to imagination and free association. In the second phase we tend the garden. Like the good artist or craftsmen lauded by Plato, we subordinate ourselves to the well-being or interest of the object.

There is a second kind of objectivity that permeates the development of knowledge, namely, the objectivity of discursive practices and conventions. What we view as knowledge is discursively structured, and, whether we like it or not, our thoughts count as knowledge only when they are articulated according to discursive rules. Fatefully, these rules · are rarely if ever neutral. In epistemology as well as politics, might tends to make right.

9.

Here is a related issue. We remember that Nancy Hartsock argued for a "standpoint epistemology," in which the worker's perspective is privileged vis-à-vis the one of the owners and a feminist perspective is privileged vis-à-vis a masculinist one. This position necessarily involves an attempt to combine particularity and universality. On the one hand, it is acknowledged, indeed emphasized, that theoretical understanding varies with social location and experience. Social knowledge would thus appear to be a mosaic of particular theories, none of which could be used as a basis for judging the truth-claims of another. On the other hand, some universal—independent and nonpartisan—standard of truth must be presupposed if a claim to epistemological privilege is to be sustained. Otherwise there would be no way of determining which of these perspectives yields a more and which a less valid knowledge of social reality.

It is possible, in principle or even occasionally in practice, to combine these positions. Marx, for example, makes a persuasive case that the standpoint of the proletariat permits one to solve problems with the labor theory of value that are insoluble from a bourgeois standpoint. But what if we attempt to generalize from such an example? Then we find ourselves clinging to the ancient hope of grasping reality itself, or in-and-for-itself, so that we can subsequently derive all particularities from the universal truth thus attained. But this human, all-too-human, project has yet to be realized. Consequently it is prudent to fall back to a more restrained position, which might be termed a contingent and (so to speak) particularized universality: In particular cases one epistemological standpoint may be more nearly universal, more validly totalizing, than another.[3]

We must enter a caveat for even this very constrained acceptance of epistemological privilege. Although abandoning the search for true knowledge usually results in a politically disengaged shrug of the epistemological shoulders, the history of racial and sexual discourse demonstrates with especial clarity how easily truth-claims can be used to de-realize lived experience.

Hence all truth-claims should come with warning labels.

10.

Our current sensitivity to the role of power within discourse and to the power of discursive practices comes more from Foucault than anyone else. This is one of the reasons why some feminists have been attracted to his version of postmodernism. It facilitates the critique of patriarchal/phallocentric discourse, even or especially when gender bias is disguised by claims to scientificity and epistemic neutrality.

Yet in my judgment it would be a mistake either to overestimate the novelty of Foucault's position or to take his style of analysis to the point where discourse and knowledge are reduced to power. In the former regard his approach is a recognizable variant of Marxist critique or Mannheim's sociology of knowledge. In the latter we may avail ourselves of Freud's rejoinder to philosophical anarchists and nihilists.[4] There is a distinction to be drawn between ether and tear-gas, and there are methodological procedures that both establish the distinction and guide the production of the one or the other. And while it is often vital to ask whose interest is served by either kind of production, it is quite pointless to deny the objectivity of the products.

11.

There is an evident difference between producing (1) ether; (2) a meaningful interpretation of Marx's methodology; and (3) an enhanced ability for self-determining action. Nor are these Habermasian differentiations the only ones that we could imagine. Examples: the location and excavation of Troy based upon a reading of the *Iliad* and the employment of archaeological techniques; knowledge of Trobriand sexual practices acquired through field research; assessment of voter attitudes through survey research; employment of statistical methods in historical research; putting an end to a prisoner's dilemma by the use of coded messages in a jail break; and so on. The paths of pluralization lead in many directions.

Still, there is some utility in a revised and simplified Habermasian triad of knowledge domains. That is, it seems worthwhile to differentiate between knowledge aimed at (1) instrumental control (science in the strict sense), (2) generation of shared meanings (communicative inter-action), and (3) individual and collective self-transformation. It is im-portant, however, not to treat the categories as determining mutually exclusive knowledge practices. As the preceding examples are meant to suggest, actual processes of gaining knowledge blend instrumentality, meaningful interpretation, and situational transformation in various ways. That on the one hand. On the other, and as the term "knowledge domains" indicates, there must be something called knowledge of which there are domains, a One that underlies or runs through the Many (or the Three).

Here is one possible approach to a conception of the unity and plu-rality of knowledge. It is a modest one. It leaves far more questions un-answered than it answers. But it is, hopefully, adequate for our purposes.

Let's say, then, (1) that knowledge in general is a function of (or perhaps a moment in) praxis and (2) that types or categories of knowl-edge are variant forms of praxis.

What praxis is not: Habermas, we remember, attempts to solve the subject–object problem of German idealism by adding the category of emancipatory praxis to the classical dyad of natural (objective) science and spiritual (cultural, subjective) science. This has the unfortunate effect of limiting the concept of praxis to unities of theory and practice having emancipatory aims. It is evident, however, that the natural and cultural sciences have practices as well as theories. Hence Habermas' usage unduly restricts the meaning of praxis. Kovel, on the other hand, overextends it. He expands the meaning of praxis to any intentional action whatsoever. Praxis becomes just another name for any- and everything we do.

Let's go back to Marx's conceptualization of praxis in his second thesis on Feuerbach (1845):

> The question whether objective truth can be attributed to human think-ing is not a question of theory but is a *practical* question. Man must prove the truth, that is, the reality and power, the this-sidedness of his thinking in practice. The dispute over the reality or non-reality of think-ing which is isolated from practice is a purely *scholastic* question. (p. 144)

Like the German idealists whom he is criticizing, Marx poses the prob-lem of valid knowledge as a subject–object relationship. Thinking is in the place of the subject, reality is in the place of the object. The relation-ship between the two is the activity of realization. Metaphysical ques-tions may be defined by their denial of this practical integument.

We may amplify Marx's text. Any ordinary action unifies a subject (an active agent) and an object (even if the object is an other, another subject, and the unity is negative, that is, destructive or hostile). Repeated, patterned, or systematic actions are practices. Theoretical knowledge begins in practices of various kinds. It aims at solving the problems posed by practice. Once practices have been theorized, further practice becomes praxis, that is, activity aiming at the realization of a theory. Within this larger setting theorizing itself (including theorizing about theorizing) may be viewed as a practice. Theorizing then becomes a means to realizing theoretical ends. We sometimes reserve the term "theory" for activity with theoretical ends, just as we sometimes reserve the term "practice" for pretheoretical or posttheoretical activity. It is important not to isolate these epistemic moments, however, but rather to recognize their interpenetration.

12.

In the preceding statement we differentiated practice from ordinary action by its relatively patterned or systematic quality. In like fashion we may differentiate theory from ordinary thinking. To theorize is to think in a relatively systematic fashion. But further, and again as asserted above, theory aims at the solution to problems, or more simply at answering questions.

W. R. Bion, who gave us a very sophisticated although unfortunately nondialectical conception of thinking, also offered us a deceptively simple conception of theory. He prefaces *Seven Servants* with the wisdom of the Elephant's Child, that creature of "satiable curtiosity" (Kipling, 1956, p. 83):

> I keep six honest serving men
> (They taught me all I knew)
> Their names are What and Why and When
> And How and Where and Who.
> I send them over land and sea,
> I send them east and west;
> But after they have worked for me,
> *I* give them all a rest.

Bion added, referring to the title of his book: "The missing one completes the seven."

Theories are systematic ways of answering these six questions. In the instance of social theory we first establish what and/or who it is we are talking about (persons, events, social structures, states of mind, ourselves, etc.). We identifiy the phenomenon in question. We then proceed to establish its where and when, its historical location. Once this is done, we attempt to determine how it develops or functions, and to explain its development or functioning. Partial determinations and explanations call for further historical investigation and delimitation of phenomena, etc.

We can build more sophisticated and abstract conceptions around these straightforward and concrete questions. Indeed, we are almost forced to do so. The questions do not yield unproblematical answers and so we question them. But we also continue to use them, even when the discourse has become very sophisticated indeed. Think, for example, of the opening moves of *The Critique of Pure Reason*. Kant begins with an abstract person, place, and time—the synthetical unity of apperception along with the sensuous intuition of space and time. These are quickly followed by explanatory categories of one kind or another. Or, in *The Phenomenology*, we begin with sense-certainty, that is, the phenomenological experience of Here and Now by a Consciousness. Thus we rely upon these six servants even when, as Tennyson would have it, we follow knowledge "beyond the utmost bound of human thought" (Tennyson, 1898, p. 88).

When Bion adds, "the missing one completes the seven," he points to an emptiness or unfilled moment in the process of knowing—the moment of silence in an analytic session, more generally the state of mind that *allows* thoughts to happen. This subjective allowance or unfilled moment has its complement in the object known. As Sartre emphasizes, human reality is incomplete, poised uncertainly between the closure of the past and the opening into the future. It is in part and always a project. We also remember Sartre's observation that our lives are irreducible to knowledge. Theory both reflects the unfilled moment in objective reality and falls behind it. There is a three-fold negativity in the positivity of knowledge: within the subject, within the object, and in the relationship between them.

13.

Marx notes the existence of "purely scholastic" questions. This does not mean that he is recognizing an autonomous sphere of scholastic or academic knowledge. His intent, it seems to me, is to puncture the balloon of conceptual purity. Once this is done, it must be admitted that there are practices associated even with the asking of metaphysical questions, and that these academic practices presuppose social ones.

At the other extreme, we may point to a variety of experiences from which we learn and which involve a kind of knowledge, but which I for one would not identify with praxis. I am thinking especially of the knowledge, mainly intuitive, involved in cultural practices such as being streetwise or writing poetry. We can develop theories about these practices, but the practices do not require theories. To the contrary, theorizing may interfere with the practice.[5]

14.

All knowledge involves the systematic interaction of subject and object. What varies among forms of knowledge are (1) the aims of the subjects; (2) the objects in and through which such aims are to be realized; and (3) the methods through which subjective aims are objectified.

Natural science is a praxis that aims at the technical control of objects that are not also subjects. If it is used, as it may be, to gain technical control over objects that are also subjects, then its aim has been perverted. The "object" has been dehumanized, "its" subjectivity has been violated.

Communicative interaction is a praxis that aims at the generation of shared, that is, intersubjective, meanings. The procedures that generate shared meanings do not establish technical control over any object whatsoever. They do, however, establish the cultural context within which technical control over objects becomes meaningful.

Transformational interaction is the praxis of self-determination, of overcoming internally and/or externally imposed individual and/or collective self-limitations. It requires something akin to the instrumental efficacy of the natural sciences as well as to the meaningfulness of communicative interaction. It cannot proceed, however, if the subject treats her/himself or is treated as a nonhuman object; nor can it be content with nontransformational but meaningful communication. It is both and neither—something other than—natural science or communicative interaction.

We may represent these relationships in a simple matrix:

Knowledge • Praxis

Practices ◄————► Theories

	Practices	Theories
Scientific		
Communicative		
Transformational		

It is important to remember that, as pure epistemological types, these distinctions are abstracted from experience; concretely, the three forms of knowing are necessarily interpenetrated. Scientific research, for example, occurs within overlapping discursive contexts, some of them narrowly scientific, some of them more broadly social. Its "truths" are necessarily inflected with meanings, and are varyingly meaningful. It has, moreover, transformational implications and its practices transform its practitioners.

15.

If we refine the conception of an epistemological modality just a bit, we may say that each form of inquiry involves a distinctive configuration or integration of scientific, communicative, and transformational methods, a synthesis of these methods determined by the aim of the inquiry.

Consider Marxism, psychoanalysis, and psychoanalytic-marxism as instances of transformational praxis.

Marxism has as one parameter or limit a scientific knowledge of economic production—scientific because economic production requires and generates natural scientific knowledge. Economic exchange, however, is already less scientifically determinate. More generally, the more one thinks to and through social and political interactions, the less scientifically determinate and the more discursive knowledge becomes. This is because social and political practices do not operate with the necessity of natural processes and the practices instrumentally attached to them. Hence there is a kind of fit between political knowledge and communicative interaction. Further, in Marxism both scientific and discursive forms of knowing move toward choices of action aimed at social transformation. The situation of choice of action is the epistemic locus of both theory and practice. One places oneself there in order to see and evaluate the praxis as a whole. And for this very reason one is forced to grant that one's knowledge will be partisan and incomplete.

Psychoanalysis has as its natural scientific parameter biological knowledge of human individuals, especially the biology of both sexual reproduction and mental function. From this limit it advances to and through the analysis of emotional interactions. The knowledge generated, including knowledge of gender, lacks the determinacy of natural science. It has, rather, the interdeterminacy of political theoretical discourse. And like political discourse it, too, moves toward a situation of action, albeit the peculiar interaction of the clinical situation. Clinical interaction is its epistemic center, the location from which one one-sidedly views the praxis as a whole.

Psychoanalytic-marxism aims, on the one hand, at the unification of these two transformational praxes. On the other, a praxis situated in choices of political action is necessarily distinct from one situated in clinical interactions. Which is not to say there is or ought to be an impermeable barrier between the two. But it is theoretically and practically disastrous to conflate political with therapeutic interaction. To take a therapeutic approach to politics is to fall victim to the illusion that one can rise above the clash of antagonistic interests. To take a political approach to therapy is to disavow the mutuality of interests that makes emotional development possible. Therefore, as the hyphen in psychoanalytic-marxism signifies, the aim of the project is a totalizing of opposed theoretical/practical modalities, not a totalization of no longer differentiable elements.

16.

"For purposes of argument," someone objects, "I'll assume you are able to solve the anthropological problem you set for yourself. You would then have a theoretical foundation that might serve equally well for political or therapeutic practice. Nonetheless a psychoanalytic-marxist praxis seems to be a contradiction in terms. It is a praxis with no practice of its own."

"Your objection is not entirely without merit," we reply, "but recall the relationship between feminism and psychoanalytic-marxism we articulated in Chapter 4. There we noted that psychoanalytic-marxism cannot and is not meant to replace feminist praxis. It is rather a means to feminist ends. It has, moreover, the same relationship to racial and class struggles. It articulates problems that each of these broad social movements needs to solve, for themselves and in their conjunction with each other."

"I see," says the critic, "psychoanalytic-marxism is midwifery."

"Just so," we reply, "but is that intended as a criticism?"

17.

If there were world enough and time we might ask the question: What counts as valid knowledge, in general and in the instances of natural science, communicative interaction, and transformational interaction? I'm not sure how good an answer we could give, but in any case, we cannot hope to answer it well in the present context. We might, however, address a narrower question of validation: What does it mean to realize a transformational theory in practice?

A clinical example is perhaps the easiest way of posing this question. A man has a persistent inhibition when it comes to asserting himself. He has been in analysis for some time. Over and over again he and I have focused upon his fear of criticism, and have linked it to abuse he received from his father. He himself recurrently introduces images of castration in this connection. I have offered him oedipal interpretations of these images, which he has found meaningful. But both of us recognize the existence of some kind of defensive barrier between his psychoanalytic insight and his everyday actions. Although less inhibited than when he began analysis, self-assertion remains extremely difficult and anxiety-provoking. He avoids it as much as possible.

One day he expresses with unusual directness and emotional force his recognition of *self*-limitation, of the internality of the barrier. I say with matching bluntness that he suffers from castration anxiety. It is hardly a new idea, but something new happens. He experiences the link between the idea of castration and the anxiety that accompanies self-assertion. Castration anxiety becomes real for him. Subsequently he is somewhat more willing and able to engage his anxiety, rather than to hide from it.

I would consider this to be a valid realization of psychoanalytic theory. It involves more than a meaningful correlation and less than a necessary causal connection between an idea and a subsequent materialization of the idea. It goes beyond the discursive validity of the patient's and my prior mutual understanding of a problem, but we could not meet scientific standards for judging the instrumental efficacy of the psychoanalytic process. Hence we might view psychoanalytic realizations as inadequate scientific demonstrations. Alternatively, and I think properly, we can recur to Habermas' claim that the signal criterion for verifying psychoanalytic interpretations is the successful continuation of a previously interrupted self-formative process, that is, the patient's development over time of a demonstrably greater capacity to engage in the struggle to overcome conditions of self-alienation.

Along these lines but more generally, a valid tranformational realization is the alteration of a pattern of activity (of a practice or set of practices) in a theoretically determined direction. Malcolm X's founding of the Organization of Afro-American Unity in 1964 fits this definition, as does the experience of my patient. But so does Stalin's elimination of Trotsky and the Left Opposition in the Soviet Union in the 1920s. Which is to say, emancipatory values are not built into the epistemological category of transformational praxis, any more than they are into natural science and communicative interaction. There is no legitimate epistemological escape from freedom.

B. Over the Line: Speculative Dialectics

1.

At the end of Book IV of *The Republic*, Socrates has completed his construction in words of the just city and the just individual and seems ready to use them as a standard for criticizing varyingly unjust cities and individuals. He is encouraged first to describe the just city in greater detail. "Words without end," he replies, "you must draw the line somewhere." Glaucon rejoins, "Draw the line at the end of life, Socrates" (in Rouse, 1956, p. 248).

Thus begins the explicitly philosophical section of *The Republic*, in which the distinction between the realms of being and becoming, true and merely apparent reality, is developed, and in which we are encouraged to take the dialectical path leading to knowledge of the Good. Then, at the beginning of Book VIII, we return to this-worldly and political concerns, guided now by a higher wisdom.

In *The Critique of Pure Reason*, Kant likewise steps over the line between phenomena and noumena. He, too, employs dialectical reasoning in the pursuit of the truth. But where Socrates seeks to transcend the world of appearances, Kant purports to demonstrate that we must be content with knowledge (albeit certain knowledge) of it. He uses dialectic in the negative or critical sense to demonstrate that all reasoning based on the ontologizing of the categories (for example, cause and effect) is necessarily self-contradictory. Where earlier he had put forth positive arguments for limiting truth-claims to the phenomenal world, here he negates the negation of his arguments. He articulates the negation of his position (the categories are objective, not subjective merely), negates it by demonstrating that it is self-negating (that it cannot be developed without contradiction), and so reestablishes the validity of the initial position. For good reason his is termed the critical philosophy.

The present section, an excursis on the Hegelian dialectic, has something in common with each of the examples. In it we cross the line from materialist to idealist dialectics. As in the Platonic instance, such a move is apparently not integral to the argument. Just as Socrates might have proceeded from this-wordly construction to this-worldly criticism, so we might proceed from social criticism to social construction. But our work requires a clearer understanding of dialectical reasoning than the one we have at present. Hegel, as Marx generously acknowledged and as we noted earlier, is the master teacher of dialectics. It is in our interest to be his students, even if briefly, and so to follow the Hegelian path toward Absolute Knowledge. We may then return to the world of the living.

But not from the realm of a higher life, a more real reality. Epistemologically, there is nothing up there. Hegelian dialectics are speculative—transcendent of the understanding, as Kant would say—and so legitimately subject to criticism. If we view Hegel's position as the negation of Kant's, it must be negated in its turn. Kant gets his revenge. He would find little satisfaction in it, however, because the negation of the negation does not restore his position. It leaves us instead in the uncertain world of actual human experience.

We consider, first, the relationship of Being and Nothing in *The Science of Logic*, then the relationship of subject and object in *The Phenomenology*.[6] Our aim in the first instance is to articulate the basic elements in a dialectical conception of developmental processes in general—of becomings. Our aim in the second instance is to articulate the basic elements in a dialectical conception of thinking and theorizing. Then, in the next section, we explore the dialectics of practical action in the context of the Hegelian problematics of recognition. In this way we give our conception of praxis a dialectical content while, simultaneously, bringing dialectics down to earth.

2.

Stated in the most general terms, a dialectical relationship is a process or passage from immediacy through mediation to realization. We begin with an apparently simple concept or thing, something as-such or that is undeveloped. As we observe it, it develops and polarizes. It has two sides instead of one, which are at odds with or mutually negating of each other. Each side exists as an object for and against the other. As we keep watching, the conflict or contradiction between the two sides resolves itself into a new unity. The new unity, the realization of the process, does not leave its process of development behind; rather, it is internally structured by the superseded conflict.

Here is figurative representation of dialectical process. It is only a distant approximation to the fluidity and complexity of actual dialectical development. But any port in a storm.

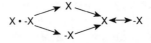

At the outset, X is not differentiated from –X. Lack of differentiation or immediacy is represented by the (•). There is a contradiction latent in the immediacy, and for just this reason there is a potential for development. Differentiation or development is then a manifestation of the latent opposition, as well as the interaction (interpenetration) of the opposites. This development in the form of opposition is sometimes termed diremption. It establishes a binary, mutually exclusive, either/or relationship between X and –X. X and –X exist for and against each other. The clash of the opposites creates a structure, X ↔ –X, a determinate relationship—represented by the double arrow—between the extremes, which serves (or can serve) as a starting point for the next phase of development.

3.

The basic terms of Hegel's ontology, as they are developed at the beginning of *The Science of Logic* (1812), may be represented by a somewhat more sophisticated version of the model:

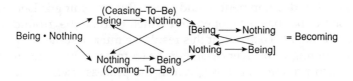

We begin in an ontological situation in which Being has not been distinguished from Nothing (Being • Nothing). The dialectical interaction of Being and Nothing (Being → Nothing; Nothing → Being) results in Becoming. Becoming is Being that has passed through Nothing and, by virtue of this passage, has become determinate. It is Determinate Being.

The beginning is Being, pure being, "without any further determination. In its indeterminate immediacy it is equal only to itself." We may say, Being = Being, but the predicate adds nothing. Indeed, nothing can be predicated of Being. There is precisely nothing to say about it. "Being, the indeterminate immediate, is in fact *nothing*, and neither more nor less than *nothing*" (*ibid.*, p. 82).

Nothing, then: "It is simply equality with itself, complete emptiness, absence of all determination and content—undifferentiatedness in itself." Yet it can be thought, in just this way, that is, as neither more nor less than Being. "Nothing is, therefore, the same determination, or rather absence of determination, and thus altogether the same as, pure *being*" (*ibid.*).

We have, it would seem, the immediate identity (•) of Being and Nothing, an absence of determination so stark that even the copula (=) says too much. But this is only the beginning, not the end, of the matter. For "it is equally true that they are not undistinguished from each other, that, on the contrary, they are not the same, that they are absolutely distinct, and yet that they are unseparated and inseparable, and that each immediately *vanishes in its opposite*" (*ibid.*, p. 83). We have actually witnessed two mirroring processes, or a double self-mirroring process, in which Being vanished into Nothing and Nothing into Being. We observed, as distinct and inseparable, a ceasing-to-be and a coming-to-be. And taken together as they must be, this emergent determinacy has a name: Becoming. Becoming is Being that has come-to-be. It is Determinate Being.

4.

Or is it? Is Hegel entitled to name the double passage of ceasing-to-be/coming-to-be or to claim that Becoming develops from it?[7]

If Becoming were *merely* a name for ceasing-to-be/coming-to-be, I for one would not object. But then no meaning would have been added and no further development would occur. But Becoming is Determinate Being, Being that has developed and which is to be the ground for further development. To arrive at this result we must assume the predominance of coming-to-be over ceasing-to-be (coming-to-be > ceasing-to-be). But no such predominance is given in the process itself. Further, once we step outside of the simple oscillation of ceasing-to-be and coming-to-be, the inverse relationship is also possible, the predominance of ceasing-to-be over coming-to-be (ceasing-to-be > coming-to-be). If on the one hand it is possible to progress toward Determinate Being, on the other it is possible to regress toward Indeterminate Being, to recoil into the void.

In other words, once we expand the simple dialectic of ceasing-to-be/coming-to-be beyond an indefinite and undeveloping oscillation, we have (1) regressive as well as progressive possibilities and (2) the need to explain how and why, in specific instances, these alternative possibilities arise.[8]

5.

In order to bring out more clearly the logical structure of dialectical reasoning, we may simplify the presentation of Being and Nothing:

Being → Nothing
Nothing → Determinate Being

Being passes into and out of Nothing, and emerges as Determinate Being. The passage is a double negation, which does not merely reproduce Being, but which determines it, limits it, and, by so doing, realizes it. Whether the transitions are necessary (Being necessarily passes into Nothing, etc.) or contingent (Being may or may not pass into Nothing, etc.), however, is not given in advance.

Any reader of *Capital, 1* will immediately recognize the isomorphism of this figure with Marx's formula for the circulation of commodities and of capital. If commodities = C and money = M, then:

Commodities: Capital:
C – M   M – C
M – C   C – M + ΔM

In one instance, a commodity is sold for money (C – M) and another commodity is purchased with the money thus acquired (M – C). This is a simple exchange of commodities. In the other, a commodity is purchased (M – C) and, in the instance of capital accumulation, is sold for more money than the purchase price (C – M + ΔM). Both processes, Marx emphasizes, are contingent: The double passage from commodity to commodity or money to money may or may not be completed. Although "commodities are in love with money, . . . the course of true love never did run smooth" (Marx, 1867, p. 202). Economic transactions resemble sexual liasons more than Hegelian identities.

6.

Yet by the end of *Capital, 1,* Marx seems to have forgotten what he asserted in the beginning: "Capitalist production begets, with the inexorability of a natural process, its own negation. This is the negation of the negation" (*ibid.,* p. 929). Marx could be, it seems, an orthodox Hegelian when he so desired.

Habermas criticizes Marx for reducing knowledge to the technical rationality of the natural sciences, as well as for a thoroughly Hegelian collapsing of epistemology into ontology. These are indeed tendencies in Marx's thinking. But Habermas misses what is perhaps the most important point. Marx, following Hegel, builds a tendency toward resolution or closure into dialectical reason. Uncertainties at the microanalytical level disappear by the time we reach the macroanalytical level. The unsettling ontological and epistemological implications of dialectical reasoning are, if not totally repressed, minimized. Dogma tends to replace doubt. It is then a secondary matter whether or not the dogma is scientific or philosophical, epistemological or ontological.

This point is as much psychological as it is methodological. If we take the dialectic of coming-to-be/ceasing-to-be as the most abstract concept from which a return to the concrete is possible, then we must accept an irreducible indeterminism in both theory and practice. The glissade in Hegel's philosophy and Marx's theory is the simultaneous engagement and disengagement with this indeterminism. For both thinkers, dialectical reason is to carry us beyond anxiety.

We, however, must go in the opposite direction.

7.

Three steps down:
• If we are concerned with a life-process and not just a conceptual one, then we are entitled to use Becoming as a frame of reference. Not

absolutely: All life-processes run down; entropy will out. And even when growth is the predominant aspect of the process, regression and negation are not absent. Becoming is, after all, dialectical. *Omnis determinatio est negatio.*

• Perhaps if Freud had read Hegel's *The Science of Logic* before writing *Beyond the Pleasure Principle,* he would have said that the concept of a drive *(Trieb)* particularizes Becoming to the human situation. Hence in its predominant aspect it is the *Lebenstrieb,* which brings things together, while in its subordinant aspect it is the *Todestrieb,* which tears them apart.

It must be added that, in the course of the life cycle, the two aspects undergo a dialectical inversion.

• So Empedocles was correct: All things mortal "never cease their continuous exchange, sometimes uniting under the influence of Love, so that all become One, at other times again each moving apart through the hostile force of Hate." It is important, however, not to transform psychology into theology. We are not the playthings of the gods. Rather, we are engaged in an unceasing struggle to bring our individual and collective affairs under the aegis of the *Lebenstrieb.* As Norman O. Brown says, life against death (Brown, 1959).

8.

So much for *The Science of Logic* and ontology; we come next to *The Phenomenology* and epistemology.

The Phenomenology is intended to be an immanent critique of all thinking that presupposes the disjunction of the knowing subject and the object to be known—of thought and being, reason and reality, subjective certainty and objective truth. All arguments based on this presupposition, Hegel contends, are self-negating. When they are systematically developed they undergo a dialectical inversion. *The Phenomenology* permits us to observe this process and to see that it is not merely negative. Each dialectical inversion is a stage in a larger process of conceptual development, in which the presupposition of subject–object disjunction is undermined and eventually the underlying subject–object identity is brought to light.

The core of Hegel's argument may be represented this way:

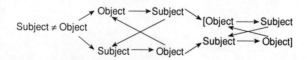

We begin by assuming or asserting the disjunction of Subject and Object. We then observe the successive unfolding of mirror-image processes. In the one Object becomes Subject, in the other Subject becomes Object. These two processes do not, however, simply pass away. They yield instead a determinate Subject–Object relationship, or structure. This structure is the process itself, grasped as a totality.

9.

We take up first the stance of Consciousness, in which the presupposition is that we wish to know the object as such, without any addition or contamination by the knowing subject. The simplest claim is that sensuous experience yields the truth, that the truth is nothing other than the unmediated object of sensation. This is Sense-Certainty. When we examine sensuous experience, however, we find that (1) it does not yield certain knowledge but only fleeting impressions and (2) when we attempt to stabilize it, it reduces to the empty universals of space, time, and existence (Here/There, Now/Then, This/That), forms of knowledge that fail to contain a sensuous content.

We then attempt to combine the universal with the shifting particularities of sensation. In Perception, we claim to know a Thing with properties or attributes. Here arises the problem of the One and the Many, which Consciousness fails to solve. The Thing is one, its properties are many. But each property is a singularity and the Thing, consisting of these properties, is manifold. Consciousness, attempting to save the objectivity of knowledge, blames this problem on itself. But interpreting perception as subjective remedies nothing. Instead, one merely finds the problem repeated on the side of the subject.

Consciousness, not yet convinced that it itself constitutes the object of knowledge, advances to the level of the Understanding. It will solve the problem of the One and the Many by *explaining* things, by positing underlying forces as the determinants of phenomena. But the same or similar problems recur, until at last it becomes clear that, behind the veil of appearances, Consciousness necessarily finds itself, its own mental activity. In its attempt to remove the taint of subjectivity from the object, it removes instead the object itself and is left with its own subjectivity.

10.

In the experience of Consciousness, Hegel offers us a dialectical and critical conception of prototheoretical knowing. We now come to the experience of Self-Consciousness, in which the subject is the real object of knowledge. At the same time, Hegel develops a dialectical and critical

conception of action. Thus the two sides of praxis—theory and practice
—begin to emerge.

In its first embodiment Self-Consciousness is mere Self-Certainty, the
claim that the truth is in the subject and not in the object. Hence the subject
or self attempts to establish itself absolutely and exclusively through successive interactions with sensuous objects that are not subjects (life and
desire); other sensuous/supersensuous subjects (the battle for recognition, lordship and bondage); and a supersensuous Being (stoicism, skepticism, and the Unhappy Consciousness). These attempts at establishing
the absolute dominion of the subject fail, and worse than fail. Each of
the three engagements depletes the subject and confers reality upon the
object [Subject → Object]. The process ends in complete self-abnegation.

11.

What are we to conclude from these two phases of phenomenological experience? On the one hand, the truth is not in the object but rather
in the subject; on the other, the truth is not in the subject but in the object.
The argument seems to move in a circle, bringing us back to the position
from which we began. But that is not the whole story. Hegel (1807) contends that just as the object was subjectified in the phase of Consciousness, so the subject is objectified in the phase of Self-Consciousness:

> There [formerly] appeared two aspects, one after the other: one in
> which the essence and the True had for consciousness the determinate-
> ness of *being* [Consciousness], the other in which it had the determi-
> nateness of being only *for consciousness* [Self-Consciousness]. But the
> two reduced themselves to a single truth, viz. that what *is*, or the
> in-itself, only *is* in so far as it is *for* consciousness, and what is *for* con-
> sciousness is also in *itself* or has intrinsic being. (pp. 140–141)

The explicit statement of this truth is the *categorical relationship* of subject
and object. This is what Hegel terms Reason (*Vernunft*).

Consciousness has grasped that reason and reality are one; but it does
not yet comprehend the dialectical process through which this compre-
hension has arisen, and which was represented figuratively in our diagram. It is we who observe the process that recognize its dialectical nature. We can see that the truth is not in the subject *or* in the object, but
rather in the double transition from object to subject and subject to object: [Object → Subject / Subject → Object]. We recognize that there is a
third term latent in the dyad of subject and object, namely, the linkage
between them. But not merely a linkage, not merely the verb joining

subject and object; the point is rather that the truth is the interaction in substance and as a whole. It is not *either* subjective *or* objective, but rather the *interpenetrating* of subject and object, the process in which each *comes-to-be* the other as it *ceases-to-be* itself.

12.

With Reason, Hegel has established the first principle of philosophical science but only, as it were, in principle. Consciousness has become Self-Consciousness, and a self-consciousness that includes the world of consciousness within itself. But to this point the self is (1) individual (albeit intersubjective) and (2) finite. So long as it is thus limited, the identification of being and knowing is incomplete. Accordingly Hegel has the self-conscious, rational individual confront first the historical world (the domain of spiritual life) and then the religious transfiguration of historical experience. In the former instance, self-consciousness universalizes itself in time and space, in the latter it overcomes its finitude. Finally, in Absolute Knowledge the infinite content of knowledge revealed by religion is reformed conceptually and, in the mode of recollection, each of the preceding stages of phenomenological development is absorbed as a moment in the infinite self-relation of being and knowing.

13.

It is evident that Hegel's dialectical interpretation of the subject–object relationship amounts to a reconceptualization of how it is possible to know anything whatsoever, a reconceptualization which seems to me both persuasive as critique and useful as modality of construction. This does not mean, however, that we must accept his conception of absolute or totalized knowledge. Although we are not truly entitled to discard it without taking up his argument in detail, we may note several problems that suggest that dialectical reasoning does not lead us to the Absolute.

• The phenomenological process originates in the critique of Sense-Certainty. Let's grant that Hegel demonstrates the instability of sensuous experience and the disjunctive relationship between that experience and the conceptual universals with which it is necessarily associated. Then it has been shown that Sense-Certainty does not satisfy even minimal epistemic standards. If such standards are to be met, one must go beyond it. But, first, there is no necessity in such an advance. One must posit an epistemic urge of some kind, a desire to know the truth, in order for the next steps to be taken; which is to say, the inquiry rests upon a contingency. Second, the advance takes place on the supposition that instability is inherent in sensuousness, not just in the relationship of the knowing subject to sensuousness. This being the case, then instability can be overcome only if knowledge is purged of sensuous content. There are such forms of knowledge, and legitimately so. But it is clear on the face of it that they are partial. Hence Hegel is left with a nasty either/or: Either knowledge is not sensuous, in which case it might be stable but is necessarily incomplete; or knowledge is (more nearly) complete but necessarily instable.

• If the dialectical advance is to be totalizing, then each transition in it must be complete. The first term must become the second without leaving a residue of itself behind. This seems to be Hegel's claim when, for example, Consciousness, in finding its own operations in the object of Understanding, replaces the object with itself. But the most that can be claimed in this and other such instances is that the subject finds itself in the object, that knowledge of objects is necessarily mediated by the epistemic activity of the subject. It cannot be claimed that the objectivity of the object has been completely surpassed or sublated. Hence Kant might object that here and elsewhere in *The Phenomenology* a semblance of epistemological self-containment is covering over a more problematical relationship between a conceptual dialectic and the object being conceptualized.

• The preceding might be termed the spatial critique of Hegel's argument. There is also a temporal criticism. For even if we grant the totality of a particular dialectical transition, or even that *The Phenomenology* is a totalization of knowledge, time marches on and we must march with it. Hence, as Sartre correctly argues, knowledge cannot be detached from practical and theoretical projects. Only by limiting knowledge to retrospect can one pretend to complete it.

• Any truth Hegel brings to light by the phenomenological process is dependent upon the process itself. Even if no internal failures of development could be found, it might be the case that the inquiry had been misframed. What if truth is not adequately problematized in subject–object terms? Then even if Hegel satisfactorily conjoins subject and object, the truth might still elude him. Or even if the framing were adequate for his time, it might not be adequate for ours.

• When we look again at our representation of phenomenological development, we note that three or more epistemological perspectives are offered: the problematical initial position, the double mirroring middle term, and the structured resolution of the problem. If the claim to totalization is to be sustained, Hegel must (1) absolutize each transition; (2) privilege the epistemic value of the third position; and (3) imagine a resolution from which no further development is possible. It is more nearly the truth, however, to say that we characteristically occupy the middle position, from which we look backward with a sense of lost simplicity and forward with an anxious uncertainty.

• In sum: If dialectical reason is genuinely to engage reality, then there can be no totalization of knowledge; if there is to be a totalization of knowledge, then there can be no genuine engagement with reality. Hegel totalizes knowledge and so disengages reality. But not completely: Like Marcuse, Hegel performs a dialectical glissade. He simultaneously engages reality and veers away from it.

14.

The Phenomenology was intended to be a solution to the problem of epistemology, that is, of the problematical relationship between the knowing subject and the object to be known. The criterion of truth is: Subject (Reason) = Object (Reality). Hegel claims to have secured this identity by an employment of dialectical reason in which, ultimately, negativity is reduced to a *"difference* which is no *difference,* or only a difference of what is *self-same. . . . "* But as we noted early on, this position excludes quite arbitrarily its dialectical complement, the sameness which is no sameness, or the self-sameness of what is only a difference. If both sides of the dialectical relationship are taken seriously, then it is necessarily an open-ended interpenetrating of subject and object, not a closed and completed identification of one with the other.

Or think of it this way. The "reality" that emerges from our critique of Hegel's ontology is inherently unstable and indeterminate; and there is nothing in "reason" that transcends this ontological or existential uncertainty. Hence the closest we come to an absolute truth-claim is the proposition that being, knowing, and the relationship between them can never be absolute.

C. Going Under: The Problematics of Recognition

1.

Our critique of Hegel's treatment of Being and Nothing in *The Science of Logic* yielded a dialectical conception of life and development. Our critique of knowing in *The Phenomenology* yielded a dialectical conception of theorizing. In the process, the speculative excesses of Hegelian dialectics have dropped away. We have returned to the world of human experience, a world in which life-processes may involve regression, fixation, and fragmentation, and in which theorizing is itself a life-process.

We come now to questions of action and practice. Again we put Hegelian conceptions to our own use, this time the problematics of recognition in the fourth chapter of *The Phenomenology*.

There are other, and seemingly more economical, ways of proceeding. But an engagement with Hegel on these issues seems almost unavoidable. Jessica Benjamin argues that they are paradigmatic for feminist theory, they are vital to Fanon's analysis of racism, and the concept of desire (through the influence of Lacan) has worked its way into diverse strands of psychoanalytic-marxist theorizing. Most of all, Hegel's conception of recognition is extraordinarily synoptic. It presents, in a highly condensed form, issues that any critical social theory must confront. Consequently bypassing Hegel's treatment of recognition would be a false economy.

2.

In both *The Phenomenology* and *The Philosophy of Mind* (that is, the section on spiritual life in the *Encyclopaedia of the Philosophical Sciences*), Hegel takes Consciousness to the point where it becomes its own object—to the stage of Self-Consciousness, symbolized by "I = I". In both treatments he posits a three-stage development of self-consciousness, from (1) appetite and desire through (2) the battle for recognition with its immediate consequence in the relationship of lordship and bondage to (3) the universality or freedom of self-consciousness. But the content of the third stage varies.

In the later work freedom is identified with mutual recognition. When each self recognizes itself in its other and the other in itself, when "I am immediately reflected into the other person and, conversely, in relating myself to the other I am immediately self-related," the result is both mutual recognition and the freedom of self-consciousness (Hegel, 1830, p. 177). This mediated unity of self and other "forms the substance of ethical life, namely, of the family, of sexual love (there this unity has the form of particularity), of patriotism, this willing of the general aims and interests of the State, of love toward God . . ." (*ibid.*). Conversely (we would add), failing such mutual recognition, social life devolves into a tenuously regulated war of all against all. In this regard our question is, under what conditions if any can stages (1) and (2) result in (3)?

In *The Phenomenology* the freedom of self-consciousness is given the content of Stoicism, Skepticism, and the Unhappy Consciousness. The position of the Unhappy Consciousness is one of painful alienation from and yearning for union with an Unchangeable Being, the Infinite One. Here our question is: What is the connection between this spiritual bondage and the prior relationship of lordship and bondage?

3.

As we remember from the discussion of desire in the preceding chapter, the self for Hegel is at first a psychophysiological organism oriented toward the satisfaction of natural desires. It is characterized by the "selfishness of merely destructive appetite" (1830, p. 170). It eats, is physically satisfied, but finds itself hungry once again and so dependent upon the objects of its desire. No lasting identity between itself as subject and its object is created; neither is its independence and freedom established. It is rather enslaved by its appetites.

Hence from one perspective "self-consciousness is caught up in the monotonous alternation ad infinitum of appetite and satisfaction, in the perpetual relapse into subjectivity from its objectification" (*ibid.*). At the same time, however, self-consciousness "has given itself the determination of otherness toward itself"—it has acted, the cycle of desire and satisfaction is its own doing—and "this Other it has filled with the 'I', has made out of something self-less a free self-like object, another 'I'" (*ibid.*). The self confronts another self and, in so doing, is confronting itself.

4.

There is an interesting ambiguity in this account of the emergence of mental life and protosociability. If one self confronts another, there must have been another self already in existence undergoing a parallel process of development. Hegel appears, however, to materialize a second self out of the experience of a first self with a merely sensuous object. Yet no matter how many times we eat apples, even when we pluck them from the tree of knowledge, the next time they are still apples. Hegel was not psychotic. He did not believe that apples were capable of subjectivity. So what is going on?

Perhaps the best approach to this question is to view Hegel as conflating three conceptions of individuality. There are, first, traces of liberal individualism, in which social theorizing begins with the experience of a self-subsisting and self-determining monad. Such a monad, as Marx argues most forcefully, is mythological. Human selfhood cannot be constituted in isolation. Nonetheless, from one perspective, Hegel seems to be telling the story of two isolated individuals who meet as strangers and, as we shall see, first interact as enemies.

Second, there is the conception of selfhood implied by the formula, "I = I". Here we have two selves-in-one, or a statement of identity. For Hegel the copula implies a difference as well: The self comes-to-be a determinate being by ceasing-to-be a merely immediate one. It is negatively self-determined. But from this perspective, there is only one individual involved.

Although it is very abstract, this is a meaningful way of framing the issue of personal identity. Empirically, however, it presupposes interaction with an other. At least developmentally, we are quite incapable of being the mirrors of our own selfhood. Hence the third conception of selfhood, that of relation and interpenetration. A self becomes itself through interaction with another self. This might be represented: "I = I" ↔ "I = I". The capacity for negative self-relation ("I = I") is a function of social interaction (↔).

Hegel's account of the origins of selfhood blends these three meanings. Hence its ambiguity. In part, this is the ambiguity of idealism, in which purely mental experiences, self-reflections, are treated as objectivities. In this regard transformational criticism is apposite. We must stage the drama of selfhood not just in an abstracted life-world but in the concrete real world. Our account, unlike Hegel's, must begin from the third conception, from the recognition that we do not exist alone and that we individuate through interaction with each other. But the ambiguity is not just an idealist misconception. The experience of personal identity contains it. We are self-determining and determined through other selves, and, when overwhelmed by this ambiguity and the anxiety it engenders, we sometimes retreat to the monadic fantasy.

5.

We may put monadology behind us. Each self confronts an Other. Each desires recognition and neither is willing to grant it. The relationship is, Hegel contends, precisely self-contradictory. The formal statement "I = I" has two, opposed meanings: I am a discrete, self-contained individual, who finds in any other individual a limitation upon and a negation of selfhood and freedom; I am a self in the same sense and only insofar as the Other is also a self, only insofar as we partake and recognize ourselves as partaking of the "universal essence common to all men" (*ibid.*, p. 171). The battle for recognition and its sequel involve the working-out and resolution of this contradiction.

More simply (perhaps misleadingly) stated, the two selves are in a scarcity situation: There is not enough recognition to go around. Either the selves are narcissistic, in fact pathologically narcissistic, so that any honor or prestige accorded to another involves a diminution of one's self-worth. Or recognition is a signifier of material scarcity, so that the battle is a variation on the first phase of the process: Eat or be eaten. These alternatives are not mutually exclusive, but rather reinforcing. If we imagine the contest taking place in a state of nature, it is one in which man is a wolf to man.

In the event, the two selves engage in the battle. One wins, one loses. If the loser dies, no further development occurs. If the loser surrenders, he becomes the physical and spiritual possession of the winner and an extension of the winner's selfhood. He grants the recognition he formerly withheld. He becomes a bondsman; the other is his lord.

Hegel takes up the relationship of lordship and bondage from each side. At the one extreme, the truth of the lord's consciousness is really "the servile consciousness of the bondsman" (Hegel, 1807, p. 117). The bondsman is the object in which the lord sees himself reflected. The lord and master may or may not be content with this show of recognition—and with having his material needs satisfied for him. In any case Hegel considers him no further.

The bondsman's experience has three aspects that enable him to develop beyond the stage of self-consciousness achieved by the lord. First, "servitude has the lord for its essential reality" (*ibid*.). The bondsman's other, his not-self, is the independent consciousness of the lord. Initially he does not recognize himself in the lord. But unlike the lord who is confronted with the image of the bondsman, the bondsman has before him an apparently autonomous self. Second, he has experienced the power of selfhood in himself, in the inverse form of absolute dread:

> For this consciousness has been fearful, not of this or that particular thing or just at odd moments, but its whole being has been seized with dread: for it has experienced the fear of death the absolute Lord. In that experience it has been quite unmanned, has trembled in every fibre of its being, and everything solid and stable has been shaken to its foundations. (*ibid*.)

The bondsman has felt the force of "absolute negativity," of "the absolute melting away of everything stable." Thus he sees the power of self-consciousness externally as the lord and feels it internally as dread. And third, in working the bondsman puts an end to the apparent autonomy of the sensuous world while simultaneously preserving what is of lasting value in it. Work succeeds in accomplishing what sensuous desire could not. In the instance of the lord's realization of his desire there was, to be sure, an "unalloyed feeling of self" (*ibid*.). But just because it was purely subjective, "this satisfaction . . . [was] itself only a fleeting one. . . ." It lacked "the side of objectivity and permanence." But work is "desire held in check, fleetingness staved off" (*ibid*.). In working, the mindless cycle of sensuous life and desire is superseded, sublated. The bondsman discovers that the thing he shapes "does not become other than himself through being made external to him; for it is precisely this shape that is his pure being-for-self, which in this externality is seen by him to be the truth" (*ibid.*). And so through "this rediscovery of himself by himself, the bondsman realizes it is precisely in his work wherein he seemed to have only an alienated existence that he acquires a mind of his own" (*ibid.*, p. 119). He is, in this subjective sense, free.

6.

There are various objections that can be brought forward against this depiction of bondage, not the least of which is that it dignifies and confers a kind of human value on the most dehumanizing and often brutal of social relationships. And whatever developmental significance it might have is entirely contingent, not necessary. But for our purposes the major point is that the relationship does not result in mutual recognition. The bondsman gains a capacity for self-recognition, and so an indifference to the external world. The lord has no reason to develop even that far. Neither of them is under any self-given imperative to grant recognition to the other. Beginning as strangers, they end as enemies.

Thus Hegel draws for us a picture of primary alienation and animosity. He can posit a third stage in which recognition is freely given by equally free individuals. And he can fairly claim that only such "universal self-consciousness" resolves the initial internal contradiction in the "I = I". But Hegel gives us no reason to think that the original "selfishness of merely destructive appetite" is completely transcended. As Merold Westphal argues, "The original demand for recognition is unmet because each individual is too concerned with winning recognition to be able to give it. There is no love, only the demand to be loved ..." (Westphal, 1979, pp. 226–227). Each self is too poor to give recognition until it receives it. Or perhaps "too poor" objectively: A hungry man is an angry man. Either way, the process of recognition turns in a vicious circle.

If this line of argument is accepted, it follows that Hegel's political philosophy is built upon the unsolved problem of recognition. As J. M. Bernstein claims, critically interpreted Hegelian history "is experienced as a series of displacements in which self-consciousness fails to recognize itself in another self-consciousness but recognizes still its being in otherness. All history is ... a variation on the lack of reciprocity ..." (Bernstein, 1984, p. 32).

And not just Hegelian philosophy: In more or less manifest, more or less attenuated, form, lordship and bondage has been *the* paradigmatic social relationship. Not, for example, "I (male) = I (female)" and "I (white) = I (black)" but "I (male) > I (female)" and "I (white) > I (black)" signify the historical nature of human relatedness. Note, however, that hierarchy and domination are not definitional in these relationships. One can think of them in terms of mutual recognition. By contrast, "I (owner) = I (worker)" is a contradiction in terms. In this instance there can only be a semblance of mutual recognition. But in all three instances social transformation is required if mutual recognition is to be a reality.

7.

If, on the one hand, Hegel sets up the problem of recognition in such a way that it can't be solved, on the other he factors in the variables necessary for its solution. Unlike Marx, who formulates questions of selfhood and freedom in one-sidedly objective terms and Freud, who formulates them in one-sidedly subjective ones, Hegel's problematic includes both work and desire. To be sure, these conceptual relationships are not worked through thoroughly and empirically. They are presented in lapidary and idealized form. But his conceptualization of work and desire forces us to recognize their interpenetration. Consequently the transformational criticism of his philosophy leads us to both Marxism and psychoanalysis—and forces us to recognize *their* interpenetration.

We return to this point in the next chapter.

8.

Thus far we have examined the phenomenology of self-certainty in its protopolitical aspect, that is, under the aegis of power and as signifying social domination. In *The Phenomenology* the quest of Consciousness for self-certainty continues, beyond or outside of social relationships, into a domain of protoreligious experience. Here we will find (to paraphrase Marx) the inverted consciousness of an inverted world and, fatefully, the beginnings of moral development.

The consciousness that has known both lordship and bondage has achieved only a limited kind of freedom and self-certainty. It has demonstrated that it is a thinking being—that it exists and knows itself to exist. It has, in its own way, arrived at the Cartesian *cogito*. But its relationship to the world of life, desire, and work is simply negative. It has withdrawn from the world into itself while leaving the world itself unchanged. It has become stoic:

> This consciousness ... has a negative attitude toward the lord and bonds-
> man relationship. As lord, it does not have its truth in the bondsman,
> nor as bondsman its truth in the lord's will and his service; on the con-
> trary, whether on the throne or in chains, in the utter dependence of
> individual existence, its aim is to be free. (Hegel, 1807, p. 121)

Consciousness maintains an attitude of indifference to the world but, in so doing, deprives itself of any objective content.

Because Consciousness is or has the power of thought, however, it can go further: It can and does demonstrate the nullity of the world. Instead of being indifferent to the world, it becomes skeptical of any claim to conjoin reality and reason. As this skeptical consciousness, it displays the world as self-contradictory, as dialectical unrest and disorder. In sophistical fashion it shows that everything is or becomes its opposite, while claiming for itself the status of self-sameness. But just as the bonds-man comes to recognize himself in and as his work, so skepticism comes to see itself in its object and operations. It itself is the "absolute dialec-tical unrest" (*ibid.*, p. 124), the oscillation between the polarities of absolute self-sameness and absolute self-opposition. Everything comes together in it and everything falls apart again. It is, and knows itself to be, "internally contradictory": "It is the dual consciousness of itself, as self-liberating, unchangeable and self-identical, and as self-bewildering and self-perverting, and it is the awareness of this self-contradictory nature of itself" (*ibid.*, p. 126). It becomes what Hegel terms the Unhappy Consciousness.

The Unhappy Consciousness contains both the self-sameness of stoicism and the dismemberment of skepticism. It experiences these two forms of consciousness within itself, that is, as internal contradiction or an inner state of alienation. But it cannot contain the contradiction and so it dirempts or (to use a psychoanalytic expression) splits into the extremes. It identifies itself as "self-bewildering and self-perverting" (the content of skepticism) and assigns free and universal selfhood (the con-tent of stoicism) to an Unchangeable Being. It then aims at establishing its unity with this most objective of objects. This can only be accomplished by self-abnegation. The selfhood it so fervently sought and so proudly asserted now stands between it and the ultimate truth. It self-consciously turns its power of negation back upon itself.

The self-abnegation of consciousness begins in an attitude of devo-tion to the Unchangeable Being: "We have here . . . the inward move-ment of the pure heart which *feels* itself, but itself as agonizingly self-divided, the movement of an infinite yearning . . ." (*ibid.*, p. 131). But yearning for unity does not produce it.

Consciousness next proceeds from attitude to action. It desires, works, and enjoys, while giving thanks to the Unchangeable for the satisfaction it obtains. Yet "even its *giving of thanks*, in which it acknowledges the other extreme as the essential Being and counts itself nothing, is its *own* act . . . " (*ibid.*, p. 134). It has not truly renounced itself.

Finally, therefore, consciousness surrenders its most precious acquisition, its freedom, the mind of its own. It gives over to a mediator (a minister or priest) "its freedom of decision" and so, too, the "responsibility for its own action." It now has "the certainty of having truly divested itself of its 'I'" (*ibid.*, p. 137). But in the form of the mediator, the affirmative relationship between consciousness and the Unchangeable Being has come into view. For the mediator is an "I", a self-conscious being, in whom the extremes of the Unchangeable and the alienated consciousness are joined. The mediator is the "middle term" in a "syllogism whose extremes appeared as held absolutely asunder." Moreover, the mediating consciousness is, in itself, directly aware of both extremes, and of connecting them. Thus the "hitherto negative relation to otherness turns round into a positive relation" (*ibid.*, p. 139). And this two-sided, negative and positive, process of self-mediation—subjectivity that has passed through an alien objectivity and returned to itself—is the freedom of self-consciousness.

9.

If we give ourselves a certain amount of interpretive license, we may say the scene has shifted from the outer world to the inner one. The stoic withdraws from social interaction, devalues it, attempts to realize itself within itself. The skeptic, within the boundaries of this withdrawal, attacks the world, fragments it, and then is attacked by it in turn. With an unrestricted license, we might even believe we are in the company of the body without organs (stoicism) and the coupling/uncoupling of the desiring machines (skepticism)—that we have entered a domain of mental experience dominated by the paranoid–schizoid position.

Be that as it may, Hegel's analysis takes us to another level of mental development, and one with its own ambiguities.

On the one hand, the Unhappy Consciousness is characterized by a painful state of mind in which the goodness of the object or other is acknowledged. There is a kind of love here, or at least a yearning for wholeness, along with a willingness to preserve the goodness of the object by taking all badness upon the self. One might be tempted to say that the Unhappy Consciousness has advanced, or at least is advancing, from the paranoid–schizoid to the depressive position. And when it develops the capacity for self-mediation, when it goes beyond the either/ or of self/not-self, then it has also solved the problem of recognition. *The self is self-recognizing, in and through the other.*

On the other hand, this "advance" could be viewed as an introjected version of lordship and bondage, an internalization of domination, a moralization of brute power. Indeed, the Unhappy Consciousness is far more surely enslaved than the bondsman. The bondsman has been forced to surrender his selfhood, but the Unhappy Consciousness surrenders willingly. The mediator—priest, political leader . . . Deleuze and Guattari would add, psychoanalyst—provides only a semblance of recognition. The Unhappy Consciousness is false consciousness.

It is evident, I think, that the second interpretation does not necessarily follow from the first. Hence it would be a mistake to reduce the experience of the Unhappy Consciousness to ideology or slave morality. But for our purposes it, and indeed Hegel's treatment of self-certainty as a whole, is best seen as a dialectic of domination.

10.

In the subsequent stages of our inquiry, Hegel's analysis of recognition will prove to be of substantive value. But for the moment we may consider its methodological implications.

From our perspective the advance from life and desire through lordship and bondage to the Unhappy Consciousness appears as a movement from action through practice to thought. The activity of merely sensuous appetite is not yet a practice. It is instinctive, spontaneous, and unpatterned. Lordship and bondage involves distinct practices, patterns of activity that count as experience, and from which it is possible to learn. Stoicism, skepticism, and the Unhappy Consciousness involve thoughtful relationships between self and other—but ones in which there is a greater or lesser alienation from practical action.

Each of these modalities of activity is dialectical. Each, indeed, is ontologically dialectical, that is, a process of becoming, or of development through negation. In contrast to the conception of ontology previously articulated, however, here development involves will and intention. It is purposeful even when it is instinctive.

Thus we emerge with four dimensions of dialectical activity: ontology in the general sense, the natural world viewed as a process of development and as the field of human interaction; spontaneous (conscious but not yet self-conscious) human activity; practice, patterned human activity; and thought, which may lead on to theory.

And a fifth: When the alienation of theory and practice is overcome—when we self-consciously orient ourselves toward realizing our theories in practice, and when we seek to learn the lessons that both successful and unsuccesful practice involves—then we have reached the standpoint of praxis.

11.

These dimensions of dialectical activity may be represented as follows:

This diagram represents the dialectical relationship of theory and practice. The relationship originates in the interaction of human beings with each other and the natural world (the interpenetration of natural and human activity). It culminates in praxis, the self-conscious unity of theory and practice. As such, it prefigures important aspects of the anthropology to be developed in the next chapter.

The scientific, communicative, and transformational modalities of praxis specified in the first part of the chapter fall within the limits of this model. They particularize our dialectical conception to discrete fields of inquiry and action.

The problematics of recognition fall within the epistemological category of transformational praxis. They might even be viewed as paradigmatic for the emancipatory instance of transformational praxis. Hence their importance for psychoanalytic-marxism. They provide a synoptic statement of the set of problems we are trying to solve.

CHAPTER 6

We Are the Problem
We Are Trying to Solve

A. Anthropology/History

1.

The methodological model of abstraction/concretion presupposes the desirability of first articulating empirically reduced or thinned out concepts and then using them to build up more complex conceptual structures. This assumption can be challenged, but at a minimum such an approach makes evident the limits and limitations of a theory. It helps to counter the tendency toward unrecognized contradiction and theoretical incoherence.

The most abstract of concepts are Being and Nothing, then ceasing-to-be and coming-to-be. One can attempt a step-by-step return to the concrete from these notions, as Hegel did; but we are only social theorists, not philosophers (or cosmologists). We are concerned with the coming-to-be and ceasing-to-be of human beings, not of metaphysical ones. Hence our need is to be as clear as possible about our own nature.

2.

For our purposes the term "anthropology" means knowledge of human nature, or of the human species qua species. It aims at providing answers to two questions. What do we and don't we have in common with other, nonhuman, species? What do we have in common with each other that permits the usage of the name or signifier, "human"?

The second question might also be stated this way: What are the necessary conditions for the possibility of any human experience whatsoever, the conditions without which human experience is inconceivable?

Note that "nature" does not mean either "biological" or "immutable." It means rather the distinctive attributes of the human species, whatever these might be.

3.

Anthropological concepts are generated by abstracting from all the particularities of human experience. We disregard any- and everything that distinguishes one person, event, time, or place from another. Human nature is what is left over. It is largely a matter of indifference whether we think of it as an essence or a residual category.

Thus anthropological concepts are universals, and quite empty ones at that. But not entirely empty: They are necessarily inflected with phenomenality. They arise by abstraction from different historical and cultural contexts. They are always the product of particular theoretical and practical interests or purposes. And there are alternative theoretical paths to knowledge of human nature that also partially determine the content of the concept.

For example: Anthropological inquiry can originate in different epistemic domains and result in correspondingly different conceptions of human nature. Thus in the natural sciences the dominant trend might be signified "body > mind," while in the cultural sciences the relationship typically is reversed.

Or consider the two transformational praxes with which we are most concerned. Marx's knowledge of human nature was based upon the analysis of actions, while Freud's derived from an analysis of intentions. Marx's method, moreover, was historical, while Freud's was fundamentally introspective. Their approaches differed with respect to both the object and the method of analysis. Their anthropologies diverged in parallel fashion.

Thus we see that, although conceptions of human nature are universals, there is no universal conception of human nature.

Yet the human species exists in reality. It really did develop along some lines and not along others. Consequently, as epistemologically awkward as it may be to say it this way, knowledge of human nature must be distinguished from human nature itself. We must content ourselves with locutions like "this is human nature as we have come to know it."

4.

There are three and only three locations for anthropological concepts in social theory:

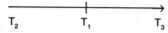

The line represents a time/space continuum, that is, history—the history of the planet. This does not mean that the planet has only one kind of history. It does mean that there is a history of the planet that includes all other histories. This general history is linear in the specific sense that, empirically, events in time/space are irreversible.

T_1 is the present, or a present, time. At this time the human species exists, as such and in relationship to other species. And at this time we theorize about it, that is, about ourselves. The knowledge thus generated might be termed anthropology in its synchronic or spatial dimension.

Our theorizing about ourselves can be extended into the past, until we reach the point, T_2, where there is no longer an identifiable human species. T_2 signifies that time in planetary evolution where and when the human species first came-to-be. Knowledge of this evolution might be termed anthropology in its diachronic or temporal dimension.

Our theorizing about ourselves can also be extended into the future, until we reach T_3, the point where the species no longer exists, because it either has simply ceased-to-be or has evolved into another species. This might be termed anthropology in its projective dimension.

These three points are the boundary markers of our species life. They delimit the field of human interaction, of our interaction with each other and with nonhuman nature.

5.

Our species life is inherently and irreducibly historical (evolutionary and/or devolutionary). Within given synchronic, diachronic, and projective boundaries it may have a certain stability, certain persistent or recurrent features. These features may transcend or cut across particular histories such as, for example, the history of the West. But they most assuredly are not fixed or absolute.

6.

At the general level there is no opposition between history and nature. The former term merely states explicitly the temporal dimension of the latter. Nature is natural history. The history of the human species is part of natural history, albeit a distinctive part.

7.

Nonhuman nature is the setting for human activity. To a far greater extent than any other species, we transform nonhuman nature and, by so doing, transform the nature of our species activity.

To a far greater extent, and in a different manner: Our transformational activity involves the making of conscious choices, albeit choices with a wide range of unintended and often uncontrollable consequences.

8.

It is important to avoid the a priori and covert particularization of the term "history." Human history is the activity of the species, period. Nothing human falls outside of it.

This isn't the case with anthropology or history as discourses. These are particularizations, distinct angles of interpretive vision. Anthropology identifies parameters of human experience, always from a particular point of view. History records and interprets particular events from particular points of view. Hence for these cultural disciplines there is an inside and an outside, a subject matter proper to them and one that is beyond their scope.

Yet disciplinary boundaries are permeable, and this in a double sense. On the one hand, fields of inquiry like anthropology (either in our sense or in the more extended academic one) and history are domains of *human* knowledge, and there are times when it is discursively meaningful to articulate totalizing visions of human affairs—although not all the time, to be sure.

On the other hand, our interpretive perspectives are interpenetrative. The various objects of knowledge blend into each other and hence can be seen from more than one angle. We might even go so far as to say that each modality of knowledge amounts to a perspective from which to interpret the whole. Not so far, however, as to collapse the whole into a part, as when Freud reduces all knowledge to natural science or psychology.

9.

It is equally important to avoid the tendency of valorizing the term "human," as in equating "fully human" with something good. I am not here referring to the ambiguity or relativity of ethical valuations. The point is rather that, unless one reduces "human" and "goodness" to a tautology, to be fully human might be quite terrible.

10.

In short: Anthropological discourse is about the natural/historical limits of what we are, have been, and might be—whether or not we like it.

B. Human Nature as Such

1.

If, in the manner of zoologists or primate anthropologists, we were to observe a small group of human beings interacting with each other and the nonhuman environment, we might note the following things about them.

All but the very young or disabled among them are capable of erect posture and bipedal mobility, which frees the forelimbs (arms and hands) for other uses. They have prehensile grip, which also facilitates manual activity.

There are two sexes, but sexual interaction is not determined by a cycle of heat and rut. Heterosexual intercourse is necessary for the reproduction of the species, but it is not the sole modality of sexual interaction.

They are mammals and nurse their young like other mammals. But the young remain in a relationship of dependence to adults for an unusually extended period of time.

For their survival they rely less on instinct and physical prowess and more on mentation than do other species.

Anatomical examination would reveal that this latter quality is made possible by a highly developed cerebral cortex.

2.

From observation to imagination. Abstracting from the historical manifold of human experience, we reach the smallest interactive and reproductive empirical unit, a man and a woman. We then ask, what do these two creatures have in common?

There is a slightly more concrete and likewise a slightly less elegant way of formulating the question: What are the common attributes of all the creatures whose activity constitutes the T_1-T_2-T_3 manifold?

By asking one or the other of these questions, we arrive at the Human Individual. The Human Individual is an abstraction. It has the same position in anthropology as Being does in metaphysics. It is an anthropological fiction or, better, a shorthand, an abbreviated notation. In referring to the individual in this universalized fashion, we will keep it in mind that there must always be more than one of us.

3.

A grim fairy tale. Nuclear Armageddon. One person survives. S/he is the Last Person on Earth. Here we have the only possible empirical instance of the Human Individual, and a very short story indeed.

4.

It's important to remember three of the constraints on the anthropological thought-experiment we are about to conduct. First, we take as given the problematic and project of human emancipation in its late twentieth-century incarnation. Second, the inquiry falls within the epistemological category of transformational praxis. Third, we are attempting to establish an anthropological groundwork for a psychoanalytic-marxist theory. These three constraints successively narrow the truth-claims that attach to our concepts. They define our Rhodes, which we have no intention of overleaping.

5.

Within these limits, we may attempt a phenomenological reduction.[1] Assume as a starting point the *conscious interactions* of human individuals with each other and the nonhuman environment. This starting point is common to both Marxism and psychoanalysis; and consciousness—meaning for the moment linguistically mediated action—is an identifiable human characteristic.

Next, by following the lead of each theory, we attempt to get beneath or behind consciousness. That is, we reduce each theory to its simplest concepts. In the case of Marxism this concept is unambiguously *work* or *labor*. The psychoanalytic case is far more ambiguous. But, so as not to unduly prolong this particular exercise, we will use *desire* as the signifier for the simplest, distinctively psychoanalytic, object of inquiry.

The phenomenological question is then: What—if anything—can serve as a common ground for these simple terms?

It is easiest to think about this question ontogenetically. As adults of the species, we can distinguish between work and desire in theory as well as in practice. A yearning to merge with someone we love is a desire, clearing rocks and weeds from a plot of land is work. Psychoanalysis theorizes the one, Marxism theorizes the other. The theories are more distinct categorically than the activities, but that need not concern us at present.

An ontogenetic reduction or regression brings us to the earliest point at which such a distinction is made by the individual her/himself. Perhaps this is when there is a conscious or at least clear perceptual awareness of the difference between a parental demand and an infantile impulse. Work is then what one must do, desire is what one wants to do. But whatever may be the case, there is a time before the distinction exists and one after it has come into existence.

Think, for example, of a baby nursing at its mother's breast. *We* might say that work, indeed vital work, is being performed, by both mother and child. A literally vital need is being satisfied. And *we* might add that not just work is being performed, that the interaction can also be interpreted from the standpoint of desire. And, following Freud, we might even link the one interpretation to the other: The gratification of desire has an anaclitic relationship to the satisfaction of need. But the infant knows nothing of this. For it, there is one thing happening that (we hope) is predominantly pleasurable.

If the nursing experience indistinguishably involves both work and desire, then it is something other than work *and* desire. To give it a familiar name, we may term it *sensuous*. Negatively, sensuousness is an experience in which work and desire are not differentiated. It is the immediacy of which they are mediations. Or, to extend the negative definition, sensuous experience is the immediacy underlying the distinctions between mind and body, and between self and other. It lies behind all three distinctions genetically and underlies all three structurally.

One might object that neonatal experience contains significant perceptual elements, that even here there is both sameness and difference (Stern, 1985). Granted: We must not project the blank spots in our knowledge of infantile experience onto the experience itself. Conversely, we must not impose the relatively stabilized and cognized distinctions of later childhood upon infancy and neonatal life. And if we complete the ontogenetic reduction by taking it to the level of intrauterine experience, we finally approach a point at which "perception" says too much. We then have something like a flux and flow, a rhythm, of sensations, a fullness of being in which there is no lack, which is not the empty Being of Hegelian metaphysics, which contains neither desiring-machines nor bodies without organs—and which we outgrow.

The preceding analysis may be represented this way:

In our discussion we proceeded from conscious interaction to the opposed modalities of work and desire, and from this opposition to sensuous interaction. At the conscious level human interactions are markedly different from those of other species, while at the sensuous level they resemble them. Work and desire link and partake of the extremes. We are not the only species in which work and desire exist as distinct modalities of interaction. We are the only species that is conscious of and consciously molds not only work and desire but sensuousness as well.

6.

Because this conceptual figure is fundamental for the remainder of our work, several remarks are in order.

• If we read the diagram from left to right, then it can represent both a diachronic and a synchronic development, that is, both the unfolding and the structuring of a self. We then have a dialectical representation of human development, in which earliest is deepest.

• If we read it from right to left, we not only retrace the path of our abbreviated phenomenological reduction, we also have an image of both regression in the psychoanalytic sense and the process by which consciousness reflexively transforms (in practice as well as in theory) its own becoming.

• Although I used ontogenetic examples in explicating the figure, I am most certainly not claiming an anthropological priority for individual development. Rather the figure is intended to be indifferently ontogenetic and phylogenetic, as well as indifferently intrasubjective and intersubjective; which is to say, it is more abstract than either of these distinctions.

• The figure is *methodologically* analogous to the concept of the commodity that we find at the beginning of *Capital, 1*. The commodity is the "elementary form" of wealth in capitalist societies (Marx, 1867, p. 125), hence also the elementary concept in Marx's critical political economic theory. Marx arrived at the concept analytically or by regression; in *Capital, 1* he unfolds it synthetically or by progression. In loosely parallel fashion we have arrived analytically at this empirical/conceptual figure, an anthropological universal containing or built from empirical or real elements. It depicts a "human individual as such"; it exists neither more nor less than a "commodity as such." And it is the point from which we attempt to construct a critical theory of our (still recognizably capitalist) society.

The analogy is, however, only methodological, *not theoretical*. The commodity is the characteristic product of alienated labor. It is a political–economic, not an anthropological, concept. If we were looking for theoretical parallels, then the analogy to our anthropological figure would be to the concept of species being. But in this regard we will not be content merely to look for parallels.

• Early on in *Capital, 1* Marx states that he must "perform a task never even attempted by bourgeois economics," namely, to show the origin of the money-form of commodities and thus to solve the mystery of money (*ibid.*, p. 139). Three or four pages later, having demonstrated how the abstract value of one commodity is expressed in the use value of another, he proclaimed the problem already solved. Long wind-up, short pitch.

We are in a somewhat similar position. Our anthropological task is to unify Marxism and psychoanalysis without, however, dissolving the more concrete distinctions between them. The conceptual figure (sensuous activity ↔ work/desire ↔ conscious activity) is intended to perform this task.[2] Perhaps it seems too simple or too easily conceived. The matter cannot be judged in advance, however; we must wait and see how things develop.

• The figure is parallel in significant respects to the triad of concepts that constitutes Self-Certainty in Chapter 4 of *The Phenomenology*, and to the earlier triad of concepts constituting Consciousness. Moreover, to some extent I have used these parallels as guidelines:

A) Sense-Certainty → Perception → Understanding
B) Life and Desire → Recognition → Unhappy Consciousness
C) Sensuous Activity ↔ Work/Desire ↔ Conscious Activity

(A) represents the phenomenological advance from the sensuous intuition of time and space to theoretical cognition. (B) represents the phenomenological advance from sensuous life-activity to self-reflection. Because Hegel wishes to progress from epistemologically less adequate to epistemologically more adequate instances of subject–object interaction, (A) comes before (B). If, however, one's concerns are theoretical and not philosophical, (A) and (B) can be folded together, as the object-oriented and subject-oriented dimensions of the same process of human development. This unification is represented by (C). Here we have, first, a world in which there are living beings attempting to satisfy sensuous appetites. Second, these beings are capable of developing the capacity for perception or, to be more concrete, for perceptual–motor activity. They learn, among other things, to distinguish between self and other. They are creatures of both work and desire, and they have entered into the field of recognition. Third, they become capable of reflecting upon things and themselves in both of these (now former) regards, and of acting/interacting in ways that are reflectively mediated. They have reached the level of understanding and (painful) self-understanding.

The conception we are developing was not and need not be derived from Hegel's; but, as was suggested in the last chapter, there is both an isomorphism and an aesthetic resonance between his notions and ours.

7.

If we duplicate the model, we have the problem of mutual recognition formulated at the level of anthropology:

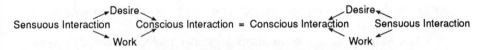

The model represents the interaction of two individuals, each of whom is a creature of sensuousness, work, desire, and consciousness. We may ask of it: Under what conditions will these individuals grant human recognition to each other, and under what conditions will their interaction be a life and death battle?

If we introduce one vital point of difference—sexual identity—we have a woman and a man. Here, too, the problem of recognition arises.

8.

The three levels of our anthropological figure structure the rest of this chapter. We will proceed from sensuousness through work and desire to consciousness. When these domains of experience have been sufficiently developed, we will have returned to the problematic signified by T_1–T_2–T_3, to the historical domain we have only apparently abandoned.

C. Sensuous Interaction

1.

In the 1844 manuscripts Marx, following Feuerbach, observes:

> Man is directly a *natural being*. As a natural being, and as a living natural being he is on the one hand furnished with *natural powers of life* —he is an *active* natural being. These forces exist in him as tenden-

Groundwork

cies and abilities—as *impulses*. On the other hand, as a natural, corporeal, sensuous, objective being he is a *suffering*, conditioned and limited creature, like plants and animals. . . . [The] *objects* of his impulses exist outside him, as *objects* independent of him; yet these objects are . . . indispensable to the manifestation and confirmation of his essential powers. (1844b, p. 115)

This statement is at once soberly empirical and exhuberantly romantic. On the empirical side, Marx quite correctly establishes sensuousness (although perhaps not in our restricted sense) as the conceptual and empirical boundary between the merely natural and the humanly natural, or as the interpenetrating of these domains. We are sensuous beings. Like all other sensuous beings, we are limited and suffering as well as empowered and active. We cannot be free in the Hegelian sense, that is, dependent upon nothing outside of ourselves. Only in imagination can there be an advance from relationship to identity.

Thus Marx grounds his anthropology in a dialectical conception of sensuous interaction, one that contains the crucial elements of activity and passivity, potency and limitation, and subject–object interpenetration. But he goes no further. He celebrates the return of sensuousness from its Hegelian exile; he does not analyze it. Most importantly, in his usage suffering is deprived of any serious implications. It means little more than to experience something passively.

Freud, by contrast, takes suffering seriously. One could even say that the experience of suffering is central to both his theory and his practice. And like Marx he theorizes both mind and body. But Marx worked dialectically while Freud thought dualistically. Hence the one can think the interpenetration of mind and body, while the other must try to think past or around a fixed, a priori, opposition of mind and body. Freud's concepts must be placed in the register of the mind *or* the body, or (like the notion of a drive) inserted into a gap between them. The possibility of conceptualizing sensuous or psychophysiological experience is all but eliminated.

Our task is determined by the limitations of these two approaches. We must do our best to take both sensuousness and suffering seriously.

2.

If we accept that in human experience earliest in time = deepest in structure, then our approach becomes genetic. If we leave to one side the evolutionary origin of the species, it becomes ontogenetic rather than phylogenetic.

Thinking ontogenetically is not risk-free. It can give rise to the illusion that babies come before adults, or that individuals precede collectivities. It also may involve adult fantasies of how infants experience the world, thus obscuring how both adults and infants experience the world. Because ontogeny is the most parsimonious modality of anthropological exposition, however, we will take the chance.

It should also be noted that ontogeny is a reality. So far as collective and individual self-understanding is concerned, we risk less by overemphasizing than by excluding it.

3.

Intrauterine life is the closest we come to purely sensuous experience. After we are born, traces of it remain, encoded in both body and mind.[3] It contributes a vital and pleasurable background sense of rhythmic continuity. Birth, by contrast, is the primal experience of discontinuity and difference. It involves a bombardment by unfamiliar stimuli, successive shocks to the organism, and an abrupt transition from umbilicus to respiration. It is painful and disorganizing. Thereafter the sense of rhythmic continuity is restored through contact with the mother's body, especially as a feeding comes to an end in a sleepy fullness.[4]

Thus we have a dialectical triad. First, there is the sensation of rhythmic continuity. We may think of it as pleasurable, especially in contrast to what follows. Second, there is the ceasing-to-be of this sensuous manifold and the coming-to-be of the mother–infant dyad, a painful or even traumatic becoming, a rupture that is also a mediation. Third, there is a new state of being, in which pleasure and pain alternate and interpenetrate.

4.

One need not follow Otto Rank in viewing the trauma of birth as the essential moment in human development. Nor can we afford to ignore it, and this for two reasons. First, the birth process is structurally isomorphic with other processes of transformation. Importantly, all historical (life historical and social historical) transformations involve a stage of travail and painful disorganization. Because there is a natural human tendency to escape from rather than to tolerate or master pain, there is a defensive or even regressive tendency built into every attempted step forward.

Second, for each of us the intrauterine and birth experiences are constituents of selfhood. It is not the case that one creature existed before birth and another after, with no connection between them. The experiences of intrauterine life and birth are preserved within the organism, as a psychophysiological terror of disintegration and a drive toward (in Marcuse's phrase) integral quiescence.

5.

The fear of death, which runs so deep in us, is in part an encoding or even memory of the experience of birth. Likewise separation anxieties.

6.

The rhythm and structure of postnatal life are established by the metabolic cycle of eating (actually, alimentation) and sleeping. Alimentation is the developmental step forward in this cycle, sleeping is an approximation to the oceanic state of intrauterine existence.

7.

A baby awakens. Partly, the need to sleep has been satisfied for the moment; partly, there is the beginning of the painful sensation we call hunger; partly, there is a hunger for stimulation. If feelings of discomfort are not too intense, a thumb might be sucked. But hunger wins out. The baby is in pain. It becomes agitated, anxious, and, fatefully, enraged. Its mother arrives. She picks it up, while talking soothingly to it. She helps it to find her nipple, relaxes as her baby suckles hungrily, even greedily. The baby's anxiety and agitation diminish and are replaced by the activity of nursing. Hunger subsides, the baby relaxes. After a bit it sinks sleepily into the comfortable sounds, smells, and other sensations of its mother-world.

In this nursery tale, we ignore all the complexities. The cycle doesn't always go so smoothly. Alimentation involves digestion and excretion, and these experiences are sensuously encoded. Babies need to be changed, cleaned, etc., as well as nursed. In our society it need not be the mother who does the nursing. There were wet nurses before there were bottles. Which is to say, infant care varies in gender-specific and culturally specific ways. As Nancy Chodorow (1978) and Jessica Benjamin (1988) both emphasize, it also expresses the subjectivity of and has meaning for the person providing the care. Amidst the variations, however, the cycle of nursing and sleeping retains its identity.

8.

We now arrive at a discursive difficulty. It is in our interest, I believe, to interpret sensuous activity in terms of drives and the principles regulating drives. Yet this involves a shift in both their location—from psyche to psychesoma—and their meaning. Retaining the terminology while shifting the meaning of the terms would seem to invite misunderstanding.

Perhaps this difficulty could be avoided by abandoning the Freudian vocabulary. But, for better or worse, I arrived at the notions that follow by rethinking Freudian concepts in the light of my own experience. It would be disingenuous to hide their derivation in a neutralized language. The alternative, which seems to me the best available option, is to be as clear as possible about how the present usages differ from the classical ones.

First, pleasure and pain. Freud, influenced by Helmholtz, Fechner, and the physics of his time, tended to identify pleasure with absence of stimulation or, at a minimum, with stimulus reduction. This is to reduce the meaning of pleasure to the absence of pain or, to put it another way, to equate stimulation and pain. Because all life involves stimulation, however, this amounts to the statement, pleasure = absence of pain = absence of life = death. Marcuse to the contrary notwithstanding, this is nonsensical. Being dead is not a human experience, nor a perspective from which human experience can be interpreted. Indeed the ordinary expression "to be dead" is oxymoronic. For any self, death = non-being. The self dies, but it cannot *be* dead.

It is true that levels of stimulation above given thresholds are painful, and that it is pleasurable when these levels are reduced. It is also true that levels of stimulation below certain thresholds are painful, and that it is pleasurable when these levels are raised. In both instances it seems fair to associate pleasure with two kinds of sensory rhythm. The simpler, that of intrauterine life, is a steady, modulated rhythm, that is, the pulse of the mother's heartbeat and the flow of her blood. It is recaptured in quiescent states and states of passive enjoyment postnatally. The more complex rhythm, characteristic of activities such as nursing and sexuality, consists of arousal and subsidence, with intense or peak stimulation at one extreme and a relative absence of stimulation at the other.

It is evident that the two forms of pleasure have a determinate relationship to each other: The earlier is the ultimate aim of the later. The pursuit of intense pleasure culminates in quiescence. Postnatally, the experience of pleasure is inherently dialectical.

The second rhythm of sensory pleasure, it might be said, represents a sublation of or triumph over the experience of birth. In both nursing and sexual intercourse, the intense anxiety of birth is transformed into

sensual excitement, as we move (is it forward or backward?) from separateness through a kind of exquisite pain to a quiescent oneness, optimally a two-in-oneness.

There is also a tertiary form of pleasure, the one closest to Freud's
definition, namely, the cessation or absence of pain. This is pleasure in a
purely negative but not meaningless sense.

9.

At the level of sensuous interaction life is regulated by the pleasure
principle: We seek to experience pleasure, as thus defined, and to avoid
pain. Moreover, at this level what gives us pleasure tends to preserve
us. What feels good tends to be good for us. The reality principle has
not yet emerged as something distinct from the pleasure principle. The
two dimensions of the principle become distinguishable only later on,
when the paths of pleasure and preservation start to diverge.

It would be odd were this not so. Imagine a creature for which painful experiences tended to preserve life while pleasurable ones were life-
threatening. Would you be willing to wager on this creature's chances of
evolutionary survival?

10.

There is a drive to experience pleasure and not to experience pain.
A drive is not just an instinct (a genetically encoded pattern of responses
to stimulation), although it may have an instinctual component. Nor is it
a "psychical representative of the stimuli originating from within the
organism and reaching the mind" or "a measure of the demand made
upon the mind for work in consequence of its connection with the body"
(Freud, 1915, p. 122). Drives precede any meaningful distinction between
mind and body. A drive is simply a *potential for activity*, specifically a
potential for sensuous activity. "Potential" in turn has two meanings.
Positively, a potential for activity is a potency or a power, as in Marx's
usual references to human powers or latent human powers. Negatively,
a potential is a pressure toward activity. This second meaning involves
the further characteristic of a resistance or a barrier, an inhibition of
potentiality. Because virtually all sensuous activities involve resistances
of one kind or another, actualization or sensuous activity itself may be
defined as overcoming resistances. A sensuous drive can then be defined
as *a potential for overcoming resistances*.

Note: The term "resistance" is not being used in the specifically
clinical sense of a defensively determined blockage of association or
insight.

11.

In different individuals and at different times, drives vary in intensity or forcefulness. They have, therefore, a quantitative dimension. It is possible to develop measures, including behavioral measures, for these variable intensities. Energy notions might be employed for this purpose. We could even redefine a concept like "libido" as the quantitative or energic aspect of a sexual drive, and then use it to map variations in potentiality for sexual activity. But such research practices and conceptual usages would have nothing in common with Freud's pseudoconceptual realm of psychical or mental energies.

12.

One implication of the preceding argument is that there is no reason to follow Freud beyond the pleasure principle. There is, however, a way of reconceptualizing the life-drive and death-drive without becoming metaphysical. Thus:

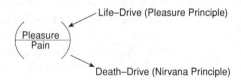

In this figure, pleasure and pain are represented as interpenetrating but distinguishable aspects of sensuous experience, such that a given experience might be essentially pleasurable or essentially painful. If it is pleasurable, then there is an attraction to it. If it is pleasurable and life-preserving, the attraction has the characteristics of a drive. This is not because we know that some pleasures are vital and others aren't. It is rather that we are formed in such a way that vital pleasures have drives attached to them. It is appropriate to term such a drive for pleasurable/life-preserving experience a life-drive, and to say that its operations are regulated by the pleasure principle.

If an experience is painful, then there is an aversion to it. The more painful a sensuous experience, the more it constitutes a threat to life, and the more the aversion takes on the characteristics of a drive. This is the life-drive in its negative form, the drive not to experience pain or unpleasure. Hence we might say that it is regulated by the unpleasure principle, simply the negative version of the pleasure principle.

That is not all. The aim of the negative form of the life-drive is to break off contact with painful stimuli. If pain exceeds certain quantitative spatial and temporal boundaries—if it is sufficiently intense and universal—life itself becomes identified with pain. The drive against pain then functions as a drive against life, a drive to end any sensation whatsoever. The life-drive in its negative form becomes life-negating. It is a death-drive. Its operations are governed by the Nirvana principle, meaning the imperative to put an end to all stimulation.

It will be objected that there is an asymmetry here. The life-drive and the pleasure principle function routinely, the death-drive and the Nirvana principle only in extreme situations. The objection is not without merit, but the asymmetry is not so great as it might appear. At the level of sensuous interaction, we are natural organisms, subject to evolutionary laws. If we survive as a species, it is because, ontogenetically, the conditions for life-sustaining interactions predominate over life-destroying ones and that, correspondingly, pleasurable experiences outweigh painful ones. Hence the death-drive commonly appears as a benign (life-sustaining, healthful) tendency to avoid painful stimulation. As the level of threat and pain rises, however, and as the situation becomes increasingly pathological, we are driven further and further away from life and toward death.

We might also think of it this way. Because pain is inherent in living, the human organism has a basic need to defend against it. Breaking off contact is the simplest of defensive operations. The Nirvana principle, conceived of as the regulator of this defensive drive, or as the principle of primary defense, is vital to sustained health and life. But under those pathological conditions in which stimulation and pain tend toward identity, the Nirvana principle increasingly dictates breaking off contact with any stimuli whatsoever. It and the drive it regulates become life-negating. Thus there is a contradiction inherent in it, a potential for dialectical inversion.

If human life were arranged for the best, if unhealthful or pathological conditions could really be disregarded in discussions of human nature, then we would not give this extreme form of organic defense a position of theoretical prominence. But there is nothing unnatural about the pathological. Although for the species overall life-sustaining conditions have predominated, it is not inappropriate to view sensuous existence as a dialectic of the life-drive and the death-drive.

13.

We might note in passing that there is a fantasy that grows organically out of the sensuous dialectic of life and death. The activity of the life-drive ends in pleasurable quiescence, in the human experience that most nearly corresponds to a metaphysical or perhaps existential Being.

The operation of the death-drive ends in death, non-being, Nothingness. It is then easy to conflate the one with the other, thus to generate the fantasy of a blissful life-in-death.

The fantasy is further animated by the sensuous encoding of pre-natal quiescence, which functions as a before-life and so supports the wish for an afterlife.

When in the course of time religious worldviews are challenged by secular ones, these fantasies migrate from the territory of the sacred to that of the profane. They become the spirit in the revolutionary flesh or the utopian impulse in critical social theories. Great and terrible deeds have been performed in attempts to realize them.

14.

There is a third drive and a corresponding regulative principle, which are analytically subsequent to but existentially coincident with the ones considered so far.

Suppose that pleasure and pain are evenly balanced and/or deeply interwoven in a situation of sensuous interaction, and that the pleasure is vital to well-being. Then one cannot simply approach or avoid it. The situation is such that an either/or response is frustrated. Both drives are called into action, or rather we have a third drive that is more complex than the other two. Pain—including the pain resulting from the frustration of the two primary drives—must be overcome in order to gain pleasure.

It is hard to know what to name this third drive, or third form of the drive. It might be termed the attack-drive, but aggressive-drive seems more in line with ordinary usage. *Here aggression means only the aim of overcoming or eliminating pain in order to experience pleasure.* It does not denote such emotions as rage, hatred, or the desire to inflict pain, although as we shall see, these emotions do have an intimate connection with it.

Let's add the aggressive-drive to the figure on page 223.

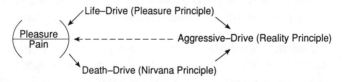

In this construction the aggressive-drive is in a position rather analogous to Becoming in Hegel's *The Science of Logic* : It is the determinate unity of the life-drive and the death-drive. It presupposes and goes beyond them.

Or, when the problem of pleasure/pain proves insoluble, it disintegrates and falls beneath them. It dissolves into a shattering frustration and rage that recreates the terror and disorganization of birth. Thus the situation of the aggressive-drive is basic both to further development and to regression.

Put another way, the situation of the aggressive-drive poses the problem of reality—of gaining pleasure and preserving the self in conditions that also contain pain and threatened destruction. The problem may or may not be solved. Either way there arises the possibility of learning from experience, or perhaps of learning to learn from experience. For the other two drives involve learning of a sort, namely, conditioning, or stimulus-response learning. But the situation of the aggressive-drive, in which the drive itself is sometimes frustrated, forces or at least facilitates the development of a gap or pause between drive-sensation and action. The negation of a driven action creates a negative moment, a delay, hence a time/space in which an alternative response to a stimulus might take form. It therefore seems fair to characterize the principle regulating this situation as the reality principle.

At this juncture it might seem that we are on familiar Freudian ground. To a certain extent, we are. The aggressive-drive does involve an incipient differentiation of mind from body, a demand for mental work, and a developing capacity for delayed gratification. It leads us to test reality. Thus the reality principle resembles one of Freud's principles of mental functioning.

There is, however, a dialectical twist that is not depicted in the Freudian tale. The reality principle is just as much the unreality principle. The aggressive-drive, in common with the other two, aims at experiences of pleasure without pain, that is, at creating a situation in which pleasure is present and pain is absent. But in reality, pleasure and pain are necessarily interpenetrative. There are sensuous interactions in which pleasure, preservation, and the life-drive predominate, and others in which pain, threat, and the death-drive predominate. But pure pleasure and pure pain are either theoretical constructions arrived at via abstraction or fantasies arrived at via splitting. In the latter regard, the first either/or, the first enacted binary judgment of good or bad, is an attempt on the part of the infant to divide the manifold of experience into either the pleasurable or the painful.

Thus the reality principle is just as much an imagination principle, while the operations of the aggressive-drive are also attempts to realize a fantasy. Still, we are capable of learning from experience, and so of distinguishing between fantasy and reality—or perhaps of distinguishing between realizable and unrealizable fantasies.

We begin to see why we might view ourselves as the problematical animals.

15.

As we have proceeded, we have been forced increasingly into the language of difference. From the postnatal beginning, in fact, we assumed an ability to distinguish between pleasure and pain. We also assumed drive-activity oriented toward the one and away from the other. It is evident, then, that sensuousness is infiltrated by perceptual–motor activity from the outset. But the experiential distinctions, the qualitative differences, that our differentiated sense organs make possible, are emergences within or crystallizations of a flow or rhythm of sensations, a Many within a One. If we grow in a healthy fashion, this Oneness is not lost. It becomes a predominantly benign matrix for experience.

We have already implied that the neonatal field of sensuous interaction becomes perceptually structured in a bipolar fashion. At one extreme is the nurturing interaction with the mother or other primary caretaker, at the other is the cessation of this activity, the lapsing back into passivity or relaxation, ultimately into sleep. The one extreme is an enactment of the life-drive and comes under the aegis of the pleasure principle. The other embodies the death-drive, optimally in its benign form, and comes under the aegis of the Nirvana principle. But because pleasure and pain are always interpenetrating in the nurturing situation, it becomes a field for aggressive interaction, of hungry attack upon the source of pleasure and life. Similarly the interpenetration of pleasure and pain in the situation of withdrawal generates fantasies of attack. In both cases sensations and percepts are accompanied by affects. If the overall situation is (as D. W. Winnicott says) "good enough," then these affects are primarily affirmative—in a very primitive sense, loving. As the level of pain increases and/or the tolerance of pain decreases, the affective state becomes more hostile. If a certain level of pain and hostility is reached, the perceptual and motoric either/or that structures sensuous experience becomes a defensive either/or that splits it. We then have the situation of the paranoid–schizoid position, that is (in my view), a particular and pathological variant of a universal stage of development. Particular, but not marginal: The dynamics of the paranoid–schizoid position exist as tendencies in all of us.

When a human organism comes into the world ill-equipped for emotional living and/or when it comes into a world insufficiently equipped for its living, it may not be able to attain the stability of even the paranoid–schizoid position. Then, in modern society, it may live in a world of desiring-machines, from which it may attempt to retreat to a body without organs. Traces of a healthy bipolarity remain visible even in this deformation of human identity, that is, in psychosis. In like fashion one can find traces of juridical procedure in the Terror of the French Revolution or the Stalinist purge trials. One would not want to build a psyche or a society on these foundations, however.

16.

As Marx said, our sensuousness identifies us with other animate species. There is very little that is distinctively human in our sketch of the sensuous stage in human ontogeny. Chimpanzees and other apes, if they were interested in such things, would recognize themselves in our portrait. Phylogenetically, too, we were sensuous beings before we became human ones. But in the course of phylogenetic and ontogenetic time, we become human, and our sensuousness becomes infused with human meanings. We also attempt, for worse as well as for better, to bring sensuousness under our technical control. Sometimes we lose ourselves in the process. We forget that we are sensuous beings, creatures vulnerable to pleasure and pain. Then, perhaps, we search for what we have lost in the society of gorillas.

But the gorillas do not search for themselves in human society. They have neither the need nor the ability to do so. They lack the taste and the imagination for it. We, on the other hand, are not limited in this fashion. We refuse to take things as they are given.

D. Work, Desire, and Recognition

1.

We have advanced to the second level of the dialectical relationship, sensuous activity ↔ work/desire ↔ conscious activity. Stated as a proposition: The interpenetrating modalities of work and desire arise from sensuous interaction through the mediation of perceptual–motor function and within the dialectic of recognition.

2.

We never cease-to-be sensuous but we come-to-be more and other than sensuous. A feedback loop between perception and motor activity exists from the beginning. Over time, it increasingly dominates the ontogenic picture. Within the first two years of life, both sensuous and perceptual–motor interactions become conscious, in the specific sense of being accompanied by spoken language. But more time must elapse before spoken language occupies the central role in human interaction. Development occurs and distinctions are made alongside and to some extent independently of language development. Indeed, thinking is not entirely dependent upon the capacity to use and understand words. And even in our adult lives, language functions in good part as mediator of nonlinguistic experience, although it is also a vital constituent of our experience.

In any case, phylogenetically and ontogenetically there is a phase between sensuous and linguistically structured interaction during which language—but not only language—develops. This is distinctively the stage in which the world becomes manifold and multiform, a unity of diverse elements, an expanding field of activity and awareness. Its content is also more variable historically. It is therefore more difficult to discuss using the limited anthropological terms we are currently employing. Increased slippage from anthropological abstraction is therefore to be expected.

3.

Within the first few months of life the indefinite unity of baby and mother (or other primary caretaker) evolves into a highly defined relationship between them. The infant also begins to distinguish, affectively and cognitively, between familiar others and strangers. Consequently from this point forward we cannot ignore the problematics of recognition. Nor can we properly refer to the preceding stage of sensuous interaction as "narcissistic." In narcissistic states one is invested in the self rather than the other. The territory of the self is expanded, the selfhood or even existence of the other is denied. Hence the "either/or" of self and other must be presupposed. In sensuous interactions, by contrast, the boundary between self and other is not yet clearly defined, much less reified. For better and for worse self and other are interpenetrated. It is ideology disguised as psychology and an inversion of reality when narcissistic states are viewed as primary and sociality is viewed as secondary. We must invert the inversion to arrive at the actual developmental order.

If we look at neonatal interactions from the mother's perspective, it is evident that questions of recognition arise from the outset. A pregnant woman has a sense of the selfhood of her child before it is born, and she interacts with it as a self after it is born. The child's selfhood is shaped in the course of this interaction, although it is not reducible to it. We are not simply imprinted or conditioned by early life interactions—not even when we conceive them interactively, or even as dialectical processes. We come into the world with certain potentialities for selfhood and not with others. Recognition of and respect for this incipient selfhood seems to be of critical importance for the development of emotional authenticity.

For the child the first other is the mother. This other is not clearly differentiated from the self. In an odd way, therefore, the ambiguity of the Hegelian dialectic of recognition captures the reality of this relationship better than more "materialist" conceptions, which insist that mother and child are separate entities. The mother both is and is not the child, both is and is not an other. She is the first mirror of the child's selfhood, but a mirror with a mind of her own.

The dialectic of recognition between mother and child emerges from and comes to frame the bipolar sensuous interaction of feeding and sleeping.[5] Hence it, too, is bipolar. At the one extreme, there is the child who actively and passionately seeks pleasure at the mother's breast and/or from her response. At the other extreme, there is the child who slips passively into a fusion with a maternal gestalt, into integral quiescence. Moreover, to a greater or lesser extent there is a (mis)shaping of the dialectic of recognition into the paranoid–schizoid position. At either the engaged or withdrawn extreme, there is a good mother–child and a bad mother–child—a dyad in which pleasure and good feelings (contentment, joy, amusement, love) predominate, split off from another in which pain and bad feelings (frustration, rage, fear, hatred) predominate. Alternatively, goodness and badness can be split up between the extremes: The good mother is the one who is present with the love-filled child and the bad mother is the one whose absence torments the hate-filled child; the bad mother is the one whose presence torments the hate-filled child and the good mother is the one who leaves the child in peace.

4.

This ontogenetically earliest dialectic of recognition, like the one we find in *The Phenomenology*, involves issues of freedom and domination. Only in pathological instances, however, is domination the principal aspect of the relationship.

Domination involves (1) a demand upon the self that (2) originates with an other—an alien demand. The other may or may not be recognized as a self.

The first demands are those placed by the (m)other upon the child. *We* might also view sensuous drives as demands. But demands that originate within the self are not initially ego-alien. The self is the demand; it is adultomorphising to think of hunger and the like as demands upon the self, or of the body upon the mind.

By contrast, when the (m)other gives form to the metabolic cycle of early life—feeding and attention at some times but not others, sleeping at specified times, activities in some places but not others, solid foods

and utensils in place of or in addition to breast or bottle, spatial and temporal control of bowel and bladder functions, bathtimes, dressing requirements,
etc.—she embodies a demand. She is necessity, against which the child's
impulse is freedom.

It is not a metaphor to say that freedom of impulse becomes freedom
of the will—determinate freedom—through the acceptance of limitation and
a kind of discipline. One learns to make demands of oneself, and to be free
in so doing. Limits are also structures of selfhood. But here the problem
of domination, open and disguised, also arises. The childhood dialectic of
recognition can be a life and death struggle, in which the child becomes the
unwilling slave of the parents-as-masters—in which their will is substituted
for hers/his. S/he is denied the possibility of self-formation and is deformed
instead. But s/he may be eager to accept this "ideological" distortion of what
has really happened because, as Nietzsche would have it, we would rather
"will *nothingness* [even or especially our own] than *not* will" (Nietzsche, 1887,
p. 97). This is not because there is a primary and irreducible will to power,
but rather because "I did it myself" is less terrifying than "they did it
to me."

5.

Contrast the cycle of neonatal life with the activities of a four- or five-
year-old. S/he has gone from creeping and crawling to standing, walking,
running, and jumping. Given half a chance s/he holds, releases, throws,
catches, puts things together and takes them apart, builds them up and tears
them down, digs holes and fills them up, climbs up onto and slides down
from things. S/he defecates and urinates at certain places and times. S/he
eats and drinks with utensils of one kind or another. S/he is interested in
and beginning to be able to manage clothing and adornments. S/he plays
with things and interactively with other people. S/he talks, yells, and sings.
And so on.

Vital distinctions emerge and stabilize: self/other, present/absent,
familiar/unfamiliar, male/female, adult/child, safe/unsafe, day/night,
permitted/not permitted, play/work, love/hate, even mind/body. At the
practical level the child is both Heraclitian and Parmenidian: in love with
the either/or but not at all troubled by interpenetrative flows—as long as
pain is not too intrusive.

6.

Along with the sophistication of perceptual–motor function comes the
complication of the dialectic of recognition. The relationship of self and other,
the primary instance of the dialectic, becomes attached to questions of

gender and generation—male/female, adult/child. What it means concretely to be male or female and the nature of the adult–child relationship is historically variable. But in all societies selfhood involves gender
and generational identity. Moreover, as selfhood becomes more complex
and internally differentiated without (in the case of healthy development)
losing its coherence, so, too, the other is pluralized without losing its unity.
The social unit that structures the individual's life world becomes a generalized other—and a constituent of selfhood.

7.

The perceptual–motor development of the sensuous organism and
its drives creates a potential for both work life and emotional life. The
classical loci of Marxism and psychoanalysis are equally the sublations
or sublimations of a sensuousness that neither theory adequately conceptualizes.

As we learn when the demands of work and desire clash, there is a
more-than-analytical distinction between them. It would be a mistake to
dissociate them, however. They both develop from sensuous interaction;
they both require adequate perceptual–motor functioning; and all conscious action combines them, albeit in varying degrees. Indeed, it is difficult to think of one without the other.

8.

Or we might think of it this way. Sensuous drives that have under-
gone perceptual–motor development constitute a *potential* for working
and desiring. The potentiality is concretized in the activity or *process* of
working or desiring. These processes result in *realizations* of one kind or
another.

The activities of working and desiring have the following formal
elements or aspects:

$$\text{Person} \longrightarrow \text{Capacity} \longrightarrow \text{Aim} \quad \begin{matrix} \nearrow \text{Subject, Self} \searrow \\ [\text{Process}] \\ \searrow \text{Object, Other} \nearrow \end{matrix} \text{Activity} \longrightarrow \text{Result/Product}$$

In this model, perceptual–motor activity is represented as a dialectical
process. We begin with a person possessing a capacity for action and an
aim to be realized through action. The action or activity itself consists of

utilizing this capacity in a process that joins (overcomes the oppositon between) subject and object, or self and other, in such a way that a result is produced—whether or not the result is a product that is separable from the process of its production.

This model is isomorphic with Marx's conception of the labor process; not surprisingly, because it is nothing more than an abstract version of that concept. Marx's analysis of labor begins with persons possessing the capacity for working. Then comes the labor process, the basic elements of which are "(1) purposeful activity, that is work itself, (2) the object on which that work is performed, and (3) the instruments of that work" (Marx, 1867, p. 284). Finally there is the product in which the process is realized or materialized. Our model simply generalizes this analysis.

Somewhat more surprisingly, the model has a certain fit with Freud's metapsychological characterization of a drive.

Freud (1915, p. 122) depicts the drives as having a pressure, an aim (discharge), an object, and a source. Pressure is one aspect of potentiality. Discharge (which Freud universalizes) is one of the possible aims of an activity. The object is the other, including parts of the self as other. And the source is the self, which Freud interprets as a physical part of the self.

With suitable modifications, we might follow Freud and apply the model to our conception of the sensuous drives. For present purposes, however, the relevant application is to desires. Desires are potential emotional interactions. They aim at some sort of gratification. They are expressed in activities which join (or separate) self and other, but in the most various ways. They yield results, if only in fantasy.

We see, then, that work and desire conform to the same metatheoretical model of human activity. Consequently the following exposition is usefully informed by it. We will not, however, apply it mechanically, forcing the manifold of work and desire into a formal identity. We will simply keep it in mind, as one of the ordering principles of the discourse.

9.

If theory adequately imitated life, we would now proceed to investigate work and desire simultaneously. But theory is a poor imitation of its object, and so we are forced to choose between them. Because work is strongly attached to sensuous needs and self-preservation, there is something to be said for advancing from it to desire. Yet work consorts with play, and play is a child of desire.

10.

Perceptual–motor development makes it possible for the child to work and play. Through working and playing, perceptual and motor skills are developed.

Both work and play involve a fitting together of impulse, activity, and object in such a way that an aim is in fact realized. And both have a drive-like quality; or rather, in work and play the sensuous drives are put to perceptual–motor and (in turn conscious) use. The life-drive is channeled into constructive activity, meaning especially the creation of unities. The death-drive is channeled into destructive activity, meaning breaking things down. The aggressive-drive, in which the life and death drives are combined, is channeled into activities in which constructive and destructive modalities are joined (such as the perceptual–motor activities noted above), and which are generally oriented toward mastery and control.

If in these respects work and play are the same, how are they to be differentiated? By their aims and their results. When the activity aims at pleasure, it is play; when it aims at preservation or is motivated by a demand, it is work. Play is willing service to the pleasure principle; work is willing or unwilling service to the reality principle. They are each instrumental, but they realize different values.

Work is activity aimed at satisfying a need—in the first instance a sensuous or vital need. Hence it must be undertaken whether it is pleasurable or not. Work tends to be pleasurable when it directly satisfies a vital need (for example, eating) and/or when it is or seems to be self-determined. Even when work is painful, the element of self-determination involves a compensatory pleasure. Especially important in this regard is the pleasure that accompanies the surmounting of a difficulty—pleasure in achievement or mastery. When this pleasure is sufficiently intense, the distinction between work and play is virtually eliminated.

The distinction between work and play presupposes that preservation and pleasure, which in the first instance are conjoined, are separable and potentially opposed. They cannot be completely opposed. Play and the pleasure it yields presuppose that the work necessary for self-preservation has been performed. Conversely, all work and no play not only makes dull boys and girls; it is also patently unhealthy.

The connection between work and preservation gives work its objectivity. Stated negatively: When work is not properly performed, there is a price to pay. But we must not forget that objective reality consists in good part of subjects—of the other or others whose demands one must satisfy, and whose demands may conflict with one's needs and desires.

Ontogenetically, the child must do the work its parents demand if it is to survive, then (in our society and many others) the work its teachers demand, then. . . .

We are not the only species that works and plays; but to cite once more Marx's condensed anthropological formulation: "A spider conducts operations which resemble those of a weaver, and a bee would put many a human architect to shame by the construction of its honeycomb cells. But what distinguishes the worst architect from the best of bees is that the architect builds the cell in his mind before he constructs it in wax." Our working and our playing are distinctively conscious—distinctively imaginative. Other species are instrumentally rational, by instinct or even by choice. They fit means to ends, sometimes in variable ways and sometimes with variable ends. But there is a transformation of quantity into quality between the capacity for creative mentation of our nearest evolutionary relatives and our own. The extent of our ability to imagine what is not given in experience, to go beyond existing reality in our imaginations, is uniquely ours. The linking of this capacity to work—to the task of transforming our nonhuman environment in our own image and to suit our own developing needs—makes us historical in a way that other species are not.

In an unorthodox fashion we arrive at an orthodox Marxist conclusion.

11.

In both Marxism and psychoanalytic-marxism the phylogeny of work is better represented than its ontogeny. To be sure, the phylogenic record largely concerns work that is mediated by language. But the history of human production, and of our self-production through production, is well documented and well developed within these theoretical traditions. The historical and anthropological ontogeny of work has been largely ignored. A beginning could be made, however, by building upon the pioneering researches of Arnold Gesell, Jean Piaget, their coworkers, and the great number of cultural anthropologists who have observed the behavior of children.

Freud was fond of commenting ironically on the academic and ideological view that we suddenly become sexual beings during adolescence, when any nurse or mother could document the sexuality of children. In a similar fashion social theorists often seem to believe that we suddenly become workers at around that same age—as if we didn't work as children, or childhood didn't matter.

When Marxists ignore the ontogeny of work, they unwittingly surrender a vital theoretical position. Because we all begin as children, and because infantile experience remains the foundation of adult character, assigning the onset of work to late childhood or adolescence consigns it to anthropological epiphenomenality. It arrives on the scene too late to be constitutive of our essential nature. This unfortunate consequence would be avoided if we traced out the developmental path of work, analyzing as we proceeded the dialectical interaction between work and desire. Moreover, by so doing we would make the creatures who inhabit our anthropology more recognizably human.

It should be added that the aim of such a project would not be to substitute ontogeny for phylogeny, or to grant ontogeny ontological priority. It would only be to include the ontogeny of work within the phylogeny of the species.

12.

All work involves pain and need. Pain is a part of working; one must be able to tolerate it in order to work, even—or especially—when the work is oriented toward overcoming or eliminating pain. Because working is necessary for preservation, the pain is in principle unavoidable. Nonetheless, work must not be conflated with alienated labor. As Freud notes, work links us to reality; as Marx emphasizes, we realize ourselves in work. To work is human. We are so constructed that we take pleasure in sensuous and perceptual–motor activity, and this pleasure carries over into, is sublated in, and sustains working. In alienated labor, pain and necessity rather than the conquest of pain and necessity become the dominant aspects of the activity. This is as true for children who labor to please punitive and overly demanding parents as it is for workers who labor to earn a wage from exploitative and oppressive bosses.

Here is a related point. There is effort but also pleasure or satisfaction in such activities as making things function, mastering a skill, performing well, or producing something that is good. These processes can be alienated. But there is a categorical difference between the activities themselves and alienated activity. Moreover, these activities are integral to play as well as to work. Which is to say, the technical or instrumental dimension of reason (1) applies as much to play as to work and (2) does not distinguish between work/play and alienated labor. Thus, in devaluing instrumental activity, critical theorists turn their backs on a vital part of human nature, the part that attaches us most firmly to reality and which contains our greatest powers of self-realization.

It might be rejoined that the object of criticism is not instrumental rationality as such but rather its universalization—the subsumption of all thought and action under the category of instrumentality. Although I think a reading of relevant texts would only partially support such a rejoinder, the substantive point is well taken. It is best taken, however, when the point is bent, that is, when we recognize in *desire* the critical antithesis to instrumentality.

13.

Certain kinds of work must be performed no matter what we desire. Desires may be expressed through work, however, and play is inconceivable without them.

A desire is not a drive, although all desires develop from drives. Desires do not have the quality of need or demand that attaches to drives, although they may give this appearance. They are free from the imperatives of reality and realization, even when they function to deny this freedom.

The distinguishing feature of desire is affect—feeling in the sense of emotion. A desire is a sensation, a percept, a remembered percept, an image, later a word or idea, linked to an affect. Desires generate not only activity but also moods and "states of mind." Thus desire is less firmly linked to action and actualization, instrumentality, and the imperatives of preservation, than is work. We may also say that desire is less constrained by the requirements of realization than is work. Hence, where work gravitates toward the reality principle, desire is pulled toward the pleasure principle. These are only tendencies, however. Work and pleasure are not mutually exclusive; considerations of rationality and reality enter into the experience of desire as well as work.

When we look at desire from the outside, we can see that it has an anaclitic relationship to work. The continuity of both sensuous existence and emotional life depends upon the performance of work, upon satisfying the demands of preservation. But viewed from the inside, work processes and relationships may appear as externalities and mere givens. Ontogenetically (and optimally) the child takes for granted the parents' provision of food, clothing, shelter, etc. And because important parts of the child's work are defined by parental demand, work itself may become identified with the outside world, or external reality. The experience of selfhood may then be centered in desire. If, however, work and play are allowed to interpenetrate and the child is permitted self-expression in these activities, then selfhood does not develop so one-sidedly.

In the discussion of work we saw that the sensuous drives are channeled into work activity, that they constitute a potential for working, and that they retain their characteristic bi- or tripolarity in so doing. The same development occurs in the field of experience determined by desire. The life-drive or sensuous appetite for pleasure becomes love. Love requires a perception of the other as other and of the other's ability to give one pleasure. And as the Kleinians contend, it involves an appreciation of or gratitude for this goodness. Love is the emotional core of mutual recognition. Correspondingly the death-drive takes on the quality of hate. Hate presupposes the perception of the other as other and of the other's ability to inflict pain. Hatred of the other is the emotional core of failures of recognition and of relationships of domination.

Like the drives from which they develop, the emotions of love and hate interpenetrate. The aggressive drive takes on the quality of ambivalence. The ability to tolerate ambivalence is necessary if love and hate are to be integrated. When this ability does not exist, typically because hatred predominates in a relationship, then love and hate, as well as the objects toward which they are directed, must be split apart. Emotional life then becomes attached to the paranoid–schizoid position.

The level of urgency in work life and emotional life is highly variable. The more the human individual develops, the more room there is for activity free from drive-like demand. But in common with drive activity, all action has its negative moment. In any action whatsoever resistance must be overcome. The negative moment is only relevant from the standpoint of experience, however, when it renders performance of the action problematical—during the phase of learning, or when the pain of resistance is sufficiently intense. Otherwise negativity is experienced only as a component of rhythm or motion.

In work life constructive and destructive potentialities are mobilized within a field of activity oriented toward efficacy. In emotional life love and hate are mobilized within a field permeated by affectivity. But despite the differences between the fields of interaction, self or subject is joined to other or object in each instance. So far as emotional life is concerned, this is especially evident in Kleinian and other object relations versions of psychoanalytic theory. There it can be seen that, not only in action but in our inner worlds as well, self interacts with other in characteristic ways (that is, through typical modes of expression and defense) and with characteristic affects.

The results of working and desiring are two-fold. There is first an objective consequence: A child learns to stack up blocks; the mother is pleased; the child is happy. Second, this specific outcome has a more general subjective consequence. It contributes to the formation of character or, in the case of adults, reinforces or challenges existing character structure.

Note that, quite apart from its emotional correlates, working contributes to the formation of character. This is not to say that working lacks emotional correlates or even determinants. The point is rather that character is structured through working as well as desiring.

14.

The transition from sensuous to perceptual–motor interactions makes us creatures of body and mind, and of body *or* mind. We have the experience of perceiving or observing bodily activity, hence of instituting a kind of subject–object relationship between mind and body. But the either/or of mind and body depends on two more specific experiences: Our mental reach exceeds our physical grasp; our mind hurts when our body doesn't. In both, we experience psychic pain. In the experience of psychic pain we come to know ourselves as creatures of desire.

First point: Intentionality becomes visible when there is a resistance to the realization of the intention. Physical limitation is such a resistance. Development occurs in the form of and by progressively resolving the contradiction, "I want to do what I am not yet capable of doing." In the process, however, the body begins to gain a relative autonomy and the mind begins to experience pain.

Second and more critical point: As a child develops and if s/he is physically healthy, s/he increasingly experiences painful feelings that have little to do with the frustration of sensuous or even bodily drives. S/he is left alone when s/he wants to be with mother or father. A parent is angry and s/he is afraid.

Two developmental paths begin in the experience of psychic pain. The child may find a solution in reality for the problem pain involves. S/he cries and the parent returns. S/he learns to stay out of the way until the parent's anger passes. Or s/he may erect psychical defenses against the experience of pain. S/he might, for example, be able to mute the affective response to the event or construct a fantasy of a returning or happy parent. Either way the child has entered the realm of mental experience. Henceforward s/he will live with a mind/body distinction— but not, except in extremely pathological instances, an absolute difference.

15.

We now come to the psychoanalytic heart of the matter: *psychic pain, defenses against psychic pain, and the dialectic of emotional development.* And to the heart of a specifically psychoanalytic Marxism: Although other psychoanalytic concepts might be used to fill in gaps in Marxist theory, the result would be of primarily academic interest were it not for the importance of psychic pain in human experience.

Because psychic pain is central to psychoanalysis in both theory and practice, all lines of inquiry proceed from it and return to it. We cannot and need not follow all these lines, or even any one of them to the end.

But we must establish a framework inclusive enough so that no area of inquiry is shut off.[6]

• There are various kinds of psychic pain—the emotional correlates of hunger or sexual frustration, impotent rage, depression, moral aloneness, etc. But *anxiety* has perhaps the strongest claim to paradigmatic status. It signals threatened physical pain or threats to preservation. It is present in any situation where pleasure is sought and the attainment of pleasure is uncertain. More generally, anxiety attaches to any situation involving a significant level of uncertainty. It is part of all emotional conflict, whether intrapsychic or interpsychic. When sufficiently intense, it can shatter psychic structure and/or be completely immobilizing. The degree of trauma associated with an event—for example, birth—is directly proportional to the amount of anxiety it induces.

• Anxiety, in common with the other affects, originates in and is a component of sensuous experience. As mind becomes differentiated from body, the affects occupy the borderline and mediate the relationship between the two. They come close to meriting Freud's characterization of a drive, as a "concept on the frontier between the mental and the somatic, as the psychical representative of the stimuli originating from within the organism and reaching the mind . . ." (Freud, 1915, pp. 121–122). Only one also would have to say: as the somatic representative of stimuli originating from within the mind and reaching the body. . . .

• The response to anxiety follows along the lines already laid out in the response to sensuous pain. The death-drive becomes a flight response, the aggressive-drive a fight response. Here we have the fight-flight response—really the flight–fight response, because fighting is rarely the preferred alternative. In the first instance this response is not distinguishable from the drives it mobilizes.

• The flight–fight response is not limited to emotional life and certainly not to intrapsychic experience. As I use the term, however, it does require perceptual–motor function, including the perception of anxiety or fear as an affective signal. Once this level of functioning is reached, the flight–fight response serves the organism as a whole.

• The more intense the anxiety that initiates it, the more the flight–fight response becomes hate-filled. Hate engenders fears of retaliation and is thus anxiety-inducing. If the anxiety is overwhelming, as it may be when it is sufficiently amplified by hatred, the flight–fight response becomes impossible and panic ensues.

• The flight–fight response can function either to master or to defend against anxiety. This is true no matter what the source of the anxiety: an earthquake, a real or imaginary threat of attack from another individual, an imagined threat of attack from another individual, an anxiety-inducing thought or impulse. The nature of its use is not given in its existence as such.

• There is a third response to anxiety: to tolerate it. Tolerating anxiety isn't "natural," but it is necessary for emotional development. When it can be tolerated, then flight–fight becomes an option rather than a driven response. It still may be used, but it also may be rendered unnecessary by transforming the anxiety-inducing situation.

Ontogenetically, the movement from driven response to problem-solving typically requires adult intervention. If, when a child is anxious, an adult can hold the situation and contain the anxiety, functioning as an extension of the child's self but not as a replacement for it, then the self begins to be able to learn from the experience of anxiety. In the absence of this learning experience, defense against rather than engagement with anxiety becomes increasingly necessary.

• In emotional life, anxiety is the signifier of contradiction, of interpenetrating and opposing tendencies within a field of interaction—maybe an intrasubjective field, maybe an intersubjective one. Take a simple instance. A child feels the need to defecate. This is a demand originating in its body, a feeling of pain or pressure for which there is an available and corresponding pleasure. But there is also the parental demand of defecating in a toilet and, we will suppose, a toilet is not available. The child wishes to please the parents and/or is afraid of their displeasure. Consequently s/he feels anxious. Anxiety signifies the contradiction: I need/want to defecate now; I mustn't/don't want to defecate now.

Again: If the parent can hold the situation by noticing the child's signs of distress and finding a toilet or by not being displeased if an "accident" happens, then the anxiety accompanying the conflict is reduced, and the child's capacity to live with contradictions is enlarged. To live with contradictions, and to resolve them: The child takes a step toward or into a dialectic of development, in which unavoidable moments of psychic pain, of emotional negation, contribute through being negated to the structuring of the self. If, however, the situation is not managed in some such fashion, the dialectical process is perverted and a defensive one supervenes.

• Laplanche and Pontalis (1973, p. 103) define a defense as a "group of operations *aimed at* the reduction and elimination of any change liable to threaten the integrity and stability of the bio-psychological individual." I would modify this definition: "A defense is an operation or group of operations aimed at the reduction or elimination of any threat to the preservation and pleasure of individuals and/or groups." Some such modification avoids the bias toward both "the individual" and stasis, while preserving the generality of the concept.

In any case, such a general definition does not differentiate between modes of defense that engage realities and those that evade them. In the former sense, defenses are in the position of the negation of a negation, and are constitutive of the structure of self or even society. That is, the "threat" is a potential negation of the self or social unit, the defense negates the negation and, by so doing, contributes to development. Because development always involves threat to preservation and pleasure, all development involves defense. Which is only to say that all development—human development—is dialectical.

The second meaning of defense reverses the developmental implication. Defense is here an avoidance of a situation in which development requires engagement, or a breaking of a link with a problematical bit of reality. One might also say that a defense is an avoidance of anxiety in a situation where tolerance of anxiety is necessary for preservation or the securing of pleasure.

Avoidance should not be confused with flight. Engagement might involve flight, while a defense might be denial of the need for flight. The fight response, which mobilizes the aggressive-drive, can be used to avoid anxiety, including the anxiety necessary for development. It might be said, however, that flight is the paradigmatic defense. And because flight involves a mobilization of the death-drive, it could be argued that the Nirvana principle is the primary regulator of defensive processes.

Defenses in the second sense are perversions of dialectical process. And this is the distinctively psychoanalytic meaning of the concept of defense. Let's restrict our usage accordingly. This precludes conflating dialectical development with its perversion.[7] In concrete instances, however, one must be careful to avoid a formulation such as "either dialectic or defense." In reality, all development combines dialectical and defensive processes.

Early on, Reich argued that symptom formation is a dialectical process. It can now be seen that this is not quite accurate. The situations that generate symptoms are self-contradictory, and if progressive development is to occur, then dialectical resolution is necessary. But symptom formation is a failure of dialectical development, a closing-off of dialectical processes in the interest of eliminating or reducing anxiety. One might say that defensive processes are idealist dialectics, pseudodialectics that seem to engage a problem while effecting a glissade away from it.

Here we have the foundation of our critique of Hegel, of the totalized dialectic in Marx, and of the various glissades we located in the Freudian-Marxist tradition.

• Flight–fight is the primary modality of defense. Other defenses are built upon and presuppose it. Some—the ones that involve breaking off contact with or attempting to destroy the threatening drive, desire, internal object, external object, etc.—are versions of it. Denial, disavowal, and, more complicatedly, repression are of this type. They behave like a perverse version of Bion's seventh servant. They create a blank opacity instead of the emptiness that receives.

Other defenses are inverse interrogatories, perverse imitations of Bion's other intellectual servants. They keep us from asking What, Who, Where, When, How, and Why. Without quite negating the threat itself, they aim at making it nonthreatening. They place it where it isn't (as in hysterical conversion) or in whom it isn't (as in projection, introjection, and projective identification). They relocate it in time (as in regression) or deny the passage of time (as in fixation). They alter its nature (split it into parts, fragment it, change it into its perceptual or affective opposite). Or they imitate explaining it (rationalization, intellectualization, obsession).

Defenses may be deployed against a threatening absence as well as a threatening presence. Hallucinatory wish-fulfillment, for example, shields us from experiences of emptiness and abandonment in the manifold of the maternal world. In time, this defensive function is refined. Fantasies supplement or replace hallucinations, daydreams grow out of fantasies. Somewhere down the line, ideologies may spring clandestinely from daydreams. Then we have the appearance but not the reality of political thinking.

This list of psychic defenses is not exhaustive, but it does suggest an important aspect of defensive processes: Defenses are not *sui generis*. They are ordinary mental processes placed in the service of derealizing painful realities.

• Defensive processes may be transitory, but for each of us they become characterological. We all have characteristic ways of defending against psychic pain we cannot master. And for each of us, as the "I" develops, an "It" develops as well—a part of the self from which we are alienated as a consequence of psychic pain. There is no It (id) otherwise, but none of us develops without some loss of selfhood. The loss may be minimal, however, or substantial. In the latter regard, there may come a time when the It overwhelms the I, when self-division becomes the predominant moment, when the self breaks down and further progressive development becomes impossible. It then becomes vital to reclaim the alienated territory of the self.

• The defenses develop over time and in distinct constellations. The paranoid–schizoid position is the first defensive posture. Here the fight response is mobilized in the engagement with the bad/threatening/powerful motherbreast, while the flight response involves breaking off contact with the persecutory object and retreating into a withdrawn state modeled on intrauterine existence—retreat to the interior of the body without organs, outside the reach of the desiring machines. The position is unstable because anxiety is generated at either extreme. Schizoid withdrawal leaves one terrifyingly alone and disconnected, paranoid interaction makes one terrifyingly vulnerable to uncontrollable forces of destruction.

If the dialectic of development predominates over defense, the self begins to emerge from the paranoid–schizoid matrix. In our culture, this is accompanied by an accentuated separation anxiety, the forerunner of the moral aloneness depicted in Fromm's *Escape from Freedom*. In a number of other cultures, the imperative of separateness is not imposed so early or so categorically. The interpenetration of mother (or motherers) and child merges over time with collective or communal identity. Selfhood is then quite different from our own, although in all cultures some version of personal identity emerges.

The Kleinians depict the second major stage in the development of selfhood as the depressive position. As in their depiction of the paranoid–schizoid position, this fuses dialectical development with the defenses that are part of and a limitation upon dialectical development. It is an appropriate designation, however, for the second crystallization of defenses.

Briefly, the child (at whatever age) begins to recognize that it exists apart from its mother and significant others, and that they exist apart from it. This is exciting and frightening. Fears of abandonment combine with an emergent sense of autonomy.

Meanwhile, sensuous modalities of interaction are supplemented with perceptual–motor modalities, sensations are supplemented with affects. Importantly, the relationship between self and other is affectively mediated. Self and other are linked through love, hate, and their affective correlates. If emergent individuality is mediated by predominantly loving feelings, then empathic bonds are created. It becomes possible for the self to experience the selfhood of the other, to know that s/he has feelings, too. The other is no longer just a function within a matrix. The phenomenon of mutual recognition begins to emerge.

But fear and hatred are inherent in the process of individuation. The self continues to interact with the other aggressively and defensively. Only now, because the other has begun to take on the characteristics of a person instead of a function, the other is experienced as liable to both sensuous and affective injury. Consequently, there arise feelings of guilt and the problem of reparation along with the experience of recognition.

• In contrast to the developmental progression depicted above, there is also developmental regression, the ordering (disordering) of pathology: dialectical development → defensive fixation or regression → traumatic undoing of selfhood. The closer we come to the end of this line, the more anxiety becomes panic.

16.

We remember that desire in the Hegelian and, even more, Lacanian usage involves the experience of a disjunction and a lack. Subject and object do not fit together, there is something missing in the experience of pleasure. We may now add that the experience of a lack has a definite affective content: anxiety.

Thus there emerges what we might term the transcendental problem of desire. Desire aims at an experience of pleasure in which there is nothing lacking in intensity, duration, or security. Only intrauterine existence approximates to a realization of this aim. Hence desire aims beyond the possible. It holds life up to an impossible standard.

We are not the only creatures who would live free from pain and anxiety if we could, but we are the only creatures who can imagine such an existence. Other species have drives and emotions, make use of the flight–fight response, and maybe make use of other, more psychological, defenses. But in our emotional lives as in our work lives, we are distinctively creatures of imagination. We alone come to believe that it is possible to live without pain and without anxiety. We defiantly refuse to accept the terms of existence. We search for happiness without end and, by so doing, put an end to the only happiness humanly available to us.

There is no basic tendency in human beings to escape from freedom, but there is a tendency to escape from psychic pain into fantasies of a world of perfect pleasure. When we attempt to live out these escapes into absolute well-being, we tend to realize them by inversion.

17.

It is past time to say something about sexuality.

In the early version of Freud's drive theory, sexuality was set off against self-preservation. The latter was given a special relationship to hunger. In the later version of the theory, self-preservation and hunger lose their autonomy. Sexuality is attached to the life-drive and set off against aggression, which is attached to the death-drive.

Our anthropology is clearly quite different from Freud's. We give sexuality a narrower role and hunger a wider one. We view sexuality as being centered in but not limited to genital experience; we extend hunger (appetite for food) to alimentation (ingestion, digestion, excretion).

Sensuous interaction is focused on alimentation, although genital sensations are part of sensuous experience. Alimentation involves the functioning of the three sensuous drives (life, death, aggression) and is regulated by the interpenetrating pleasure, Nirvana, and reality principles. As perceptual–motor function advances, alimentation becomes an experience structured by the problematics of recognition and mediated by working/desiring. Construction and destruction, love and hate, person and thing, self and other, feelings of pride and shame are fused and confused in alimentary experience. In our culture this is especially evident

in bowel and bladder training, with its associated meanings of performance (voluntary, on demand, only apparently voluntary), production (quantitative and qualitative), gift-giving, yes-saying and no-say-
ing, etc.

Genital sexuality emerges gradually from its sensuous and alimentary integument. As it does, it inflects pleasurable sensuousness with the
quality of sensuality. The genitals are the center of sensual feelings but,
optimally, these feelings are not genitally limited. In certain circumstances
they may even fuse with the encoded sense of unbounded quiescent pleasure that is the legacy of prenatal life.

As in hunger and alimentation, the sensuous drives and their regulatory principles are integral to sexuality; likewise the problematics
of recognition and the field of interaction defined by desire. But sexuality involves an intensity of sensation that sets it apart from other
domains of perceptual–motor experience. And because it involves not
only intensely pleasurable sensations but also equally intense sensations of pressure, it combines freedom from necessity with the quality of
demand.

To put it another way, sexuality is peculiarly self-contradictory, and
its contradictory quality gives it a particularly important position in the
interactional fields of desire and recognition.

18.

For whatever reason, all developmental roads except those reserved
for self-preservation lead to sexuality. Love and hate, which are the basic
modalities of desire, are sensualized in the course of human development,
and sensualized love and hate are among the most important objects of
defensive operations.

Sensuality involves a subtle interplay of mind and body. Although
sexuality is at first a sensation, an experience of the whole organism, it
becomes experienced as something in and of the body, to which the mind
responds. At the same time, the body and its sexual parts become a
vehicle for the expression of mental (ideational and affective) meanings.
Unavoidably the genitals, in which intense sensations originate, attract
mental processes and gain meaning.

There are two signal consequences of sensuality-qua-genitality. On
the one hand, we come to know ourselves and others as creatures who
have a penis or who have a vagina. The one form of knowledge is more
manifestly available than the other. And, fatefully, the one form of genital may be more valued than the other. It is not just in our culture that
little boys are infatuated with their penises. Be that as it may, genital

sexuality and the difference between the sexes becomes an irreducible dimension of human recognition.

On the other hand, the genitals occasion not only intense excitement and pleasure but also intense anxiety. They become the locus of the intergenerational struggle for recognition. Selfhood is expressed in terms of sexual desire, specifically the desire for sensual gratification from the parent or parenting figure of the opposite sex. The same-sex parent becomes a rival, powerful and feared, who is imagined to operate by the principle, "thine eye offends me and I will pluck it out." The "eye" is here the genitals, which the child fears will be lacerated. There is a conventional name for the boy's fear: castration anxiety. This name is not appropriate for girls, nor is it any good to replace it with the fear of abandonment or loss of love. The latter is universal, the accompaniment of individuation, the legacy of separation anxiety. The girl's fear that her genitals will be or have been lacerated is something else.[8]

Thus we arrive at Oedipus and the triangulation of desire. As Deleuze, Guattari, and Gayle Rubin remind us, however, the oedipal triangle is not only an expression of desire but also a defense against it. We are inherently bisexual. Our sensuality reaches toward both mother and father; we desire the sensual experience of our sexual opposite. The oedipal triangle defends us against the terrors and delights of an undefined and unbounded sensuality.

19.

When we reflect upon the unfolding of desire in relation to work, we can identify three kinds of interaction:

• Work and desire develop through and are mutually constitutive of each other. Working helps to structure the self and create a location for the play of desire; satisfying demands reduces anxiety and so has an affective yield; desires are tied to work and gratified through it, etc.

• Work and desire are mutually compensatory. The pain of ungratified desire is alleviated through work or play; the difficulty and stress of work are relieved through the gratification of desire.

• Work and desire are mutually exclusive and/or mutually destructive. Pathologies in one sphere carry over into and pathologize the other. The demands of work overload and constrict the field of desire; disruptions in the field of desire make work difficult or impossible.

In the second and third instances various fantasies arise, including the one that the work demanded of one has been freely chosen. This is an emergent form of false consciousness.

In what ways these various possibilities are realized is a matter of history, not anthropology—a matter of history, and of praxis.

20.

Here is another way of looking at the dialectic of development.
- All development originates in the quiescent pleasure of intrauterine experience. Because this experience is sensuously encoded, it is the synchronic as well as diachronic point of origin. Earliest is deepest.
- Paradise is lost and cannot be regained. Postnatal life necessarily involves pain, anxiety, and threats to preservation.
- Healthy ontogenetic development is dialectical. In it, dialectical processes predominate over defensive ones. An essential openness—a totalizing but not totalized quality— is maintained. Anxiety and conflict are tolerated as conditions of growth.
- Pathological ontogenetic development is antidialectical. Here, defensive processes predominate or threaten to predominate over dialectical ones. At the limit, totalization is required as a defense against panic and a chaotic destructuring of the self.
- A fantasy may develop that anxiety, conflict, and the need for defense do not or need not exist. Characteristically, pleasure and sensual gratification are split off from work and pain. The encoded experience of intrauterine, oceanic oneness is brought forward as a defense against real world difficulties. At the level of consciousness there emerges a vision of life after death, a lost golden age, or a golden age yet to come.

21.

In *The Phenomenology* work, desire, and recognition are initially configured as a life and death battle, then as a relationship of lordship and bondage. It is a fair criticism of Hegel that, if he meant to depict the origins of human sociability, he erred in what we might term a Kleinian fashion. He mistook a developmental perversion for the conditions of development as such, substituted the pathological side of development for development overall. But like Klein, by so doing he revealed with unusual clarity the dark side of our nature.

22.

Up to this point we have ignored the distinction between conscious and unconscious mental processes and, along with it, the role of language in human interaction. Because the discourse follows a roughly ontogenetic line, we are increasingly called upon to explicate these features of our species life. First, however, we focus our attention on the problem of domination in early development and, along with it, on the emerging structure of the self.

No human being grows up without a struggle and without the experience of domination. Overtly or covertly, minorly or majorly, the development of selfhood is a battle of wills, and a battle within which the will is formed. A child learns that it has a mind or will of its own through the negation of its intention by an other, and through its reassertion of this intention despite the negation.

The self is structured in the process. It contends with the other, the not-self. The battle, initially intersubjective, becomes intrasubjective as well. The alien presence is internalized, becomes a part of the self that is not the self—not only the not-self but the negation (even more, negating) of the self. It, the alien presence, becomes the demand that the self be self-negating, that it give up that part of itself that is rebellious, that resists the imposition of alien power and authority. Manifestly the self complies, accepts its bondage, acquiesces to domination, grants recognition to the will of the internalized other, allows a part of itself to be split off and alienated—less extremely, repressed. Part of the I becomes an It, parallel to and the opposite of the internalized other, the moralized persecutor of the self. Resistance to authority goes underground, vowing silently, "I will return."

In this way the self takes on its characteristic tripartite form. We may retain the names ego, id, and super-ego for the component parts if we are mindful of the following points. First, our anthropology excludes conceptions of primary narcissism, of a selfhood that somehow, mysteriously, precedes intersubjectivity. We maintain that there cannot be a self without an other. Second, we are not assuming a primordial id from which the ego develops, but rather a self-developing sensuous organism that is structured through conflict in the course of its development, an "I" that develops an "It" and not an "It" that somehow becomes an "I." And third, we include the dynamics of work and play within the structuring of character and selfhood.

With these reservations in mind, we may picture the emergent self this way:

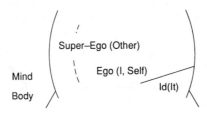

This representation is a modified version of the ones used by Freud in *The Ego and the Id* (1923) and *New Introductory Lectures on Psycho-Analysis* (1933a). The self, which is latent or potential in the field of sensuous inter-action, becomes manifest at the level of perceptual–motor interaction. At the former level mind and body, self and other, are not differentiated; at the latter level they are—but they are also interpenetrative. Further, as the self emerges it is internally differentiated in the manner described above. The internalized other compels the self to alienate a part of itself while, conversely, the alienated self presses its claims to expression, seeks its return and repatriation.

The human self thus bears the marks of lordship and bondage, of domination. It is structured, partially, through the deployment of defenses. But the divided self we encounter in critical social theories comes into existence only when defensive trends distort and pervert the dialectic of development. In more favorable circumstances, when inter-subjective conditions of mutual recognition predominate, the self is able to unify and affirm itself through negative self-relation.

The question then becomes, how big a part, for individuals and col-lectivities, do relationships of domination play in development? In any given instance, is lordship and bondage paradigmatic of social interac-tion or a subordinate aspect of relationships of mutual recognition?

And now we really can go no further without attending to the dis-tinction between conscious and unconscious.

E. Conscious Activity

1.

Consciousness is a discursively overloaded concept and we ought not to add to its burdens. To the contrary: Let's see if we can lighten the load.

The simplest meaning of consciousness is awareness; of unconscious-ness, lack of awareness. At the level of sensuousness, these two mean-ings are scarcely differentiable from being awake and being asleep, respectively. At the level of perception, being conscious is attending to something in particular, being unconscious is not attending to that thing. When there is a self with a history, the past experiences of the self become possible objects of perceptual/conscious attention or inattention.

From the ontogenetic beginning, oral communication—the sending and receiving of meaningful sounds—is an aspect of experience. And early on oral communication gains a verbal form. For the child words are first "passively" experienced as sensations, then as percepts bearing meaning, and eventually as signifiers and symbols that need not have a one-to-one relationship with percepts and sensations. Active language use follows in the train of passive language use. The active or expressive use of language is not, however, simply the result of internalization or learning from example. It is driven from the inside. Words become a vehicle through which the individual seeks self-preservation, pleasure, the satisfaction of needs, the gratification of desires, and recognition.

Once language has been sufficiently established, it permeates all subsequent sensuous and perceptual experience. Consciousness is then linguistically mediated. So, too, is unconsciousness, as we know most of all from dreams. Memory of percepts, affects, and actions may extend, however, to the period before language, and recoverable sensations may extend to the period before birth. Diachronically as well as synchronically language is only a part of human experience.

Lacan claimed that the unconscious is structured like a language. This may be so. But if so, it is because language is first structured like the unconscious, that is, by sensuous and perceptual experiences that precede and partially determine the advent of language.

The use of language is, however, fundamental to our identity as a species. The imaginative quality of our working and desiring, our ability to go, first mentally and then concretely, beyond the existentially given, depends upon our linguistic capability. In his own way Aristotle makes this point very well. "The mere making of sounds," he claims in *The Politics*, "serves to indicate pleasure and pain, and is thus a faculty that belongs to animals in general. . . . But language serves to declare what is advantageous and what is the reverse, and it therefore serves to declare what is just and what is unjust" (Barker, 1958, p. 6). Being moral and political animals requires the use of language.

Aristotle goes on to say, "Man, when perfected, is the best of animals; but if he is isolated from law and justice he is worst of all. . . . if he be without virtue, he is a most unholy and savage being, and worse than all others in the indulgence of lust and gluttony" (*ibid.*, p. 7). Hence the title of this chapter: We are the problem we are trying to solve.

2.

There is some utility in restricting the idea of consciousness to sensuous and perceptual activity that is characterized by awareness or attention and that is mediated by language. Then we can say that, so far as the self is concerned, deeper and earlier experience tends to be less conscious than more superficial and recent experience.

On this basis we can also identify three distinct modes of communication and interaction. At the level of consciousness we communicate and interact through language. Beneath the conscious level comes communication through perception, action, and empathy (affective interaction). And at the deepest level we share sensations.

Later on, when we come to the interpretation of psychoanalytic practice, it will be important to distinguish these levels of interaction from each other. For the present their enumeration serves as a safeguard against the reduction of communication to linguistic interaction.

3.

Conscious activity has (relatively) active and passive dimensions. This may be represented so:

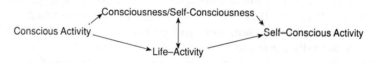

Conscious activity is here divided into the doing of things (life-activity) and the awareness of things (consciousness), including in the latter category awareness of oneself and one's activities (self-consciousness).[9] When one's actions are mediated by self-awareness, the action itself is self-conscious.

Further, when thinking about things involves systematic problem solving, conscious activity becomes theoretical. When activity is systematic or patterned, it becomes practice. Self-conscious activity proceeding from the interaction of these extremes is praxis.

Praxis as thus defined is historically universal, anthropological. All societies, from the most "primitive" to the most sophisticated, possess praxes of various kinds. Individuals, who are always within societies, have their selfhoods determined by these praxes, whether or not their own thinking and doing qualifies as praxis.

Under certain circumstances, individual and collective praxis can be self-determining. We must not make the mistake, however, of isolating praxis from the developmental manifold in which it originates. Praxis is never free from the problematics of sensuousness, work, desire, and recognition. It is a characteristically academic illusion, parallel to the illusions accompanying linguistic imperialism, to believe that praxis can be self-contained and self-sustaining. When we are genuinely self-determining, it is because we engage and act upon our preconscious determinants.

4.

Implicitly, we have now posed the question that is so vital to both Marxist and psychoanalytic theory: Under what conditions, and with what degree of distortion or falsification, are things capable of becoming conscious? How, moreover, do we judge between distorted and undistorted, true and false, rational and irrational, forms of conscious activity?

Note that in raising this question we move away from ontogeny, with its focus on individuals in dyadic or triadic relationships. When we recognize that consciousness and unconsciousness are collective experiences, and that the conscious and unconscious experience of collectivities is widely variable, the historical manifold from which we have abstracted begins to come back into view. And we may then remind ourselves that even the earliest ontogenic experiences are culturally determined.

5.

It might seem like a contradiction in terms to raise questions concerning distortions of consciousness at the theoretical level of anthropology. The content of consciousness is historically, indeed individual life-historically, variable. How could there be universal principles of rationality (or, for that matter, of morality) in the face of the great multiplicity of worldviews and belief systems? Isn't any universalization of right and reason ideological, the imposition of the One upon the Many, a disguised act of domination, power in the form of knowledge?

In all respects but one, I think this objection must be sustained. Even the one exception is not beyond argument. For present purposes, however, it will suffice to assert it: No form of conscious activity can be seen as rational if it undercuts the possibility of human existence. Or, positively, it is rational to preserve the conditions that make it possible for the species to live and flourish as sensuous, perceptual, and conscious beings.

This minimalist notion might be termed a conception of "anthropological rationality." Because anthropology is merely the articulation of necessary historical conditions for distinctively human experience, it might equally be termed "historical rationality." And because all history is ultimately natural history, a third designation would be "ecological rationality."

Unless one rejects the preservation of the species as a good or a value, anthropological rationality is also an ethical grounding principle. As Albert Camus (1956, p. 6) said from his own perspective, from "the

moment that life is recognized as good, it becomes good for all men."
For all people, we would say.

Yet it is important not to beg the question. It is entirely possible to
reject the preservation of the species as a good or value. Individuals and
collectivities might also enact such a rejection, whatever their conscious
intent.

If our fairy tale of the Last Person on Earth becomes a reality, we
will have conclusively demonstrated our anthropological irrationality.

6.

Or we might picture the situation this way:

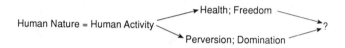

In the diagram, "Human Nature" stands for the diachronic and synchronic unfolding of our species life. Hence human nature = human activity. The historical process is then two-sided. A tendency toward health
and freedom is opposed by a tendency toward perversion and domination. Just because we are relatively free—because we are creatures of
consciousness and imagination—this dialectic does not work itself out
organically, as an undifferentiated part of the dialectic of nature. Rather,
it is beyond nature, in both good and evil. Consequently the dialectic of
human development is open-ended. Although we determine ourselves
teleologically, we are not teleologically determined.

7.

It is evident that our notion of anthropological rationality poses a
problem rather than offering a solution. Will we survive and flourish, or
won't we? And then other problems: Will we survive but not flourish?
Will some of us survive and flourish but not others? Will your survival
be at the expense of mine?

It could not be otherwise. We are problematical animals. But we are
also creatures of project and praxis, experimenters and problem-solvers.
Time will tell if we ourselves are the one problem we cannot solve.

CHAPTER 7

Social Production

1.

What if, as a step down from anthropological abstraction, we place the relationship of sensuousness, work, desire, and consciousness under the sign of domination, more specifically of capitalist domination? Then we might put forward the following three propositions:

• Capitalist production necessarily involves a profound disruption of sensuous and metabolic processes. It perverts these processes and, in so doing, induces levels of pain that strengthen the death-drive in relation to the life-drive. It places us in a state of war.

• As both cause and effect of sensuous disruption, work and desire operate antagonistically. Work becomes alienated labor, in which the forces of destruction predominate over those of construction. Desire is frozen into the paranoid–schizoid position, in which hate predominates over love. When stabilized and interpenetrated, we then have relationships of lordship and bondage: parents > children; men > women; owners > workers; elites > masses; one race > another race.

• At the level of consciousness, however, these relationships of domination take on the guise of mutual recognition, of free individuality. In advanced capitalist societies, we live lives of liberalized domination.

2.

There is another characteristic form of consciousness in (although not just in) capitalist societies. Born into a world of pain, we long for rebirth into a world of pleasure—of bliss. But the image of life reborn is derived from the sensuous memory of life unborn, of intrauterine existence. Hence this spiritual yearning is profoundly regressive, and its object is unattainable.

We recognize in this sketch the image of the Unhappy Consciousness—also of certain forms of utopian consciousness, with their ambiguous desire to go beyond.

The problem is to go beyond capitalism without falling behind it.

3.

If capitalism is a disguised state of war, then the praxis of liberation is a life and death struggle, a battle. We require a map of the battlefield. The purpose of this chapter is to provide one.

4.

We inherit from Marx—and indirectly from Hegel—the concept of modes of social production. A mode of social production is a set of interpenetrating practices, including institutionalized practices, that structure the life-world of a given population. For both Hegel and Marx the structuring of these practices is assumed to be dialectical. Social conflict is built into the synchronic dimension of the concept, while diachronically conflicts and contradictions are seen as resulting in the transformation of modes of production.

Given Hegel's and Marx's conceptions of dialectics, the structuring of modes of social production becomes attached to the notion of totality. Simultaneously social transformation is viewed as rational and progressive. Moreover, the imperatives and contingencies inherent in choices of action are transformed into the reassurances and certainties of absolute historical knowledge.

We do not presume to such wisdom. Our conception of dialectic is filled with the uncertainties of everyday life. Correspondingly our notion of modes of production yields a much looser articulation of social practices, albeit one in which its ancestry is readily apparent.

A. History/Anthropology

1.

The further one goes in the development of anthropological concepts, the less anthropological and the more historical they become, and this in a double sense. We become increasingly aware that complex social practices are implied in the notions being articulated. Simultaneously we recognize the variability of these practices in time and space.

In a theoretical groundwork such as the present one, it is quite impossible to either represent or interpret world history. We can, however, develop a set of categories that (1) mediates the relationship between anthropology and history and (2) enables us to analyze the social practices of capitalist societies.

2.

I do not see how it is possible to argue meaningfully against the following propositions: Human individuals always live in social units; all social units have something in common; no two social units are exactly alike; social units vary quantitatively and qualitatively in time and space; the size and complexity of social units, along with the level of interaction between them, have tended (but only tended) to increase over time.

The first two propositions are anthropological; the other three are historical. Or, one could say, human history is anthropological variation; anthropology is historical invariance. No doubt this categorization is more controversial than the propositions categorized.

3.

Within this simple historical/anthropological framework, it is possible to develop a substantial body of empirical data. There are sophisticated, even scientific, techniques available for gathering and testing the accuracy of such data. Consequently we possess a large quantity of knowledge about historical events—what things have and have not happened, when and where they took place, who was and was not involved. This knowledge is not complete or absolute. There are meaningful questions of facticity in historical inquiry. But there is also a great deal that is definitely known and which it is not meaningful to question.

4.

The same cannot be said for the categories we use to organize and interpret historical data. Even the simplest of such categories is a forming of the object of inquiry. Moreover, categories are necessarily attached to worldviews and often to theories. They are at least pre-interpretive. This does not mean that they are arbitrary or that the data of experience can be categorized and interpreted just as we please. We form objects when we interpret them but—when we do the job well—along lines suggested by the objects themselves.

Thus the categories that follow should not be mistaken for either unproblematical orderings of historical experience or arbitrary impositions upon it. One might say that they are intended to correspond loosely to data we are interested in categorizing.

5.

As I am using the term, categories mediate the relationship of data and concepts. Categories organize or classify data; concepts interpret or explain them. Or to use a convenient analogy: The manifold of historical events resembles natural resources; categorization converts these resources into the raw materials of conceptualization.

Yet there are no categories without concepts nor concepts without categories. In laying out categories, concepts necessarily emerge; wherever there are concepts categories are presupposed.

6.

Here again is the simple historical/anthropological figure presented at the beginning of the last chapter:

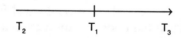

Synchronically, human history = the interaction of human individuals with each other and nonhuman nature during a given period of time. Diachronically, human history = the interaction of human individuals with each other and nonhuman nature over time.

In both regards there is a question of geographical variation. Not so long ago all concrete history was local. The idea of world history was nearly as abstract as that of human species identity. Universal history was a part masking as the whole, as in Eurocentric interpretations, or a pulling together of empirically disjoined histories through the use of interpretive categories and concepts—or both simultaneously. Marx, following Hegel, is sometimes universalizing in this ideological and abstract fashion. But as he both depicted and predicted, the bourgeoisie "creates a world after its own image" (Marx & Engels, 1848, p. 477). The totalization of social relationships against which Foucault and others protest is increasingly an international or transnational reality. Increasingly, but not completely.

As indicated above, for the most part we must forego discussion of the variations in capitalist systems and content ourselves with a depiction of the generality.

7.

We locate ourselves, therefore, at T_1, our own time, hence with a society sufficiently complex so that (1) economic production has been differentiated from human reproduction (from the household, as is classically said); (2) cultural practices are not merely mediations of production and reproduction; (3) collective formations such as social classes exist, as do (4) individuals who cannot be identified simply by their position in such collective formations; and (5) politics has its own institutional framework.

Given these conditions, social relationships can be pictured in various ways. Here is one of them:

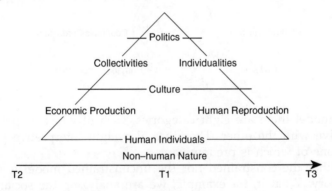

This is a model of social production. It presupposes both nonhuman nature and human individuals as they exist in a given present time. These individuals interact with nature and each other in terms of various practical modalities, which are structured at varying levels of generality. There are, first, the general conditions for social action, the ones that are common to all individuals of a society—the mode of economic production, human reproduction, and culture. Second, these general conditions are particularized along both collective (social class, emotional group) and individual (social role, character type) lines. Third, at least in societies like our own, there is a relative totalization or integration of the first two levels through political and, especially, bureaucratic practices. And at all levels there are corresponding forms of consciousness and ideology.

Like the model articulated in Marx's preface to the 1859 *A Contribution to the Critique of Political Economy* and in *The German Ideology*, this one is built from the bottom up.[1] And like Marx's model, it is neither unidirectional in its determinations nor indifferently interactional. It is rather constrained from bottom to top. Nonhuman nature as it exists at T_1 is a constraint on any human action whatsoever; the nature of human individuals at this time constrains economic production and human reproduction; and so on.

Because this model depicts social relations as constrained from bottom to top, it also constrains our interpretive perspective. Foundational issues tend to loom larger than any others, and we are predisposed to work from these issues to the others.

So long as these constraints are not merely theoretical artifacts—so long as social action is actually constrained in this fashion—such a model is of heuristic value. It is important, however, to think about social reality without its constraints. Thus:

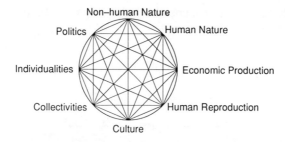

In this model there are eight categories, each of which is potentially interactive with the other. There are also eight interpretive perspectives, none of which is predominant.

Neither the constrained nor the unconstrained model is entirely satisfactory. What if, for example, we are analyzing the social reality of African-Americans? African-Americans are a specific collectivity, a people with their own culture, work, and familial patterns, roles and character types, and political interests. Looking at the situation from the general standpoint of capitalist production tends to occlude the particularity of their experience. Ignoring the structural constraints of capitalism, however, engenders illusions concerning the rational choices of action actually available to them.

Although we cannot simultaneously privilege the standpoints of particularity and generality, we are not forced to choose between them. We can start from one and work toward the other, as the need arises. Assume, for example, that the model of constrained social action generally or abstractly corresponds to social conditions. Without independent demonstration this is only an assumption, but it is not an implausible one. In any case, on this assumption the model of constrained social action provides a framework for analysis, a map of the territory. Actual analysis, however, is conducted from within the categories. Each category then functions as a locus of interpretation, so that social production appears as structured but not totalized, and the particularity of each domain is preserved.

Or we might consider the matter more methodologically. In the process of abstraction or phenomenological reduction we generate abstract or universal concepts. When we reverse the process and advance synthetically toward the reproduction of the concrete, universality becomes relative to emergent particularities. More concrete concepts and categories are relatively particular, less concrete ones are relatively universal.

In this context, Sartre's complaint against lazy or dogmatic Marxists is that they always work from pre-established universals to particulars, or substitute universals for particulars, instead of starting again with particulars and allowing the course of the inquiry to determine which, if any, of the pre-existing universals is relevant to the inquiry.

The same could be said for lazy Freudians, or lazy psychoanalytic-marxists.

8.

Here is another way of approaching the matter. Class, gender, and race each provide standpoints for the analysis of and struggle against domination. None of these collective (and complex) social interests can be reduced to or privileged over the other. Hence critical theory must be constituted from at least these three perspectives:

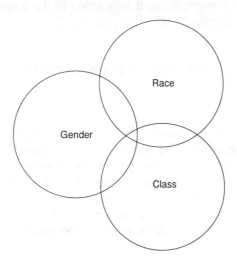

This diagram shows three loci of struggle. In the domain of gender, the struggle is against sexism, including the hegemonic imposition of hetero-sexuality. In the domain of race, the struggle (in the United States) is against white racism. Native-Americans, African-Americans, various Latino peoples, and various Asian-American peoples have a common enemy but do not constitute a single oppressed community. And in the domain of class, the struggle is against late capitalistic or bureaucratic capitalistic domination.

Each standpoint can be used to analyze social production as a whole, each other standpoint, and (reflexively) itself. The intersections between standpoints also define loci for analysis and action. Thus there are social locations where the problematics of race and gender, race and class, and class and gender converge, as well as those where all three must be con-fronted simultaneously.

Note that this categorization of collective interests presupposes our map of the social battlefield. If we were to analyze the issue of abortion rights in the United States, for example, we might approach it first from the standpoint of gender. But we would be thinking and acting in a vacuum if we ignored the systemic context within which the issue arises and the other collective interests that it involves.

Conversely, the model of constrained social production maps a battle-field because capitalism pits collectivity against collectivity, within and across the boundaries of race, class, and gender.

9.

In this chapter, we will explicate the constrained version of the model. In the next, we will use it as a guide to the analysis of capitalist, sexist, and racist domination.

B. Generality of Social Production

1.

Human nature has already been discussed and nonhuman nature requires little discussion at this juncture. It is sufficient to note the tension between them. Nature can never give us everything we want, if for no other reason than that it is in our nature to want what we cannot have. At least in capitalist systems desire reaches beyond the possibilities of gratification. Fatefully, its reach is instrumentally rational and efficacious. Nature pays the price for our inability to recognize and live within its metabolic limits.

Are we not reminded of the wisdom of Anaximander of Miletos, who said that all things "make reparation and satisfaction to one another for their injustice according to the ordering of time" (Burnet, 1930, p. 52)?

2.

In the first instance economic production is work—work in the sense of human activity aimed at the satisfaction of needs. It necessarily involves the transformation of natural resources into objects suitable for human use and consumption. It is also the modality of human interaction most firmly attached to and determinative of the content of the social reality principle. Moreover, the satisfaction of needs is the foundation of social interests, of individual and collective advantages and disadvantages. In all of these respects it has a special connection to instrumental forms of reason.

These features of economic production are transhistorical. They are as universal as human nature itself and are scarcely distinguishable from it. It is only in quite special historical circumstances, however, that economic production is institutionally distinguishable from human reproduction and the other categories of social production.

Economic production deserves the honor that Marx bestowed upon it, namely, of being the historical category par excellence. One can read the story of historical transformation more clearly in the development of means of production than in any other modality or product of human interaction. This does not imply anything approaching an historical-cum-economic determinism. But economic analysis would not offer us such great interpretive leverage if economic production were not of such great practical importance.

Marxism is far from being the only theory of economic production, and it is most assuredly not beyond criticism. Indeed, the contributions upon which Marx most prided himself—the theory of value in general and surplus value in particular—are the ones that have drawn the most critical fire. Strictly economic debates lie outside the boundaries of our inquiry, however, and we shall find that precisely the most debated of Marx's concepts retain their heuristic value. These concepts remain determinative of social character even if they are not strictly determinative of market prices. It must be added: Their heuristic value depends upon the recognition that even self-interested economic actors are creatures of desire.

The last is by now a familiar point, but perhaps it is worth a further comment. Marx accepted from the classical political economists a conception of scientific specialization that permitted him to present individuals and classes of individuals as simply the bearers or embodiments of economic relationships. Their subjectivity was limited to the interests that result from these relationships. Insofar as capitalism does in fact tend to reduce individuals and collectivities to economic functions and objective interests, this methodological one-sidedness had an empirical justification. But only a limited justification, and this for two reasons.

First, even in the sphere of production, individuals and collectivities retain their subjectivity, no matter how deformed by the objective circumstances in which they find themselves. This would not be theoretically significant if there were no recoil of subjectivity upon the objectivity of economic processes. But one only needs to observe the role of panic in economic life to recognize that desire is itself an economic force.

Second, as we know, Marx carried this one-sidedness over into his anthropology. The only attributes of human individuals he *conceptualized* were those related to work and production. Other attributes might be observed or introduced ad hoc, but they had no theoretical status. Consequently the noneconomic dimensions of social life were necessarily interpreted economically.

Our anthropology is intended to counter this one-sidedness. Whatever the sphere or institutional domain of social life, our approach is to recognize the interplay of sensuousness, work (or interests derived ultimately from work relationships), desire, and consciousness.

3.

The function of human reproduction is institutionalized in familial or kinship relationships of one kind or another. For the greater part of human history these relationships have framed economic production as well as human reproduction. Manifestly, then, they have involved the interplay of work and desire. In modern societies, however, economic and human reproductive functions are increasingly separated. The former slide toward the public sphere while the latter, in parallel fashion, are privatized.

Various consequences follow from this division. Perhaps most importantly, the functions historically performed by women lose their (official, ideological) status as work. At best these functions are characterized as "women's work," that is, not real work. This facilitates a rather vicious form of circular reasoning: Because women's work is not real work, it merits no payment; the proof that women's work is not real work is that it is unpaid. Indeed, the fact that women *do* things becomes virtually invisible. They are seen, rather, as the embodiment of emotional life—as creatures of feeling rather than of thought and action. At the same time, and especially in psychoanalysis, familial relationships in general are viewed exclusively through the optic of desire.

Just as our approach saves us from a one-sided construal of economic production, so it saves us from the opposite one-sided construal of human reproduction. Whatever its relationship to directly economic production, we see human reproduction as a work relationship, and not just an emotional one.

Perhaps, however, it is fair to see the relationship between work and desire in these two spheres as mirroring each other. The differentiating factor is the nature of the work performed. Economic production turns on the making of the things that satisfy needs. Its standard of rationality is instrumental; rational action requires the subordination of desire to these instrumental aims. This does not mean that economic activity is *in fact* instrumentally rational, but instrumental rationality is the norm. Familial relationships, on the other hand, center on persons rather than on things. The central modalities of interaction are the sexual/emotional relationship of men and women, and child rearing. Desire is central to both of these familial modalities. One might well say, for example, that child rearing is the most demanding of all jobs—but in contrast to working in an office, where emotional factors are normatively secondary, the demands of the job are as much emotional as they are technical. To put it crudely, people are the product, not the byproduct, of the activity.

Hence the sphere of production might be signified work > desire, while that of reproduction might be signified desire > work.

A parallel line of analysis can be followed with respect to the analysis of gender. Neither the formation nor the consequences of gender are limited to the sphere of human reproduction. Indeed, in certain ancient societies it would be fair to characterize the mode of economic production as patriarchal. In modern societies the time is long since past when woman's place—and questions of gender along with it—were in the home. But *Anti-Oedipus* to the contrary notwithstanding, there is an especially intimate connection between familial relationships and the problematics of gender.

Given these parallels, it is all the more important not to conflate the analysis of desire with that of gender. The designation "patriarchy/ phallocentrism" is intended to remind us that gender in the mode of domination has two interpenetrated dimensions: the subordination of women to the interests and power of men; and a psychology that infiltrates and supports this relationship of lordship and bondage.

4.

A culture is a way of life, the basic or everyday practices of a given society. The historically most fundamental and ubiquitous of these practices are those associated with economic production, human reproduction, and the linkages between them. In this sense, culture is a summary expression or a totalizing of economic and familial relationships. Culture is never, however, reducible to this immediacy. It also involves a discrete set of practices that mediate social relationships more generally.

Cultural practices might be divided into the categories of use and production. The former involves people's use or consumption of goods and services resulting from economic production, that is, the use of food, clothing, shelter, and health services, along with the available means of transportation, communication, education, and recreation. In secular societies religious participation would also fall into this category.

The concept of cultural production is somewhat more problematical. Insofar as the category of culture expresses the generality of the primary spheres of social production, all production is cultural production.[2] More narrowly, the production of consumer goods and services has cultural utilization as its aim. But there is a further and more distinctive kind of cultural production, namely, productive activity that has a reflexive (critical or affirmative) relationship to social production as a whole. Classically, this refers to the spheres of art, religion, and philosophy; but the category can be broadened to include most productive activity in the spheres of education and recreation.

Because academic activity is cultural in the above sense, there is an understandable academic tendency to locate cultural production above and outside the field of social production in general. This tendency is not limited to academia. It extends to the elites in the cultural professions and to those who have the privilege of being the sophisticated consumers of cultural products. Taken together, these groups become the high priests of culture, a self-designated aristocracy looking down with open or concealed disdain upon popular culture, the way of life of the Many.

From the beginning Marx was critical of any such Platonizing of cultural production. In his view cultural production was neither disengaged nor disinterested. He contended, rather, that (1) the "mode of production of material life conditions the social, political and intellectual life process in general" (Marx, 1859, p. 4), and (2) the "ideas of the ruling class are in every epoch the ruling ideas" (Marx & Engels, 1845b, p. 172). The activity of cultural elites is shaped by and serves to perpetuate the existing conditions of social production. Thus we have the concept, often identified with Antonio Gramsci, of cultural or ideological hegemony—of the production of forms of consciousness that both are woven into the fabric of everyday life and serve the interests of the ruling class or classes.

In this way we also arrive at the issue of true and false consciousness. False consciousness must be differentiated from incidental and, especially, harmless error. The term is used, rather, to denote systematically distorted thinking, especially when the distortions induce people to act against their own interests.

The concept of false consciousness necessarily presupposes a standard of truth—of thinking that reflects and facilitates action in terms of actual interests. Yet it is only rarely the case that the objectivity of social interests is beyond dispute. More frequently advantages and disadvantages are complex and criss-crossing, with the result that judgments concerning interests are problematic and probabilistic. Moreover, as Foucault emphasizes, it is difficult to locate a domain of truth lying beyond the reaches of power. Truth-claims, judgments of truth and falsity, tend to be servants of social interests and weapons of political warfare. Hence those who articulate these judgments should not claim to be noncombatants. Or to put the point more civilly, theorists of false consciousness should apply their categories to themselves. If they do, they may open a space in which a meaningful discourse about the truth becomes possible. It might even be the case that something worthy of that venerable name would emerge through such a discipline of self-knowledge.

C. Particularity of Social Production

1.

We come now to the particularization of social production: collective social formations on the one hand, individual modes of interaction on the other.

Three points might be noted in advance.

• These particularized collective and individual formations are structured or conditioned by the generality of social production. In like fashion, the individual formations are determined or limited by the collective ones. We therefore take up collective formations before issues of individuality.

• Freud and most of his followers accept uncritically a liberal conception of "the individual"—of a self that is constituted and conceivable outside of social relationships. This conception, appealing though it may be ideologically, lacks any and all empirical grounding. It is an instance of false consciousness. But it is not so obviously ideological to identify psychology with individual states of mind. To do so is nonetheless mistaken, specifically the mistaking of a part for the whole. Psychology certainly includes the domain of intrapsychic experience, and psychoanalytic psychology includes the unconscious region of that domain. Psychologists are necessarily explorers of the inner worlds of individuals. But on the one hand, even the most sealed off of inner worlds is populated: Selves within the self interact with others within the self. On the other, individuals are bound together in patterns or structures of desire, some of which are conscious and some of which are unconscious. *All psychology is therefore social psychology.* This being given, social psychological analysis can be conducted on the levels of individuals, dyads, triads, small groups, and varyingly large groups.

Our concern here is with large groups, specifically with emotional formations that complement and contradict social class alignments.

• In the analysis of collective action, as in social analysis generally, needs and interests precede emotions and desires. The relationship between objective and subjective factors is not, however, that of cause and effect, or independent to dependent variable.

Consider two situations.

In the first, collective survival depends upon a high degree of instrumental rationality. Desires must be neutralized or brought into line with interests *if* the collectivity is to survive. But it is not given in advance that this condition for survival will be met.

In the second, the survival of the collectivity is not directly at issue. The necessity for instrumental rationality is therefore weakened; the reality constraints on action are reduced. Action that is not collectively self-interested remains irrational, but the field of irrational action has been enlarged.

Or think of it this way. If human beings lived by interests alone, a positive science of social action would be possible. We would all be rational actors and game theorists, differing from each other only in skills, training, and resources. But we are also creatures of desire. Desires are inherently multivalent, and they cannot be reduced to interests. Moreover, it is precisely our capacity for rational action that frees us to be creatures of desire. We determine our own indeterminacy.

One final way. We begin with objectivities (the imperatives of self-preservation—work, production, interests, instrumental reason) because they constitute the necessary conditions for both human survival and transformational action. We might end with them, if they constituted the sufficient conditions as well. But the gap between necessity and sufficiency, the lacuna signified by the hypothetical (*if* we are to survive, *if* we are to be free), opens up the territory of desire.

When starvation approaches, we dream of food, but we also have been known to kill and die for love.

2.

We will take up collective interests, then collective desires, and finally the relationship between the two.

In Marxist theory the analysis of collective interests and action centers on classes. This is because class divisions are internal to economic production in all relatively complex societies. There cannot be, for example, a capitalist society without capitalists and wage laborers. But classes are not the only collectivities with social interests. Moreover, class membership is not necessarily economically determined. It might be determined on the basis of race, ethnicity, or gender, in other words, on the basis of other collective social interests. Hence the appropriateness of concepts such as a sexual or racial division of labor.

We do not mean to privilege the concept of class over race and gender. We cannot ignore class, however, and we need to clarify our usage of the term. Hence we will begin by following Marx's lead and focusing on class interests. Later we will broaden the discussion to include other collective interests.

3.

Marx offers us the following two complementary and mutually reinforcing propositions:

> At a certain stage of their development, the material productive forces of society come in conflict with the existing relations of production. . . . Then begins an epoch of social revolution. (Marx, 1859, p. 4)

> The history of all hitherto existing society is the history of class struggle. . . . [Throughout history] oppressor and oppressed stood in constant opposition to one another, carried on an uninterrupted, now hidden, now open fight, a fight that each time ended, either in a revolutionary re-constitution of society at large, or in the common ruin of the contending classes. (Marx & Engels, 1848, pp. 473–474)

For the moment we leave aside the question of the historical rationality of these processes. We may also put aside the chicken and egg question of which comes first, the mode of economic production or class struggle. Class divisions are built into the mode of production and so, too, is conflict between social classes. Class action, conversely, reacts upon and possibly transforms existing forces and relations of production.

It is customary and useful to view classes from three perspectives: economic, social, and political. In the economic sense a class is a collective relationship—ownership, control, or the lack thereof—to means of production. In the social sense a class is a cultural entity, a collectivity not only with a distinctive role in economic production but also with its own familial relationships and way of life. In the political sense a class is (directly or through representatives) oriented toward participation in and/or the transformation of public institutions.

In all three respects classes have a double nature. On the one hand, all individuals in a society, no matter what their class position, are conditioned by the generalities of social production. There may also be a general interest, a set of mutual advantages, that unites all members of a society, at least (or especially) vis-à-vis other societies. On the other hand, members of a class live the generality of social production in a particular way. The particularity of the class corresponds to its class interest—its advantages and disadvantages vis-à-vis other classes.

It is always in the interest of ruling classes to persuade ruled classes that their particular interests are comprised within the general interest. If this is not in fact true, and if members of ruled classes accept it as the truth, we have the classic instance of false consciousness. The emancipatory task is then to demonstrate the falsity of the universalizing claim, that is, to bring into consciousness the opposition between particular and (so-called) general interests.

The concept of class as thus delineated must be differentiated from the statistical or merely classificatory notion of class, as in the division of a population into upper, middle, and lower classes. At a minimum, the use of one term for two quite distinct phenomena is confusing; and when the latter notion is used in place of the former, the result is to obscure underlying structures of ownership, control, and power. Hence we will reserve the term "class" for structural social divisions and adopt the term "strata" for the statistical or merely descriptive ones.

Marxists tend to treat social strata as secondary matters. There is some justification for this practice. Social stratification is largely a product of class divisions. But politically, strata may be more important than classes. This is most evident with respect to the issue of the so-called middle class or classes. Marx argued that capitalist production tended toward social polarization, in part because small-scale independent producers—the traditional yeoman farmer, artisan, shopkeeper, tradesman—lose out to and are replaced by large-scale producers.

Hence over time capitalist society "is more and more splitting up into two great hostile camps, into two great classes directly facing each other: Bourgeoisie and Proletariat" (Marx & Engels, 1848, p. 474). This is not just a dialectical fantasy. Traditional petty-bourgeois classes decline in size and importance in the course of capitalist development; capitalist societies are structurally divided into those who own and control large-scale means of production and those who don't; and the interests of these two great classes are fundamentally opposed. But in specifiable circumstances, capitalism also spawns a broad middle stratum that cuts across class lines. Such a middle stratum is no more fantastical than the polarized structure it mediates.[3]

If this line of argument is accepted, then two points follow. First, so long as a capitalist economy is able to generate and sustain a broad middle stratum, the political consequences of class polarization—open class conflict—will be minimized. Second, when a capitalist economy is not able to sustain this condition, then open class conflict will tend to occur.

4.

We have developed the concept of collective interests narrowly, simply in terms of class. But even when we extend the concept to include sexual, racial, ethnic, or national interests, it still fits within an essentially Marxist framework. And if nothing more were required for the interpretation of collective action and the realization of emancipatory interests, then there would be no *political* need either to hyphenate Marxism or politicize psychoanalysis. But collectively no less than individually, people are capable of acting in opposition to their interests.

It seems evident (although one finds little evidence of it in the psychoanalytic-marxist literature) that a psychology of individuals, even a social psychology of individuals, cannot solve the unsolved problems of a class analytic theory.[4] A social class is a structural component of a social system, not an aggregation of individuals. Likewise class consciousness (whether true or false) is a collective mentality that shapes and constrains the thinking of individuals. One does not arrive at it by adding up or averaging the opinions and beliefs of individual members of the class. Accordingly a genuinely group psychology is required for mediating the relationship of class and consciousness.

Freud (1921, p. 116) defined a "primary group" as *"a number of individuals who have put one and the same object in the place of their ego ideal and have consequently identified themselves with one another in their ego.*" The object here is a leader or leading idea. The identificatory relationship with this object is hypnotic. It, as well as the mutual identification of the group members, is effected through aim-inhibited libidinal bonding.

Freud's concept is open to a variety of objections (Wolfenstein, 1990a, 1990c), but it also opens the way to thinking about collective emotional structures—and picturing them[5]:

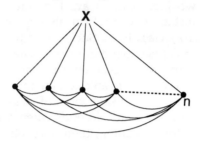

The representation consists of three elements: the leader or leading idea (X); the members (•), the number of which is extended indefinitely; and a double set of affective bonds (–). These bonds are both within the individuals and between them. If they are sufficiently well established and/or intense, individuals entering the group will experience them as their own feelings. Thus the group as a whole is the unit of analysis, not the psyches of the individuals comprising it.

In this representation the group is hierarchical. The members are united by their relationship to something experienced as higher or greater than they are. Historically most groups have been of this type. But unless the group is reduced to a dyad, it also contains the egalitarian relationship of the members to each other. If this egalitarian dimension is conceptualized as a distinct social formation, we then have a group in which the leading idea is the absence of a leading idea, or simply the idea of group membership itself:

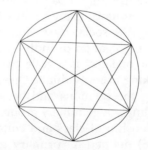

Here the identificatory and other affective bonds are at least potentially those of mutual recognition. Occasionally friendships and communal relationships are of this kind.

Freud viewed groups as regressive, irrationalizing, and deindividualizing. W. R. Bion, who did not share Freud's fear of and hostility toward collectivities, has a more subtle and dispassionate view of them.

Bion recognizes, first of all, that human beings are group animals: "No individual, however isolated in time and space, can be regarded as outside a group or lacking in active manifestations of group psychology" (Bion, 1959, p. 132). Within organized groups he distinguishes two interpenetrated levels of functioning: that of the work group (which is instrumentally rational) and that of the basic assumption group (which is not). He identifies three such basic assumptions: dependency, in which the group exists "in order to be sustained by a leader on whom it depends for nourishment, material and spiritual, and protection"; fight–flight, in which the group exists to "fight something or to run away from it"; and pairing, in which the group exists to witness (especially the imagined sexual) interaction of a couple, from whose union a messianic leader is expected to be born (*ibid.*, pp. 146–153).

Bion views the basic assumptions as having the "characteristics of defensive reactions to psychotic anxiety" (*ibid.*, p. 189). Hence they have something in common with "mechanisms described by Melanie Klein . . . as typical of the earliest phases of mental life" (*ibid.*, p. 141). This does not mean, however, that groups function at a pre-oedipal level. Indeed, there are at least traces of a developmental line from the dependency situation, for which the prototype is mother and infant, to the pairing situation, for which the prototype is witnessing the primal scene.

Because there is a tendency in psychoanalytic discourse to equate "primitive" emotional relationships with pre-oedipal ones, we might take a moment to clarify the terms. At least as I see it, we may distinguish between two dimensions of emotional development, as in a matrix of this type:

	Dyadic (Not-Oedipal)	Triadic (Oedipal)
Paranoid–Schizoid Position		
Depressive Position		

The vertical dimension of the matrix uses Klein's characterization of defensive constellations to specify whether emotional function is more or less primitive. The horizontal dimension specifies what kind of self–other relationship is involved. One may then investigate at what level of emotional sophistication and within which self–other relationship the basic assumptions are being played out. More generally, one could use

the matrix as an aid in assessing a group's level of emotional functioning and its capacity for reality testing/work group activity.[6]

It might also be noted that work group function may be either
supported or undermined by the emotional life of the group. In this
regard an especially important group configuration occurs when apparently sophisticated work group function is actually being unconsciously
determined by primitive versions of the basic assumptions. The production of thermonuclear weapons is a case in point.

Although dependency, flight–fight, and pairing may be viewed
simply as orientations toward a reality of some kind, we have seen that
Bion emphasizes their defensive function and primitive nature. In his
view, each of them aims at preventing the group from experiencing
intense psychic pain, that is, psychotic or psychotic-like anxieties. But
psychotic anxieties are not always present in collective emotional
experience. Hence we might introduce a variant interpretation: The
higher the level of potential anxiety the group is called upon to manage, the greater will be its tendency to rely on primitive versions of
defense.

We should also mention a rather more surprising and politically
important countertendency: Sometimes a rising level of anxiety will
break through existing group defenses and make possible more sophisticated and progressive work group functioning.

Groups may be threatened, in fact or in fantasy, from within or
without. Or both: As is well known, a group may deal with its internal anxieties by displacement and projection, so that an outsider or
Other (be it individual or collective) is created as the source of the
danger. We then have not only a fight–flight (or flight–fight) group, but
group experience in the paranoid–schizoid position. It may be, however, that the intergroup drama is simultaneously played out in oedipal terms. The group is then experienced as a family presided over by
a protective parent (usually the father), while the Other is cast in the
role of Satan or a barbaric horde.

Leaving aside for a moment the distinction between work and
basic assumption groups, it is useful to identify at least four kinds of
group experience:

• *The group at the level of a society.* Here the group is most often
manifest in patriotic feelings, especially those focused upon a leader
who incarnates the spirit of the nation.

• *In-group/out-group formations coinciding with or cutting across objective lines of social division.* For example, a class, if it has begun to
coalesce politically, is also a group; the political emergence of a class
may be precluded by cross-cutting group formations of race or ethnic
identity.

• *The group in the form of institutions.* Institutionalized white racism is an obvious example. Here an in-group/out-group structure is crystallized in a set of institutional practices, so that it operates not only unconsciously but also impersonally. More generally, social institutions are group structures, composites of work function and the enactment of the basic assumptions. Witness behavior in any bureaucracy.

• *The group as a dimension of mass movements, especially those in which the leader–follower relationship is not institutionally routinized.* This is what I—following Weber—term "charismatic group-emotion." Charismatic group-emotion can be seen as a breakdown product of or challenge to institutionalized group structures. Conversely, in studying social institutions one may often trace in them the paths by which charismatic group-emotion has been routinized.

5.

The more one specifies the features of group experience, the more obstrusive become questions of social reality. For example: What concretely determines the level of sophistication of group functioning? Under what conditions do in-group/out-group formations come into existence? When is group-emotion charismatic, and why? Further, the notion of work group function pushes against the limits of a purely psychoanalytic theory. Yet Bion, like Klein, seems scarcely to recognize the existence of an extrapsychoanalytic world.

By contrast, a theory of groups is securely placed within the present version of psychoanalytic-marxism. First, the work group function is ontogenetically grounded. Work, instead of being an externality grafted onto the psyche via an ill-defined sublimation, is seen as the developmental complement to emotional life. Hence it has a psychological weight of its own. Second, and reciprocally, the notion of work group functioning insures that, psychologically speaking, work can be analyzed as a collective process, and not just as aggregated individual efforts. Third, it is basic to our theory that work relationships are objective as well as subjective. Accordingly, we can link the analysis of groups, in both their emotional and their work aspects, to the analysis of interests—and especially to the analysis of collective interests. In this way we locate group psychology in the field of social inquiry and action.

6.

Collective interests (and here we no longer limit the concept of collective interests to social classes) and desires are concretely joined in choices of action. Choices of action raise the interpenetrating issues of rationality and realizability.

There are then three meanings of rationality attached to collective interests. First, it is rational for members of a collectivity to act so as to realize their mutual interests, that is, to maximize or optimize their collective advantages, and to eliminate or minimize their collective disadvantages. It is irrational not to so act, either by not acting or by not acting with this orientation. Second, it is rational for members of a collectivity to choose means that tend toward the realization of their interests, irrational to choose means that tend away from the realization of their interests.[7] Third, it is rational to attempt to realize an interest if it is in fact potentially realizable, irrational to attempt to realize an interest that is inherently unrealizable.

Questions can be raised about all three types of rationality. Critical theorists object to the utilitarian quality of the first, especially when it is conjoined to the instrumental quality of the second. Despite the bland assurances of some game theorists, it is rarely easy to determine the means that are most likely to secure the desired ends. And it is especially difficult to know if a collective interest is realizable, either within or through the transformation of an existing mode of production.

In the present context we must bracket these questions in order to raise another: How is irrational action possible? Plato noted long ago that one does not intentionally act to one's own disadvantage. Hence if irrational actions do not proceed from simple ignorance, it would seem that their irrationality must be disguised. They must appear to be rational despite their actual irrationality.

As Reich argued, it is at this juncture that Marxism requires psychoanalysis. And as we have argued, it requires a psychoanalysis of groups.

Let's narrow the focus to the third standard of rationality. We may then put forward the following propositions:

• An unrealizable collective interest will be acted upon only when its irrationality can be concealed by group-emotional formations in which basic assumption functions predominate.

• A realizable collective interest, just because it is realizable, need not be mediated by basic assumption functions. It may be predominantly mediated by work group function.

• A realizable interest does not necessarily generate action in terms of work group function. It may be irrationalized and rendered unrealizable by the intrusion of basic assumption functions.

The first and third propositions provide explanations of false consciousness. The second establishes the criterion of true consciousness, by which the falsification of consciousness is to be judged. With this in mind, they may be restated in this form:

- True Consciousness = f (Realizable Interest + [Work Group > Basic Assumption Group]).
- False Consciousness = f (Realizable Interest + [Basic Assumption Group > Work Group]) *or* (Unrealizable Interest + [Basic Assumption Group > Work Group]).[8]

We have already acknowledged the difficulties involved in judgments of true and false consciousness. It is tempting to avoid them by opting for a kind of epistemological agnosticism in which all such judgments are avoided. But we do not live as epistemological agnostics. We enact judgments of truth and falsity even when we are not conscious of them. To put it another way, it is only when we disassociate theory from practice that we have the luxury of begging questions of rationality and realizability. Yet engaging these questions does not mean that we absolutize their answers. It is rather the case that making rational choices requires the ability to tolerate uncertainty and anxiety and to learn from one's mistakes.

7.

If we think for a moment about the imperatives of mass movement, perhaps the first thing that comes to mind is membership. No members means no movement, no matter how organizationally skilled and clear-thinking potential leaders might be. More generally, in complex societies in which there is a private realm, individuals may choose to participate or not participate in public activities, as such or of particular kinds. It may then be that some forms of participation are in their interest and others are not, and that they may or may not be able to distinguish one from the other. Moreover, on the basis of characterological predisposition, individuals will be varyingly motivated to participate in public activities.

It is at this point, and only at this point, that the problem of "the individual and society" legitimately arises. Individuals are always members of society. There can never be a question of participating or not participating in social life in general. But there can be a question of whether or not to participate in politics. Consequently, when one investigates collective action, one comes upon individual choices of action at the same time.

Alternatively, it is a matter of common sense that there can be no societies without individuals to be their members. And there are times when it is appropriate to look at things (whatever they are) from the perspective of a solitary part, or to raise the question of how the individual part is related to other parts of the whole, or to the whole itself. But one must keep this perspective in perspective.

Who are the individuals who now enter the theoretical picture? They are not: human individuals as such, individuals at the level of anthropological abstraction; members of the species at a particular point in its historical evolution; participants in economically productive, human reproductive, cultural or class/group processes. They are the products of all of these determinations and relations, but they are not reducible to them. Nor are they necessarily the actual, historically existing individuals who are acted upon and in turn act upon this manifold of social relations. They might be, rather, individuals conceptualized in terms of social roles and character types. As in the early work of both Reich and Fromm, social roles defined by class, occupation, gender, generation, race, ethnicity, nationality, religion, etc., are linked to character types derived from one version or another of psychoanalytic theory: obsessive–compulsive, hysterical, narcissistic, schizoid, paranoid, depressive, etc.

I would not go so far as to say that these typological studies are a waste of time, but I do think they are a relatively bad investment. On the one hand, they are an attempt to make something determinate out of individual action, which is inherently indeterminate. On the other, they substitute categories for concrete individuals. This is especially unfortunate in the instance of clinical theory and practice. A patient is in for a bad time of it if the analyst views her/him through the optic of diagnostic categories. And so are individuals who are the objects of historical and biographical research, although the practical stakes are not so high in this discursive context.

It might be added that, whatever the level or type of social research, there is always at least one individual involved: the researcher. If s/he is not conscious of the wealth of social determinations of which s/he is a product, then s/he may inject this individualism into the object of the research. And if s/he is not conscious of the research as an individual project, s/he may claim for it a universality and objectivity it cannot possibly possess.

D. (Relative) Totalization of Social Production

1.

The practical problem of "the individual and society"—mobilizing private individuals for public action—carries us into the political realm. From one perspective, all psychoanalytic-marxist theorizing is political theorizing. This is because the theory is tied to the project of human emancipation, a project that requires collective action aimed at the possession of state power for its realization. Hence one can find in it varying, and varyingly sophisticated, answers to Lenin's question of what is to be done. But if by "political" one means a theory of governments and governing, of the state itself, then psychoanalytic-marxism is relatively deficient.[9]

I am not going to attempt to make good the deficiency. Instead I will narrow the focus to one critical topic: the political totalization of social relations.

2.

Briefly, this is how the issue—no, the ideological form of the issue—arises.

In classical liberal theories of politics, the state is given a restricted role to play. Individual rights, including the right to the private ownership of property, are viewed as preceding the compacts that found civil society and institute governments. If, therefore, we were to convert our constrained model of social production into one of normative constraints on political action, it would look like this:

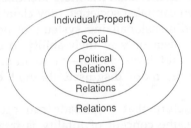

Social relationships are a subset of individual ones, often viewed as anchored in natural law, and political relationships are a subset of social ones. Governmental functions are thus doubly limited. Moreover, within the political domain legislative functions tend to be given priority over executive ones. In this way, the power of the One is to be subordinated to the power of the Many, while the power of the Many is to be exercised only within the limits of the law.

We need go no further with this sketch, which is or ought to be familar to every schoolchild. Nor need we rehearse the Marxist criticism of liberalism as bourgeois ideology or detail the many ways in which reality necessarily departs from the liberal ideal. But neither should we deny that constitutional limitations on the exercise of political power have existed and do exist in certain societies at certain times.

The Third Reich is the obvious and historically crucial twentieth-century counterexample to societies in which state power is constrained and a private realm is protected. The Nazi mobilization of and control over social resources in support of its political and military aims, coupled with its use of treachery, terror, and propaganda, rendered meaningless the distinction between public and private. Hence the appropriateness of the term "totalitarian," even before one takes into account the absolute horror of the final solution to the Jewish question.

We note, then, that two meanings are joined in the idea of totalitarianism: the collapsing of the distinction between public and private, and the penetration of what would otherwise be the private realm by unrestrained power. Totalitarianism is totalized tyranny, political domination taken to its limit, a universalized relationship of lordship and bondage in which paranoid tendencies have been pushed to or beyond the point of insanity.

Very few would go so far as to collapse the distinction between liberalism and totalitarianism, but there are many who would narrow it. Leaving aside right-wing libertarian criticisms of the so-called totalitarianism of the so-called welfare state, left-wing critics have been quick to identify fascist tendencies in polities that claimed to be democratic. One could also identify fascist tendencies in left-wing parties that claimed to be revolutionary and emancipatory. And the critical theorists went a step further than the mere identification of totalitarian tendencies: Advanced capitalist societies, they claimed, were dehumanizing totalities, one-dimensionalizing systems of domination that differed from totalitarianism only in their ability to change the balance between cooptation and intimidation—more fraud, less force; more persuasion, less terror; more disguised thought control, less crude indoctrination.

It is at this juncture that a glissade can occur. In some postmodernist discourse, the concept of totality is treated as a synonym for totalitarian. It is assumed that any totalizing of social relationships is coercive and malign. Where for Marcuse or even Adorno there is an imaginable "good totality," for certain postmodernists there are only bad ones. To say "totality" is to say "bad totality." Consequently Hegel and Marx are thrown into the pot along with Hitler and Stalin, and these purportedly left-wing critics of domination cook up the same tasteless stew they would not eat when it was served to them by the right-wing libertarians.

3.

An unfortunate consequence of this ideological debate is that it obscures an important empirical/conceptual issue: What is meant by a totalizing of social relations, and what is the role of politics in the process?

If by a totalizing of social relations one means the closing of a system or the completing of a process, then it is evident that social relationships are never totalized. The tensions and contradictions within and between the domains of social production are never simply a "difference which is no difference, or only a difference of what is self-same." But it would not be meaningful to speak about a system or a nation if social relationships were completely pluralized—random or chaotic. Even when social systems break down and cease functioning, some order remains within the disorder.

To put it another way, complex societies never attain the degree of identity we find in organisms. Nor do they reach the degree of difference we find in, say, explosions. At least, not if they survive.

The issue, however, is not totality, but totalization. By totalization we do not mean simply that a society is an open system or a structured set of social practices. We also mean that it consists of a number of discrete practices that are pulled together into a unity. In this sense, societies are (necessarily incomplete) processes of unification, not just unities.

Although the matter is no doubt debatable, we assume, first, that complex societies require processes of totalization and, second, that they are totalized from two primary directions. On the one hand, they are totalized from below, especially but not exclusively by economic laws (those of production as well as those of the market). As Marx emphasized, these laws operate whether or not we are conscious of them. They are analogous to the laws of the unconscious adduced by Freud. On the other hand, societies are totalized from above, through political practices aimed (minimally) at the preservation of the society.

Various relationships between these two modes of totalization are possible. They may act in concert or in opposition. Now one, now the other, may dominate the historical picture. But theories that claim we can do without one or the other—laissez-faire theories at one extreme, centralized state planning theories at the other—are both prescriptions for societal breakdown.

4.

Clearly, we are on familiar ground. Totalization turns out to be another term for structural and political integration. There is the added implication that integration and disintegration are dialectical processes. This, too, is a familiar idea; but then, novelty is not the aim of the inquiry.

If we were Hegelians, the concept of totalization would have the further implication of overcoming contradictions and universalizing interests. If we were orthodox Marxists, we might be content to say that social contradictions are carried over into the political sphere and that, if and when they are politically resolved, the resolution is in the interest of the ruling class. Universality is a semblance, an ideological veil thrown over the particular class interests that are realized by the existing social and political arrangements.

Although the Hegelian instance is not ruled out in principle, it would be difficult to find an historical case in point. Which is not to say there are no historical examples of general interests being served by the totalizing of social relationships. To the contrary: In all societies some general interests must be served if the society is to survive. Moreover, the extent to which particular interests usurp universal ones is highly variable. Yet when all is said and done, it is not realistic to side with Hegel against Marx.

Nor, as we have repeatedly seen, is it possible to accept an orthodox Marxist explanation of ideological hegemony, or even a psychoanalytic-marxist one that relies on conceptions of social character. Politics always involves a complex play of collective interests and desires. Hence political analysis involves working out the situational relationship between emotional group formations and the structure of social and political interests.

5.

In some premodern societies discrete political institutions do not exist. Political practices are integrated into social practices more generally, and no one pursues politics as a sole vocation. But in modern societies discrete political institutions do exist and politics is a possible vocation.

Here we come to the political meanings of the concept of class. First, a political class is the political form or organization of a social class. In this sense its political interests are determined by its social ones. But second, a political class is a collectivity with an interest of its own. Moreover, those who make politics their vocation come to share a way of life, one which tends to identify them with their social class enemies and separate them from politically inactive members of their own social class. Consequently it is rarely the case that social class interests are translated directly into political actions and public policies. Rather they are, in a strong sense of the word, mediated by political processes. Yet it is even more rarely the case that political actions and public policies have no determinate relationship to social class interests. Ralph Milliband's conception of the "relative autonomy of the state" thus seems about right (Milliband, 1977, p. 74 ff.).

The obvious exception to this rule is the case of the totalitarian penetration of society by the state. But even in this instance one does not arrive at the absolute autonomy of the state. For one thing, and as noted above, political totalization can never replace or overcome the limitations imposed by structural totalization. For another, there can be no enduring totalization of politics itself. Ultimately there will be a falling-out among thieves.

The last point is important because we often encounter a tendency to treat the state or, for that matter, a political movement as a monolith. If the political entity is seen as embodying our interests, then the monolithic vision is a wishful group fantasy, perhaps operating from the basic assumption of dependency. If the political entity is perceived as an enemy, then the monolithic vision results from a group fantasy in which the basic assumption of fight–flight predominates. In fact, all political entities, even concentration camps, are complex structures built out of oppositional tendencies.

6.

Although political structures are not monolithic, they are, to varying extents, bureaucratic. The more complex the political functions that need to be performed in the interest of social totalization, the more extensive the bureaucracy. The more extensive the bureaucracy, the less effectively it functions.

So it goes.

7.

Although we assign politics a specific position within the model of social production, it must be admitted that the specificity is difficult to maintain. Social forces push upward and are played out politically. Political forces push downward and are played out socially. Bureaucratization, which is so notable a part of modern societies, is obviously not limited to the political sphere. Indeed, public and private bureaucracies intertwine and interact in so many ways that the lines between them tend to become indistinct.

There are other ways in which the line between politics and society becomes blurred. If, for example, we identify politics with the exercise of, or struggles over, power, then all social relationships, including intrapsychic ones, are political.

Such an identification no doubt goes too far. It pushes social structural issues too far into the background. It defines social life as a more or less open war of all against all without paying any attention to the terrain on which the battles will be fought. But in a world of opposed interests and often tyrannical desires, there is an undoubted strategic value in the following orientation toward reality:

• Do you have or seek the power of commanding my activity against my will?

• If so, then you have placed us in the situation of Hegel's life and death struggle for recognition. Or to vary the political theoretical reference, you have initiated a state of war, in which I am left with no choice but to defend myself or submit to slavery.

• Alternatively, if you do not seek power over me, then there is no battle and we can be friends.

• But how can I be sure?

8.

The preceding discussion yields three meanings of politics: public institutions and the practices associated thereto; the penetration of politics in the first sense into the private sphere; and what might be called the politics of everyday life, the bureaucratic and power-oriented dimensions of nominally nonpolitical modes of interaction.

There is a fourth meaning of politics, as when we refer to ourselves as Americans, English, Chinese, etc. These collective self-identifications usually include a directly political component, that is, a sense of self that is associated with citizenship, rights of political participation, etc. But national or political identity is far more totalizing. Although it does not go so far as to constitute a spirit of a people in an Hegelian sense, through group psychology it often approximates to the Hegelian word made flesh.

It may be that the spirit of the nation is a fantasy, but that doesn't mean it isn't real.

9.

If, in the various ways adumbrated above, a society or polity is held together by processes of totalization, then in the first instance political transformation must be detotalizing. This is not the case if nothing more is involved than the replacement of one set of rulers by another set of rulers, especially if the rivals are factions within the same political class. But if the transformational aims extend from politics into society, and especially if the aim is the transformation of the mode of production as a whole, then the breaking up of existing patterns of totalization is required.

It is from this perspective that the constrained model of social production is also the map of a battlefield. Each category specifies a location for engagement, indeed a multiplicity of such locations: workplaces, homes, cultural settings, collectivities, social roles, etc. Any of these may become a possible site of guerrilla warfare. But if the political aim is the overall transformation of a society, these local struggles are not enough. There must be an overall theory of society and a related conception of rational choices of action. Most of all, there must be a sufficient force to mount an effective attack. The relative totalization of the existing mode of production must be matched by a parallel totalization of the revolutionary opposition.

Then what? Unless the ruling political classes have fallen victim to internal division and/or unless social relations have been destabilized by economic crisis, war, etc., they command the heights. They control the modalities of interaction through which political totalization is achieved. These may be used to fragment the opposition—by brute force, by propaganda, by divide and conquer, and so forth. Muliplicity in this instance is a death-knell and not a rallying cry, proof that the revolutionary movement has been shattered and scattered before it could storm the citadel.

Nonetheless citadels do fall and new social/political orders come into being. For better and for worse.

10.

Discussions of political conflict eventually lead to questions of social transformation, hence to a shift from a synchronic to a diachronic perspective. Better put, there is an expansion of the synchronic into the diachronic, and this in two respects. First, for any society or mode of production the structure of social relationships is historical. It stretches backward into a manifold of past events and forward into the constrained possibilities of the future. Second, the synchronic interaction between societies points to the history of these interactions and to the criss-crossing of diachronic lines that is the history of the species.

To put it another way, diachronic and synchronic are not alternative perspectives but interpenetrating dimensions of the same perspective, the historical equivalents of the sensuous intuition of time and

space through which Kant hoped to escape from . . . the reality of time
and space. Or rather, they delimit the realiti*es* of time and space: Even
now, we must speak of the histories of the world. But perhaps not for
long.

11.

Various divisions of the histories of the species are possible. The
most general would probably involve the application of a threefold
categorization of modes of production: preagricultural, agricultural,
and industrial.

Marx, following Hegel, offers us a set of categories that are almost
as general as the above: In "broad outlines Asiatic, ancient, feudal, and
modern bourgeois modes of production can be designated as progressive epochs in the economic formation of society" (Marx, 1859, p. 5).
This only goes to show how dangerous it is to be guided by the wisdom of a master. It's as if Marx had been mesmerized by the epic tale
of the World-Spirit's journey from East to West, of the advance from
oriental despotism toward occidental freedom, and so forgot what he
had learned from experience, namely, that one cannot arrive at historical knowledge "by using as one's master key a general historico-
philosophical theory, the supreme virtue of which consists in being
supra-historical" (Marx & Engels, 1975c, p. 294).

If we wish to be historical, we must abandon Marx's schema. It
incoherently mixes geographical, temporal, and social categories. It
obscures the similarities among all preindustrial societies and fails to
recognize the differences among them. It treats the histories of the
world as if they were a single history. And it gives this invented world
history a progressive or evolutionary quality for which there is only
one piece of evidence, namely, an overall record of increasing technological potency.

So far as historical research is concerned, this piece of evidence is
one among many. So far as our present history is concerned, it is *the*
one among many. And the one last, ironic signifier of historical dialectics: Like an chicken developing within its shell, we are approaching
the limits of incubation; but unlike the hatchling chicken, we have no
place else to go.

PART THREE

CONSTRUCTIONS
AND
CONFIGURATIONS

CHAPTER 8

Lordship and Bondage

1.

The preceding chapters have supplied us with anthropological/historical and social theoretical categories and concepts. In this and the following chapters, we seek to give these concepts and categories a particular realization. We will arrange a passage for some number of human individuals through the realms of economic production, human reproduction, culture, collective experience, individual experience, and politics. They will not emerge unscatched, but rather twisted and deformed by the experience of domination.

2.

We inherit from Marx the technique of transformational criticism and from Freud techniques for the analysis of defenses. They will help us to distinguish between the gaudy appearances and the grimy realities of the capitalist carnival.

We will also keep in mind that domination is not just another roadside attraction—not a trope, metaphor, text, discourse, conversation, or theatrical performance.

3.

The limiting instance of domination is when one person or party—or part of the self—has absolute power over another. There are, however, various degrees and forms of domination. Correspondingly, there are various situations of resistance and forms of liberation. For this and other reasons, the theoretical and practical problematics of domination and emancipation can be formulated in a variety of ways. Hegel's conceptualization of failed and mutual recognition is only one of many. But it is highly synoptic. As we know, it links sensuous appetite, work, desire, and consciousness to questions of freedom and domination. Hence we will configure the matter in this way.

These are the terms of the problem of recognition. Like Kant, Hegel identifies freedom with the autonomy of the will—with self-determination, independence, and nonsubservience. At the same time he sees selfhood as intersubjective: My selfhood requires your affirmation of it, and vice versa. Freedom and selfhood thus appear to be mutually exclusive, contradictory. But the incompatibility is not absolute. My autonomy does not require freedom from any limitation whatsoever, but only from imposed or alien limitation. If I find myself (my self) in you as you find yourself (your self) in me, if "I = I", then our mutual dependence confirms our independence.

To put it another way, I am morally autonomous when I give the law to myself. It is moral heteronomy if you impose your law on me. If, however, we accept the same law as both binding and expressive of our will, then we have secured our mutual freedom through the law. Moral autonomy becomes a constitutive and constituted element of ethical community.

The psychoanalytic-marxist appropriation of this problematic involves the claim that history is primarily characterized by failures of mutual recognition ("I ≠ I"), failures that take the form of relations of domination ("I > I"), the superiority of one self to another. Domination may be either outright, as in relationships of lordship and bondage proper, or disguised/attentuated, as in relationships where formal freedom is combined with substantive domination. Psychoanalytic-marxism explores the objective and subjective reasons why selfhood is a battle, why it results in relationships of domination, and why it is attended by falsified and alienated forms of consciousness. It then considers the ways in which mutuality of recognition might be achieved.

4.

The emancipatory political struggles of the 1960s and early 1970s, which did so much to reanimate and transform Freudian-Marxism, had as their principal objects racial, sexual, and class domination. These forms of domination will be our theoretical objects, conceptualized in terms of failed recognition: "White > Black"; "Male > Female"; "Owner > Worker".

Where are these relationships located on our map of social production?

Although class relationships extend through the other categories, they are based in economic production. Gender relationships have an affinity with human reproduction, at least insofar as the issue of sexual difference is most evident in this domain. Race (in the United States) is best placed in the categories of cultural and collective (class/group) experience. Hence these categories structure the present chapter.

By way of anticipation: Psychoanalytic practice fits into the category of individual experience; the state and revolutionary struggle are political matters. When we take up these topics in the last two chapters we will simultaneously complete our exploration of the capitalist battlefield and consider how emancipatory battles are to be waged.

5.

Like the philosophical "moments" we find in *The Phenomenology*, the conceptual figures or configurations to be developed in this chapter are abstract, highly condensed, and at a remove from empirical reality. But in contrast to Hegel, we will not deny the distance or disjunction between reason and reality. We do not lay claim to knowledge of an ur-reality that renders knowledge of our reality merely phenomenal. We recognize instead the epistemological priority of life-worlds.

To put it another way, these constructions or configurations are heuristic merely. They are not propositions or hypotheses that we might verify evidentially. They are too tentative, incomplete, and speculative for that. Yet they are not fantasies, fictions, literary devices, or philosophical daydreams. They have an anthropological foundation, an historical and social theoretical framework, and conceptual elements derived from historical and clinical research, as well as from political practice. Hence with their aid we might learn something about the real world.

So far as validity is concerned, two points seem relevant.

First, the fit of these concepts with empirical data is a function of the totalization of capitalist social relations. Assuming that the concepts themselves accurately reflect aspects of the capitalist mode of production, it follows that the more universal capitalism is in its breadth and depth, the more nearly these concepts would be expected to correspond to reality.

Second, if we recognize ourselves and our world reflected in these constructions or if they seem worth talking about, then they have a discursive meaning and so a kind of validity. But precisely then we must remind ourselves that understanding the world is not a substitute for transforming it. Although there is a real comfort in shared meanings, there can be no real contentment in shared bondage.

A. Commodities All

1.

One building block of psychoanalytic-marxism is the notion that class structure determines character structure and that character structure in turn subjectively reinforces class structure. The concept originates with Reich, who saw character as the psychical location where external and internal reality coalesce. It was further developed by Fromm in the notion of social character.

We represented Fromm's notion of character structured by the desire to escape from freedom this way:

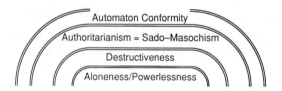

Destructiveness, authoritarianism as a sado-masochistic relationship, and automaton conformity are pictured as successive defenses against the experience of powerlessness and moral aloneness. We were more impressed by Fromm's orchestration of defenses, however, than by what they were presumed to be defenses against.

Michael Schneider offered us a further particularization of the notion of social character, which also lent itself to figurative representation:

Commodity Structure:		**Character Structure:**
Exchange/Abstract Value		Consciousness
———————————— (Alienation = Repression) ————————————		
Use Values/Sensuousnes		Desires/Sensuousness

Commodity structure and character structure are isomorphic. Each involves a vertical split in which sensuousness is devalued. Schneider did not get much further than a mechanical pairing of the two modes of analysis—unlike, for example, Deleuze and Guattari, whose notion of desiring-production suggests a deeper (and more explosive) bond between self and society. But he did take seriously and put to good use the method of analysis we find in *Capital, 1.*

None of these efforts is grounded in a satisfactory anthropology. All of them tend to conflate character in the abstract with the personalities of individuals in the concrete. Taken together, however, they point us in a promising direction.

The immediate task, then, is to explore the problematics of recognition at the level of character structure and in a world of commodities. By way of beginning we will ask, how does Marx explain the value of money? Answering this question will lead us to an understanding of the fetishism of commodities and the devaluation of selves.

2.

For Marx the interpretive key to the value of money is the "simple, isolated, or accidental form of value" (1867, p. 139), the simplest relationship between one commodity and another. We are presented with this statement: x commodity A = y commodity B, or 20 yards of linen = 1 coat. Each commodity in the relationship is a use value and, as such, the product of useful labor. Each is also an exchange value, more exactly, an abstract value and, as such, the product of abstract labor. In the former regard the two commodities are qualitatively distinct and lack a common measure of value. In the latter regard they are qualitatively identical. Abstract labor, reduced to socially necessary labor time, functions as a measure of value. If x commodity A contains the same amount of abstract labor as y commodity B, then the two commodities are of equal value. If they contain different amounts of abstract labor, they are of unequal value.

The two commodities, each of which is a use value and an abstract value, confront each other. Each commodity in the relationship is capable of expressing its own use value. Neither knows its own abstract value. This lack of self-knowledge is not because abstract value is external to the commodity, something added to it through the process of exchange. To the contrary: Its abstract value exists in it, in-itself, so to speak, or as a potential. It is intrinsic; it is not created in the exchange relationship. But unlike use value, it is supersensuous, precisely abstract. It comes to exist for-itself, becomes visible and recognizable, only in the relationship of one commodity to another. Only when two commodities meet does it become possible for one of them to ask the other, "How much am I worth?"

When this question is asked and answered, the qualitative and quantitative aspects of each commodity are divided between them. In the relative form of value commodity A, the linen, is equated to commodity B, the coat. The coat is the equivalent of the linen, the value of the linen is measured by or is relative to the coat. The coat "counts as the form of existence, as the material embodiment" of the abstract value of the linen (*ibid.*, p. 141). The linen's abstract value is objectified: The "linen's own existence as value comes into view and receives an independent expression. . . ." Thus "the natural form of commodity B becomes the value-form of commodity A, . . . the physical body of commodity B becomes a mirror for the value of commodity A" (*ibid.*, p. 144).

It is not just a flight of fancy or an imposition on our part to say the two commodities are engaged in a process of recognition. At this point in the text Marx notes, with delicious irony:

> In a certain sense a man is in the same situation as a commodity. As he neither enters into the world in possession of a mirror, nor as a Fichtean philosopher who can say "I am I," a man first sees and recognizes himself in another man. Peter only relates to himself as a man through his relation to another man, Paul, in whom he recognizes his likeness. With this, however, Paul also becomes from head to toe, in his physical form as Paul, the form of appearance of the species man for Peter. (*ibid.*)

One might think Marx would say it the other way around, that is, that there is a sense in which commodities are in the same situation as people. But commodities are the subjects, the effective agents, in the capitalist drama. Human beings function merely as "bearers" of economic values: "The characters who appear on the economic stage are merely personifications of economic relations . . ." (*ibid.*, p. 179). They exist for each other as guardians, representatives, and owners of commodities, as "persons whose will resides in these objects" and who "recognize each other as owners of private property" (*ibid.*, p. 178). Further, the juridical relationship of the contract mirrors and is determined by the economic relationship. Hence the simple form of value, x commodity A = y commodity B, contains the basic terms of the problem of recognition in a world of commodity relations.

It is evident that we have been placed inside a world of alienated social relationships. But for the moment what concerns us more is the alienation of the commodity itself. For in the value relation of commodity A to commodity B, the "natural form of commodity A figures only as the aspect of use value, while the natural form of B figures only as the . . . aspect of value. The internal opposition between use value and value, hidden within the commodity, is therefore represented on the surface by an external opposition . . ." (*ibid.*, p. 153). A and B are no longer both use values and abstract values. The one is only a use value, the other only an abstract value.

When this diremped value relationship is universalized, we emerge, through three steps, with the relationship of commodities and money.

First, the simple form of value is expanded: (x commodity A = y commodity B) becomes (z commodity A = u commodity B or = v commodity C or ... etc.). The expanded form of value may also be presented this way:

$$20 \text{ yards of linen} = \begin{cases} 1 \text{ coat } or \\ 10 \text{ lb. of tea } or \\ 40 \text{ lb. of coffee } or \\ 1 \text{ quarter of corn } or \\ 2 \text{ ounces of gold } or \\ \tfrac{1}{2} \text{ ton of iron } or \\ \text{etc.} \end{cases}$$

The linen has escaped its limited and parochial relationship to the coat. It is now a "citizen of the world" (*ibid.*, p. 155). But it suffers from a fresh limitation: Each time it meets another commodity, it once more has to establish its value relative to the newcomer. Its two aspects are divided up, again and again, in an endless series of discrete transactions. Hence the next step is taken, roles are reversed, and the linen becomes the equivalent to all other values:

$$\begin{cases} 1 \text{ coat} \\ 10 \text{ lb. of tea} \\ 40 \text{ lb. of coffee} \\ 1 \text{ quarter of corn} \\ 2 \text{ ounces of gold} \\ \tfrac{1}{2} \text{ ton of iron} \\ \text{etc.} \end{cases} = 20 \text{ yards of linen}$$

The linen now functions exclusively as the abstract value or universal equivalent of all other commodities; all other commodities function exclusively as use values. As use values, they can only consort with each other by passing through the linen, while "the physical form of the linen counts as the visible incarnation, the social chrysalis state, of all human labour" (*ibid.*, p. 159). But the linen is not perfectly suited to this role. Another commodity, gold, could play it better. Thus we take the third step and arrive at money:

$$\begin{cases} 1 \text{ coat} \\ 10 \text{ lb. of tea} \\ 40 \text{ lb. of coffee} \\ 1 \text{ quarter of corn} \\ 20 \text{ yards of linen} \\ \tfrac{1}{2} \text{ ton of iron} \\ \text{etc.} \end{cases} = 2 \text{ ounces of gold}$$

Gold now "confronts the other commodities as money" but "only because it previously confronted them as a commodity" (*ibid.*, p. 162). "The simple commodity form is therefore the germ of the money-form" (*ibid.*, p. 163). Money is a commodity that has alienated its use value to all other commodities and now serves as the measure of their abstract value.

Let's pause to get our bearings. The process of human recognition involves the confrontation of two selves, each of whom is likewise an other ("I = I"). As sensuous beings each has needs. Each works to satisfy those needs. Both might find it advantageous, even mutually advantageous, to exchange the products of their labor. This is a barter relationship, an object-mediated relationship of recognition. But in the world of commodities, its terms become inverted. The commodity is the master of the man. Its will be done.

The situation is further complicated by the introduction of money. We then have the basic transaction of capitalism, where commodities (C) have intercourse with each other through the medium of money (M). Thus (C – M – C). Money here functions as measure of values and means of circulation.

It is evident, I think, that a kind of recognition can occur when commodities are exchanged through the medium of money. A fair exchange, equivalent for equivalent, is mutual recognition in the world of commodities. The subjectivity of human individuals, however, is not recognized. The value that they gave to the commodities through their labor appears instead to be an attribute of the commodities themselves: "The commodity reflects the social character of men's own labor as objective characteristics of the products of labour themselves, as the socio-natural properties of these things" (*ibid.*, p. 165). The process through which the value of commodities comes into existence and through which one commodity comes to play the part of money—the process we (following Marx) have just recapitulated—"vanishes in its own result, leaving no trace behind" (*ibid.*, p. 187). Consequently individuals do not recognize themselves in their products, that is, as the creators of value, but rather attribute value to commodities and money themselves. Thus instead of self-recognition we have money worship and the fetishism of commodities.

3.

I do not think we can be satisfied with Marx's explanation of commodity fetishism. Let's put to one side any criticisms we might want to make of the theory of value. We'll assume that commodities have an abstract value that is the product of abstract labor, and that money is the incarnation of abstract labor value: (labor → value of commodities → money). It is a necessary condition for commodity fetishism that the links (→) between labor and money be unavailable to consciousness. Instead of a chain of determinations, there then appears to exist three separate entities having no organic connection to each other. Consequently the value of commodities and money seems to be intrinsic to them. But it is not clear how this economic amnesia is produced. It does not seem adequate to attribute it to lack of scientific knowledge. It seems better to view it as resulting from the ideological suppression of the linkages. This, however, leaves us with the task of understanding the mental processes through which ideological tendencies become subjectively effective.

Second, the fetishistic relationship of individuals to commodities has an evident affective dimension. This comes through to some extent in Marx's use of figurative language: The "objectivity of commodities as values differs from Dame Quickly in the sense that 'a man knows not where to have it'" (*ibid.*, p. 138); "commodities are in love with money, but . . . 'the course of true love never did run smooth'" (*ibid.*, p. 202), and so forth. Marx creates a drama in which the commodity is the protagonist—now lover, then citizen, sometimes Christian or Jew. Commodities have desires, aims, ambitions, etc. Moreover, Marx creates a mood of something mysterious and fascinating about money. The "riddle of the money fetish," for example, "is . . . the riddle of the commodity fetish, now become visible and dazzling to our eyes" (*ibid.*, p. 187). Hence we might take him to be implying that a misplaced desire is a feature of commodity and money fetishism. But the affective dimension of fetishism has no role to play in his substantive analysis.

Marx's analysis of fetishism, in other words, is part of the problem as well as part of the solution. As problem it has the two aspects of broken linkages between ideas and displacement of affect. When we have solved this problem, we will have a better understanding of the durability of capitalist social relations.

4.

Although Marx may not entirely explain the broken linkages in our understanding of economic reality, he is nonetheless intent upon restoring them. He has restored them horizontally, on the surface of society or at the level of the market, in the analysis of the relationship between commodities and money. He then goes on to establish the critical link between the "primitive," that is, more fundamental, forces of economic life and the manifest forms in which these primitive forces are expressed and disguised. This relationship can be represented as follows:

The Sphere of Circulation

↑

The Buying and Selling of Labor–Power

↑

The Production of Surplus Value

The buying and selling of labor-power is the link between the sphere of circulation and the realm of production. At the one extreme we have the "very Eden of the innate rights of man . . . , the exclusive realm of Freedom, Equality, Property and Bentham" (*ibid.*, p. 280). Buyers and sellers of commodities contract as free persons, who are equal before the law. To be sure, each looks only to his own advantage, and "the only force bringing them together, and putting them into relation with each other, is the selfishness, the gain and the private interest of each. Each pays heed to himself only, and no one worries about the others" (*ibid*). But the contracting parties are, as indicated, formally free and equal; and as long as we stay within the sphere of circulation, there is an appearance of mutual advantage and even of the realization of the common interest. But this is only an appearance, a semblance, a structure of relationships that contains and disguises an underlying reality. The analysis of the buying and selling of labor-power makes it possible to pass from appearance to essence, from one extreme to the other. And at the other extreme, economic life is comparable to lordship and bondage, not to mutual recognition.

Enter Mr. Moneybags, would-be capitalist, the King Midas of our time. He loves money for its own sake, as an end in itself. He desires to have his money make more money. He gives himself over to this aim, and he makes any and all commodities a means to its realization.

Viewed from the perspective of Mr. Moneybags, the world looks like this: $(M - C - [M + \Delta M])$. He wishes to buy commodities (C) for some amount of money (M) and sell them for a larger amount of money, $[M + \Delta M]$. And so we, looking over Mr. Moneybags' shoulder, can see that a further inversion has taken place. $(C - M - C)$ has become $(M - C - [M + \Delta M])$. The problem of recognition has become the problem of surplus value.

This problem cannot be solved in the sphere of circulation, where values are at most redistributed, nor in that of production, where values but not self-valorizing values are produced. It is solved in practice by the transaction through which labor-power, a commodity belonging to the worker, becomes labor (and the product of labor), a commodity belonging to Mr. Moneybags. It is solved in theory by the analysis of that transaction.

Mr. Moneybags proceeds as follows. He uses his money to purchase labor-power (l. p.) and means of production (m. p.). He combines them in such a way as to create commodities that have a greater value than the commodities he purchased. This is possible because and insofar as the value of labor-power is less than the new value of the products that actual labor produces. He sells the commodities thus produced at their value and makes a profit . . . and so on to infinity.

Mr. Moneybags' view of the transaction can now be represented this way: $(M - C\ [_{l.\,p.\ +\ m.\,p.}] - [C + \Delta C] - [M + \Delta M])$. He has invested his money (M) in factors of production $(C\ [_{l.\,p.\ +\ m.\,p.}])$ that have generated commodities containing a surplus value $[C + \Delta C]$, and he has sold these commodities at their value $[M + \Delta M]$.

From the worker's perspective the transaction looks like this: $(C\ [_{l.\,p.}] - M - C\ [_{u.\,v.}])$, where [u. v.] = use values of various kinds. The worker's commodity is labor-power $(C\ [_{l.\,p.}])$, which s/he sold for a wage (M). Her/his wages were then used to purchase commodities for use $(C\ [_{u.\,v.}])$.

According to the law governing the exchange of commodities, the worker has been paid for the value of her/his commodity, that is, for its cost of reproduction. S/he has gained enough money to regenerate her/his labor-power. Mr. Moneybags has gained the use of this commodity for employment in a labor process. Because the worker is the owner of her/his labor-power and so long as we do not examine the transaction too closely, the labor contract looks like a free choice on the part of both parties, hence an act of mutual recognition. But more closely and/or contextually considered, it is evident that the worker is forced to sell her/his labor-power, if not to Mr. Moneybags then to his cousin. The labor contract masks a power relationship, one in which Mr. Moneybags' ownership of means of production insures his dominance. In accepting the labor contract, the worker has lost the battle for recognition and has accepted the position of bondsman. Mr. Moneybags has emerged as lord and master.

So long as Mr. Moneybags can deal with workers as individuals rather than as an organized collectivity, his position as lord and master is assured. Under unfavorable conditions in the labor market (shortage of supply relative to demand), he may have to pay more for his bondsman's service, and he must compete with his capitalist cousins. He nonetheless commands his worker's recognition, in the form of the latter's deference no less than in his labor. Consequently:

> When we leave . . . [the sphere of circulation] a certain change takes place . . . in the physiognomy of our *dramatis personae*. He who was previously the money-owner now strides out in front as a capitalist; the possessor of labour-power follows as his worker. The one smirks self-importantly and is intent on business; the other is timid and holds back, like someone who has brought his own hide to market and now has nothing else to expect but—a hiding.[1] (*ibid.*, p. 280)

The apparent identity of capitalist and worker as owners of commodities dissolves. In its place we have a difference—a division of labor that is simultaneously a relationship of domination.

Along with this change in dramatic characters comes a change in theme and mood. Hitherto the mood has been set by various images of civility: the commodity as citizen, as lover, etc. We now enter a barbaric and brutal region, a house of terror haunted and controlled by vampires and werewolves.

5.

Our concern, like that of Mr. Moneybags, becomes the production of surplus value. Again, a structure of relationships is involved:

$$M - C_{(l.p. + m.p.)} - (C + \Delta C) - (M + \Delta M)$$
$$\updownarrow$$
$$c + v + s = C + \Delta C$$
$$\updownarrow$$
$$\text{Labor–Power} \rightarrow \text{Labor Process} \rightarrow \text{Product}$$

The production of surplus value (the valorization process) is a middle term linking the buying and selling of labor-power (and of the means of production), at the one extreme, to the labor process (the production of use values, which is also the worker's life activity) at the other. Stated differently, the labor process takes place within the valorization process, which in turn takes place within the capitalist circulation of commodities. Money is the limit of this set of social relationships and, for this reason, may be viewed as the signifier of social reality.

In the representation of the valorization process (c) stands for constant capital—raw material and instruments of production, that is, dead labor, labor materialized in the form of means of production; (v) stands for variable capital—wages, the price of living labor-power; and (s) stands for surplus value. Constant capital transfers its value to the product, but does not itself vary in value. New value is produced through the employment of living labor. Hence (s) is inversely proportional to (v), and the interests of workers and capitalists are intrinsically opposed. The opposition is most dramatically evident in the struggle over the length of the working day. Assume that the value of (v) = \$50, that is, that the worker requires \$50 each day to regenerate her/his labor-power. Assume further that linen is produced at a rate of \$10/hour, so that \$50 worth of linen can be produced in five hours. Thus in five hours the worker replaces the amount of wages s/he is being paid. The amount of surplus value generated therefore will depend upon the number of additional hours the worker can be forced to work. A ten-hour day will yield \$50 of surplus value, an eight-hour day \$30, a twelve-hour day

$70. The worker will attempt to limit the working day, the capitalist to extend it. Each can appeal to the laws of exchange to justify her/his position. Hence there is an antinomy, a struggle of right against right and "between equal rights, force decides" (*ibid.*, p. 344).

As in the fourth chapter of *The Phenomenology* we are once again at the scene of a battle. The one confrontation sheds light on the other.

We remember that in *The Phenomenology* the first stage in the development of self-certainty involves the gratification of sensuous desire, as in eating. When oral gratification does not yield a sense of autonomy and self-certainty, consciousness attempts to gain recognition of selfhood from another consciousness. A battle results. Hegel, however, is a bit hazy about the reasons for the antagonism. The two selves might, after all, become friends and freely grant recognition to each other. But if we add a condition of material scarcity to the Hegelian situation, then (1) the two phases of the process can be combined and (2) the struggle for recognition is simultaneously a battle over scarce resources. The same idea can be extended to the contest between capitalist and worker, but at a more developed political level: The battle over scarce resources becomes class struggle, and the struggle for recognition becomes the opposition between state power and revolutionary movement.

The parallel is not, however, exact. Revolutionary class struggle develops within a prior situation of lordship and bondage. As indicated above, in the first instance the worker has lost the battle for resources and recognition, Mr. Moneybags has won. He controls both the labor process and the length of the working day. And in his role as capitalist,

> he is only capital personified. His soul is the soul of capital. But capital has one sole driving force, the drive to valorize itself, to make its constant part, the means of production, absorb the greatest amount of surplus labour. Capital is dead labour, which, vampire-like, lives only by sucking living labour, and lives the more, the more labour it sucks. (*ibid.*, p. 342)

With the cloak of civility removed, Mr. Moneybags is revealed to be vampire-like, a creature with a "voracious appetite" (*ibid.*, p. 344), a "boundless thirst" (*ibid.*, p. 345), a "werewolf-like hunger" (*ibid.*, p. 353) for surplus labor. His "appetite for surplus labour appears in the drive for an unlimited extension of the working day . . ." (*ibid.*, p. 346). The working day is extended into the night. But this "only slightly quenches the [capitalist's] vampire thirst for the living blood of labour" (*ibid.*, p. 367). The factory arises as a house of terror, in which the worker is subjected to the power of a "vampire [that] will not let go 'while there remains a single muscle, sinew or drop of blood to be exploited'" (*ibid.*, p. 416).

Marx's analysis of capital does not end at this juncture. In *Capital, 1* he goes on to the analysis of relative surplus value, capital accumulation, etc. But for our purposes we need follow him no further. The point has been made, and the problem has been posed. The appearance of freedom and equality (of mutual recognition) found in the sphere of circulation has been stripped away. We have reverted to the battle, and to the relationship of lordship and bondage. And our descent into the realm of production has introduced us to a new dramatic character, the capitalist vampire, a creature with an insatiable appetite for living labor. To be sure, Marx is using the language of a primitive orality metaphorically. But what if we take him more literally? Perhaps the capitalist's greed has a double origin—in the depths of the psyche as well as the depths of society.

6.

What would be the character structure of an individual whose inner world mirrored this historically specific external reality?

Let's begin again with money. In the world of Mr. Moneybags, money is a commodity that functions, in relationship to all other commodities, as the universal equivalent, the standard of price or value, and the means of circulation. When we move from this, the external world, into the internal world, it continues to perform these functions but with an emotional content. Reciprocally, this new content attaches itself to money in the external world.

First, then, money circulates all values, be they physical or psychical. It is a conduit of values in and between the external and internal worlds. It can perform this function because, second, it is the universal equivalent not just of linen and the like but also of all psychical values. Some of these are more prominent than others, such as the components of anal fantasies. But money may be equated with anything. And not just with objects but also with affects. Two such affective equations are of particular importance: (Money = Love) and (Money = Hate). Hence when money (objective money) is received it may be subjectively experienced as the bearer of love and/or hatred.

Third, money is the measure or standard of psychical as well as physical values: Money is the measure of the man. This implies that psychical values are akin to commodities. This commoditization of the inner world extends to the ego itself. Money, that is to say, takes up residence in the super-ego or ego-ideal. The super-ego is monetized. The ego, which is judged by and measures itself against the super-ego, is thus commoditized. Dimensions of selfhood that are not commoditizable—that can not be measured by money—are alienated and devalued.

This configuration I term the *commodity-character structure* of the individual in bourgeois society. It may be represented thus:

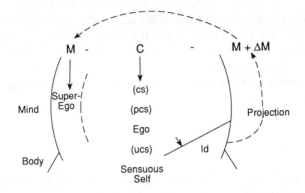

The external world is represented as a circulation of commodities aimed at the production and realization of surplus value; the inner world, according to the model of selfhood developed in Chapter 6. Taken together, they represent an individual for whom the structure of the external world has become the structure of the internal one. This involves a double process. On the one hand, the super-ego is progressively monetized and the ego commoditized as the child becomes an adult, as in the developmental sequence (milk at the breast → praise in exchange for proper defecation → presents as rewards for good behavior → grades in school as reward/punishment for academic performance → money for job performance). On the other, the relationship of commodities and money regresses (sinks deeper) into the structure of the self. Later experiences attach to and lend additional meaning to earlier ones. The consequence in both regards is that desires that do not have an exchange value are alienated. These include most importantly the polymorphous perverse desires of infancy.

Let's take an accessible and appropriate example. Loss of job and/or income produces anger. If, however, there is nothing that can be done with the anger, it is repressed and turned against the self. The consequence is depression and lowered self-esteem. Moreover, all prior issues of self-esteem are likely to be reactivated within this context. The adult re-experiences the child's hunger for healing, affirmative recognition. But this desire for recognition remains unrecognized. It is repressed along with the individual's impotent rage. Both desires are covered over by a kind of amnesia. All that the individual consciously experiences is worthlessness. And because the link to the ego has been severed, these alienated desires have no direct outlet. But they do have an indirect one: *The individual projects onto money the power of realizing repressed desires.*

Money gains a *surplus psychical value,* an affective (ΔM), it would not otherwise possess. Money has been fetishized and, with it, commodities. Hence they "appear as autonomous figures endowed with a life of their own, which enter into relations with each other and the human race" (*ibid.,* p. 165). Or to recur to *The Phenomenology*: Money takes on the features of the Unchangeable Being, the ultimate object of desire. The individual is then in the role of the Unhappy Consciousness, yearning to possess a source of bliss that remains perpetually and tantalizingly just out of reach.

7.

So much, then, for the meaning of money and the failure of self-recognition at the level of the circulation of commodities and its enacted ideology. Our next task is to consider the psychical meaning of the buying and selling of labor-power. If this were a free and equal exchange, then psychoanalysis would have nothing distinctive to say about it. Alternatively, if the worker is overpowered but not overawed, defeated but not persuaded, then, too, the psychoanalyst remains silent. If, however, the semblance of a fair exchange is mistaken for the real thing—as it is in bourgeois ideology and very often in bourgeois actuality—then we have what might be termed a "sado-masochistic contract."

The sado-masochistic contract is a version of the relationship analyzed by Fromm in the instance of fascist authoritarianism and by Benjamin in her interpretation of *The Story of O.* It involves an objective situation of domination that is subjectively mediated by a surrender of freedom, an act of self-abnegation, a voluntary giving over of one's will to the other. In the extreme instance the contract establishes the roles of torturer and tortured, with the specific proviso that the torture victim is to love and identify with the torturer. Out of love, s/he is to accept brutal necessity as if it were her/his own choice. Through identification with the oppressor s/he is to take pleasure in the pain s/he also suffers. Or, to make use of our model of commodity-character, the sadist's role is taken over by the individual's super-ego, the masochist's role by the ego. Thus the infliction of suffering is moralized. A relationship of domination takes on the appearance of a relationship of rightful authority. Or, as Nietzsche might have it, in this way the victim makes a virtue out of necessity.

Clearly, sado-masochistic transactions are not limited to the labor market, and labor market transactions are not necessarily agreements to torture and be tortured. Yet one might think it fiendishly clever that in capitalism a structural relationship of domination is mediated by subjective freedom. The apparently independent owner of labor-power agrees to become a wage slave—and to whistle while s/he works.

In sum, when the worker confronts the capitalist in the buying and selling of labor-power, the generality of commodity-character is particularized. The position of the super-ego, occupied by the capitalist, emerges as a monetized and moralized slave-driver. The position of the ego, occupied by the worker, emerges as a commoditized and morally devalued slave.

Slave-drivers have a creed, a quite inclusive one: Spare the lash and spoil the _____ (fill in the blank). Marx was not exaggerating when he commented that the worker, in bringing his hide to market, had nothing to expect but a hiding!

8.

As noted earlier Marx's metaphors in the chapter on the working day suggest that a primitive and destructive orality is involved in the production of surplus value. We may add that in their vampire-like hunger for surplus value capitalists devour not only the lives and energies of their workers but also each other: Big fish eat little fish. And Marx comments elsewhere that the capitalist economy turns on the wheel of greed—on "*avarice* and the *war amongst the avaricious—competition*" (Marx, 1844b, p. 71).

Because we wish to learn about greed, we will take a bit of instruction from Melanie Klein. This requires a brief visit to the nursery.

Klein (1952) draws a picture of infantile life that makes Hobbes' state of nature look like shelter from a storm. Although the infant is sustained by the experience of the mother as a good breast, s/he inevitably—under the influence of frustration and hatred—also experiences her as a bad breast:

> [In this instance] we find that the hated breast has acquired the oral destructive qualities of the infant's own impulses when he is in states of frustration and hatred. In his destructive fantasies he bites and tears up the breast, devours it, annihilates it; and he feels that the breast will attack him in the same way. As urethral- and anal-sadistic impulses gain in strength, the infant in his mind attacks the breast with poisonous urine and explosive faeces, and therefore expects it to be poisonous and explosive toward him. . . . [And since] the fantasied attacks on the object are fundamentally influenced by greed, the fear of the object's greed, owing to projection, is an essential element in persecutory anxiety: the bad breast will devour him in the same greedy way as he desires to devour it. (pp. 63-64)

For Klein, this paranoid interaction of infant and bad breast is onto-logically grounded and therefore historically unproblematical. We, by contrast, see the destructiveness of the fantasy as a function of intense pain and frustration, hence as both problematical and pathological. Pathology, unfortunately, is neither unnatural nor unhistorical.

When formulated as a process of recognition, the situation can be represented as "I (infant) = I (mother)". The infant is a protoself not yet differentiated from the mother. Lack of differentiation is indeed one of its distinguishing features. In its experience need is not distinguished from desire nor mind from body. It is a psychophysiological or sensu-ous organism that experiences various admixtures of pleasure and pain. The mother is the emergent and ultimate object of need/desire, of the infant's appetite. When she is able to provide pleasure and elimination of pain and to take pleasure in so doing, she provides the infant with the first experience of mutual recognition. When the interaction ends, the infant takes away something good and gains an element of affirmative selfhood. But the infant brings pain (hunger and other discomforts) into the interaction. Pain is accompanied by anger, even rage. Hence contact with the mother engenders anxiety. If the infant is in sufficient pain and/or if the mother is excessively frustrating through her inability to ease pain, then the interaction becomes paranoid. This is the first instance of nonrecognition. The conclusion of the interaction is then experienced as (1) a retreat from a hostile situation and (2) an attack on linking and on the mother. The resulting self is negatively defined. It is also schizoid. It is based upon a broken link to the (m)other, and it has left behind the self that interacts with her. It is a duplicated or divided self.

Let's now go from the nursery to the factory, from the production of selves to the production of surplus value. Mr. Moneybags lets fall the cloak of his (merely apparent) humanity and stands revealed as the vam-pire he really is. But he is a capitalist vampire, hence a machine—the machinery of production, machines as such and mechanical processes, objective forces that function with a subjectivity and will of their own. Workers are subjected to the will of these voracious mechanical mon-sters. They may fight back or try to defend themselves by sabotage and rearguard actions; or they may retreat to a stance of stoic indifference, in which they maintain their freedom by psychic flight from an intoler-ably dangerous and dehumanizing situation.

By way of (to be sure, an extreme) illustration: In its final sequences, the movie *Brazil* offers us an alternative ending to the destruction of Winston Smith's selfhood in Orwell's *Nineteen Eighty-Four* (1949). The protagonist is being tortured, but his mind is elsewhere. He has fled into fantasy and there he feels no pain. The State is not his lord and master; he still has a mind of his own.

There is a continuum between such an escape into fantasy and the benign daydreams that are woven into the fabric of everyday life. When life is torture, however, or to the extent that life is torture, these day-dreams crystallize into a zone of withdrawal and safety. Psychologically we are then, again, in the paranoid–schizoid position, on the borderline, occupying the last line of defense against the insane flux and flows of desiring-machines and bodies without organs.

In this instance the paranoid–schizoid position is the intersubjective or intrasubjective relationship between a persecutor on the edge of madness and a persecuted whose only recourse is adherence to the Nirvana principle (death to all stimuli). It is the ultimate, most pathological, structure of failed recognition. To fall beneath it is to experience the death of the self altogether.

Mr. Moneybags relishes the expression, "the bottom line." We have just drawn it.

9.

We may summarize our analysis through consideration of the following figure:

Falsified (Pseudo–Happy) Consciousness
Unhappy Consciousness
Circulation of Social Values & Commodity–Character Structure
Buying & Selling of Labor–Power = Sado–Masochistic Contract
Production of Surplus Value/Paranoid–Schizoid Position
Horrors of War

This figure has the same form as Fromm's conception of social character, and some of the same content. It does not, however, represent a typical individual member of a capitalist society—commodity-character structure occupies that position. Instead, it models, from a psychoanalytic-marxist perspective, capitalist forces and relations of production.

On the surface, we seem to have selves inhabiting "an Eden of the innate rights of man." At the center, we find a war of all against all. In between we have a multilayered defense against, or social relationships structured against, the horrors of this state of war. At the same time, the layers of the structure are stages or forms of the battle. Defenses are battlements.

It would take us beyond the limits of our current project to develop this configuration in detail. But here are some of the main points.

• Although the state of war is not unique to capitalism, capitalism is, as Marx says, the war of the avaricious. However, this state of war is not human nature. It is rather a deformation of our nature, anthropology-cum-pathology.

The horrors of this state of war are not objective *or* subjective. They go deeper; they penetrate to the sensuousness of human existence. The precarious and precious balance of the basic drives is tilted toward death and aggression by painful disruptions of the rhythms of life. In part and for defined populations, the disruption is a function of literal material scarcities, to say nothing of literal wars. In part and for other populations, the disruption results from the substitution of mechanisms for life-processes. Either way, it generates both rage and anxiety—terror. Hence like all war, its true divinity is Panic. The dialectic of the One and the Many tends to fragment or explode. The structures of selfhood develop in response to the threat of disintegration and chaos.

• Around this maelstrom crystallizes the double structure of the paranoid–schizoid position and the production of surplus value. At this level there is a distinction between objective and subjective, that is, between desire and work. Neither side is reducible to the other, but neither is the relationship between them symmetrical: Social interactions and states of mind characterized by the paranoid–schizoid position may or may not exist without surplus value production, but the production of surplus value necessarily produces the paranoid–schizoid position. As Marx's metaphors reveal, the production of surplus value transforms work itself into a persecutory object or Other, from which flight and fight are the only possible responses. Thus the capitalist form of lordship and bondage is rooted in the production of surplus value and the paranoid–schizoid position.

• The buying and selling of labor-power with its affiliated sado-masochistic meanings is the fundamental social contract in capitalist society. It institutes the distinctively capitalist division of labor. It contains two possibilities: selling oneself into bondage or purchasing a slave. It is an alienating of the self that results in the alienation of the self. It recapitulates or replays the life and death battle of recognition, but in a legitimated form.

• At the individual level commodity-character structure contains the more primitive and brutal elements of the system. At the social level there is a systematic circulation of social values in general, surplus values in particular. Commodity-character structure and the circulation of values are, moreover, mutually determining—mutually fetishizing.

• Each layer of social interaction preserves and disguises the reality beneath it. By the time we reach consciousness we experience the horrors of war without being horrified. As if hypnotized—which in a sense we are—we mistake self-limiting and self-defeating defenses against pain for self-expressive pursuits of pleasure and the good life. Only intermittently do we recognize ourselves in the figure of the Unhappy Consciousness. Most of the time we live our lives in the position of the Pseudo-Happy Consciousness.

10.

We may add a note on the meaning of money. There is no money in the nursery, but ontogenetically the meaning of money originates there. For the infant the mother's body contains all good things. It is the ultimate source of value. The good breast, to use Klein's terms, is the source of the milk of life and lovingkindness. But the persecutory breast is projectively filled with urine, feces, and all things hateful. Money, via the processes previously described, takes on both meanings. Further, when the infant is confronted by the recurrent contamination of the good breast by its oral sadistic impulses, it turns the good breast into an "'ideal' breast which should fulfil the greedy desire for unlimited, immediate and everlasting gratification" (Klein, 1952, p. 64). Thus in the shape of the ideal breast we find the ontogenetic foundation of the mystery of money—and so, too, the animating spirit of the Unchangeable Being. Money is who we are not.

B. Sexual Parts and Part-Objects

1.

In the preceding exploration we implicitly bracketed the issue of gender. One could make the argument that it should have been our starting point. After all, the separation of the sphere of economic production from that of human reproduction is an historical latecomer. Phylogenetically and ontogenetically, kinship structures precede market structures.

If, however, our aim is to develop the problematics of recognition in the present tense, then we have appropriately begun with economic production. Just as the production of surplus value mobilizes and gives historically determinate form to emotional life in general, so it mobilizes and gives historically determinate form to sex/gender relations in particular.

Thanks to Jessica Benjamin we have already come some distance in the exploration of gender and recognition. It is possible, I think, to go a bit further: Within the orbit of capitalist production, selves tend to be reduced to sexual parts or, more accurately sexual part-objects. These sexual part-objects are then commoditized, monetized, and fetishized. In the place of Aphrodite a golden phallus arises from the seas.

2.

Part-objects are a Kleinian discovery or invention. Typically the object is a real/fantasized body part, such as a breast or penis, which is endowed with the agency of a person, hence a part mistaken for a whole. Part-object relationships are viewed as characteristic of the paranoid–schizoid position, while the capacity to relate to whole persons is assigned to the depressive position.

There is a double conflation—adult with infant, pathological with healthy—in the typical Kleinian articulation of this concept.

Consider the instance of nursing. In the Kleinian view, the infant experiences the mother's breast as a part-object within a paranoid–schizoid relationship. Assume for a moment that the infant does experience the unit, mother = breast. Then there are at least three possible meanings of the experience. First, the infant does not distinguish between mother and breast. They are one, a matrix. The breast is then not a part-object, but simply an object. To be sure, if an adult did not distinguish between woman and breast, s/he would be imagining or perceiving a part-object. But the superimposition of this interpretation onto the infant's is plainly adultomorphic. Second, the matrix of experience having the perceptual form of a breast is replaced by a breast within a void, a breast with a life of its own and lacking the fullness of a sensuous manifold. Here we do have a part-object and a paranoid–schizoid experience. Third, the infant has become an individual capable of distinguishing between a woman as a whole and her breasts as parts of a whole. While maintaining the distinction, s/he emotionally reduces a woman to her breasts, so that her breasts and *not* the woman are the objects of desire. This, too, is a part-object relationship and a paranoid–schizoid experience.

Thus the preceding proposition may be restated: In capitalism gender identity is normatively established as a part-object relationship in the paranoid–schizoid position. Apparent recognition between persons covers over the fantasmal interaction of body parts, all of which have monetary equivalents.

It must be added that the exchange is unequal. The vagina never has the same value as the penis. Rather, the denial of the vagina as presence and as locus of desire is the foundation upon which the phallocentric structure is (of course) erected.

3.

Here are two war stories.

Electra. A woman is waging a psychoanalytic battle. She has a well-developed capacity for concern. She has a tense and sometimes hostile relationship to her mother, an admiring and loving relationship to her father. She is also profoundly not-sexual. A good part of the time she has no feeling in her clitoris and vagina. When she does have sexual sensations, they sometimes bring her close to panic. They threaten her with the remembrance of things past. She lives alone.

Don Juan. A man is waging his version of the analytic battle. He spends much time helping his many friends. He does his best to distance himself from his parents. He is both sexual and seductive. He lives to give and get sexual pleasure. He is only happy when he is with a woman. Yet he cannot sustain an intimate relationship. Somehow either women betray him or he betrays them. His most intimate relationship is with his penis. He gets very anxious when he has to be alone.

Moral of the stories: Gender identity, no less than social character, develops in response to the horrors of war, a war in which penis = weapon and vagina = wound. In the language of body parts, the domination of the phallus = the violation of the vagina.

4.

The contemporary version of male dominant or patriarchal ideology makes one of two claims: Men and women have the same rights, responsibilities, and opportunities; men and women have different—but complementary—rights, responsibilities, and opportunities. Earlier versions were more forthright: Men are different from and superior to women. To be sure, this claim transformed might into right, the facts of domination into the values of a patriarchal order. But it had the virtue of not denying the facts themselves.

It would be foolish to make the counterclaim that nothing has changed in relationships of gender. Nonetheless it remains true that women on average earn less than men, that women's jobs are less well paid than men's jobs, and that housework and child-rearing are unpaid and devalued. Women are predominantly characterized as consumers and not producers. Alternatively, as can be seen in the related instances of advertising and pornography, they themselves are the commodities. And when women manage by their actions to pierce the veil of ideology, they are either condemned as unfeminine or, in rare instances, given this much recognition: "A man couldn't have done it better."

Perhaps the same was said of Clytaemestra. The more things change, the more they stay the same.

5.

In her exploration of gender, Rubin followed the familiar Marxist path from exchange through the division of labor to production. We followed more or less the same path in our exploration of commodity-character, and will now follow it again. But Rubin developed her conception of sex/gender systems by analyzing precapitalist social relationships. This had the advantage of bringing kinship structures into focus. But one of the features of the capitalist mode of production is that it inverts the relationship between kinship and economic relationships. Instead of economic relationships being one of the mediations of kinship, kinship becomes one of the mediations of economic relationships. To make contemporary use of Rubin's analysis, therefore, it must be refocused.[2]

A very simple kinship model of exchange might look like this:

Here we picture two elementary kinship units. Men are represented by the phallic part-object (Δ), women by the mammary, vaginal, or uterine part-object (○). The units are to be linked through the exchange of women. We presume that the fathers arrange the transaction, which also might be accompanied and symbolized by an exchange of gifts. The sons are subject to the power and authority of the fathers. Even when, as children, they were subject to their mother's commands, this was only by delegation of authority from the fathers. When the transaction is completed, they will have dominion over their wives, as did their fathers before them.

When formulated in this fashion, we have an exchange of women within a patriarchal structure. Not just men but fathers occupy the positions of ultimate power and authority. It stretches the term to designate as patriarchal other relationships of male domination. If men are exchanging or sharing women without regard to generational standing, or if men take possession of women on an individual basis, then objectively we no longer have the rule of the father. Even so patriarchy is preserved (what does it mean to say "preserved"?) in the oedipal configuration.

These considerations lead us to modify our conceptualization patriarchy/phallocentrism. Instead of characterizing patriarchy as simply objective, we view it as objective in the first instance. The oedipal configuration can then be seen as the subjective reflection of this objective relationship. Phallocentrism, by contrast, originates in the sphere of subjectivity and desire. Yet it is a component of the oedipal configuration, hence indirectly a product of patriarchy. And it has quite objective realizations, that is, phallocentric social practices, including those clustered around castration anxiety and penis envy.

The expanded conception of patriarchy, in which the role of the father is placed in the background, permits a simpler representation of the exchange of women:

$$\text{Man—Woman}$$
$$\text{Woman—Man}$$

Each man gives and receives a woman. He alienates himself from a woman he cannot use, perhaps as a result of the incest taboo, and gains one that he can. At the same time he establishes a relationship of recognition with the other man: Each man recognizes the other as the rightful possessor of the woman who was exchanged. Which is also to say, each man's individual interest in the possession of women has become a mutual interest. The exchange of women thus secures two relationships simultaneously: the mutual recognition of the two men and the denial of recognition to the two women.

The form of this relationship is familiar to us from Marxist political economy. The two men are in the position of commodity owners and the women are in the position of commodities or money: $C - M - C$. This is not to say that the two transactions can be identified with one another. It is clear enough that the precapitalist or at least nonmarket exchange of women is not an exchange of commodities, and the capitalist exchange of commodities is only incidentally an exchange of women. Nor, however, are the two relationships merely analogous. Rather the exchange of women is the prototype for the exchange of commodities. In our society commodities must perform the linking functions formerly performed by women. And just as patriarchal relations are preserved in the oedipal configuration, so the exchange of women is preserved symbolically within the exchange of commodities.

The following formula represents the last point, that is, the capitalist exchange of women. The prime (') is used to symbolize augmented or surplus value of whatever kind. The other symbols retain their former meanings. Thus:

$$(M = \Delta) - (C = \bigcirc) - (M' = \Delta')$$

This symbolic relationship combines a patriarchal circulation of sexual values ($\Delta - \bigcirc - \Delta'$) with the capitalist circulation of labor values (M – C – M'). For brevity's sake we will work out the two relationships in the combined form.

Initially we have the symbolic equation, money = man, or more precisely, money (M) = penis (Δ). Exchange is thus a man's act no matter what the biological sex of the one performing it. And it is not the action of a person, but rather of a part-object. Just as individuals function within capitalist exchange merely as the bearers of the values of commodities, so they function as the representatives of part-objects.

The monetized penis then takes possession of a commodity, of a value that is a source of value, that is, a breast (commodity = breast, C = $\bigcirc$). Because the valued object is also the contents of the mother's body, there is also a hint of the equation: commodity = vagina or uterus. But castration anxiety renders this meaning void.

Finally, enriched by the content of the commoditized breast, the monetized penis emerges with augmented value. Money becomes capital, the penis becomes a phallus, and the one is equated with the other (M' = Δ'). The phallus is thus not a penis, a biological organ, but rather a fantasmal penis, a penis that contains and is covertly maintained by a full breast and that, as a consequence, is perpetually erect, invulnerable, and self-reproducing. Phallus = penis + breast. When the phallus is then fused with capital it becomes not only hard but metallic. It glitters like gold and is as unbending as steel. Reciprocally, money becomes potent, indeed omnipotent—divine and persecutory. Thus human subjectivity becomes an objective force, or part-objective force, more subjectively powerful than the human subjects who created it.

The interpenetration of the processes circulating commodities and part-objects could be refered to as capitalism/phallocentrism. Capitalism may or may not be patriarchal, in the restricted sense of the term; it is always phallocentric, symbolically male dominant. And it is usually both. Older men rule over both women and younger men, in corporations and in governments no less than in families. When women do rule, they do so only as Clytaemestra—with Orestes waiting off-stage.

Yet when the dominion of the fathers is secured through capitalism/phallocentrism, it is subject to a counterforce. A commodity, as Marx says, is a "born leveller and cynic": It will exchange itself with anything or anybody (Marx, 1867, p. 179). It has no respect for age or generational status, nor even for biological sex. Clytaemestra will do just fine, so long as she is the bearer of the phallus.

6.

The circulation of monetized and commoditized sexual part-objects engenders and is reproduced by a social character structure that, following the model of commodity-character, might be pictured this way:

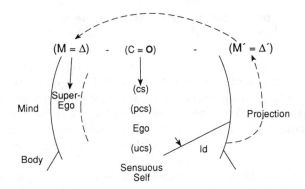

In this model the super-ego is simultaneously monetized and masculinized. The ego is then not only commoditized but—in the stereotypical sense—feminized. Its value is assessed by a standard of *monetized masculinity*. It is, indeed, subjected to this standard. The ego gives but does not receive recognition. Like the woman O in *The Story of O*, it is deprived of agency, of active selfhood. Any expression of selfhood on its part would be an unlawful challenge to masculine authority—a challenge lacking not only justification but even a language of protest. In a word, the ego's self-activity is alienated, repressed. But there is a self-defeating return of the repressed, a projection of repressed feminine desire into the fetishized representations of monetized masculinity. And so the cycle repeats itself.

7.

So much for gender at the level of exchange—for monetized masculinity and the capitalist circulation of sexual part-objects. We come next to the social contract that legitimizes patriarchal domination, namely, the marital agreement.

In precapitalist societies the marital agreement is arguably the fundamental social compact. In capitalist systems, this role is taken over by directly economic contracts, most importantly by the contractual relationship of labor and capital. But market relationships have kinship meanings—witness the frequency with which business transactions are characterized as courtships, marriages, or divorces. And despite the displacement of and assault upon the family by the market, the marriage contract remains one of the basic social bonds. It also retains its economic significance, as is especially evident in the instances of divorce and inheritance when substantial property is involved.

In the buying and selling of labor-power, there is an appearance of mutual recognition (a contract freely entered into between equals) masking a relationship of domination. The same interpretation applies to marriage argeements. Assume that the contract centers on sexual privileges. Then, on the surface, two individuals alienate the right to have sexual intercourse with anyone other than the partner to the agreement, in exchange for which they gain an exclusive right to the partner's sexual services. But if we step back from the contractual act to the context of the act, the picture changes. The generality of gender relationships is male domination, "Male > Female" and "Men > Women". Hence as a rule, marriage signifies or formalizes a woman's acceptance of male dominance.[3]

It is possible for a given couple to achieve a relationship of mutual recognition despite this structuring of gender, but such exceptions do not disprove the rule. More commonly, women wage the battle for selfhood and freedom within and despite the structural asymmetry of marital institutions. But men tend to feel cheated when their wives refuse to be slaves. They also tend to get angry. The uppity wife is likely to be the beaten wife.

In developing a critique of male domination it is important not to damage the case by overstating it. After all, not every family romance is a concealed horror story. There are authentically joyous anniversary celebrations. But it is fair to ask—and this is an empirical question—how often this occurs, especially how often it occurs in proportion to unhappy marriages, divorces, and violence against women. Further, it is arguable that the marital contract, like the labor contract, has a sado-masochistic content. This is manifestly true in the all-too-common relationships in which wives accept abuse from their husbands as their just desert. But sado-masochism is not just a matter of physical or sexual abuse. As Jessica Benjamin emphasizes, it is just as much a relationship of one will to another. In this instance, I (male) demand that you (female) relinquish your will in favor of mine; I (female) voluntarily relinquish my will in favor of yours (male); and each of us is to take pleasure in the act of submission.

Viewed from another angle, the marriage contract solemnizes the sexual division of labor between the partners. Thus we may paraphrase Marx: When we leave the wedding feast, a change takes place in the happy couple. The groom emerges as lord and master, the bride as help-mate and devoted servant.[4]

8.

Once again, we have come to the sexual division of labor, hence also to the question of sameness and difference, and of recognition.

Take two selves whose relationship to each other is immediate or indeterminate. Insofar as each of them is a self, they are the same. Using the usual notation, "I = I". Insofar as they are discrete entities, they are different: "I ≠ I". Hence the immediate relationship of selves involves both identity and difference, "I =/≠ I", and neither aspect is predominant. One cannot say that the two selves are essentially the same or essentially different, nor is there any reason to do so.

Take a man and a woman. They each possess definably human biological attributes and so are the same. In equally definable biological ways they are different. Abstractly, there is no reason to privilege either sameness or difference. Men and women both are and are not the same, are and are not different.

These observations are not very interesting, and that is precisely the point. Abstract determinants such as sameness and difference or the One and the Many are politically innocent. It is their connection to activities, interests, and desires that makes them political. It is a glissade or dis-placement to debate the concepts themselves instead of their concrete employment.

We can make things a bit more concrete by specifying certain fea-tures of men and women that have social functional implications. They are few. As noted in Chapter 4, they cluster around human reproduc-tion. The species must be reproduced through the sexual intercourse of men and women, although our biological sexual programs are not limited to this function. Only women can bear and nurse children. Women menstruate, have vaginas and uteruses, and breasts that can lactate. They do not have penises. Men do not menstruate, and do not have vaginas, uteruses, and breasts that can lactate. They do have penises.

In a society as technologically sophisticated as our own, this set of similarities and differences has extremely minimal *necessary* social func-tional implications. For the species to reproduce itself, some number of women must become pregnant and bear children. The time and experience involved are collectively (but not individually) unavoidable. For individuals, reproduction is an option. Assuming use of birth control techniques, this is even true for sexually active male/female couples. And for the women who do bear children, even breast-feeding is optional.

So long as women are not disadvantaged or devalued for performing these minimally necessary reproductive functions, the difference between men and women in the sphere of human reproduction is hardly more germane to politics than the abstract concepts of similarity and difference. The same could not be said about the performance of these functions in less technologically advanced societies, that is, in societies in which most women necessarily spent a very substantial part of their lives bearing and taking care of children. In these societies anatomy was something close to destiny and the sexual division of labor was perhaps the fundamental economic principle. This does not mean that child-rearing was exclusively a female role, that women's labor was devalued, or that men were masters and women were slaves. But the sexual division itself was a matter of necessity and not of choice. Whatever the modalities of recognition between men and women, they took form within these limits. One necessarily participated in collective life as a woman or a man. No longer. Necessity has become freedom or, more modestly, a social given has become a problem. We must work out for ourselves the parameters and implications of the sexual division of labor.

Regrettably, we must also abandon the idea that we are free to work out these parameters and implications, guided only by concerns for individual and collective well-being. In fact, women's work is devalued, and women are disadvantaged in and as a consequence of performing it. The sexual division of labor is hierarchical as well as functional.

Why should this be the case? Not, I think it can be safely said, because male domination is human nature, and certainly not because it has always been that way. Any such use of history and human nature begs the question. But there are undoubted advantages that accrue to men as a result of a male dominant sexual division of labor, including directly economic and political ones. Men have an interest in keeping women in the servant's role.

Yet engendered interests are not unambiguous. It could be shown that men and women would mutually benefit from a proper valuation of parenting functions and an equalization of gender roles. But something other than or in addition to individual and collective self-interest is involved. The sexual division of labor is accompanied by characteristic placements and displacements of desire, by a psychology and ideology of the masculine and feminine. Men and women see themselves, each other, and the work they perform through a screen of gender stereotypes. When passed through this filter, men become males, women become females, creatures not merely different but alien from one another, embodied fantasies, walking and talking part-objects. It was Freud's great contribution to bring this phantasmagoria into focus and make it accessible to analysis. To be sure, he himself was deeply under its influence, so that his analysis of gender took the form of a defense of maleness. But when feminists turn to psychoanalysis, it is because there at least *our* problem can be found: Who are we, as male and female? How are we produced psychologically? And what can we do about it?

9.

We may add two further comments on gender identity and difference before we descend into the realm of gender production.

• It could be argued that capitalism minimizes gender differences— but in a way that further disadvantages women. The precapitalist position of women in the cycle of human reproduction gave them a defensible bastion against the incursion of masculinity. Maternity was a power/knowledge position, as well as a basis for self-respect, self-recognition, and—between women—mutual recognition. If women were imprisoned in maternity, they also possessed a kind of freedom through it.

Capitalism batters the walls of this fortress/prison. Childbirth is medicalized, child-rearing is scientized. Which is to say, the political and epistemological standpoint of human reproduction is coopted and masculinized.

The implication? So long as capitalism, patriarchy, and phallocentrism remain, even emancipatory potentialities tend to be realized inversely.

• In a patriarchal/phallocentric discourse, the argument that men and women are essentially the same becomes the claim that women are the same as men. To use an analogy from American racial politics, the argument becomes integrationist. Maleness remains the standard of selfhood and the only available form of recognition. Women, in pursuing equality with men, are struggling for the right to distort themselves into males. It may be in their interest to do so, but it leaves them unrecognized as women. Hence the appeal of a politics of difference. Within patriarchy/phallocentrism, however, difference implies separation. Again to use the racial anology, it amounts to either segregation or separatism. If men determine the difference, women are segregated. They are confined to private life or women's jobs. If women determine the difference, they become separatists who surrender any hope of mutual recognition between the sexes and seek for authentic selfhood exclusively in the company of other women. Something important can be gained in this kind of relative isolation. Something important can also be lost.

In other words, the meaning of sex/gender sameness and difference is distorted by patriarchy/phallocentrism. The distorted meanings won't change until the system is changed.

10.

It is easy to slip into thinking that the production of gender is a family affair. In one sense, this is obviously true. Ontogenetically we live first within family units of one kind or another. The elementary kinship combinations—the mother–child dyad, the mother–father–child triad, and the various more extended forms that include, most importantly, sibling relations—are consequently fundamental to human and gender identity. But this is only a part of the story. Familial relationships are themselves determined by the mode of social production and the particularity of the family's position within it. Further, other domains of social interaction intrude upon family life directly and early on. In our society, for example, children are exposed to the mass media practically from birth and to public (nonfamilial) education from no later than the fifth year. And perhaps most importantly, gender is not simply produced in the family and consumed elsewhere. It is rather produced and reproduced in all domains of social interaction.

Thus we are entitled to talk about a capitalist production of gender and to put forward the substantive claim that it mirrors the production of commodities. Psychologically, commodities are part-objects. They are function-performing elements of the metabolism of production that have been split off from the whole and, via projection, endowed with a life of their own. To say that there is a fetishism of commodities is also to say that commodities function as part-objects. If the self is monetized and commoditized, then it, too, functions in the manner of a part-object. Because gender is an attribute of selves, gender relationships will likewise establish relationships between things instead of persons, between sexual part-objects instead of persons who are in part sexual.

The commoditization of gender does not mean that all sex/gender interactions are part-object transactions. To use an analogy from classical political economy: Just as market prices can rise above or fall below the costs of production of a commodity, so the actualities of gender may deviate, for better or worse, from the capitalist standard. But normatively, or insofar as gender is determined by capitalist social relations, we know ourselves as hierarchically ordered body-parts.

11.

From the feminist writers discussed in Chapter 4 we know quite a bit about how a patriarchal and phallocentric sex/gender system is produced and reproduced. But the analysis is incomplete if we fail to recognize that phallocentrism is in essence the denial of the vagina, the negation and negating of vaginal experience.

I hope I will not be misunderstood. It's not my intention to replace or challenge one part-object with another. As Jessica Benjamin rightly argues, simply "finding a female counterpart to the phallic symbol will not work; it is necessary to find an alternative psychic register" (Benjamin, 1988, p. 125). The mutual recognition of selves, not the contestation of genitals, is the aim of a critique of sex/gender relationships.

Yet it hardly seems possible to deconstruct phallocentric discourse if the vagina is unspoken. Think, for example, of Lacanian theory, which makes the vagina into a lack, an absence, a no-thing for which there is no word. The vagina is disavowed and disallowed. And what follows? Women exist only as the Other, the mysterious feminine negative of male discourse.[5]

It seems worthwhile, therefore, to think about the production of gender from the standpoint of vaginal experience.

12.

In each of us there is registered the sensuous experience of intrauterine existence. We retain, to a greater or lesser degree, a sense of a pleasurable space that we once occupied. Retain it, and yearn for it: What Freud termed the oceanic feeling and what Hegel termed the Unchangeable Being have their ontogenetic origin in the quiescent pleasure of intrauterine experience.

The vagina is the passageway to and from the interior of the mother's body. As the passageway into the mother's body, it is the entrance into a state of bliss. As the passageway from the mother's body, it is filled with the memories of the primal voyage, of a journey that was anxiety-filled, disruptive, and terrifying. Hence the ubiquity of children's games in which one thing is placed into another or the child her/himself wiggles, creeps, or crawls into a closed space. The birth process is reversed, the anxiety it involved is imaginatively mastered, and the pleasurable and safe intrauterine past is recaptured.

At this depth of experience our mothers are the world. We are contained by this world, then inexplicably expelled from it into another, alien one. In games and fantasies we re-enter it through our own efforts.

When we are fortunate, a further development occurs. Something of intrauterine experience is transferred to the outer world, which then can serve as container and matrix of further development. And because both maternal worlds exist before life becomes conscious and historical, they have an ontological or natural appearance. Thus the symbolic equation: mother = world = nature.

Here we have the prehistory and most basic meanings of uterus and vagina—not yet, however, as part-objects, rather as whole ones; but also not yet as persons or parts of persons. At its origin a kind of impersonality and a sense of indestructibility attach to our experience of the maternal world. When, in later life, the maternal world is embodied in women, these two qualities create an opening for failures of recognition and outright abuse by men. The vulnerability and selfhood of women, along with their own needs and desires, disappear into the uterine ur-reality. Women become objects to be used, used up, and misused—at will. In parallel fashion the fusion of the maternal world with the natural world facilitates the greedy and destructive use of environmental resources.

Meanwhile the maternal world becomes endowed with personality in the course of development. Partly, by making use of projective identification, we attribute selfhood to the other, both women and nonhuman nature. Partly, the independent actions of mothering persons make us aware that they, too, possess a will. We more nearly enter the field of recognition. Then, however, a new issue arises: The mothering person becomes available as an object of blame, as the one responsible for our fall from grace. She is the place from which we have been exiled. Because she is also the world, she is the source of our pain. And especially in our sensuous interaction with her, she is also the ultimate source of both pleasure and security. Hence, as Dinnerstein argues most forcefully, she becomes the object of our most intense ambivalences. For women, to win is to lose.

There is some plausibility to the argument that shared parenting reduces the focal intensity of these feelings, spreading them more evenly over biological mothers and fathers. One might go further: At this juncture maternity is not yet engendered; there is no paternity to which it might be opposed. Nor is the child in this domain psychologically a boy or a girl. Shared parenting would mirror and reinforce the not-yet engendered nature of the experience. But sharing can only be taken so far. For the child to flourish maternity must be personal. Mothering does not have to be monadic, but neither can it be purely communal. And no matter what the distribution of mothering functions, the intensity of the primary maternal experience cannot be eliminated. It is developmentally catastrophic when parents deny and impose upon their children a denial of sensuous reality. In this and other respects, the basic question is less who does the mothering and more how the mothering is done.

13.

Although the intensity of need and desire does not diminish absolutely during the first few years of life, it is reduced relative to our capacity for containment. Boys and girls alike develop an inner space and passageways to and from the outside. They begin to be able to contain the experience that formerly contained them. This process is modeled on alimentation; the mind initially functions as an alimentary process. But as the typical infantile confusion of defecation and birth shows, there is only one internal space, which is experienced indifferently as stomach or uterus. Thus we all have, so to speak, an alimentary uterus and vagina.

Then comes the discovery of the sexual organs. Both sexes become capable of localizing sexual sensations in their genitals. From one standpoint it doesn't matter if we call it a vagina or a penis. But it invariably comes to matter, although with varying degrees of urgency. Two sexes come into being. To outward appearances one has a sexual part and one does not. Boys become differentiated from girls, fathers from mothers, haves from have-nots.

This is not the whole story, but in orthodox psychoanalytic theory this is where the story ends. Boys become phallocentric and anxiously castratable men, girls become phallocentric and resentfully castrated women. And not just in psychoanalytic theory: In a male dominant and/ or patriarchal society this is how, normatively speaking, it must end. Patriarchy engenders phallocentrism.

As we saw earlier, the phallus is a penis held erect by an introjected breast. We may now add that its foundation (or, better, pedestal) is the denial of the vagina as absence and as presence—as the absent penis and as the terrible passage leading from integral quiescence into a world of trial and trouble. Its social production likewise involves an absence and a presence—the absence in the capitalist mode of production of structural relationships of mutual recognition, the presence of an underlying state of war that recurrently evokes extremely primitive terrors and hatreds.

Phallocentrism is at once oppressive and repressive, an instrument of domination and a defense, something to wield against the other and something to hold on to. Better to have a phallus as a self than no self at all. And this holds, in its own way, for women as well as men. Lacking a phallus of her own, a woman is expected to be grateful to the man who lets her borrow his.

Free advice: Neither a borrower nor a lender be.

14.

From our present position there is something more to say about the relationship between phallocentrism and fetishism.[6]

As we know, a fetish is a thing with magical powers. It gains these powers through an unconscious process of attribution. This holds even when the thing is an idea, such as the idea of God.

Freud had a more specific conception of fetishism. The sexual fetish, he believed, "is a substitute for the woman's (the mother's) penis that the little boy once believed in . . ." (Freud, 1927b, p. 152). Unable to bear the sight of her genitals, which appear to him to be the site of castration, he shifts his gaze and erotic interest to an object that (1) can symbolize the maternal penis and (2) function to deny the possibility of castration. Further, Freud contended, fetishism involves a splitting of the ego (Freud, 1940, pp. 276–277). One part of the self accepts and can testify to the reality of the situation; another part disavows it.

Freud's analysis makes a contribution to the critique of both capitalism and phallocentrism. If we are correct in identifying the commodity and the phallus as fetishes, then each of them is a substitute for the mother's penis and a defense against the anxiety produced through the recognition that she doesn't have one. But fetishism is also a defense against a presence, and this in a double sense. The fetish that one possesses denies both the life-giving power of the maternal breast that one does not possess and the maternal space of safety and integral quiescence to which one does not have access.

Thus the fetish is a denial both of what the mother lacks and of what she possesses. It is, further, a defense within the paranoid–schizoid position. If on the one hand it animates inanimate objects, on the other it reduces whole objects to part-objects. It subjectifies the thing by thingifying the subject. And because the ego is split in the process, a conscious self comes into existence that acts as if things were people and people were things. Eminently realistic and rational, the conscious self is unaware that its thinking is an exercise in fetishism, and even less aware that its commodity fetishism and phallocentrism consist of magical defenses against the maternal experience of life and desire.

15.

We have not yet gone beyond a phallocentric perspective. Think back to our two war stories, the experiences of Don Juan and Electra. The former would recognize himself in the analysis thus far conducted. He might also acknowledge the desire for revenge against women that originates in infantile helplessness. But not just infantile helplessness: He would add that he was the victim of oedipal betrayal, and that the mother must be punished for her infidelities.

Be that as it may, Electra would find the essence of her experience missing from our analysis. Karen Horney (1933) would help her to understand it. Speaking of certain of her women patients, she conjectures that

> when these patients were children and indulged in onanistic play, they were led by vaginal sensations to the discovery of the vagina itself, and that their anxiety took the very form of the dread that they made a hole where no hole ought to be. (p. 156)

For these women the dread of having injured themselves is so intense that both the memory of the masturbatory experience and their knowledge of the vagina is repressed. Typically direct "genital masturbation is given up altogether, or at least confined to the more easily accessible clitoris"; and "the fiction is conceived and long maintained that the vagina does not exist. . . ." Thus *"behind the 'failure to discover' the vagina is a denial of its existence"* (*ibid.*, p. 160).

Horney is not, it should be emphasized, devaluing or denying the erotic significance of the clitoris. Rather she is calling attention to the *defensive* substitution of a part for a whole, of the clitoris for the manifold of feminine genital experience. In the instances with which she is concerned, the little girl's clitoral experience covers over the hole she fears she has made in herself. She defends herself against intense anxiety, but only by cutting herself off from a vital source of feminine desire. Moreover, she now treats her clitoris as if it were a phallus. This means she has entered into a competition with boys that she must necessarily lose (*ibid.*, p. 161)—entered into the world of penis envy and (we would say) phallocentrism. Only the recognition of the vagina, by contrast, will empower her as a woman and enable her to be centered in herself.

16.

There is another and more terrible possibility for the Electras of our world. What if it was her father and not the little girl herself who discovered her vagina? What if her father's penis, which is frightening enough in her imagination, is actually an instrument of penetration and domination? How is she to recover from this life and death struggle, from this shattering violation of selfhood?

In such an eventuality the stories of Don Juan and Electra would merge. The father's rape of the daughter, or more generally Don Juan's mistreatment of women, would be the son's revenge against the mother.

To repeat: Our sex/gender system is a war in which penis = weapon and vagina = wound.

17.

This last analytic step changes the meaning of the preceding ones. Hitherto the denial of the vagina was seen as a defense against unconscious fantasies and anxieties. Now we see that, from a feminine perspective, the fears are not necessarily generated by fantasies. Labeling them as fantasies is rather the act of denial.

The meaning of the denial also changes from the masculine perspective. A Don Juan might be intensely aware of and interested in vaginas. What he would then deny is his need and desire to damage them—that is, the women possessing them.

18.

The reality of erotic domination gives our sex/gender system its characteristic paranoid–schizoid structure.

At the paranoid extreme, we have the act of sexual violation. The man plays the part of sexual attacker, the woman of the sexually attacked. These roles have their roots in the relationship of infant (male or female) to maternal breast and body. But they are now distributed in binary fashion. The woman occupies the mother's place, the man that of the hungry and ruthless infant.

At the schizoid extreme, the participants have withdrawn from the scene of violation. They deny the reality of what has happened, either totally or through a misrepresentation of its meaning. For men, this denial maintains an appearance of innocence. For women, it functions as a defense against intense psychic pain.

Once it has been established, the paranoid–schizoid sex/gender system distances men and women from the immediacy of erotic violation. At the same time it freezes and reifies sexuality, limits it to a play of fetishes and part-objects. Within this macabre dance of body parts, the penis is valorized. It has swallowed up the maternal life-world and feminine desire and, via this process of incorporation, has become the phallus. The vagina vanishes. It has been emptied of power and desire, and it is now an absence, a hole instead of a whole.

Or think of it this way. In the instance of erotic violation, the male is persecutory and destructive, the female is persecuted and in danger of being destroyed. If she cannot fight back, and if she is not emotionally shattered, she must retreat from the scene of violation to an inner space. Her true self finds refuge in the womb of her own being, deep within her own mental body. But it is now a body without organs. Meanwhile her physical body, and her physically embodied self, is violated. She has been split apart, a split which her vagina comes to symbolize. And if the pain is sufficiently intense, the entire experience vanishes from consciousness. Then the phallus arises from the amnesiac haze and covers over the gap in memory.

Thus we might represent our sex/gender system by the equation, "phallocentrism = the denial of the vagina." But we will not forget that this relationship signifies a paranoid–schizoid defense against the reality of sexual violation.

19.

It might be objected that it is unfair or overstated to be constructing a model of gender identity from this standpoint. Not all little girls are sexually molested, not all women are raped—not all vaginas are lacerated by phallic intrusion. It seems to me, however, that fear of being the victim of sexual violence is the paradigmatic feminine anxiety in most societies, including most emphatically our own. And it is not, in the first instance, a neurotic anxiety, a fear spawned by a girl's oedipal imagination. There are indeed such anxieties, and it would be a great mistake to overlook or deny them. But it is a far greater sin to deny the reality of sexual violation.

A second form of the objection. We have been depicting sexual interaction in the paranoid–schizoid position. But by our own account, this is a pathological formation. The preceding description is therefore of gender pathology, not gender itself.

Fair enough. But what if, in our society, "gender itself" is a thing-in-itself, a mere ought-to-be, an abstract essence? Or to put the point in less extreme terms, what if pathologies of gender tend to be the rule rather than the exception? Then we would see ourselves more clearly in the stories of Don Juan and Electra than in narratives of mutual recognition.

20.

We might expand our argument in the manner suggested by ecological feminism and say that the combination of capitalism and patri-
archy/phallocentrism involves the systematized, rationalized, and legitimized violation of the mother-world—of the women who bear us and
the earth that contains us. The relationship of men to women and of
humankind to the natural world is one of technologically rational and
morally sanctified rape.

21.

There is an evident parallel between our analysis of patriarchy/
phallocentrism and our prior analysis of capitalist social relations:

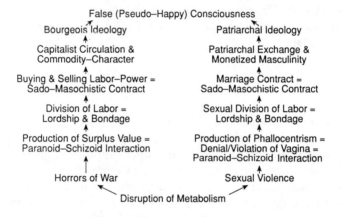

This diagram represents the foundations of capitalist social production.
It presupposes the anthropological manifold of sensuous interaction,
work/desire, and conscious interaction. But it is a perverse, unhealthy
development of anthropological potentialities. At one extreme sensuousness has become disrupted metabolic processes. Nonhuman nature and
our own nature are a torn-up battlefield. Both of these meanings—the
ecological and the social one—may be expressed in the concept or metaphor of a greedy, ruthless violation of the mother-world or maternal
body. At the other extreme this devastation is denied in a pseudo-happy
consciousness. The polarities are mediated by capitalist and patriarchal/
phallocentric social relationships, each set of which involves multiple
pathological deployments of work and desire.

Stated another way, the diagram represents a pathological developmental process, one in which defensive modalities predominate over dia-

lectical ones. In it we see social reality as successive defenses against and expressions of an underlying life and death struggle. On each side of the diagram, that is, in each modality of social interaction, a contractual arrangement is the passageway between an upper realm of exchange and apparent recognition and a lower realm of production and domination.

Although the upper regions consist of appearances, they are not unreal. Even their ideological articulations—bourgeois and patriarchal ideologies—are not simple lies and fabrications. Hence the "I = I" of exchange is not reducible to the "I > I" of production. But the surface of society conceals its depth. Ideologies disguise underlying social practices. They also infiltrate virtually all social practices, so that it becomes quite literally true that we do not know what we are doing.

We need not go down the sides of the diagram step by step—that is precisely what we have been doing in this chapter. And it would take us beyond the limits of our present inquiry to work out in detail the processes of interpenetration through which capitalist production and patriarchy/phallocentrism come to constitute a destructively totalizing system of social production. One point might be emphasized, however, before we turn to the analysis of racial relationships.

We have taken over from Klein the concept of the paranoid–schizoid position. Unlike Klein, we've viewed it as a pathological version of a potentially healthy developmental process. In this incarnation it plays a critical role in our theorizing. On the one hand, we recognize it as our most basic defense against unbearable, self-fragmenting psychic pain. On the other, our social interactions seem to be fixated at this developmental level. And we deny the fixation. We put on the masks, the false selves, of mutual recognition. Then we try to persuade ourselves that we are what we pretend to be.

C. Epidermal Fetishism

1.

Culture in capitalist societies involves the circulation and consumption of commoditized sexual part-objects. The continuous and disrupted flow of these part-objects both reveals and conceals capitalism's war of all against all, and its engendered rapacity. Maintaining the flow passes as sanity, questioning its rationality is seen as a kind of madness. Like a borderline psychotic who clings desperately to the paranoid–schizoid position as the only defense against psychic chaos and terror, so social character in capitalism is structured to defend against a presumed malignancy, a monstrous greed, in human nature. But here the analogy fails: In capitalism the defense is the disease. The insatiability of desire is as much consequence as it is cause.

Piero Sraffa characterized capitalism as the production of commodities by means of commodities (Sraffa, 1975). He forgot to add: phallicized and epidermalized commodities.

2.

We come now to the problematics of race and recognition, specifically to the phenomenon of white racism in the United States. By way of reorientation let's refer back to our map, the constrained model of social production.

We might think of its categories from the dual standpoint of patterns of activities and the agents or actors involved in these activities. Economic production requires economic producers, human reproduction requires agents of human reproduction. If we ignore all the real-life complications, we also may say that the capitalist division of labor requires that these producers be either owners or nonowners of the means of production, while human reproduction involves a division of labor between men and women.

Although economic production and human reproduction involve distinguishable patterns of activity, the agents in the one are also (actually or potentially) the agents in the other. Women and men are involved in economic production, as either owners or nonowners of means of production. Owners and nonowners of means of production engage, as women and men, in human reproductive activities.

What happens if we add in the factor of race or ethnicity, for example, the distinction between European-Americans and African-Americans? From the standpoint of agency we have simply added another dimension. Thus, in analyzing economic production and human reproduction, we add white and black to the divisions between owners and nonowners, men and women. The matter is not so straightforward, however, from the standpoint of patterns of activity. Although owners and nonowners are not limited in their actions to the category of economic production, they have an integral relationship to it, as do men and women with respect to the category of human reproduction. But race is not tied in this way to either of these categories of activity.

Race does, however, have an affinity with the categories of culture and collectivity. When race organizes or structures lived experience, it necessarily involves a distinctive way of life. Likewise, it only has this structuring effect when it is a collectivity defined in opposition to another racial collectivity. Thus, although the lives of black people are shaped by the relations of economic production and human reproduction characteristic of American capitalism in general, the black experience also involves a distinctive pattern of class and gender relations, as well as customs and modalities of social interaction that depart from and challenge the dominant culture. Moreover, black people have common interests as a people, as a collectivity, and not just as class-defined members of American society.

In seems, therefore, that we are the least likely to obscure the lived experience of racial or ethnic identity when we center the analysis in the categories of culture and collectivity.

3.

In the United States the problematics of race and recognition are of various kinds, each shaped by the particularities of the collectivities involved. Native Americans, Latinos, African-Americans, Asian-Americans, etc., have distinctive cultures and experiences of oppression. America, the land of many racisms—in which the one fixed point is the whiteness of domination.

Whiteness is, first, skin color, or rather an oppositional way of describing skin color. It is a relative term, defined over and against darkness. It is a social designation from the outset, no matter how much its sociality is denied. Like maleness only more so, it is history disguised as biology.

Whiteness is, second, an attribute of language. Languages have skin colors. There are white nouns and verbs, white grammar and white syntax. In the absence of challenges to linguistic hegemony, indeed, language *is* white. If you don't speak white you will not be heard, just as when you don't look white you will not be seen.

Proper names can also have skin colors. At certain times and places, for example, Scandinavian or Middle European names have been non-white, although in these instances pigmentation is mutable. If you work at it, acculturation may make you white eventually.

Sometimes word magic will do the trick. In Los Angeles the pursuit of racial integration in education led to the busing of black children into white areas. Predominantly white schools were required to have a designated percentage of minority students. As immigration, birth rates, and white flight changed the racial demography of the city, however, the racial minorities became the majority. Consequently more white children were needed to maintain racial balance.

A boy of racially mixed parentage living in a black area had been bused to a white elementary school, where he did very well. His presence helped to integrate the school. When the time came for junior high school, he was found to be racially ineligible for continued busing into the white area because the junior high school was becoming racially imbalanced by the lack of white students. In an interview between his parents and the school administrators, it came out that his racial heritage was evenly divided between white and black. The sensible administrator thereupon reclassified him as white and admitted him. Once again, this time as a white boy, his presence helped to integrate the school.

Rationality within irrationality: a comment on the idiocy of white racism.

4.

So-called white people come in a variety of colors; likewise so-called black people. It is only by a radical decolorization that we see a relationship of white and black.

Sometimes we reject racial dualisms. Then we become trinitarians: "If you're white, you're all right; if you're brown, stick around; if you're black, stay back."

5.

A thought experiment. We remove the category of race from our minds and let our eyes wander over the surface of the globe. We see a complex pattern of pigmentations and other biological features, so complex as to make classification extremely difficult. We decide it isn't worth the effort.

Closer inspection would bring us into contact with cultures of various kinds. We would find that they, too, defy any parsimonious classification.

Then we notice that in many of these cultures a line is drawn between "us" and "them." We are struck by the way in which this binary logic functions to organize and simplify things—the way it creates identities where there were no identities, differences where there were no differences.

We are reminded of the category of race, which we had so recently discarded. We note how it slides along the lines of cultural oppositions, reifying and intensifying them. We recognize the need to think *about* it, but we no longer wish to think *with* it.

"Too abstract," you say. "You can't be empirical without thinking in racial terms."

Objection sustained, but with reservations. First, thinking in racial terms is not risk-free. All racial thinking involves a potentially dangerous degree of simplification. Second, if we must think in racial terms, then it's important to differentiate between racism and racialism. Racialism is collective self-assertion, as in Black Power and Black Pride. It does not entail claims of racial superiority. Racism, by contrast, is inherently supremacist. Third, racist attitudes may or may not be actualized in relationships of domination. There is nothing logically or sociologically contradictory about being simultaneously racist and oppressed.[7] But, fourth, it is not racism when members of an oppressed race hate their oppressors. It is rather an appropriate affective complement to a negated interest. But the oppressor will label it as racism—the pot calling the kettle . . . white.

6.

The language of white racism is a composite structure. It devalues Asians one way, Latinos another, Arabs yet another. White racists are virtuosos of denigration. Optimally we would match their denigrative virtuosity with a deconstructive virtuosity of our own. But for present purposes we limit ourselves to elucidating certain aspects of the binary discourse of white and black.

Within this discourse there is a fixed signifier of negation: "nigger."

In the first instance, "nigger" is a term of abuse. When a white man calls a black man a nigger, he is articulating a sado-masochistic message: "Say 'yes, sir,' and like it." The black man may or may not be forced to accept the assigned role and appear to be happy with the assignment. If he is forced to comply, he may or may not internalize the role; it may or may not become part of his character structure.

There is a second instance. Sometimes one black man might say of another, "He's a bad nigger." This may be a moral or prudential judgment: "He is evil or destructive, stay away from him." But it might also mean: "He is unbroken and free; he does not bend his knee to the white man, or any other man."

"Look out, Whitey! Black Power's Gon' Get Your Mama!"[8]

7.

When it is subjected to even the most cursory analysis, the language of white racism reveals a state of war. Most of the time, however, the battle is denied. People speak politely across racial lines and pretend to believe in the American dream. The atmosphere, as Malcolm X claimed, becomes filled with "racial mirages, clichés, and lies" (Malcolm X, 1966, p. 273).

Malcolm knew full well that the denial of racial antagonism was not just a matter of conscious deceit. White racism is rather a mental disorder, an ocular disease, an opacity of the soul that is articulated with unintended irony in the idea of "color blindness." To be color blind is the highest form of racial false consciousness, a denial of both difference and domination. But one doesn't have to be color blind to be blinded by white racism. Hence we find commonalities of speech among the analysts of white racism. The hero of Ralph Ellison's novel is invisible to white people and, for many years, to himself. He only begins to know himself when he recognizes his invisibility. Frantz Fanon's analysis of white racism is entitled *Peau Noire, Masques Blancs—Black Skins, White Masks*. Black people see themselves in white mirrors, white people see black people as their own photographic negatives. W. E. B. DuBois argues that "the Negro is a sort of seventh son, born with a veil, and gifted with second-sight in this American world—a world which yields him no true self-consciousness, but only lets him see himself through the revelation of the other world" (DuBois, 1903, p. 8). No need to read Hegel if one is born with black skin.

8.

Just here an epistemological question arises. Malcolm X often said that no one knows the master like the servant. Black people are in a position to see through the public guises and disguises of white people. The relationship is not reciprocal. Because black people are the servants, they remain unseen by white people. But for this same reason, and as DuBois indicates, they only see themselves in relation to the Other. They are denied an integral point of self-reference.

If we assume the validity of such an analysis, then two tasks must be performed. For black people it becomes necessary to look away from the white mirror, that is, to develop a praxis of cultural reflexivity or self-consciousness. For white people it becomes necessary to stand behind the veil—that is, to attempt to see black people as they see themselves, and to see themselves as they are seen by black people.

Black people have come a considerable distance along their epistemological road; white people have advanced only stumblingly along theirs.

9.

White racism precludes mutual recognition. It involves an inter-action of pseudo-selves, a dumbshow or pantomime of racial stereotypes (Wolfenstein, 1990c, pp. 354-355).

The form of this interaction is "Whiteness > Blackness". Racial stereotypes interact, people don't. As to content, the White Self is gener-ally defined as mind, the Black Other as body. More specifically, the White Self is clean, odorless, cold, restrained, intelligent, hard-working, moral; the Black Other is dirty, smelly, warm, sexually unrestrained and violent, stupid, lazy, and immoral. The White Self is and must be master; the Black Other is and must be slave.

We note in this pairing a certain lack of originality. It is yet another version of the hierarchicalized split of mind and body, reason and pas-sion, that is characteristic of capitalism, patriarchy/phallocentrism, and indeed Western culture generally.

The Man, it seems, just can't get it together.

10.

On each side of the stereotypical divide there is a further divi-sion, along with a typical pairing across the divide. There is the bene-volent paternalist, the good white master, who is served by the good Negro, the house Negro, the loyal servant. And there is the malevolent paternalist, the slavedriver, who is hated and feared by the bad nigger, the field nigger, the runaway or rebellious slave. These roles may be distributed between persons, but there is also a structuring of roles within persons, with the more civil attitudes masking the underlying hostilities.

When a white person comes in contact with a black person, s/he sees the other through this two-fold veil. At best s/he will see the other in relation to the veil—as an exception, as different from the rest. Likewise the black person, when s/he comes in contact with some-one who is white. Neither is free to interact with the other as a self like oneself. They are not, however, equal in their lack of freedom. The arrangement is hierarchical. It reflects the differential social power of the two racial collectivities. Hence for white people the stereo-types function as a shield, while for black people they function as a cage.

Yet even the bars of the cage can be used to some advantage. On his deathbed the invisible man's grandfather says:

I never told you, but our life is a war and I have been a traitor all my
born days, a spy in the enemy's country ever since I give up my gun
back in the Reconstruction. Live with your head in the lion's mouth. I
want you to overcome 'em with yeses, undermine 'em with grins, agree
'em to death and destruction, let 'em swoller you till they vomit or
bust wide open. (Ellison, 1947, p. 16)

11.

Commodity fetishism, phallocentrism . . . finally, epidermal fetishism.

Epidermal fetishism is the attribution of powers to skin color that it
does not inherently possess. At the same time it reduces personhood to
skin color and, by so doing, renders the person invisible. Like the commodity and the phallus, the epidermis here functions as a magical part-
object.

Whether or not specific individuals are afflicted by it, epidermal
fetishism is a form of social character. Like commodity-character and
monetized masculinity, it is formed within a process of exchange or
circulation. If we put to one side its interpenetration with these other
registers of social value, we might represent it as a process of the whiten-
ing out of selfhood:

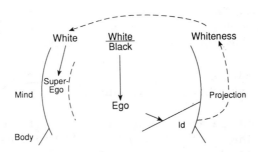

White constitutes the standard of social value, self-worth, and morality,
hence the substance of the super-ego. The ego, in turn, must be white
if it is to be affirmatively reflected in the super-ego. Blackness must
be repressed. It becomes identified with the unwanted or bad parts of
the self.

At the level of social character, white racism is self-limiting for white
people, self-destructive for black people. White people alienate their sensuous potentialities from themselves. They are devitalized and sterilized.
Blackness, officially devalued, comes to embody their estranged life and
desire. They are able, however, to see themselves reflected in the mir-

rors of selfhood. But if black people have their selfhood structured by the whitened-out form of social character, they become fundamentally self-negating. Their blackness, hated and despised, must be hidden away. Hair straighteners and skin lighteners testify to the desire to go further and eradicate blackness altogether.

In the analysis of commodity-character and phallocentrism we emphasized the way in which repressed or split-off desires contributed to fetishizing objects, giving them a psychical value they would not otherwise possess. The valorization of white skin is produced in similar fashion. Invisibly, blackness is subsumed within whiteness, giving whiteness its incorporeal luminescence.

In addition, white racism calls our attention to the other side of this process, the displacement and exclusion of hated components of the self. Workers (the masses), women, and black people become the containers of everything bad, destructive, and dirty. At once scapegoat and safety valve, they reduce the pressure within the system, permit it to circulate sanitized and idealized values—abstract values, as Marx says. To vary the frame of reference, the circulation of valorized part-objects is an alimentary process. The sensuous energies of workers, women, and black people are voraciously consumed. What cannot be digested is excreted.

It is something more than a metaphor when oppressed people say they are treated like shit.

12.

If via projection black people come to contain the "badness" of white people, then via a transvaluation of values "badness" becomes a signifier of power. After a particularly effective speech, Malcolm X said to a friend, "Was I bad, or was I *bad*!"

Once again, negation is determination. Marks of oppression have a way of becoming signifiers of rebellion.

13.

When white people disburden themselves of their emotional excrement, they empty themselves of their sensuality at the same time. Hence their peculiar double attitude toward blackness. They both despise and lust after it.

Take the example of Malcolm X and the white woman he calls Sophia (Malcolm X, 1966, p. 67 ff.; Wolfenstein, 1990c, pp. 158-164). Malcolm was a ghetto youth, cool and wild. Sophia was a middle-class

Constructions and Configurations

white woman who came to an all-Negro dance, alone and looking for excitement. They were immediately attracted to each other. She was after a black man; he was drawn to her because she was white.

What were they each hoping to find? Biographically, it's difficult to be certain. But we might imagine a white woman and a black man who resemble them.

The white woman wishes to be black, which means to overcome her inhibitions, release the sensuality repressed within her whitened-out character structure. She is mesmerized by images of black manhood, tantalized by violating a racial taboo. By violating the taboo she is being "bad"—a fallen and free woman. Her triumph over her repressive whiteness lies in her surrender to his phallic blackness.

The black man, by contrast, wants to be white, to have the power and prestige of the white man. The woman's sexual surrender serves to affirm his manhood and his whiteness. It is also his triumph over the white man—not only a violation of the white man's taboo but also a conquest of his woman.

This relationship has various meanings. It is a case of epidermally mediated erotic domination, an epidermally mediated double violation of the oedipal incest taboo, an epidermalized sexual rebellion against a repressive social morality. It is also an epidermalized experience of the Unhappy Consciousness. The fetish of skin color signifies the identification of the Unchangeable Being with race. For the white person, blackness contains the promise of happiness; for the black person, whiteness. Each strives to overcome her/his alienation through sexual merger with the other.

There are other versions of epidermalized sexuality. But whatever its form and whatever its particular meaning, it is not a relationship of mutual recognition. This does not mean that individual men and women are fated to play their roles in the stereotypical dumbshow. But they will come to recognize themselves and each other only if they are able to cast off their racial masks.

14.

The deconstruction of epidermal fetishism is not a word game, but oppressed people can neither recognize themselves nor struggle against domination without a language of their own.

For example: Black people have found it necessary to reject any name given to them by the White Man. Thus in the 1950s and 1960s the Nation of Islam led a movement to replace the term "Negro" with "Black Man." Moreover, members of the Nation replaced their given family names with an "X." The "X" symbolized that they were ex-Negroes, that is, that their selfhood was not conferred upon them by the white people. It also symbolized that their true African names were no longer known.

What was lost individually could, perhaps, be regained collectively. Malcolm X, after he left the Nation of Islam, advocated the use of the term "Afro-American." More generally, by the middle of the 1960s a strong cultural nationalist movement developed. Many black people Africanized their names and attempted to Africanize their minds—and their bodies: African styles of dress became popular, and "natural" hair styles were called "Afros."

A later generation of black people identified "Afro" with its cosmetic rather than its cultural meaning and therefore rejected the term "Afro-American." They replaced it with "African-American." Even "African-American" seemed too assimilationist to some people, who began calling themselves simply "Africans."

This incessant renaming, it seems to me, is partially word magic—as if one could change reality simply by changing language. But at a deeper level, it is a response to co-optation in the domain of speech. The officially sanctioned participants in public discourse are the real word magicians. Their language games are con games, intended to make the reality of racist domination disappear. Now you see it, now you don't.

In their attacks upon each successively legitimized name, black people are waging a linguistic struggle for survival.

15.

More is at stake, however, than the verbal form of self-recognition. There is also a matter of cultural content. Across the generations black people in the United States have struggled with an experience of hyphenation. Their lineage and heritage is problematically both African and American. Neither source of cultural identity can be disregarded without a loss of reality, but the point of cultural interpenetration is also a locus of anxiety.

The problem signified by the hyphen is expressed in a cultural dialectic of separation and assimilation. The separatist position, characteristically pan-Africanist and Afrocentric, stresses the difference between black and white in the United States, along with the sameness of black people everywhere. In its most extreme form it calls for a physical as well as spiritual return of black people to Africa. Its advocates view assimilationists (integrationists) as self-deluded or worse. By contrast, the assimilationist position is grounded in the historical experience of black people in the United States. It stresses American identity and the otherness of Africa. Hence its advocates see Afrocentrism and pan-Africanism as escapist and abstract. They insist upon their rights as Americans, and they struggle to realize their interests through reform of the existing social and political system.

Thus assimilationists and separatists place the qualities of sameness and difference on opposite sides of the hyphen. Assimilationists assert, "We are Americans and (no longer) Africans. We believe in the American dream and must struggle to realize it." Separatists assert, "We are all Africans and never were Americans. The American dream is a nightmare and it's long past time we awaken from it."

There has been an ongoing and heated struggle between these two positions. But we would be misrepresenting them if we did not recognize their common ground. The hyphen in "African-American" signifies the pain of oppression and not merely the tensions of cultural particularity. Although the polarization of assimilationist and separatist positions reflects a tendency toward splitting induced by this suffering, neither participant in the discourse of black liberation denies the reality of oppression. Both sides recognize that they are engaged with the problematics of white racist domination. In their confrontation with each other they are searching for solutions.

16.

Especially in the United States it is easy to forget that capitalism involves the domination of one collectivity by another. Because men and women populate all social classes, it is even easier to ignore the fact that the sex/gender system is a relationship between collectivities. But it is manifestly absurd to think of white racism as purely systemic (universal) or purely individual. The signs of collectivity are etched into its every feature.

Although by definition racism is intercollective, we noted above that it is not necessarily a relationship of domination. We also distinguished it from racialism, from collective self-assertion and self-consciousness—collective self-recognition. Knowing myself to be European-American and you to be African-American is not racist and does not preclude mutual recognition.

White racism is not racial self-consciousness. Nor is it merely a set of racist attitudes. It is a relationship of domination. This is evident even at the level of exchange. The entry of black people into American life involved no social contract, at least not one to which they were a party. They entered as property, not as persons, and this dehumanization has been maintained in one way or another ever since.

In our investigations of capitalism and patriarchy/phallocentrism we proceeded from exchange to the division of labor and production. Here we proceed from culture to collectivity. Within the category of intercollective relationships, however, we will encounter a racial division of labor and the social process through which white racism is produced.

17.

White racism involves a complex interplay of collective interests and desires. But a rather simple relationship underlies the complexity. Briefly expressed: *mass (group) motives serve ruling class interests.*
We may represent this relationship as follows:

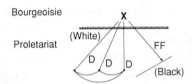

This diagram combines three elements. There is, first, a binary representation of class structure. Above the line is the bourgeoisie, the owners of means of production; below the line is the proletariat, the non-owners of means of production. The former are advantaged and the latter disadvantaged within this relationship. From the standpoint of interests, they are enemies.

Second, there is a demographic element. The population is racially divided between a white majority and a black minority. The great majority of both racial collectivities are working class; the great majority of capitalists are white. From the standpoint of class interests, black and white workers are on the same side. The white bourgeoisie is their common enemy.

Third, a group-emotional structure is superimposed upon the class–racial matrix. The white working class is bound to the white capitalist class in a dependency group formation, and it is formed into a flight–fight group in opposition to black people. For white workers class consciousness has been replaced by white racism. Black people are then constrained to defend themselves from their racial enemies. Consequently the class game is not played. It is replaced by the game of divide and conquer, here in the form of racist domination.

From the standpoint of ruling class interests white racism is a rational means to collective ends. It is irrational and a form of false consciousness for the white working class. Once it exists, it circumscribes rational action for black people. It becomes rational for them to act in terms of their racial, rather than their class, interests. If they do not recognize their situationally defined racial interests and mobilize work group function in order to realize them, however, their struggle may be subverted by the intrusion of one or more of the basic assumptions—including the possible formation of a dependency group with the White Man as leader. In this instance a struggle must be waged against false consciousness within black communities.

18.

In the preceding analysis we omitted the petty bourgeois classes and the middle strata of American society. Because there is an underlying bipolarity to class structure and because group emotion washes across class lines and, by so doing, simplifies intercollective relationships, this simplification is not a falsification. But the analysis becomes more concrete when we add in the problematics of the middle classes.

On both sides of the racial divide the middle classes consist of three separate strata: upper-echelon managers and executives in public and private organizations; independent entrepreneurs and professionals; and relatively highly paid workers. Of these three segments, the first two are aligned with the capitalist class, the third is aligned with the rest of the working class. But culturally the three strata have a good deal in common, and they are, on balance, economic beneficiaries of the system. They mediate its extremes and reduce the intensity of class antagonisms.

Yet there is a racial divide within the middle class, and it makes a difference. Prior to World War II the black middle class was a small percentage of the black population. Such as it was, it was excluded from participation in the white side of the economy, from white society, and from political office. In the aftermath of the war its size increased, but its segregated status did not change. Hence the integrationist aspirations of the Civil Rights Movement, which expressed the interests of this class.

The leaders of the Civil Rights Movement claimed to be speaking for all black people. In purely racial terms there is some truth in this assertion. But socioeconomically the claim cannot be sustained. Although the movement served the economic interests of the black middle class, it left the economic condition of the black masses unchanged.

The racial division of labor places the greater percentage of the black population in low-paying and economically vulnerable jobs. Moreover, changes in American capitalism—notably, the decline of the blue-collar industries along with economic policies favoring the very wealthy—have mired the black masses ever more deeply in poverty and a variety of related social pathologies. The Civil Rights Movement did not and could not alter these structural features of the system. And the more the integrationist aspirations of the middle class were realized, the more its members became separated from the less advantaged members of the race. Thus the middle-class dream became a mass nightmare.[9]

Earlier, when we used the status relationships of the plantation system as a way of defining roles in the stereotypical dumbshow, we were borrowing our analytical categories from Malcolm X. In his usage these terms had both psychological and sociological meaning. Modern house Negroes were assimilationist and middle class. They received crumbs from the white man's table and they identified with their oppressors. Their consciousness had been whitened-out. They no longer knew who they were. Their racial leadership was really mis-leadership. But the masses, the modern equivalent of the field nigger, recognized the master as their enemy. They refused to be misled. They were ready for action and always on the lookout for a way out. They were inclined toward separatism and black nationalism.

Malcolm viewed the racial situation from the standpoint of the black masses. Even if we don't accept his political stance, however, we can see that the antagonism between the assimilationist and separatist positions in the black liberation struggle expresses a class difference within the black community. All black people are bound together by an interest in ending white racist domination; but the middle classes can hope for an assimilationist solution to their problem, while the masses require separation from or a transformation of the existing system in order to solve theirs.

19.

There is another standpoint from which to analyze white racism and black liberation, namely, that of black women. Along with other women of color, black women carry the burdens of class, racial, and sexual domination. Consequently they see American life from a position that no other collectivity occupies. An epistemic position, and a battle position: They are forced to wage a war on three fronts, and their allies in one engagement may be their enemies in another. Perhaps most importantly, they struggle together with black men against a combination of capitalism and white racism. But they are often subjected to male supremacist ideologies and practices by these same black men.

As to the first point, think of the roles assigned to black women in the stereotypical dumbshow. Again, they originate on the plantation. Miss Ann, the white mistress, is served by Sally, her slave gal. Sally must be respectful and do her job properly. She must try not to get Miss Ann angry. But she will fail, and then she must accept the consequences.

At night, in the slave quarters, the white master takes sexual possession of her. He will find her irresistibly sensual. In his mind she is the embodiment of a jungle fever. His wife leaves him cold; Sally makes him burn. In her mind he is a monster of whiteness. But he is the master, and he will have his way. Better to suffer the rape than to die. And if she gets pregnant? Then her children will be his children—and his slaves. Maybe they will grow up to be house slaves, in distorted recognition of their paternal lineage.

As Sally gets older, she will tend to Miss Ann's children. She will be their Black Mammy, all warmth, comfort, and common sense, their dark earth mother in contrast to their pale celestial one.

These roles have lingered on, partly sustained by a tradition of domestic service as an occupation for black women, more recently maintained within the mythology of white racist culture. Either way, they signify a position of solidarity with black men and against white women and men, in the struggle against white racism.

As to the second point: Paula Giddings (1984) aptly characterizes the 1960s as "the masculine decade" (p. 314). To a large extent the liberation movement was oriented toward Black Manhood. The White Man must be forced, in a life and death struggle, to give recognition to the Black Man. Black women were largely sympathetic to this struggle. They nurtured it, so to speak. But their own aspirations for recognition were in part negated within it. When women in SNCC (the Student Nonviolent Coordinating Committee) challenged organizational assumptions of male superiority, they were told that the "only position for women in SNCC is prone" (*ibid.*, p. 302). And on the separatist side of the movement, the Nation of Islam proclaimed that "black women must become chattel once again, with good and loving masters, to be sure, but chattel nevertheless" (*ibid.*, p. 318).

Enough said.

20.

We now see that the roles in the stereotypical dumbshow reflect class and gender as well as racial relationships. We must not forget that they are pathologized character types and not simply constellations of social interests. They are particularizations of white racist character structure. And white racist character structure, in which a devalued sensuality is split off from white people and projectively identified with black people, is generated by group emotion.

It should be emphasized that group emotion operates unconsciously. Stereotypes are conscious or preconscious manifestations of unconscious group processes. In part because these processes are unconscious, they tend to be hypnotic. Epidermal fetishists are hypnotized by skin color.

In the discourse of Freudian-Marxism, Fromm was the first to observe that the apparent free will of individuals can mask an underlying, societally induced, hypnotic domination of the will. Even earlier, as we noted in Chapter 7, Freud argued that the emotional connection between group leader and group members was hypnotic. White racism unifies white people in this fashion. If we do not struggle to free ourselves from it, we act in obedience to its unconscious collective commandments. Although we are seemingly awake, we are actually living in a dream world—and we are elements of the dream, not the dreamers.

In the next chapter we will see that hypnotic phenomena originate in prenatal and neonatal experience. Not surprisingly, therefore, W. R. Bion (1959) believes that psychoanalytic investigation of group experience arouses dread because "the group approximates too closely, in the minds of the individuals composing it, to very primitive phantasies about the contents of the mother's body" (p. 162).

Within the Manichean world of white racism, blackness signifies the maternal body, whiteness the collective self that yearns for union with and is terrified by this most profound and unchangeable of beings.

21.

We find ourselves in a familiar position. Each of our three explorations of social production reaches the place where work and desire merge into sensuousness, where the maternal world is the life-world. In each instance we see that relationships within this world are destructive and persecutory. The potential for a healthy social metabolism is realized inversely, pathologically, that is, in paranoid and schizoid patterns of interaction. All three relationships converge, moreover, in a greedy, assaultive, and rapacious relationship to the nonhuman environment. To borrow from liberal political theory, our state of nature has become a state of war. We must see if there is some way to restore the peace.

22.

When it comes to questions of war and peace, we might take a page from the book of the invisible man.

We first encounter the invisible man holed up in a basement cave, his place of retreat from the racial wars. Wounded in battle, he continues the fight from his refuge. He has illuminated his cave with 1,369 lightbulbs, which drain power from Monopolated Power and Light (Ellison, 1947, p. 7).

On one level, we have here the schizoid solution to the problematics of the paranoid–schizoid position. The invisible man couldn't stand the pain of social interaction and so he went underground; from this position he plays the part of saboteur—an internal saboteur, to borrow (and bend) W. R. Fairbairn's expression, for he has not escaped from society despite his withdrawal from it (Fairbairn, 1954, p. 101). On another level, as the allusions to a subterranean existence imply, the invisible man resembles the protagonist of Dostoevsky's *Notes from Underground* (1864) not so much in his state of mind, but in his failure to solve existential problems of recognition. On a third level, by telling his story to us and to himself, he is attempting to solve the problem, to heal himself from the wounds of invisibility.

The novel traces the path of its protagonist from his adolescence in the rural South through his young manhood in Harlem. It is a tale of growth and disillusionment, or growth *through* disillusionment. The invisible man, quite like Candide, begins in a state of innocence, almost willful innocence or blindness. His desire to be a success in life robs him of the ability to understand the causality of his own fate. His grandfather understood the situation, as his deathbed speech reveals. He was a saboteur in his own way. But the invisible man refuses to take the point, even when it is presented to him in a dream:

> I dreamed I was at a circus with . . . [my grandfather] and that he refused to laugh at the clowns no matter what they did. Then later he told me to open my brief case and read what was inside and I did, finding an official envelope stamped with the state seal; and inside the envelope I found another and another, endlessly, and I thought I would fall of weariness. "Them's yours," he said. "Now open that one." And I did and in it I found an engraved document containing a short message in letters of gold. "Read it," my grandfather said. "Out loud!"
>
> "To Whom It May Concern," I intoned. "Keep This Nigger-Boy Running." (*ibid.*, p. 33)

The invisible man had received the brief case as a reward for reciting an accomodationist speech to local white notables, after first undergoing an experience of the most abject humiliation at their hands. This experience should have taught him not to seek for himself in their recognition. But he was unable to learn the lesson. False consciousness, we might say. In any case, his grandfather had known better. And the grandfather inside him knew that, so long as he did not search for himself in himself, other people would keep him running in circles, running away from himself in his attempts to realize himself.

Eventually the invisible man gets to Harlem, where his oratorical abilities bring him to the attention of the Brotherhood (the Communist Party, or one very much like it). The Brotherhood is integrationist, so to speak, an organization that claims to represent the interests of all oppressed peoples. The invisible man becomes a member and its principal Harlem organizer. His chief rival for the hearts and minds of his black brothers and sisters is Ras the Exhorter, a West Indian black nationalist. Thus the political stage is set with the familiar conflict between assimilationist and separatist solutions to the problem of white racist oppression.

A black member of the Brotherhood—actually a former or fallen member who was struggling with his own invisibility by selling Sambo dolls on street corners—is killed. The Harlem masses are enraged and the invisible man gives voice to their anger. But the Brotherhood tells him that the party line has changed and he is to quiet things down rather than stir them up. Consequently the stage is left to Ras, now Ras the Destroyer, who whips the masses up into a destructive frenzy of looting and rioting. Harlem erupts chaotically. The rage contained by white racist character structure explodes. The latent paranoia of the social situation becomes manifest and deadly. The life and death battle is fought and lost. The insurrection is violently put down by the forces of law and order.

Too late, the invisible man understands: An uncontrolled riot and the wanton shedding of black blood were just what the Brotherhood had ordered. Black lives were to be the raw material for its propaganda machine. Hence his advice to us, echoing his grandfather's advice to him: "Beware of those who speak of the *spiral* of history; they are preparing a boomerang. Keep a steel helmet handy" (*ibid.*, p. 6). Advice, and (as we saw in Chapter 4) a black existential critique of whitened-out Marxism.

Yet if the spiral of history is a boomerang, so the boomerang may be a spiral. Trying to escape from the chaos, the invisible man falls into a coal cellar. As he gropes through the darkness, he finds the underground room he transforms into his cave. Brightly illuminated though it may be—the Enlightenment is not his enemy—it is the womb of his recreation.

Two dreams reveal his pilgrim's progress. The first, induced by smoking marijuana and listening to Louis Armstrong playing and singing "What Did I Do to Be So Black and Blue," takes him into a cavern of the past, where he asks an old slave woman the meaning of freedom. She is confused and can't tell him. Her sons, the slave master's sons, drive him away. But in his passage through the maternal body of blackness and the inferno of slavery, something profound and archaic comes alive in him.

In the second dream he is trapped by all the men, white and black, who have victimized him and kept him running. They castrate him and ask him how it feels to be free of illusions. "Painful and empty," he replies (*ibid.*, p. 569). But then he starts to laugh. His castration, he realizes, is "all the history" they have made (*ibid.*, p. 570). They are truly impotent and, despite the dream, he is whole. They have not achieved potency by their attempt to destroy his. The lord gains no real recognition through the service of the bondsman.

In chronological time this second dream came first, just after the invisible man fell into his hole. The dream we are told first, near the beginning of the story, comes chronologically at its end. "The end was in the beginning," as he tells us (*ibid.*, p. 581).

23.

When the story began, the invisible man was in schizoid withdrawal from a persecutory society. As it ends, he is about to emerge from his cave. What, we might ask, has his hybernation accomplished?

The question has two answers. On the plane of personal experience the invisible man has learned something about himself and partially healed his wounds. Freedom was not defined for him by his maternal archetype. We might infer that he learned to look for it in himself. He also recognizes that the men were castrating themselves when they were attempting to castrate him. They have been demystified and their hold over him has been broken. Through his reclusive labors he has won for himself a mind of his own.

To put it differently, the invisible man is no longer *personally* trapped in the paranoid–schizoid position. Then again, his occupancy of the paranoid–schizoid position was never just—or even primarily—personal. One might even say that he was not sufficiently paranoid and schizoid: Despite his blindness he was never lacking in empathy and compassion. His inner world only imperfectly mirrored the external world. But the latter, the social reality of white racist domination, was truly paranoid–schizoid. For as Foucault, Deleuze, and Guattari might observe, the paranoid–schizoid position is a social structure, a placement and deployment of power, a combination of real persecutory forces. An impersonal slavedriver, it whips oppressed individuals into identification with the oppressor, retreat, or—by dialectical inversion—rebellion.

The invisible man has passed through each of these stations. He has broken the chains of mental slavery and overcome the temptations of isolation and seclusion. He has re-entered the world as a rebel. But he is an existential rebel, not a political one. And this brings us to the second answer. In his retreat the invisible man discarded Marxism as hyper-rational, hypocritical, and manipulative. He rejected black nationalism as irrational if sincere, and as self-destructive in its simplicity and rage. Consequently he has left himself with no political options, at least none that are sufficiently radical, none that cut to the heart of the matter. He may no longer be running, but others will be compelled to run in his place.

Or, if they have stopped running, they will have to pick up the historical boomerang, find an opening, and throw it into the gears of the white racist machine.

CHAPTER 9

Transferences and Transformations

1.

When we consult our map of the social battlefield, we find that our exploration of race and recognition leaves us on the border between collective action and individual identity. To experience the problematics of recognition at the level of individuality, we must cross the line. And because we are interested in the emancipatory praxis of clinical psychoanalysis, we will take the consulting room as our field of inquiry.

2.

The psychoanalytic consulting room is a quite peculiar space. It involves constraints and liberties not found in other loci of social interaction. It is created by a process of abstraction or phenomenological bracketing, as a consequence of which the social foreground is placed in the background and the intrapsychic background becomes the foreground. But this bracketing of social reality is itself a moment of social reality.

Although not so brightly illuminated, it has a distinct resemblance to the invisible man's basement.

3.

We begin with a few remarks on the distinctive features of the psychoanalytic situation. We will then proceed to consider the record of two clinical experiences. The first centers on uncovering and elucidating the paranoid–schizoid foundations of personal identity, the second on self-hood and the struggle for recognition.

A. The Psychoanalytic Situation

1.

As noted, psychoanalytic practice falls into the category of social action at the level of individuals. It is also an epistemologically distinct type of social action, namely, emancipatory praxis. We have discussed the epistemological dimension of the psychoanalytic situation previously (in Chapters 4 and 5), and we will exemplify it below. Hence our first concern is the social location of psychoanalytic practice.

The practicing clinician looks at psychoanalysis from the inside out. Social reality is an externality, manifest content that must be analyzed for its latent meanings, for the desires trapped within and beneath it. But for us psychoanalysis, including this characteristic and appropriate psychoanalytic perspective, must be looked at first from the outside in. Psychoanalysis exists in particular historical and social locations, without an understanding of which it is not comprehensible.

Psychoanalysis originated in European bourgeois culture, although somewhat to the east and somewhat later than Marxism. Its history is part of the history of capitalism. The individuals engaged in its practice, as patient and as analyst, have personal identities structured by the social character of this mode of production. These identities vary by class, gender, and ethnicity (race, geography, nationality, etc.). Hence psychoanalysis does not investigate human individuality as such, but rather determinate social types of individuals. Yet it is not sociology. Patient and analyst are actual individuals, not concepts and categories. The clinical process begins and ends with two people interacting with each other and with themselves. Hence we might think of it as an inter- and intra-subjective encounter within determinate social limits.

More narrowly, the context of the clinical encounter is either a commodity transaction or a bureaucratic one.[1] Bourgeois and petty bourgeois individuals needing therapy freely contract for the services of a (presumably) skilled professional. The contracting parties may or may not collude to remain unconscious of the commodity fetishism that binds them together. In any case their relationship begins with the freedom and equality of the marketplace. But especially in the United States, workers and poor people receive treatment within public or semipublic institutions. Exceptionally, they receive good treatment. Typically, they are treated like raw material for the functioning of bureaucratic machines.

2.

And so we enter the consulting room. We will assume that analyst and patient recognize their situation and know that their inner worlds are structured and populated by the outer one. Hence we will save ourselves the trouble of analyzing any possible resistances to knowledge of social reality. We will also suppose that they each know that interpretations at the level of social reality can function as resistances to experiencing intrapsychic reality.

We further suppose that the two parties have entered into the relationship voluntarily, although the one of them must necessarily earn a livelihood and the other is motivated by psychic pain. And they both know the rules. They will meet at predetermined times and at a specified location. There is a fee for service which is to be paid in a timely fashion. The patient will recline and will do her/his best to say whatever comes to mind. The analyst will sit in some proximity to the patient and will do her/his best not to censor whatever comes to mind. Except perhaps for a handshake, they will not touch each other physically. They will most assuredly touch each other emotionally and intellectually.

"I (analyst) =/≠ I (patient)": Need it be said that here we have a situation or problematic of recognition?

3.

We may represent the relationship between patient and analyst this way:

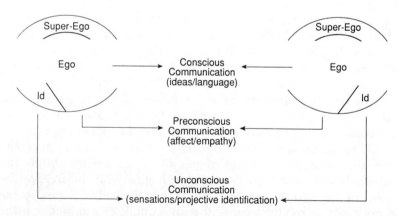

Two selves are placed in a situation where they will interact on three levels and in two modalities.

The selves are structured in the same way, if for the moment we disregard differences of class, gender, race, and age. For each, the ego or "I" is a manifold extending from sensuousness/unconsciousness to consciousness and self-consciousness. Each has a super-ego and, proportionately, an id or "It," a domain of alienated selfhood.

Manifestly patient and analyst will interact at the level of conscious communication. They will speak and listen. But they must learn to "hear" more than words. At a preconscious level they communicate affectively. They, and especially the analyst, must have the empathic capacity to experience this affective flow.

It may be added that communication at the preconscious level will tend to be in the depressive position. It presupposes selves who are capable of experiencing and becoming conscious of sadness, joy, longing, grief, guilt, etc.

At the unconscious level, the relationship moves along the borderline between mind and body. Affects blend into sensations, empathy gives way to projective and introjective processes. Here the interaction is formed within the paranoid–schizoid position.

At the deepest level, there is a vortex formed by a pull toward the integral quiescence of intrauterine existence and a repulsion from the absolute terror of absent selfhood.

And at each level each self will encounter both anxiety and defenses against it. The imperative of the process is to reach these points of anxiety, tolerate being there, and so be able to learn from and go beyond them.

As to modality: Patient and analyst are members of a dyadic work group, bound together by a mutual interest in understanding and transforming the patient's inner world. They are also members of shifting basic assumption groups, that is, of a dyad that moves within the field of transference and countertransference. They will find it difficult to know which modality they are in at any given point in the process.

4.

In most respects the two selves engaged in the relationship resemble each other, but they have different roles to play. The patient is there to confront and overcome unconscious bondage. The analyst is there is facilitate this process.

In order to be adequate to the task, the analyst must fulfill three requirements. First, her/his internal boundaries, the lines of demarcation between ego, super-ego, and id, must have been previously explored, so that s/he now has the capacity for self-exploration. Second, s/he must possess a knowledge of psychoanalytic theory, including the theory of technique. And third, s/he must be able to forget what s/he knows.

As to the third point: Freud recommended an "evenly-suspended attention" as the analyst's complement to the patient's free association (Freud, 1912, p. 111). How is this state of mind to be achieved? He advised his colleagues to model themselves "on the surgeon, who puts aside all his feelings, even his human sympathy, and concentrates his mental forces on the single aim of performing the operation as skilfully as possible" (*ibid.*, p. 115).

As we noted in Chapter 4, W. R. Bion goes further. Genuine psychoanalytic experience requires, he contends, the analyst's "disciplined denial of memory and desire" (Bion, 1970, p. 41). The analyst must not be concerned with what has happened in the patient's past, or in past sessions; and s/he must not burden the present with hopes, fears, or fantasies about the future.

"Memory and desire" have a poetic resonance:

> April is the cruellest month, breeding
> Lilacs out of the dead land, mixing
> Memory and desire, stirring
> Dull roots with spring rain.
> Winter kept us warm, covering
> Earth in forgetful snow, feeding
> A little life with dried tubers. (Eliot, 1934, p. 37)

These are the first lines of the section entitled "The Burial of the Dead," from T. S. Eliot's *The Waste Land*. I don't know if Bion intended to direct us toward them, but they evoke the mood of his terse communication. Analysis, like April, is cruel. It awakens memories and desires, recreates the pain of what did happen and what didn't, renews hopes and also disappointment. To tolerate the pain of the patient's awakening and to open a space for it in her/his own mental life, the analyst must cover her/his feelings "in forgetful snow," put them to sleep. S/he must undergo what amounts to an emotional death.

We might also state the point this way. During working hours, analysts must guide their conduct by the Nirvana principle. So far as their own emotional lives are concerned, they must be able to suspend temporarily the operations of both the pleasure and reality principles. They must reduce or eliminate their own internal sources of stimulation. In this way they create an emptiness, an absence of selfhood, that makes it possible to experience the selfhood of the other. And because they are nonetheless living and desiring creatures, they will always at least partially fail.

5.

As noted earlier, the following two accounts of clinical experience are focused at different levels. To use Hegel's terms, one is primarily concerned with questions of life and desire, the other with lordship and bondage. Thus between them they anchor psychoanalytic-marxist theory at its clinical end.

These cases also played a central part in shaping my clinical perspective. There were times during the course of the first analysis when I would find myself becoming hypnotically sleepy. Understanding my patient required developing an understanding of this phenomenon. It also led me to the conception of the paranoid–schizoid position and its relationship of the pleasure, reality, and Nirvana principles that I presented in Chapter 6. The second case was majorly concerned—for both patient and analyst—with issues of selfhood and recognition. It confirmed the lessons learned in the earlier case, as well as the practical utility of conceptions of negative self-relation and dialectical development.

6.

Psychoanalytic-marxism is a public matter. It functions through pedagogy, publication, and political participation. Clinical psychoanalysis is a private, some would say an esoteric, experience. Yet psychoanalytic-marxism depends upon the knowledge we gain from it. If we are to avoid cultishness, that is, the granting of epistemic privileges to psychoanalysts, then we must open the domain of psychoanalytic experience to public inspection.

Thus when we said earlier that we were entering the consulting room, this was something more than a figure of speech. One aim of this chapter is to place the reader inside such a room, so that s/he can share actual clinical experiences and join in the attempt to learn from them.

"Actual clinical experiences": This is misleading. The two reports fail to convey even my own experience of these analyses, much less the experiences of my patients. There are various reasons for this failure, of which two are most evident.

First, the case reports must carry the weight of conceptual communication. But actual analyses have nothing to do with conceptual elucidation. They are rather attempts at self-transformation. If a patient is burdened with the analyst's conceptual interests, this attempt will fail.

Second, in these reports clinical events have been formed into narratives, with the analyst in the position of narrator. This means that the patients do not get to tell their side of the story. Yet even if they did, a problem would remain. For then they, too, would be functioning as narrators. Clinical psychoanalysis is not, however, a telling of tales any more than it is an elucidation of concepts.

Hence we would do well to heed a postmodernist warning as we temporarily leave the public realm behind: Beware of clarity and closure![2]

B. Heart of Darkness

1.

"The nearer the analyst comes to achieving the suppression of desire, memory, and understanding, the more likely he is to fall into a sleep akin to stupor" (Bion, 1970, p. 47).

2.

The first clinical record has two dimensions. Both parts are aspects of the patient's character and of the transference configuration. Partially, they unfolded sequentially in the analysis, reflecting the fact that one of them was defended by and was more deeply buried than the other. Partially, they were displayed side by side, as oscillating polarities throughout the duration of the analysis. In the former regard they can be viewed as schizoid defenses against the emergence of the paranoid–schizoid position, ultimately as defenses against the possibility of a paranoid interaction. In the latter, they can be seen as a paranoid–schizoid process of interaction.

3.

A man in his late twenties, whom we shall call Mr. P, presented himself for analysis. He had academic pursuits to which psychoanalysis was relevant. He was somewhat bothered by a sense of being damaged. He thought he had the capacity to do significant, even great, things; but the idea of realizing his potential was connected in his mind to images of disaster.

Mr. P was his parents' only child. He remembered his earliest years as being happy. But his parents were divorced when he was six, and such happiness as he had known came to an end. He was a good athlete, however, and did very well in school. He began having difficulties with his school work and with school authorities in early adolescence, and more or less dropped out. He lived alone with his mother, was virtually unable to leave their apartment, looked to her for comfort but received none. She was dutiful and took care of his physical needs, but there was no emotional contact betwen them. When he would try to talk to her, after long and lonely days spent in isolation, she would fall asleep. As the crisis deepened he was permitted to see his father, with whom contact had been severed at the time of the divorce. This did not improve matters.

Eventually Mr. P worked his way out of his state of isolation. He kept a journal and wrote poetry. His writing released him from enough of his pain to permit re-entry into society. He gained admission to a university, did excellent work, was active in on- and off-campus politics. Still, there was a recurrent pattern of doing well until a crisis would develop, after which a form of activity would be dropped, and he would have to start over at something else. His intellectual development, however, was steady, indeed impressive. He possessed a powerful, highly organized, intellect. He could master the most abstract and philosophical materials. And he lived a kind of philosophical life. Although he had no close attachments, he had a wide circle of acquaintances. He was always willing to listen to their problems, both intellectual and personal, and to help them out when he could. He asked nothing in return. He was stoic and uncomplaining about the absence of pleasure in his life.

At the beginning I found Mr. P mildly agreeable. He did not evoke strong feelings one way or the other. He did make me sleepy. This happened first as he was telling me his life story. I had been listening in a not uninterested fashion when he came to his parents' divorce. I became intensely sleepy and did not really awaken until he began talking about his adolescent identity crisis.

In many analyses there is an early moment of interaction between patient and analyst that foreshadows the course of the analytic relationship and provides a preliminary definition of the central transference and countertransference issues (Leonard J. Comess, personal communication). For example, with Mr. I—the patient in the next case—I remember a sudden relaxation of muscular tension and a look of boyish hope, when I made the unexpected (but I think warranted) comment that he would like to think I cared for him. His response, which was also unexpected, led me to think he hoped that I could or would care for him, in the double sense of taking care of him and having caring feelings for him. Moreover, the hope and/or sense of my caring for him made him feel good. The analysis turned upon and was sustained by this hope, and by his capacity to feel good when he felt cared for. The sleepy-making interaction with my philosophical patient was quite a different matter, but it did prove to have prognostic value: Sleepiness and I became intimates.

Here is a typical instance. I would be feeling well rested and alert as the hour began. Mr. P would be talking about an event in his present life, the previous session, a dream. He would seem to be intensely involved with his subject matter, although there was a sense of his moving in circles within it. His style of communication would be orderly, logical, somewhat repetitive. His tone of voice would be well modulated within a narrow range. He would lie motionless. For my part, I would be following what he was saying with more or less relaxed attention. Then, quite suddenly, I would feel as if I had been injected with a sleep-making drug. I would find myself trapped between antithetical imperatives: I must go to sleep! I must stay awake! When the session ended, I would feel worn out and out of it: worn out from the effort of trying to stay awake, out of it from the after-effect of the "injection." Within a few minutes I would come to myself again. A varying degree of weariness might linger on.

It was evident that my weariness was a function of the analytic interaction. It did not correlate with feeling physically or emotionally depleted, although weariness would somewhat increase my susceptibility to it. But even when I was tired I would not feel sleepy during the preceding and succeeding analytic hours. It was not clear, however, what it was about the interaction that was making me sleepy.

The available literature, taken in conjunction with the data of Mr. P's analysis, suggested various possibilities. There was the fact that Mr. P's mother had fallen asleep when he when he tried to discuss his problems with her, during his troubled adolescence. This suggested the possibility of a "reciprocal identification," in which the analyst experiences "the attitude or feelings that would be appropriate for the transference source in . . . [his] patient's past and its counterpart in . . . his own inner object-representations" (McLaughlin, 1975, p. 367). But if I were identifying with his mother, this raised a further question: Why did I identify with her, and how did this identification occur? Moreover, I couldn't take it as given that I did identify with her. There were various additional or alternative possibilities. My sleepiness might express an "unconscious resentment at the emotional barrenness of the patient's communication" (Brown, 1977, p. 483), leading to a "talion response" (Racker, 1968, p. 139). He was withdrawn, rendering my analytic efforts useless. Unconsciously feeling helpless and hostile, I withdrew in turn from "a seemingly insoluble problem where sleep and the hope for a better tomorrow seem to offer the only solutions" (Alexander, 1981, p. 49). Perhaps also the patient's "general character defenses and areas of specific conflict" were too similar to my own, again leading me into an avoiding reaction (McLaughlin, 1975, p. 373).

These hypotheses amounted to the view that my sleepiness was countertransference in the narrow sense, that is, a defensive response requiring the analysis of the analyst. But it might be the case that my sleepiness was integral to the analysis. What if I were experiencing Mr. P in me, containing him or some part of him (a maternal introject, most obviously) in the space created by maintaining the analytic stance? My sleepiness might then represent "a primitive splitting in which a whole part of the self is dissociated. By a process of projective identification, the analyst feels depleted and half alive, and thus disoriented and out of touch with the bases of what is most alive or would be most alive at the time if the patient were truly there" (Brown, 1977, p. 490). Perhaps one could say that "the analyst's mental ego is eclipsed by the patient's body ego" (*ibid.*), or that the patient is suffering from "a functional ego defect which casts a shadow on the perceptual functions of the analyst's ego" (*ibid.*). On the basis of these hypotheses one could say that the patient was engaged in an attack on linking or was unable to establish an emotional link to me, but that I was properly connected to his disconnection.

Yet if the sleepiness originated with Mr. P and I was experiencing it, then ipso facto it was a link between us. Perhaps it bespoke a "powerful urge to merge" (Brown, 1977, p. 491), the wish to fuse with me as the nurturing mother. It could also express a more or less hallucinatory experience of being merged with me. Or it could be a statement of a problem the patient had been unable to solve, a statement in the language of the problem itself. What if the patient had been exposed to a "major trauma in childhood during which time . . . a hypnoid state was used defensively" (Dickes, 1965, p. 400)? The patient might now be putting me into a hypnoid state, not only to avoid a repetition of the trauma but also to communicate to me the nature of the catastrophe that had occurred. There might also be a dream or a fantasy within the hypnoid condition, which might only be accessible through my own reverie. If this were true, attempting to dispel the sleepiness would be the real countertransference response.

Thus there were various plausible and often quite contradictory interpretations of my sleepiness. No a priori resolution of the matter seemed possible or desirable. I, and Mr. P along with me, would have to try to learn the meaning of the phenomenon as we went along.

4.

For quite a while Mr. P talked and acted as if he were trying to get on with things, to make progress with the analysis and in the rest of his life. These efforts seemed inauthentic and false, even though Mr. P was very invested in them. His conscious fantasy life, replete with Gothic and other images, was similarly unconvincing. It was not possible to tell, however, whether this sense of falsity arose from the content of his communications, his defensive relationship to their content, or his difficulty in relating to me. In any case, beneath this layer of self-presentation another world was coming into view:

> This is the dead land
> This is cactus land
> Here the stone images
> Are raised, here they receive
> The supplication of a dead man's hand
> Under the twinkle of a fading star. (Eliot, 1934, p. 57)

The movement from consciousness toward the unconscious brought me an impression of desolation and destruction. This seemed true in two ways. There seemed to be an absence of significant internal and interpersonal object-relations; and I found only the slightest traces of emotional life. I concluded that Mr. P had suffered a virtual emotional death at the age of six, when his father left, and that he had been moribund even earlier. Mr. P both did and did not share this understanding. He, too, believed that his parents' divorce had occasioned a radical rupture in his development. He also began to acknowledge that there had been problems before the divorce. He could see these things—but so far as I could tell, he could not feel them. Interpretations aimed at possible emotional reactions to his early losses or toward interruptions in the analysis (weekends, vacations) were useless. Grief, anger, and anxiety were dead issues. Pointing in their direction produced neither free associations nor affective responses. Moreover, although the picture of his world contained a self-image, he looked at himself and his world from the outside. And if this were called to his attention, it tended to multiply the images. He would then be observing himself observing himself in the cactus land of his mind.

It was becoming evident that Mr. P relied upon a "splitting of the ego in the process of defense" (Freud, 1940). His reaction to the divorce was paradigmatic. Here is how he described the final breaking up of the marriage:

> On the day of the separation my mother told me to get some toys and then say good-bye to my father. I thought we were going to spend a few days with my [maternal] grandparents, although I think I knew there was something more serious happening. I selected a pair of roller skates and a wooden sword my father had made for me, and went to him. He saw the sword and said, "to remember me by." I didn't know what he meant. I went outside to wait in the car. I heard sounds of fighting coming from inside the house and saw lots of people coming.

> Then I don't remember anything until a day or two later, at my grand-parents' house. Somehow I also learned that my father had really lost control and had physically attacked my mother.

We will examine the latent content of this memory in a moment. For now its form claims our attention. As Mr. P and I came to view it, it represents the process through which one ego and mode of self-organization becomes two. At one extreme he is in the house with his parents. He is, however tenuously, connected to them and to his feelings. He is confused, but not so confused that he fails to perceive something is wrong. At the other extreme he is in exile at his grandparents' house, a stranger in a strange land. In between there are two moments or stages of detachment. First, he is outside the house and inside the car while his parents are fighting. This represents the adoption of a schizoid defense against the feelings aroused by their real or fantasied interaction. But the defense is not adequate. Even in the car he can hear them fighting, that is, even in his withdrawn state he experiences painful and terrifying feelings. Thus there is a second moment. He blanks out, becomes amnesiac. He goes into the psychical equivalent of a state of shock. This corresponds to Dickes' depiction of a hypnoid state used defensively. Here we see the hypnoid moment as a stage in the development of a schizoid character structure.

Mr. P, in short, could not tolerate the pain of the separation. He withdrew from the scene, leaving behind the self who had an emotional link to his father. He continued to have a relationship to his mother, but he now experienced her as emotionally dead and ungratifying. She was alive only in what he characterized as "hysterical" fits of rage. He continued to want her love and to desire contact with his father, but these desires had now become ego-alien. They were the demands of the self he had left behind and a threat to his fragile character structure.

He responded to the threatening return of his dissociated self in two ways. On the one hand, he was recurrently able to put the desiring self to sleep. He would unconsciously reproduce a hypnoid state and use it as a defense against emotional stimulation. He then would be in a kind of reverie or trance, one aspect of which was not knowing that he was in a trance. He was neither awake nor asleep or—to put it another way—he was apparently awake but actually asleep. On the other hand, he utilized processes of denial or disavowal to ward off any consciousness of desires attached to memories. In this regard he resembled children who have experienced the death of a parent: "Feelings of protracted grief are avoided and the finality of the loss is denied" (M. Wolfenstein, 1969, p. 432). His presenting self was predicated upon this denial of unfinished business with his past. The appearance of a normal self was created, but because the process of its creation had dropped from sight, Mr. P mistook the semblance for the reality. Moreover, the process, from with-drawal to denial, was repeated each time he encountered a painful experience. Thus around the wound of the divorce layer upon layer of psychical scar tissue developed. To vary the metaphor, he used the dead-ened remnants of his object relationships to build a labyrinth around a tomb. In the tomb was a stone image of his father, which indeed received the "supplication of a dead man's hand." Here also lay his potential for creative and assertive living. The trick of the labyrinth, and of its effec-tiveness as a defense, was that in it all meanings were inverted. Within the analysis, when he would acknowledge the truth of something, this would mean he was unconsciously denying it. When he thought he was struggling to get closer to the center of the labyrinth, he was really try-ing to get away from it. Conversely, when he denied the significance of something, this was more nearly an acknowledgment of its importance. When he tried to get away from something, he brought himself closer to it.

The rule of inverted meanings was not without exception. Conse-quently neither Mr. P nor I could rely upon it for the purpose of decod-ing his communications. This was actually a blessing, if a bit in disguise. The exceptions were moments of direct communication. These increased in number and became increasingly recognizable as time went by. Corre-spondingly, the absence of direct communication could then be identi-fied and its functions analyzed. We were more able to determine when speech constituted a link between us (and, if so, what kind of link) and when it served to break a connection (or to deny the fact that there was no connection) between us. But this was later in the treatment.

I have yet to mention the most striking, and also most elusive, fea-ture of Mr. P's inner world, as I was now perceiving it. This was the almost total absence of pleasure in his life—past, present, and anticipated future. Pain and his characteristic defenses against it were readily noted. But only gradually did it emerge that, at best, he found things not pain-ful. From his vantage point, on the basis of his experience, Freud was correct in equating pain and stimulation. The Nirvana principle and the pleasure principle were identical. But from my perspective, it was the absence of pleasure in his life that led to the conflating of these two prin-ciples of mental functioning. He avoided stimulation and emotional life because to live meant to be in pain. He was missing the leavening of experienced pleasure, which makes the pain of living bearable.

Here is another way of looking at the matter. Mr. P was experienc-ing Freud's postulated identity of the pleasure and Nirvana principles: stimulation = pain; absence of stimulation = pleasure. This identity was not accompanied by psychic health, however, but rather by a pervasive feeling of malaise or even morbidity. Recognizing in this condition his alienated selfhood, Mr. P struggled against it with every life-force available to him. Something was missing which, despite his interminable nomadic wandering in the dead lands of his mind, he still hoped to find. If Freud were correct, this would have been a false hope and the analysis a fool's errand. But another interpretation was possible. If the Nirvana principle was (1) distinct from the pleasure principle and (2) a defense against pain, then both Mr. P's suffering and his struggle were intelligible.

5.

As the dead land of Mr. P's inner world was becoming visible to us, I continued to be intermittently sleepy. Partially, my sleepiness was clarified by my understanding of his inner world; partially, it was the vehicle through which I entered his inner world.

His inner world seemed to have this structure:

• The identification of life and the possible pleasure in living with intolerable pain, making necessary adherence to the Nirvana principle.

• The equation of any significant other, internal or external, with pain.

• Withdrawal from the source of the pain through a splitting of the ego and the defensive use of a hypnoid state.

• Recurrent use of the hypnoid state as a defense against the return of the desiring self or ego.

• The creation of a false self predicated upon the denial or disavowal of its own process of creation.

Mr. P's personality thus was constituted through a series of broken links, of which the most dramatic was the hypnoid, or amnesiac, moment. A broken link is, however, still a link. Like any defense, it is also an expression of what it defends against.

My sleepiness was a function of the broken links in Mr. P's personality. Because there were broken links, I became sleepy. But also, because I became sleepy, I could experience the link that had been broken, the desire that had been denied.

This general statement can be reduced to three more specific propositions. My sleepiness was a function of: (1) a break in affective linkage, with a resultant lack of empathic resonance; (2) a hypnotic interaction; and (3) the patient's use of projective identification.

For example: One day Mr. P began a session by saying he was dealing with "almost uncontrollable, gut-wrenching emotions" resulting from his involvement with a young woman and his jealousy of a rival. He related his feelings to his parents' divorce and his anger at his mother, who was at this time emerging as the villain in the piece. He felt he wanted to attack the woman, as his father had attacked his mother. He knew he wouldn't actually do it. In fact and instead, he made a date with another woman.

Despite his apparent involvement in what he was saying, I felt detached from the narrative. When he came to his decision to date someone else, I became sleepy. As he continued talking, images of the apartment he had shared with his mother floated hazily through my mind. I could visualize him talking to her, with apparent intensity, while she lapsed into sleep. As this image was crystallizing, he began to talk about a desire or hunger for wholeness, and about his fear of that desire. My sleepiness faded and I remarked that I was reminded of his interactions with his mother, when she would fall asleep and leave him unsatisfied. He replied, "It is painful to realize that it was not satisfying with her, that I would spend days [I had not seen him the previous day] waiting for her, but knowing in advance that it wouldn't work."

In interpreting this interaction, I will presuppose that Mr. P's desiring self was painfully involved with the woman (although not at the manifest triangular level) but that his withdrawn self was describing the event to me. He was detached from his feelings toward the woman and any feelings he might have toward me. The intrapsychic and interpersonal link had been broken because it involved "gut-wrenching" pain. There was a void where feelings might have been and hence no possibility of an empathic connection between us. The lack of empathic resonance, of a pathos or feeling of suffering that I could share, left me with nothing to do or say, and so I became sleepy.

The broken affective link explains my detachment from the narrative and, partially, why I became sleepy when I did: When he described breaking off contact with the woman who caused him pain, he was simultaneously breaking off contact with me. I was a frustrating object of desire, the recipient of a maternal transference. He withdrew from me out of anger and to preserve me from his anger. But this interpretation does not adequately account for the sudden, invasive quality of my experience. Nor could I find the basis of my response in myself, that is, as a countertransference reaction in the narrow sense. Neither in this instance nor in general did variations in my narrowly countertransferential feelings correspond to variations in my sleepiness.

Thus I come to the second proposition. It seemed plausible that Mr. P was unconsciously engaged in autohypnotic activity. His absolute physical immobility and the modulated, subtly rhythmic quality of his voice suggested as much. Moreover, I am inclined to interpret the break in his narrative as signifying a hypnoid moment. On this supposition, my sleepiness would be a result of his autohypnosis, in one of two possible ways. It might be the incidental byproduct of that activity and so devoid of further meaning. But the transference situation and the images in my mind suggested that he was unconsciously intending to put me to sleep, as he had his mother.

We shall see that there are several reasons why Mr. P might want to put me as his mother to sleep. One of them was because the self who desired "wholeness" was attached to her. This self threatened his withdrawn self with almost uncontrollable emotions. If, therefore, in putting himself to sleep he was hypnotizing his mother, in hypnotizing his mother he was also putting himself to sleep.

The second explanation accounts for the intensity of my experience, but not for why it was my experience and not his. He was not falling asleep, I was. This brings me to the third proposition. The self who was linked to his mother was a burden and a threat. He therefore availed himself of the opportunity presented by the analysis and disburdened himself of it. Via projection, he identified me with that self and emptied himself of it. In the space created by the analytic attitude, I received the projection. I felt hypnotized and stupefied, but I also gained access to the dream within the sleep and to the dreamer of the dream. Within my drowsiness my inner world became the apartment containing himself and his mother. This visualization was the equivalent of his memory, dream, or fantasy. When I was able to report the "dream" to him in the form of an interpretation, he was able to experience the feelings attached to it. He realized how deeply disappointed he was in his mother, and how hopeless interaction with her made him feel.

In this painful way we advanced beyond, or perhaps returned from, the Nirvana principle.

6.

The schizoid side of Mr. P's character structure was built in obedience to the Nirvana principle. At the same time he lived in defiance of it. He struggled to awaken and to stay awake, but he had so little experience of pleasure that the struggle seemed pointless. Nonetheless he waged it, and so I had an ally in the analytic enterprise. But my ally, who was as much Kurtz as Marlow, was not entirely reliable.

Kurtz and Marlow are the protagonists in Joseph Conrad's *Heart of Darkness*. Often in the half-sleep induced by the analysis I would find myself in their company, deep inside their world. I communicated this experience to my patient, who found in Conrad's tale a depiction of his analytic experience.

Marlow is a seaman with a fascination for and an understanding of the "dark places of the earth" (Conrad, 1902, p. 493). As he talks to his companions, night falls. They can hear his voice without being able to see him. In *this* darkness he tells of the voyage up an African river that brought him to Kurtz.

Kurtz is an agent for a trading company. He, too, has a fascination for Africa, and he, too, is a voice in the darkness. He is Marlow's shadow, the "nightmare of . . . [his] choice" (*ibid.*, p. 583). But where Marlow has the inner *restraint* to explore the darkness without getting absorbed by it, Kurtz does not:

> Mr. Kurtz lacked restraint in the gratification of his various lusts. . . . [The] wilderness had found him out early, and had taken on him a terrible vengeance for the fantastic invasion. I think it whispered to him things about himself which he did not know, things of which he had no conception till he took counsel with this great solitude—and the whisper proved irresistibly fascinating. It echoed loudly within him because he was hollow at the core. (*ibid.*, p. 573)

Kurtz discovers too late that at bottom he is pure appetite. In an attempt to satisfy his hunger, he turns cannibal. Perhaps he even becomes addicted to the eating of human flesh. Consequently Marlow, after he finally reached him, could not "break the spell—the heavy, mute spell of the wilderness—that seemed to draw . . . [him] to its pitiless breast by the awakening of forgotten and brutal instincts, by the memory of gratified and monstrous passions" (*ibid.*, p. 585). He could only listen to Kurtz's last words (the horror! the horror!) and assimilate as self-knowledge what the other man had learned, too late, about himself.

I need not belabor the psychoanalytic point. Because Mr. P did not believe his Marlow was strong enough to be relied upon, he had fled from the heart of darkness into the dead land. The Nirvana principle was his substitute for restraint. By contrast, the Kurtz in him was hypnotically powerful. If we were now to re-enter the Africa of his mind, leaving world-weary Europe behind, he was afraid the wilderness would draw him to its pitiless breast—that in the darkened analytic consulting room, where he could hear but not see me, the analysis and the analyst would cruelly awaken his forgotten and brutal instincts, undermine his schizoid defenses, and leave him to face the horror alone.

Mr. P's struggle with the wilderness is well represented in the following dream:

> I leave an amphitheater, where some women are talking, and go into a wood. I see my father by a waterfall. I try to exhort the child in me to talk to him but I remain silent. My father slips into the water, goes over the falls, and dies.
>
> There is a change of scene. I'm an African explorer leading a group away from the waterfall. This me is also you [the analyst]. There is a me watching, who has set traps in the river and knows the other me is

going the wrong way. Finally I lead the group back to the waterfall. But the explorer is still afraid to drill for oil in the pool. He is afraid of monsters in the water.

The dream concerns the divorce and its aftermath. Mr. P's mother (the waterfall) destroyed his father. He could have and should have saved his father, but he was immobilized by anxiety. Afterwards and in the analysis he appears to be looking for his father, who also represents his manhood. But the search is actually a retreat, the analysis is misled and misleading. Yet he is also learning to unravel his schizoid defenses (the traps) and to risk the confrontation with his mother. At this juncture, however, he is still afraid to enter her, because he believes she contains something monstrous.

His further associations led into dressing rooms near lakes or swimming pools, when he was a small child. He would undress with his mother and was erotically stimulated by the sight of her naked body. We therefore would conclude that the monster was his desire for erotic fusion with or immersion in his mother. Yet it was his father who slipped over the waterfall. This suggests that his father was the monster in the pool, who threatened his son with death or castration. Either way, the monster was a penis, a projected and dissociated body-part—no longer a stone image within a labyrinth but rather a living instrument of destruction, waiting angrily in the womb of creation.

If on one level the dream reflects the situation of the divorce, with its elements of oedipal conflict, on another it represents a pre-oedipal situation. Mr. P is attempting to individuate, to free himself from a fused, confused, and hypnotic relationship to his mother—his actual mother and the mother of his fantasies. He attempts to become himself by running away from her, disguising his flight as maturation. Eventually he realizes he must re-enter her to free himself from her.

7.

As Mr. P's schizoid defenses were elucidated, we were able to reverse the path of his withdrawal from the scene of the divorce. We could then re-enter his parents' house, at the time of and prior to the divorce. The major episodes in the transference drama took place in this heart of darkness. They had four principal forms:

• He as his father is attacking me as his mother. The attack is sadistic, a fusion of sexual and aggressive aims. Its intense aggressive quality proceeds from frustration and lack of pleasurable experience. In part Mr. P wants me to be asleep, so that I won't be able to defend myself; in part I want to be asleep so that, ostrich-like, I won't see/experience what is happening. But if I am asleep, emotionally dead, then his sexuality is reduced to necrophilia. He is once more frustrated and unsatisfied. Catch-22: to win is to lose. His attack is simultaneously deadly and impotent. He as his father goes mad and is driven into exile. I as his mother survive, a living corpse, a robot.

• In the first transference configuration Mr. P plays his father's role in the primal scene. The roles were sometimes, and sometimes simultaneously, reversed. Then he as his mother is attempting to put me as his father to sleep, so I won't assault him.

• At a deeper level, I am his infantile self and he is his mother or his mother's breast. I am starving. He fears this hunger will destroy him. I must be put to sleep to avert the danger. Withholding his true substance, he feeds me on hypnotic dreams, puts me into a state of hallucinated satisfaction.

• He is the infant who is assaulting the breast. It is an assault because he has been hungry for so long. He wants to be nourished, to be comforted, to be filled with good sensations. But to satisfy his hunger is to destroy the source of satisfaction. Besides, the satisfaction seems to be withheld. He becomes increasingly frustrated and enraged, and the situation becomes terrifyingly persecutory. To save himself and to save the possible source of pleasure for himself, he withdraws. But the withdrawal is modeled on the breast that withholds. It is an act of vengeance, motivated by an intense bitterness, and consecrated to the goddess Nemesis. To acknowledge this, to feel the bitterness, is madness. It draws him back into paranoia. Hence Nemesis gives way to Thanatos. A stoic indifference covers the emotional ground, feeding only a little life with dried tubers, until his hunger is once again so strong that there must be a second coming: "And what rough beast, its hour come round at last / Slouches toward Bethlehem to be born?" (Yeats, 1921, p. 185). Not Christ but Kurtz this time.

We also remember that the drama in the house had an audience, one that could hear but not see: Mr. P waiting in the car. This represents the son's exclusion/protection from the sado-masochistic primal scene, as well as the time (a time filled with hallucinatory satisfaction or paranoid dread) in the metabolic cycle of infantile life when the child is awake, alone, and waiting to be fed. The drama also has an end—Mr. P's exile to his grandparents' house. This represents both the bitter end of his oedipal struggle and the equally bitter end of his symbiotic relationship with his mother (weaning). Finally there are the sword and the roller skates. These symbolize his genitals, part-objects that he inherits from his father, which were lifeless and mechanical but which the analysis is reanimating and perhaps even reintegrating.

Let me add two points about the divorce. First, as indicated above, it was a screen memory for Mr. P's experience of weaning. He had been breast-fed for more than a year. He did not protest directly against the end of the nursing relationship, but he did suffer from asthma and other symptoms of anxiety and suppressed rage during and after weaning. He distinctly remembered being fed prepared baby food, not liking it, but eating it without manifest protest. He also retained an hallucinatory or dream image of one last drop of milk falling from his mother's breast. The divorce thus signified the loss of his mother's breast and of the nursing relationship. The one loss concealed as well as revealed the other.

Second, Mr. P believed that prior to the divorce his mother had been alive emotionally, his father had been responsive to him, and he had been happy. Afterwards his mother died emotionally, his father was represented to him as a monster, and he was lost, unloved, and unguided. I both accepted and rejected this view. On the one hand, the divorce was a real, destructively painful break in Mr. P's intrapsychic and interpersonal life. But he idealized his early childhood, and his interpretation of the divorce served to protect the idealization. Even before the divorce there had been a good (loving and caring) and bad (emotionally dead and absent) mother, a good (present and involved) and bad (depressed, withdrawn, and absent) father, and a good (loved and loving, affirmed and self-affirming) and bad (neglected, enraged, and destructive) son. This spatial or structural set of splits was displaced, via the divorce, into a temporal dimension. The "either/or" characteristic of the paranoid–schizoid position became a "before/after," and this in a double sense: before and after the divorce, before and after weaning. In this way, his life history was transformed into the familiar theological drama of a fall from grace or the expulsion from Eden.

Paradise lost. . . .

8.

Despite their paranoid nature, Mr. P took some pleasure from the numerous interactions in which I was experienced as a breast and he as the voracious child. If he succeeded in communicating with me and I proved this by understanding his communication, he felt potent, comforted, cared for, and nourished. At first this initiated a new split in his object representations, in which I was the good mother and his actual mother was the bad one. This was a development within the paranoid–schizoid position. But in time, as the split was analyzed and he began to experience our relationship as a source of both pleasure and pain, he became curious about his earliest relationship with his mother and decided to ask her about it. This was a step beyond the paranoid–schizoid position. It was predicated on the hope that he and his mother had really been alive, once upon a time, and it required the courage to face the possibility that this hope might be disappointed.

He asked his mother what it had been like when he was a nursling. She told him she had been very happy with him. She loved nursing him. It was very satisfying to both of them. *He would fall asleep at the breast and she would fall asleep, too.*

This fact was not in itself remarkable. To the contrary, it is a commonplace of the nursery world. But it illuminated the heart of darkness. At the center of my patient's personality and of the transference relationship was the experience of merging with his mother. This experience had, however, at least three interpenetrated meanings: It was his most intense desire, a trap, and a defense.

As the object of desire, it may be understood as a moment (a timeless one) of quiescent gratification, or as the point where the pleasure, Nirvana, and reality principles coincide. The sensation of merging into the mother's body, filling one's mother as one is filled by one's mother, is pleasure itself, or as close to an "in-itself" as human experience permits. As we stated in Chapter 6, it is our nearest postnatal approximation to prenatal experience. It is a timeless moment from which pain has been banished. Because it is real, and because it is not experienced as continuous in time with moments of pain, the pleasure and reality principles converge. And in the sleepy pleasure of satiation, as Hypnos casts its spell, the program of the Nirvana principle is nearly fulfilled. Here pleasure becomes an absence of tension and, in the sweetness of sleep, an absence of stimulation as well. This sleep is indeed the "balm of hurt minds, great nature's second course, chief nourisher of life's feast" (Shakespeare, 1605, p. 977).

A gratification at one stage of development can be a confinement at the next: From the standpoint of the emergent, percipient, and motor-active self—the self craving recognition of its autonomy and potency—fusion with the mother is a seduction and a violation of selfhood. It is an "unbecoming," as Mr. P put it with his characteristic insight and precision. It is an experience of domination via hypnosis. The percipient self is being put to sleep, veritably destroyed. Insofar as the merger experience is (1) pleasurable and (2) an ending of pain (hunger, alimentary discomfort), the self seeks its own annihilation. But insofar as (1) there is pleasure in being awake and active and (2) the merger is infiltrated or even filled with the pain it also brings to an end, it is a trap. The paranoid fantasies so richly detailed by Melanie Klein are partly a response to this existential dilemma, although (as we have emphasized and as was true in this instance) existential problems must become life-historical traumas before paranoid states of mind dominate the developmental picture—which, unfortunately, they often do.

The meaning for Mr. P of merger as a trap is illustrated in the following dream:

> I'm making love to my mother. My mouth is at her vagina. It's pleasurable, but it's more like being at the breast. It turns into sleepiness—like breathing carbon monoxide fumes.

He commented: "My mother is putting me to sleep with carbon monoxide. It's carbon monoxide because I don't want to go to sleep. And it's carbon monoxide because I'm fuming with rage."

The sleepy union with the mother is here experienced as a state of war. Mr. P's hunger is an attack upon his mother; she repels the attack with poison gas. The interaction is toxic, filled with hostility. Early in the analysis, when I felt poisoned by sleepiness, it was because he was projectively identifying me with the self who was merged with his mother and was fuming with rage. Later on, when his anger had subsided, sleepiness felt less poisonous and more seductive.

If fusion with the mother was a trap, it was also a defense. Again, a dream is of illustrative value:

> My mother [also the analyst] takes me to the backyard to show me something. There is a tree, with the horrible sight of dead bodies hanging from it. One of them, a young woman in a shroud, is not quite dead. I recognize her.
>
> I send my mother back into the house. I start to fall asleep, nodding off in the dirt. I manage to get into the house. I lie down on an uncomfortable couch and try to figure out what it meant.

In his associations to this dream Mr. P focused upon the dying woman and his sleepiness. The woman is his mother. What is he to do about her? Cutting her down will not save her. Should he kill her, for mercy or revenge? What then, make love to the corpse? Confronted by these painful choices he becomes immobilized. He severs the affective link to his dying mother. He begins to fall asleep, but stays sufficiently awake to attempt the analytic interpretation of his experience.

In this dream sleepiness signifies a regression from object choice to identification. Mr. P is disconnected from his mother/analyst and from his internal object representation of his dying mother. Instead of having contact with them he falls asleep at a fantasied breast. This regressive fusion with his mother's body is the hypnoid moment in the dream and is the fantasy that accompanies the use of the hypnoid state as a schizoid defense. Additionally, the convergence of sleepiness as regressive fusion with the hypnoid moment suggests that hypnotic phenomena derive from the earliest interaction between mother and child. Dickes (1965) observes that the "newborn infant at the breast is subject to the rhythmic sounds and vibrations of the maternal heartbeat. Crooning, lullabies, rocking, and stroking are all parts of the loving care given to infants and . . . these all have potent hypnotic overtones" (p. 397). In the interaction with me, I often experienced Mr. P's manner of speaking as a kind of crooning and my sleepiness as its consequence. As himself-qua-infant I was being lulled to sleep; as himself-qua-mother I was being invited to fall asleep with him. Finally, these sleepy states signified the fantasy of an intrauterine state of bliss, desirable in itself and even more as a way of avoiding both ordinary unhappiness and hysterical misery.

9.

In the course of his analysis, Mr. P and I traversed the path from his natal home to his place of exile many times. Eventually, the painful reality occluded by his amnesia reappeared. He remembered the hotel room he and his mother occupied the night following the scene of separation. He could see himself washing his hands in a sink, the soap and soap bubbles—a cleansing that failed. Finally, he recalled the repressed moment itself. He had seen his father being led from the house, looking defeated and bewildered. He was not able to go to him or say anything to him. The dream of the waterfall captured this moment precisely, locating it in the heart of his personal darkness.

As Mr. P noted at the beginning of his analysis, he had been damaged by his experience in life. This damage could not be undone, but his work in the analysis went some way toward repairing it, toward healing the wounds in his psyche. The healing was sufficient so that, after the analysis ended, Mr. P was able to involve himself in activities where his intelligence, organizational abilities, and high moral values could be put to practical use. It is not just a bon mot to say he advanced from philosophy to praxis.

C. He Who Loses His Self Shall Find It

1.

Although Mr. P's character structure was split between its schizoid and paranoid extremes, his adult selfhood was never seriously in doubt.

He could become paralyzed by his internal antitheses, but he remained self-same. Mr. I, to whom we now turn, had no such assured if limiting structure. He lacked the selfhood with which Mr. P was burdened.

2.

Throughout this inquiry, we have assumed the meaningfulness and empirical reality of selfhood. A postmodernist might view this asumption as atavistic and, unkindest cut of all, as not psychoanalytic. After all, in the beginning and as the name implies, psychoanalysis aimed at the dissolution of the conscious and self-conscious subject, the "I" of both philosophy and everyday life. Isn't a return to issues of selfhood a regression to an outworn pre-Freudian position?

Freud most assuredly subjected the self to intense scrutiny. Although he acknowledged the existence of an "I" having some aspects of agency and a degree of synthetical power, the psychoanalytic ego is more subjected to the powers of others than it is a subject in its own right. It serves the three jealous and antagonistic masters of the external world, the id, and the super-ego. To be sure, the ego is not the equivalent of the self. But Freud and his early followers only used the term "self" in a non-technical way, to refer to a person as a whole. The first hint of a *concept* of the self—and it is only a hint—is in an essay by Hartmann (1950), in which he postulates "narcissism as the libidinal cathexis not of the ego but of the self" (p. 85), meaning by the "self" either "one's own person" or its mental representation. Jacobson (1964) accepts Hartman's usage, defining the self as "the whole person of an individual, including his body and body parts as well as his psychic organization and its parts" (p. 6). But the ego, not the self, remained the focus of analytic theory and practice.

Thus, although classical psychoanalysis is not entirely self-less, J.-B. Pontalis (1981) is largely justified in his claim that it is not a psychology of the self:

> From the discovery of the "multiple personality" which marks the accession of psychoanalysis to the notion of the *Ichspaltung* (a split of the "I" or the "me" . . .) which concludes the Freudian works, one can validly claim that three quarters of a century of analytical experience undermines the illusion of a totally monadic subject, a person totally sure of *belonging to himself.* (p. 127)

Consequently he views with considerable skepticism the emergence of a concept of the self, first in Winnicott's distinction between a true and a false self (1965) and then in the work of Harry Guntrip. For Guntrip, the "most profound problem in human life" is "how a human being develops out of his original total infantile dependence and helplessness a sense of becoming a secure, inwardly stable self, strong enough to stand up against the external pressures of life in adult years" (Guntrip, 1971, p. 149). In the face of such statements, it is no wonder that Pontalis is inclined to view the resurrection of the self as a "return of the *repressing* rather than a return of the repressed: a return masked by nostalgia, a nostalgia for the good old self which would have been lost through too much analysis: *'He is quite his old self again'*" (Pontalis, 1981, p. 127).

3.

If Pontalis senses a touch of nostalgia in English middle school psychoanalysis, he would find its presence overwhelming in the self psychology of Heinz Kohut and his followers. In Kohut's work a cohesive, conflict-free self seems to be a birthright. Conflict and/or fragmentation of the self reflects a lack of empathy on the part of the caretakers ("selfobjects") of early childhood. The concepts of classical psychoanalytic theory, from drives through the oedipal configuration, are viewed as derivative or secondary phenomena, the effects of empathic failures rather than the cause of psychopathology. Thus the language of psychoanalysis so carefully articulated by Laplanche and Pontalis (1973) almost disappears. And so does the spirit animating it. The sober and dispassionate analysis of psychic pain that characterizes the best of psychoanalytic work gives way to evocations of health and a functioning self in which "ambitions, skills, and ideals form an unbroken continuum that permits joyful creative activity" (Kohut, 1977, p. 63).

4.

Still, the conventional emphasis upon psychic dissection ought not to have a privileged status. The free development of psychoanalytic knowledge is impeded as much by fixation upon the *corpus* of Freud's work, that is, by the institutionalized necrophilia of organized psychoanalysis, as by regression to pre-Freudian positions. We may therefore ask: Are there valid reasons for returning to the idea of an integrative self?

The question must, I think, be answered in the affirmative. First, and as Pontalis notes, if a number of psychoanalysts, of varying metapsychological persuasion, have resurrected the self, "they did it to find an answer to problems posed by some of their patients" (1981, p. 128). The case we are about to consider testifies to the accuracy of this contention. Second, there *is* a sense in which the self has been lost through too much analysis.

We might think of it this way. The starting point of analytic inquiry is a conscious self with the capacity to say "I" and to reflect upon the meaning of saying "I." If I understand him properly, when Kohut argues for an empathic stance on the part of the analyst, he is emphasizing the importance of recognizing the thoughts and feelings of the self in this sense, that is, the "I" that speaks for itself—the conscious and preconscious self. In so doing he begins well. It is not clear, however, that his method leads on to analysis proper, namely, to the psychoanalytic deconstruction of the "I," a deconstruction without which it cannot be reconstructed.

Conversely, and more to the present point, the splitting apart of the conscious self in the psychoanalytic process is not an end in itself but rather a mediation, a means to an end. We aim at the elucidation of the ruptures and faultlines in the psyche in order that they may be transformed into self-maintaining internal boundaries, psychical structures that ground the "I." In this sense, although not in Kohut's, psychoanalysis is a psychology of the self.

We can also approach this point from an Hegelian direction. In the preface to *The Phenomenology* Hegel contends that the real issue or what really matters in philosophy is "not exhausted by stating it as an aim, but by carrying it out, nor is the result the actual whole, but rather the result together with the process through which it came about" (1807, p. 2). Three aspects of philosophizing are thus indicated: aim, process, and result. Process or mediation has in turn a double, positive and negative, aspect: Consciousness "wins its truth only when, in utter dismemberment, it finds itself" (*ibid.*, p. 19). Dismemberment results from the exercise of the Understanding (*der Verstand*), the "power of the negative," from analysis. Psychoanalysis is analytic in just this sense, as Pontalis reminds us. It dismembers the conscious self through free association and the interpretation of resistance, revealing thereby what the self is not. A psychoanalysis not employing analysis is not worthy of the name. It really is a kind of nostalgia or edification. But it must not be forgotten that the dissolution of the self is in the interest of its higher unity. Which is to say, the negative moment in psychoanalysis is an aspect of a dialectical process of self-transformation. And "the negative, which emerges as the result of the dialectic, is, because [it is] a result, at the same time the positive; it contains what it results from, absorbed into itself, and made a part of its own nature" (Wallace, 1904, p. 152). The "I" that enters psychoanalysis is premised upon self-negation. The conscious self is opposed and undermined by an unconscious repressed not-self. The dismemberment of the pre-existing unity of self and not-self is thus the negation of a negation that creates the possibility of self-affirmation.

Selfhood in psychoanalysis, like selfhood in Hegelian phenomenology, is a process of negative self-relation.

5.

In what follows, I hope to show that Mr. I and the "I" of Hegelian self-certainty are brothers in arms. It may be useful, however, to consider two of the objections to such a proposition:

1. The process of recognition involves two selves equally undergoing development. Yet in the psychological development of the individual and in psychoanalytic treatment, intersubjectivity is not symmetrical. Only one of the two selves (child, patient) is the subject of the developmental process.

2. The Hegelian self develops through an encounter with the Unchangeable Being, that is, with a phenomenological forerunner to God. This accords with Hegel's purpose but not with the aims of psychoanalysis. After all, Hegel is an idealist. He wishes to demonstrate the absolute identity of being and knowing. Psychoanalysis, by contrast, views idealism as an illusion and the idea of absolute knowledge as grandiose and untenable.

As to the first objection, one could counter that parent and analyst continue to develop in their relationship with child and patient. But this would be to evade the criticism, for their development is incidental to the aims of the process of which they are a part. Indeed, if we take Hegel to mean that there are two empirically distinct selves equally undeveloped and developing, the objection must be granted. We are then immediately in the domain of political theory, concerned with the origins of civic order. And no doubt Hegel has this issue in mind. But as he also observes, the process of recognition is characterized by an ambiguity or duplication (*Doppelsinn*). The other, the second party to the interaction, is not the self, and so is an alien being, but in the other the self is only seeing itself, that is, itself in the form of otherness. One self interacts with another, not knowing that in so doing it is interacting with itself. Here we are in the domain of a psychoanalytic psychology. The self is internally ruptured, split, although at first the *Ichspaltung* may not be manifest. But when the self encounters the other, the intrasubjective diremption becomes intersubjective. The internal Not-I, the repressed or even disavowed self, is projected and identified with the other, the analyst. Insofar as the Not-I is also the "true Self," the self that remains as subject may feel the loss of itself in the object. What it loses through projective identification it then attempts to regain through introjective identification. These are among the basic modalities of the transference interaction of patient and analyst. Hence the process of recognition anticipates, sheds light upon, and is illuminated by the dynamics of the transference.

This brings me to the second objection. For if on the one hand Hegel advances beyond his philosophical predecessors in acknowledging the intersubjectivity of the self, on the other the ambiguity in the relationship of self and other is never completely resolved. In fact it deepens. One cannot be sure in reading *The Phenomenology* that one has escaped from the philosopher's inner world, albeit an inner world into which the variegated content of the external one has been reflected. Thought is progressively identified with being, but at the expense of being. There is, indeed, only one being that can be entirely identified with thought and that is God, the Unchangeable. The Unchangeable is the idealized projection of the philosopher's own mind, the self in the form of a perfect other. Thus when Hegel proceeds from the process of recognition to the experience of the Unhappy Consciousness, there is an unacknowledged retreat from intersubjectivity to intrasubjectivity. It is a subtle retreat: Through the agency of the mediator, the self and the Unchangeable are recognized as polarities of an internal relationship. But the consciousness for which the relationship is internal has been extended to include all reality. One might say that the phenomenological process manifestly intended to supersede the experience of life and desire instead embodies it. Hegelian philosophy cannibalizes the objective world.

This objection is valid, as far as it goes. Indeed, we have insisted upon it all along. We are not Hegelians, not even young Hegelians, but rather psychoanalytic-marxists whose notions of salvation are limited to the possibilities and bounded by the necessary disjunctions of human experience. Yet the idealization of reality, which from one standpoint mystifies the process of recognition, clarifies it from another. Psychoanalytically interpreted, absolute idealism is the matrix of the transference, the undifferentiated or fused relationship of mother and child that converts the analytic consulting room into a psychical womb. More narrowly, the phenomenon of the Unhappy Consciousness can be taken as signifying a basic transference fantasy: The self is painfully separated, alienated, from the Being that would complete it, make it whole, heal its wounds. The analyst is either that Being or the mediator, the link between a self filled only with yearning and a maternal object (especially a breast) containing life itself.

In short, the process of recognition and the experience of the Unhappy Consciousness may be interpreted, for psychoanalytic purposes, as related forms of a basic transference configuration.

6.

If there was one thing Mr. I did not feel, it was self-same. When he first entered analysis, he felt he had hardly any self at all. He was, at that time, in his late twenties. He was intelligent, articulate, quick-witted, good-looking, and extremely likable. He was able to form close and long-lasting friendships, and he had an outstanding record of academic achievement. He was also depressed, intensely anxious, and immobilized. He lived with an exquisite and excruciatingly painful sense of his own inadequacy and worthlessness. Consequently he was hyper-sensitive to other people's opinions of him, and he was always ready to hear criticism in their voices. He felt he did not have a skin thick enough to tolerate the abrasions of everyday living. Nor did he have sufficient substance to tolerate withdrawal from contact with others. When he was alone, he was beset by a terrifying experience of nothingness. Death seemed to be an immediate presence. He would lie in bed, bracing him-self against the sensation of being sucked into a void, or of seeing/being a tiny point of light disappearing into absolute darkness. To ward off the horror of it, he would put himself into a "stupor," a kind of half-sleep filled with erotic images and sensations. The stupor prevented the slip into nothingness—and prevented the free use of his many abilities. He experienced it as chemically addictive and as a shameful substitute for being a self in the adult world.

Mr. I's lack of self-certainty had evident roots. His father, whom he resembled physically, was a long-term alcoholic. He had been a success-ful businessman during Mr. I's earliest childhood, but had been on a downhill course ever since. He verbally abused all the members of his family, especially his son. No matter what Mr. I did or accomplished, he would berate him and belittle his actions: "Mr. Smart Guy, you think you're so smart. You're a piece of shit, just like me." He was monstrous in his rage. Then the rage would be turned inward, or turn into depres-sion. He would beg Mr. I to help him. At least once he begged Mr. I to kill him and end the whole dirty, worthless business. He was therefore a weak, ruined monster. Because he was a monster he was feared, because he was weak he could not be attacked. Indeed, anything that Mr. I did in his own interest or to his own credit was felt to be an attack upon his father. He could only become himself by destroying his father—and he was uncertain that he had a self to become. Maybe he was just his father all over again.

One of the father's accusations against Mr. I was that he had caused pain to his mother. His mother was a pleasant but weak woman who had very little confidence in herself and little to give to her son. What-ever strength of mind she possessed was more than expended in trying to cope with her husband. For almost as long as Mr. I could remember, she had been depressed and intermittently suicidal. She felt helpless when confronted with any indications of emotional distress in her son. As he grew to manhood, she increasingly called upon him to rescue his father, or rescue her from his father. He would respond to these calls for help, but with reluctance and anger. He did not want to think of himself as his parents' child, yet he was intensely preoccupied by his relationship to them. Moreover, the center of his sexual fantasy was a dark-haired woman who sometimes loved and sometimes tortured him. As the analysis proceeded he came to recognize that the fantasy image was derived from early memories of his mother.

Mr. I shielded himself from the disorder and sorrow of his family's life as best he could. Early on he vowed not to be like his father. He spent long hours alone in his room where he would lose himself (and preserve himself) in sexual fantasy but also in his schoolwork. He was never absent from school, no matter how ill he might be. He aimed at perfection in school performance. He viewed academic achievement as a way of escaping from his family and his father's fate. He tried to create an identity, for himself and by himself, other than the one given to him by birth. He tried to become someone other than his mother's and his father's son. This put him in a hopelessly self-contradictory position. On the one hand, he aspired to selfhood, by which *he* meant several things: the ability to be alone, work productively alone, be self-organizing, withstand criticism, make choices, have and assert an opinion. Stated negatively, he wished not to be weak, disorganized, and scared. On the other hand, he disavowed who he *in fact* was, the life-historical substance of his identity. His selfhood was therefore reduced to a form without content. This had the further consequence that he could only see himself as others saw him, or judge himself as others judged him. Other people were mirrors in which he saw himself reflected. When he was alone, he ceased to exist. That is, the Mr. I who aspired to autonomous selfhood ceased to exist. There emerged instead the weakened, terrified victim of familial devastation, precisely the antithesis, the not-self, of the self he desired to be.

7.

For our purposes I need not describe the early years of Mr. I's analysis. It will be useful, however, to say just a few words about the then-current status of psychoanalytic theory and interpretive technique. For it could be argued that, in the United States at that time, psychoanalysis lacked a self, or perhaps had an oversupply of them.

This had not always been the case. If we leave aside terminological disputes, we can say that classical psychoanalytic theory has a quite simple notion of the self, albeit one that gives rise to a variety of questions. It postulates a self divided by repression and defended by resistance. The self is driven by dangerous or unacceptable desires, wishes, and fantasies. These are repressed and withdrawn from consciousness. When the individual approaches the territory of the unconscious repressed, s/he experiences resistance. In the analytic situation the unconscious repressed self is encouraged to emerge. Resistance is encountered by patient and analyst. The resistance is interpreted and, as its meaning becomes apparent, tends to dissolve. The patient thus becomes self-conscious—aware of the self that has been repressed and of how (the defensive operations through which) repression has been maintained. The territory of the conscious self is enlarged, that of the repressed self is diminished. Internal alienation is, to a greater or lesser extent, overcome.

So long as the classical position is unquestioningly accepted, the analyst has, in principle, a kind of self-certainty. The analyst's role is clearly defined and recognizable, at least to the analyst her/himself, beneath its multiform transference transmutations. But this position has been challenged, and the conceptions of the self appropriate to patient and analyst have become correspondingly less well defined.

In Kleinian/object relations theory, the interpretive focus tends to shift away from the triad of drive–repression–resistance to the process of interaction in the patient's inner world. The analytic consulting room, via the transference, is the inner world externalized. One then asks: Who is doing what to whom, by what means, and with what associated feelings? The patient's various self–other representations are more likely to be an object of attention than in the instance of classical theory and practice, and the analyst must monitor not only what comes into her/his mind in response to the patient, but also into *whose mind* it is coming.

Despite the orthodox psychoanalytic hostility to Kleinian psychoanalysis, the Kleinian/object relational position does not fundamentally alter the psychoanalytic situation. Both orthodox and Kleinian variants of psychoanalytic theory guide the analyst toward the transference interpretation of the patient's intrapsychic conflicts. By contrast Kohut's self psychology does involve a radically revised conception of psychoanalytic work. This is not because the self and narcissistic transference formations become major foci of interpretation. In this regard self psychology simply adds a dimension to classical psychoanalytic theory, as did object relations theory before it. The critical point is rather that, in self psychology, the self is not self-formative. The self is formed from the outside in, as a result of empathic or unempathic parental response to needs. By contrast, in classical theory and most versions of object relations theory, the self is largely formed from the inside out. If one takes self psychology seriously, therefore, the relationship of patient and analyst changes in at least two ways. First, the explanatory emphasis is placed upon what happens or has happened to the self, rather than on what the self, through conscious and unconscious intention, makes happen. Second, the transference phenomena that in classical and object relations theory are interpreted as derivatives of the patient's intrapsychic conflicts tend to be viewed as resulting from the analyst's empathic failure—even if what constitutes an empathic failure is determined by the transference itself.

To some extent these three theoretical positions are like the proverbial three blind men and the elephant. Each contains important elements of truth without being the whole truth; each errs in claiming to be the whole truth and nothing but the truth. Because, however, useful analytic interpretations stay close to the patient's level of conscious awareness and are usually articulated in the patient's language, the analyst may be able to develop insights derived from each position without having to confront their ultimate lack of theoretical compatibility. This was true throughout the early phases of Mr. I's analysis. Although I did not think of myself as eclectic, I had no need to probe into my own psychoanalytic identity. But when we reached the decisive point in Mr. I's self-transformation, this approach was no longer sufficient. The coherence of his emerging self depended in part upon the coherence of my interpretion of the transference situation. He needed to recognize himself not only *in* but also *as* the process of psychoanalytic self-transformation—that is, *as self-mediating*. For this purpose I required a theory of the self capable of ordering the various contradictory elements of Mr. I's experience. And I needed to be able to contain it as well. Thus the analysis became a testing ground for the self-certainty of each "consciousness"—his and mine— constituting it.

8.

By the time this point was reached Mr. I had come a long way. He had overcome the stasis in his life and the "stupor" was losing its addictive quality. He had found employment in an area that pretty well suited his interests and abilities. He had established an intimate relationship with the woman he was eventually to marry. He no longer felt so worthless or so defined by his relationship to his father.

As the analysis had progressed Mr. I had evolved a metaphorical representation of his inner world. The basic structure in it was a hollow cannonball. It was partly modeled on the room of Mr. I's childhood, partly on fantasies of a womb, and partly on the vehicle driven by Mad Max in the film *Road Warrior*. Outside the cannonball was the world of castrative men, the world of his father. Mr. I could leave the cannonball and confront the fathers. That is, he could work, to some extent assert himself and make decisions. But it made him anxious to do so. The interior of the cannonball was, by contrast, safe. Its lines were walled with the visible proofs of Mr. I's existence. For example, Mr. I kept a complete record of my bills. These proved that the analysis existed—that he was of sufficient value to me for the analysis to exist. Such things were provisions, pieces of selfhood that could be ingested if the day came when he could no longer be part of the outer world. They were also dead matter, feces, the excremental refuse of life's feast.

Mr. I was not alone inside the cannonball. He had the company of the dark-haired woman, the thinly veiled representation of the beautiful and desirable mother of his early childhood. When the world was too much with him, he could retreat to her for comfort. She would alternate between nurturing him and tormenting him sexually. Thus Mr. I was pushed into the cannonball by his fear of the castrative father and pulled into it by the allure of the nurturing–tormenting mother.

Contrary to his own opinion at the beginning of the analysis, Mr. I had discovered that he had a self. He was no longer so completely divided between the aspiration to selfhood and a life history he could not acknowledge as his own. The "cannonball self," as he termed it, joined the extremes. It had both the form and content of selfhood. To be sure, it left something to be desired. It was selfhood constituted at the level of the paranoid–schizoid position. The cannonball was his body without organs and the world outside was filled with thinly veiled desiring-machines. But it was immeasurably better than a chaotic absence of selfhood. Moreover, Mr. I was spending more time outside the cannonball. The "I" of the cannonball self was gradually getting stronger and more autonomous.

Then Mr. I was offered a job with a different company. He had to decide between remaining with his present employer, whom he experienced as a good father, or taking the new position, which seemed less secure although better paying and more exciting. The analysis became focused on the required decision: What were the various meanings of remaining with the present job or taking the new one? What would I think of him in the one case or the other?

Over a period of some weeks, Mr. I struggled to make a decision. At last he decided to remain where he was, which meant where he knew he was appreciated, where the environment was nurturing, and where his growth toward selfhood could continue. But the allure of the other job grew stronger, especially as rumors began to be heard that his company was failing and that the fortunes of the other company were on the rise. He overcame his fears and self-doubts, called the head of the other company, and said he was available. Too late! The position had been filled. Mr. I fell apart. He felt completely shattered and undone. It now seemed that his one chance for security and selfhood was gone. He had failed and the analysis had failed him. He felt like killing himself in the consulting room, as a warning to the world to avoid psychoanalysis. He was enraged, terrified, and out of control. He couldn't sleep and he couldn't work. His inner world and the real, external world had become fused and overwhelmingly confused. He felt that the little bit of self he had been able to develop had been destroyed. And it was my fault!

Mr. I was obviously in a state of intense psychic disruption. The question was, why? Two mutually exclusive explanations suggested themselves. Along the lines of self psychology, Mr. I's breakdown would be interpreted as the product of a defective self structure. Despite the compensatory work of the analysis, the weakness of his mother and the assaults of his father had left Mr. I with deficits in the area of autonomous functioning. He had been called upon to make a decision he was not up to, he hated himself for being so weak, and he was furious at me for not making him stronger. I had let him down, as had his mother before me (his most bitter reproaches were delivered to me by telephone on Mother's Day). Our task was therefore to work through the disappointment and anger, until his self could be restored to some semblance of its previous order.

This view fit the manifest facts, especially the *affective* facts, of the matter. It conformed to Mr. I's expressed belief that he had a weak self and would always need propping up. At a minimum, however, the issues of selfhood were more complex. Mr. I had attempted to use what he termed "cannonball thinking" to make the decision. But cannonball thinking was premised upon a contradiction: The cannonball was created to protect and nourish his self, yet the imperative of its organization was self-denial. The cannonball said, "Stay inside of me and you'll be safe; I will take care of your needs." But Mr. I needed to be an autonomous self, to be strong and self-assertive. Cannonball thinking imposed upon Mr. I the necessity of *trying to realize his interests by negating them.* His inability to make the job decision revealed this contradiction, the fatal flaw of the cannonball self. In his rage he smashed it. It then seemed to him that he had no self at all, that the analysis had betrayed him, tricked him into destroying his only possible way of being in the world.

Once the crisis is seen as the product of an internal contradiction— of cannonball thinking—the second way of interpreting the situation comes into focus. The smashing of the cannonball was not an externally caused shattering of a weak self, but rather the emergence of the protoself, the potential self, that the cannonball suppressed and denied. With the analysis as midwife, Mr. I was giving birth to himself. It was a condition of becoming himself, however, that all the ghosts of his past walk again. Consequently the future appeared to him in the form of the past. This did not signify the defeat of the analysis. It meant, rather, that for the first time the battle for selfhood had been truly joined. But—and this was the crucial point—the struggle came without assurances of victory. Mr. I would determine his destiny for himself.

If one compares these two conceptualizations of Mr. I's situation, it is apparent that, although they are not compatible, the second subsumed the facts upon which the first is based. It also permitted the specific interpretations suggested by the first, but it was not limited to them. Rather it contained them within a problematic of struggle. This did not guarantee its validity. It might have been a countertransference fantasy, an un-self-conscious mirroring of Mr. I's unrealizable desire for psychic freedom. No certainty was possible on this score. The truth or falsity of the position would have to be demonstrated in practice.

In the event, I framed particular interpretations of Mr. I's situation with the general conception that he was deeply involved in a dialectical process of self-transformation. I communicated this conception to him, substantially as I have presented it here. He needed, I believed, to be self-conscious of the struggle he was waging. The two sides of his personality congealed in the cannonball self, the aspiraton to autonomous selfhood and the self negatively defined by interaction with his parents, had split apart. The negatively defined self was now visible as never before. He needed to be able to experience the strength of his aspiration to selfhood as well. This meant that he had to recognize both the creation and the destruction of the cannonball as his own action. Only if he could experience his subjectivity in his negated selfhood and in the negating of that self-negation would he be able to claim all of himself for himself.

Gradually, painfully, Mr. I began to see the job decision as the enactment of a transference drama. Before he turned down the job and was then turned down, it represented the world of his father. Self-assertion in that world meant castration, according to the symbolic equation penis = self. Once the job was irretrievably lost, its meaning was inverted. Mr. I now saw it as the one place where he could be secure and nurtured. It was the lost paradise of union with the Unchangeable Being. More concretely, it represented the perfect mother, with whom he could be the perfect son, and from whom he was now permanently cut off. Not taking the job was an act of autocastration. And I, the analyst, was a replication of his weak mother, whose lack of confidence in him had ruined him. Here, in short, was the experience of the

Unhappy Consciousness except that, within the transference, I had failed to perform adequately the role of mediating minister.

9.

If Mr. I's alienation from the ideal union of mother and son is a variation on the theme of the Unhappy Consciousness, the paternal dimension of the transference was an enactment of lordship and bondage. His father's actual relationship to him had been extremely narcissistic. He demanded that Mr. I satisfy his, the father's, needs, including his need to see in Mr. I a mirror of himself. Manifestly Mr. I rejected the role that had been thrust upon him. But unconsciously he was his father's bondsman. He lived in terror of his father the castrating monster, and of being his father the ruined, weak, castrated monster. He was, moreover, deeply ashamed of his bondage, and he was in an ongoing state of indirect rebellion against it. Nonetheless he served his lord and master. His boss at work, who formerly had seemed to be a good father, took on the guise of his weak, alcoholic father. Mr. I hated working for him. He felt like he was on a sinking ship with a drunken captain. Worst of all, he had been thrown a life preserver and had refused it. How could he be so stupid, so self-destructive? How could I have permitted him to destroy himself?

I offered him two answers to this question. Within the transference (and as noted above), I was his weak and frightened mother, who had not supported him in the assertion of his manhood. His experience of analysis as destructive was therefore comprehensible. But analysis was destructive in another sense as well: Between us we had shattered the cannonball. The cannonball had functioned to contain and limit the effects of the emotional reality he was now experiencing. But this had always been his world. He had lived his life in the fear of being overwhelmed by it. The cannonball was based on that fear. It had been necessary for his emotional survival when he was growing up. But, as we had seen in the instance of the job decision, it was self-limiting. It had broken down and the outer world had become flooded with its contents. As painful as he found this to be, it gave him the possibility of mastering the psychical reality that had always been his master.

10.

Mr. I's struggle for himself was painful and protracted. I will note two moments in it.

From early on in the analysis Mr. I had formed the fantasy of a white room where he could be purified, healed, and made strong. This was another version of redemption through union with the Unchangeable Being, of magical rebirth through infinite maternal solicitude and love. The fantasy was now connected to the idea of psychiatric hospitalization. This connection derived from the fact that Mr. I sometimes had been forced to institutionalize his father. He now felt as crazed, scared, and destroyed as his father, and so he considered the possibility of hospitalizing himself. One morning he drove to the hospital. Then he drove away. He had confronted himself with his worst fear, namely, that his father was right, that the two of them were just the same. But he found within himself the will to struggle on. Whatever the cost, he was determined to be himself, not his father.

From this time, Mr. I began to reinternalize the elements of himself he had projected into the external situation. Then came a second important moment of self-affirmation. He was in a theater watching a movie when he had what he described in his ironical fashion as "a little epiphany." It was actually true: The forces of the past, especially his relationship with his father, had prevented him from taking the job. What we had discovered in the analysis was *him*, not just a hypothetical way of looking at him. The transference drama that had unfolded around the job offer was really the story of his life.

11.

Through his psychoanalytic labor, Mr. I was coming to have a "mind of his own." As in the case of the Hegelian bondsman, this truth was being established through a process of self-objectification and resubjectification, of alienation and the supersession of alienation. This was most dramatically demonstrated in the transference enactment described above; but in a less intense way, it characterized the analysis from first to last. Step by step, Mr. I appropriated lost dimensions of his selfhood. These losses originated, as the self psychologists emphasize, in the psychopathogenic environment created by his parents. But their world had become his. His own desires, his vital energies, his capacity for love and hate, had been formed (deformed) through interaction with them. These patterns of interaction, with the associated affects, constituted his inner world. The full flowering of the transference transposed the inner world into the external one. The opposition between self-aspiration and self-alienation contained and disguised by the cannonball was then starkly, painfully, revealed. Mr. I was faced with the necessity of mediating the extremes if he were to become more nearly self-determining. He proved equal to the task.

12.

At the beginning of this chapter we considered the relationship between psychoanalytic practice and social reality. The comparison between Mr. I's experience and that of Hegelian self-consciousness permits a further comment.

Mr. I's experience supports the claim that clinical psychoanalysis shares with the fourth chapter of *The Phenomenology* and with Marxist praxis the telos of freedom, that is, that it is most of all a process of self-emancipation. Hence it also accords with Habermas' characterization of psychoanalysis as an emancipatory praxis. The freedom sought in psychoanalytic experience should not, however, be confused with political freedom. It is both more limited and more complete.

In the former regard, psychoanalytic experience has the same relationship to politics that self-certainty has to spiritual life (history and culture) in *The Phenomenology*. Hegel states the point this way:

> Spirit [the historical world] is . . . the self-supporting, absolute, real being. All previous shapes of consciousness [Consciousness, Self-Certainty, Reason] are abstract forms of it. They result from Spirit analysing itself, distinguishing its moments, and dwelling for a while with each. This isolating of those moments *presupposes* Spirit itself and subsists therein; in other words, the isolation exists only in Spirit which is a concrete existence. (1807, p. 264)

Self-certainty is the moment of being-for-self, of the relationship of one self to another. It is reached by abstracting from the totality of social interaction and is comprehended or concretized by being reabsorbed as a moment or aspect of the social order. The same can be said of psychoanalytic experience. Both patient and analyst are members of a given social order. They create a microcosm, a domain of interaction in which, to a greater or lesser extent, the interests and conflicts of interest of the macrocosm are suspended. Thus they are able to give their full attention to the project of individual self-liberation—but only to individual self-liberation. The freedom they create extends to but not beyond the point at which social reality has been bracketed.

In the latter regard, the psychoanalytic experience of mutual recognition and intersubjective freedom transcends the limits of political life. Here I have in mind a parallel to Hegel's portrayal of evil and forgiveness. Evil and forgiveness is the ultimate moral issue. It arises at the end of the treatment of spiritual life, when the phenomenological consciousness has moved beyond the alienation and conflict of political and cultural experience; and it helps to effect the transition to the sphere of religion.

Once again, two selves confront each other, the one as judge and the other as evil-doer. Thus we have the authentic moral sequel to lordship and bondage. The evil-doer asks for forgiveness, but "his confession is not an abasement, a humiliation, a throwing-away of himself in relation to the other . . ." (*ibid.*, p. 405). To the contrary: The sinner recognizes in his judge a sinner like himself; he seeks compassion, true mutual recognition. It then falls upon the judge to find within himself the evil-doer, so that in accepting the confession of the other he is just as much making the confession himself. In this "reciprocal recognition" there is at last "reconciliation" and true self-sameness.

There may be moments in political life that approach the experience of evil and forgiveness. But these are the exceptions, not the rule. In analyzing politics we properly approach it from the direction of lordship and bondage. To characterize politics in moral terms is, unfortunately, to dissemble. If an analysis is successful, however, there may come a time when patient and analyst can experience the pain they have inflicted on each other with mutual forgiveness—and, in that forgiveness, with mutual gratitude. In this instance morality is not dissemblance.

Thus *The Phenomenology* helps us to situate the clinical encounter within the manifold of social life. On the one hand, the psychoanalytic struggle for freedom and self-certainty leaves the structures of political domination unchanged. Like the fourth chapter of *The Phenomenology*, it is prepolitical. On the other, it undermines internalized and moralized structures of domination and, in this symbolic way, stands in a critical relationship to the political world that encompasses it. Sometimes it even enables its participants to experience each other as persons instead of part-objects and to repair the damage that the one has inflicted on the other. In this sense, it is postpolitical.

The last point implies, among other things, that psychoanalytic knowledge is not directly or immediately political knowledge. When patient and analyst uncover the relationship of lordship and bondage in the transference, they learn something important about domination. But because the conflict of objective and collective interests that structures political life has been bracketed, neither they nor we can move directly from this understanding to political knowledge. Political conflict may creep into the consulting room, as in the instance of the bureaucratic or institutional misuse of an ostensibly therapeutic relationship; and it is always there in the background, in the social character and class/group formations that structure individual selfhood. But at its best, clinical psychoanalysis is not a political experience. Hence the knowledge derived from it is not political, although it does have political implications.

CHAPTER 10

Taking the Cure

1.

When we emerge from the clinical consulting room and enter again upon the public stage, the social conflicts bracketed by the psychoanalytic compact likewise re-emerge. Conflicts of interest and relationships of domination, which are transferential fantasies in the one setting, are substantial realities in the other.[1] Conversely, the mutuality of interests that constitutes the psychoanalytic relationship is largely an ideological distortion of political ones.

Sometimes psychoanalysts, accustomed as they are to the peculiar illumination of the consulting room, see only fantasies and transferences where others see interests and ideologies. If they do not counter this reductionistic inclination with a willingness to learn from political experience, they will find themselves denying the objectivity of political oppositions and suggesting unrealistic therapeutic resolutions for political conflicts.

On the other hand, although politics is not a therapeutic process, it does tend to be a psychopathological one. Psychoanalysts are rarely mistaken when they see transferential relationships and, especially, group fantasies in the political world; they err only in leaving out of account the objective determinants of these pathologies.

As we know, orthodox Marxists err in the opposite fashion. They are habituated to the light of the objective world and so have difficulty perceiving its psychological shadows. Their eyes are sharp and subtle enough to pierce the gloom of factories and sweatshops; but they tend not to see the ghosts and goblins of desire hidden inside the machines.

No doubt these mirrored portraits are overdrawn or, if not overdrawn, outworn. We have traveled too far down the road of theoretical integration to go back to a naive and unmediated antithesis. But our time

389

spent in the clinical environment serves to remind us that an unmediated joining of psychoanalysis and Marxism is equally naive. Even if we have succeeded in constructing a theoretical groundwork and a modality of social analysis in which the "either/or" relationship between the theories has been adequately sublated (dialectically resolved), clinical and political practice retain their autonomy. There can and should be a movement back and forth between them—a movement both in theory and in practice. But politics cannot be therapy and therapy should not be politics.

How, then, to heal political wounds?

2.

The Marxist and psychoanalytic-marxist answer to this question is political transformation. "Political" is used here in its relatively totalizing sense to include both the mode of social production in general and activity at the level of public institutions in particular. And because the political is linked to the aim of transformation, it locates us within a field of thought and action signified by the familiar terms "state" and "revolution."

We will begin with Hegel's theory of the state, as articulated in his *The Philosophy of Right* (1821), and this for two reasons. First, we will find that Hegel's political philosophy retains its interpretive value down to our own time. In crucial respects we recognize our political selves in it. Second, the critique of Hegelian political philosophy is the theoretical point of origin of Marxist praxis. Here, therefore, we locate the dividing of the ways between liberal and radical political theory, the beginning of the path along which we are still traveling.

Next we will turn to Marx's *The Eighteenth Brumaire of Louis Bonaparte* (1852; hereafter *The Eighteenth Brumaire*). In part we will find in it a continuation of Marx's critique of Hegel and of the modern state. It also will provide a concrete demonstration of the utility of class analysis for understanding political processes. And it is strikingly psychological, indeed almost psychoanalytic, and this despite Marx's antipathy to psychology. Most of all it will permit us to take up the problematics of revolutionary movement, including the knotty issues of true and false consciousness.

Finally, we will turn our attention directly to our own times, the twilight of modernity, and an anxious age if ever there was one.

3.

Here is another formulation of the problem.

Hegel presents us with an image of the modern state cloaked in robes of virtue. Marx strips away this disguise, conceptually and concretely.

Just as in the critique of political economy, here, too, Marx reveals a war of all against all and a relationship of domination beneath the appearance of freedom and mutual recognition. Bonapartism gives the lie to Hegelian and liberal notions of sovereignty. It is the psychotic kernel concealed within the politically rational shell.

Thus Marx views the modern state, both in its usual and degenerated forms, as a disease. He offers us proletarian praxis as a remedy. We concur in the diagnosis, but entertain some doubts about the efficacy of the cure.

4.

And one more.

A man, while in Rome, boasted that he had performed a mighty leap in Rhodes. He was told, "*Hic* Rhodus, *hic* saltus": Here is Rhodes, here's your jump. Don't tell tall tales; prove it in the here and now.

Hegel cites this proverb in the preface to *The Philosophy of Right*, He then comments that it is "just as absurd to fancy that a philosophy can transcend its contemporary world as it is to fancy that an individual can overleap his own age, jump over Rhodes" (1821, p. 11). Yet philosophy is not the counsel of despair. For with "hardly an alteration" the proverb would run, "Hier ist die Rose, hier tanze: here is the rose, dance here!" The Rosicrucians, from whom Hegel is borrowing, see a rose in the cross, the resurrection and salvation in the moment of the crucifixion. In like fashion philosophy permits us to "recognize reason as the rose in the cross of the present and thereby to enjoy the present . . ." (*ibid.*, p. 12). "*What is rational is actual and what is actual is rational*" (*ibid.*, p. 10). There is no need, in the Sartrean sense, to go beyond the world as it exists.

Marx, by contrast, wishes to go beyond the existing world. Yet he, too, believes that rationality equals reality, and so finds a rose of his own in the cross of the present.

We, on the other hand, see neither crosses nor roses—only Rhodes, and the imperatives of project and praxis.

A. Political Perversion

1.

Hegel considered the modern state and its philosophical reflection to be a remedy for ancient political ills. This position is developed most fully in *The History of Philosophy* (1892). The context is an analysis of *The Republic*. For Hegel, *The Republic* is the paradigmatic work of Greek political philosophy (see also Pelczynski, 1984b, p. 57). He argues that its central construct, Callipolis, is not a "chimera," an unreality, a mere "ought" having no practical relationship to actual Athenian political life. To the contrary: "The main thought which forms the groundwork of Plato's Republic is the same which is to be regarded as the principle of the common Greek morality . . . ," namely, unreflective ethical life, in which the individual citizen is "moved to action by respect and reverence for the institutions of the state . . ." rather than by autonomous moral deliberation (Hegel, 1892, Vol. 2, p. 98). The latter, the "principle of subjective freedom," is a "later growth," the "principle of our modern days of culture" (*ibid.*, p. 99). But it "entered into the Greek world . . . as the principle of the destruction of Greek state-life." Hence Plato, who grasped the underlying reality of Greek ethical life, excludes from his Republic "freedom of conscience, according to which every individual may demand the right of following out his own interests" (*ibid.*).

According to Hegel, Plato's exclusion of subjective freedom is achieved by the fact that in the *Republic* "all aspects in which particularity as such has established its position . . . are dissolved in the universal,—all men simply rank as man in general" (*ibid.*, p. 109). Three institutional arrangements secure this immediate identification of individuals with the universal. First, Plato "does not allow individuals to choose their own class," but rather has the guardians place them into the class for which they are suited. By contrast, in the modern world individuals are free to determine their own vocations, hence also their class positions, on the basis of inclination and choice. Second, Plato "abolished in his state the principle of private property" (*ibid.*, p. 110). "Personal property is a possession which belongs to me as a certain person, and in which my person as such comes into existence, into reality; on this ground Plato excludes it." Third, Plato abolishes marriage "because the family is nothing but an extended personality, a relationship to others of an exclusive character" (*ibid.*, p. 111). Through these measures Plato "believes he has barred the door to all the passions," and that he has safeguarded the polis from the forces undermining it. For "he knew very well that the ruin of Greek life proceeded from this, that individuals, as such, began to assert their aims, inclinations, and interests, and made them dominate over the common mind" (*ibid.*, p. 114).

Thus Hegel contends that (1) free subjectivity perverted the polis, and (2) Plato, recognizing that it was destructive of Greek ethical life, excluded it from his Republic by abolishing choice of vocation (class position), private property, and the family. Although one can question both of these contentions, I think this much might be granted. Plato linked the perversion of the political animal to the displacement of universal interests and the public good by the pursuit of particular (individual and/ or class) interests and personal advantage. The institutional arrangements and educational program of Callipolis were intended to cure this disease. Likewise, it can be argued that Aristotle, in the first book of the *Politics*, links the perverse form of acquisition (acquisition in which money becomes an end in itself instead of a means to the satisfaction of human needs) to the corruption of both the constitution of the state and the character of its citizens. True justice is perverted, relativized, by a vicious circle of insecurity, greed, and gain. Aristotle does not, to be sure, analyze political perversion in narrowly economic terms. Nonetheless he, like Plato, recognizes the corruptive influence of free subjectivity (self-interested activity) when it is conjoined to the unlimited pursuit of wealth.

2.

The diagnosis of the political disease by Hegel and his philosophical forebears is, if not identical, at least convergent. The conceptions of treatment are, however, widely divergent. We will leave the dispute between Plato and Aristotle to one (the classical) side. For against them both, Hegel argues that in the modern state the unlimited pursuit of wealth is constitutive rather than corruptive of civic virtue—private interests and passions serve rather than undermine ethical life.

"The principle of modern states," Hegel contends, "has prodigious strength and depth because it allows the principle of subjectivity to progress to its culmination in the extreme of self-subsistent particularity, and yet at the same time brings it back to the substantive unity and so maintains this unity as the principle of subjectivity itself" (1821, p. 161). As we have seen, in Hegel's view Plato could secure ethical universality only by eliminating the mediating institutions and practices through which free subjectivity and self-interest could be expressed, that is, class mobility, private property, and private family life. The modern state, however, secures its universality through the incorporation of precisely these mediating institutions and practices. Civil society, the realm of self-interested economic action, becomes differentiated from the family, on the one hand, and the political state, on the other. Particularity is given full rein within its own sphere but, limited to that sphere, it serves to constitute rather than to corrupt the ethical life of the state.

One might think from these statements that Hegel was blind to the dark side of modernity, but this is not the case. He was, in fact, an acute observer of capitalist development, and from early on he recognized the alienation and dehumanization that accompany it (see also Avineri, 1972;

Benhabib, 1984; Plant, 1980, 1984; Riedel, 1984; Schmidt, 1981). In the 1802/1804 "Philosophy of Spirit" he comments that man saves himself labor through the use of machines. But "this deceit that he practices against nature . . . takes its revenge upon him; what he gains from nature, the more he subdues it, the lower he sinks himself" (Hegel, 1802/ 1804, p. 247). His own laboring becomes more machine-like and the value of his labor diminishes. Money comes to embody the universality of need and labor, so that need and labor "form on their own account a monstrous system of community and mutual interdependence in a great people; a life of the dead body, that moves itself within itself, one which ebbs and flows in its motions blindly, like the elements, and which requires continual strict dominance and taming like a wild beast" (*ibid.*, p. 249). This line of analysis is sustained in the 1805/1806 "Philosophy of Spirit," with the additional comment that modern industry creates both great wealth and severe poverty; and this "inequality between wealth and poverty, this need and necessity, lead to the utmost dismemberment of the will, to inner indignation and hatred" (Rauch, 1983, p. 140). It was clear to him, however, that there was no turning back of the economic clock, just as there was no possibility of suppressing the principle of subjective freedom that was so closely linked to a market economy.

3.

How, then, to substantiate the claim that the modern state can both contain and put to good use these destructive tendencies?

Hegel's answer, as put forward in *The Philosophy of Right*, takes the form of a dialectical unfolding of social relationships. He begins from the presupposed notion of the free will, which is displayed objectively in the form of abstract right (property, contract, and wrong) and subjectively in the form of morality (purpose and responsibility, intention and welfare, good and conscience). The former establishes the concept of the person, a will that secures its objectivity and freedom through the possession of property, and that grants recognition to and receives recognition from other persons through the alienation of property in contractual relationships. Abstract right preserves much of the content of natural law theory, along with a critical subsumption of Roman law into the concept of right. Morality is partly the critical appropriation of Kantian morality, partly a consideration of free subjectivity abstracted from the totality of ethical life. Ethical life, in turn, consists of the family, civil society, and the state, the social institutions of which abstract right and morality are elements.

4.

The family is treated as "ethical mind in its natural or immediate phase" (Hegel, 1821, p. 110). Its essence is love. Love is a "feeling," and so something merely "natural" (*ibid.*, p. 261). But at the level of feeling, it is a further development of the process of recognition: Love is "the consciousness of my unity with another, so that I am not in selfish isolation but win my self-consciousness only as the renunciation of my independence and through knowing myself as the unity of myself with another and of the other with me" (*ibid.*). The family begins with marriage, conceived of as an ethical bond and not a mere contract, proceeds through the use and preservation of family property and capital, and eventuates in the having and rearing of children.

Rudolf Siebert (1980) claims that according to "Hegel's social ethics, the truth of a more rational and freer marriage and family type of the post-bourgeois world consists in the dialectical unity of marital decision and sexual inclination," in which "marital decision no longer represses sexual inclination" as in the ancient world, and "sexual inclination no longer explodes marital decision" as in bourgeois modernity (p. 208).

A closer look at the matter undermines any such claim. Although the home is ostensibly the realm of sexual desire transformed into ethical feeling, of love as a relationship of mutual recognition, men and women do not function as equal marital partners. Men think, women feel; men are "powerful and active," women are "passive and subjective"; men "correspond to animals, while women correspond to plants because their development is more placid and the principle that underlies it is the rather vague feeling of unity" (Hegel, 1821, p. 263). Which is to say, Hegel gives us precisely that sentimentalized view of women and the bourgeois nuclear family, of the modern version of patriarchy, that feminist scholarship has done so much to debunk. He dresses it up in the robes of mutual recognition, but what could be more bourgeois than that?

5.

Consequently it comes as no surprise when Hegel claims that the family's boundaries are the limits of a woman's world, while men are meant to transcend those limits and step forth from the family into the public realm. A woman "has her substantive destiny in the family, and to be imbued with family piety is her ethical state of mind," but a man "has his actual substantive life in the state, in learning, and so forth, as well as in labour and struggle with the external world and with himself . . ." (*ibid.*, p. 114). The imperative of self-development as well as the need to earn a livelihood carry him into civil society.

The concept of civil society is the key to Hegel's theory of the state. Civil society is "the world of ethical appearance" (*ibid.*, p. 122), where "ethical life is split into its extremes and lost . . ." (*ibid.*, p. 267). Free subjectivity is taken to its limit and the narrowest of self-interests holds sway. Yet in the pursuit of their individual ends men come to a recognition of universal interests. Beginning as economic agents, as "bourgeois" (*ibid.*, p. 127), they end as citizens. Moreover, Hegel argues, civil society contains ethical universality within itself. It consists of three subsystems: the system of needs, work activity, and social classes (including the "universal class" of civil servants); the administration of justice as the regulatory principle of civil transactions, as abstract right now recognized as law; and the police (public authority) and corporations, which together educate economic actors in their civil responsibilities, aggregate them into consciously organized social units, and compensate for the unavoidable excesses and failings of a competitive economy.

We see, then, that the state does not impose itself upon civil society from above but is rather operative in it all along. The family, too, is a constituent of the state in this extended sense, and it plays its part in preparing individuals for political participation. The state is "the end immanent within . . . [the family and civil society], and its strength lies in the unity of its own universal end and aim with the particular interest of individuals, in the fact that individuals have duties to the state in proportion as they have rights against it" (*ibid.*, p. 161). It is evident here that Hegel uses the concept of the state in a double sense, that is, that he distinguishes the political state from the state as the immanent universality of ethical life. In the former sense, the state is differentiated into various powers (Legislative, Executive, and Crown) that are mutually constitutive rather than mutually exclusive or merely "balanced." Hegel does not deny that there can be conflict between and within the powers of the state. But it "is one of the most important discoveries of logic that a specific moment which, by standing in an opposition, has the position of an extreme, ceases to be such and is a moment in an organic whole by being at the same time a mean" (*ibid.*, p. 197). The powers of the state must be conceived as mutually mediative. Indeed, even the state in the extended sense can be conceived as a process of logical mediation. In the version of his logic to be found in *The Encyclopaedia of the Philosophical Sciences* Hegel claims that "the state is a system of three syllogisms" (Wallace, 1904):

(1) The Individual or person, through his particularity or physical or mental needs (which when carried out to their full development

give civil society), is coupled with the universal, i.e. with society, law, right, government. (2) The will or action of the individuals is the inter-mediating force which procures for these needs satisfaction in society, in law, etc., and which gives to society, law, etc. their fulfilment and actualisation. (3) But the universal, etc., that is to say the state, govern-ment, and law, is the permanent underlying mean in which the indi-viduals and their satisfaction have and receive their fulfilled reality, inter-mediation, and persistence. (p. 340)

Presumably the logic of mediation could be extended to include the fam-ily. States in this broad sense, as self-mediating ethical totalities within which the political state functions as the integrative moment, are (we might add) the real historical actors. History parades before us a succes-sion of states which, through internal and external conflict, constitute the great march of freedom through the world.

If Shlomo Avineri (1972) is correct—and I think he is—Hegel has here propounded the "theory of the modern state." The state is the realiza-tion of the free will. Within it the "I" takes on the successive meanings of person, subjective agent, family member, economic agent, and citizen. The self finds its freedom in the life of the state. The state itself is a com-plex, internally structured organization, replete with private property, private families, a capitalist market economy, social classes and class mobility, state regulatory agencies, a state bureaucracy, parliamentary institutions and electoral politics, constitutionally protected rights, etc.

What Marx wrote in 1844 remains true today: "German *philosophy of right and of the state* [i.e., *The Philosophy of Right*] is . . . *al pari* with the *official* modern times" (Marx, 1844a, p. 58).

6.

It is time for a final settling of our accounts with Hegel. We need not repeat our criticisms of his speculative and totalizing use of dialecti-cal logic. Our concern is with civil society and the state.

Following Marx's lead, we begin with the category of political medi-ation. As we have seen, Hegel portrays the interaction of powers of the state (the branches of government) as one in which extremes change places and function as mutually mediative. It is as if, Marx says,

a man were to step between two fighting men and then again one of the fighting men were to step between the mediator and the fighting man. It is the story of the man and his wife who fought, and the doc-tor who wanted to step between them as mediator, when in turn the wife had to mediate between the doctor and her husband, and the husband between his wife and the doctor. . . . One can see, it is a society which at heart is spoiling for a fight, but is too afraid of bruises to engage in a real fight. . . . (1843a, pp. 87–88)

What Hegel sees as mediation constitutive of the political state Marx sees as attenuated conflict that paralyzes it.

It might be rejoined that just because Marx sees it this way doesn't make it so. Indeed, it is possible that in given instances the powers of the state might be mutually mediative or that public life might be a realm of freedom. For example, it could plausibly be contended that in the United States, Great Britain, and a number of other states there exists, for citizens, a matching of rights and responsibilities. Further, one might interpret the relationship of citizens to each other or of the individual citizen to the state as a process of mutual recognition and so affirm, via Hegel, Aristotle's claim that we are political animals.

At the level of political process, in other words, a given state might or might not conform to Hegel's theory. The claim that the modern state solves the problem of political perversion might be sustained in some instances. But politics is a matter of substantive freedoms as well as formal ones, and, at the substantive level, the claim is a good deal harder to sustain. Moreover, the indefiniteness and contingency of the interpretive situation is reduced when we shift our attention from political process to political interests, and to the corresponding socioeconomic interests of civil society. For by his own admission, Hegel's state contains a large number of impoverished citizens who are substantively disenfranchised and who are condemned to a life of alienated labor or outright beggary. In civil society "conditions tend to multiply and subdivide needs, means, and enjoyments indefinitely" (Hegel, 1821, p. 128). At the same time, "dependence and want increase *ad infinitum*, and the material to meet these is permanently barred to the needy man because it consists of external objects with the special character of being property, the embodiment of the free will of others, and hence from his point of view its recalcitrance is absolute" (*ibid.*).

The modern state tends toward social polarization. At one end of the social scale there develops the "concentration of disproportionate wealth in a few hands"; at the other there emerges a "rabble of paupers" (*ibid.*, p. 150). The rabble are not simply poor. Although there might be poverty in nature, "against nature man can claim no right" (*ibid.*, p. 277). But in society "poverty takes the form of a wrong done to one class by another" (*ibid.*, p. 278). The poor become a rabble, in which "there is joined to poverty a disposition of mind, an inner indignation against the rich, against society, against government" (*ibid.*, p. 277). Hegel considers the possibility that charity and publically sponsored work are solutions to this problem, but he argues that the one damages the self-respect of the individual and the other intensifies the economic problem it is meant to solve. He believes that membership in corporations has an ameliorative effect, but here his arguments are unconvincing. He also comments on the role of foreign trade and colonization as outlets for surplus goods and labor. To his credit, however, he acknowledges that the resources of civil society "are insufficient to check excessive poverty and the creation of a penurious rabble" (*ibid.*, p. 150). When, therefore, we examine civil society from the perspective of the relationship between the rich and the poor, we see that the formal process of recognition involved in contracts and the alienation of property masks a substantive social antagonism and lack of mutual recognition (see also Kortian, 1984; Plant, 1980, 1984).

Thus the economic phenomena Hegel observed and commented on in his earliest versions of the philosophy of spirit remain empirically unchanged in his mature philosophy. They have been given a new locus, a determinate position within the theory. But neither in theory nor in practice does the modern state solve the problems of social justice resulting from (in Hegel's terms) the full expression of subjective freedom or (in Aristotle's) perverse acquisition. The modern state may have a kind of coherence, the coherence that accompanies the universalization of production for exchange; but according to the standard of interests, the modern state is just as perverse as ancient Athens. Indeed, one is strongly reminded of Aristotle's depiction of a polis lacking a strong middle class, in which the poor "are ignorant how to rule and only know how to obey, as if they were so many slaves," and the rich "are ignorant how to obey any sort of authority and only know how to rule as if they were masters of slaves." The result is "a state of envy on the one side and on the other contempt" (Barker, 1958, p. 181).

Beneath the show of mutual recognition we find the substance of lordship and bondage, including its familiar antipathies and antagonisms. And as Aristotle remarks, nothing could be further than this "from the spirit of friendship" on which the "temper of a political community depends" (*ibid.*).

In sum: Hegel's theory of the state properly locates us in our own time and place. But it is the problem and not the solution, the disease and not the remedy.

B. Bonapartism

1.

The Eighteenth Brumaire can be read as a continuation of Marx's critique of Hegel's political philosophy. The position he argued abstractly in his comments on *The Philosophy of Right* is argued concretely in his analysis of the Bonapartist state.

We shall see that (1) Marx fails to lay his Hegelian ghosts entirely to rest and (2) he himself teaches us how to interpret the failure.

In the latter regard, Marx offers us a virtually psychoanalytic marxist conception of ideology or false consciousness: Political uncertainty generates anxiety; we tend to repress—alienate from consciousness—painful and anxiety-producing aspects of reality. Thus we might say that false consciousness is objectively determined individual and collective psychopathology.

In the former regard, Marx wishes to limit the application of this conception to bourgeois ideology and such phenomena as Bonapartism. Conversely, he identifies the consciousness of the proletariat with his theory of history, and his theory of history with history itself. Like Hegel before him, he projectively identifies his worldview with the world itself. This is a tendency toward false consciousness within a theory of false consciousness, a tendency explicable by the theory itself.

What's sauce for the goose is sauce for the gander. As Karl Mannheim observed, "there is no reason why we should not apply to Marxism the perceptions which it itself has produced, and point out from case to case its ideological character" (Mannheim, 1936, p. 125).

2.

"Hegel remarks somewhere that all facts and personages of great importance in world history occur, as it were, twice. He forgot to add: the first time as tragedy, the second time as farce" (Marx, 1852, p. 103).

This is Marx's opening statement in *The Eighteenth Brumaire*. It expresses his intention of explaining the revolution of 1848 through comparison with the revolution of 1789. The comparison and the Hegelian reference were suggested to him by Engels. On December 3, 1851, the day after Louis Bonaparte's successful *coup d'état*, he wrote to Marx:

> But after what we saw yesterday, the people cannot be relied upon for anything and it really seems as if old Hegel in his grave were acting as World Spirit and directing history, ordaining most conscientiously that it should all be unrolled twice over, the first time as a great tragedy, the second time as a wretched farce. (Marx & Engels, 1975c, p. 56)

Engels, and Marx after him, would not win Hegel's approval for their appropriation of his idea. Hegel had actually remarked that "a political revolution is sanctioned in men's opinion, when it repeats itself. . . . By repetition that which at first appeared merely a matter of chance and contingency, becomes a real and ratified existence" (1956, p. 313). The second event is as necessary and serious as the first. But Engels and Marx do not accept this sanguine judgment. The second event is not the ratification but rather the caricaturization of the first.

Although Marx's portrayal of the first French revolution as a tragedy and the second one as a farce is partly a matter of aesthetic judgment and partly one of polemical intent, it also has a theoretical or historical content. The earlier revolution, Marx contends, was historically progressive, both because it performed the task of "unchaining and setting up modern *bourgeois* society" (1852, p. 104) and because it moved "along an ascending line":

> The rule of the *Constitutionalists* is followed by the rule of the *Girondins* and the rule of the *Girondins* by the rule of the *Jacobins*. Each of these parties relies on the more progressive party for support. As soon as it has brought the revolution far enough to be unable to follow it further, still less to go ahead of it, it is thrust aside by the bolder ally that stands behind it and sent it to the guillotine. (*ibid.*, p. 124)

A new social order has been ratified by these political events and the events themselves, that is, the revolutionary process, mirror this fact. The later revolution, by contrast, is politically regressive: "Instead of *society* having conquered a new content for itself, it seems that the *state* only returned to its oldest form, to the shamelessly simple domination of the saber and the cowl" (*ibid.*, p. 106). Correspondingly the revolutionary process moves along a "descending line." Each "party kicks back at the one behind, which presses upon it, and leans upon the one in front, which pushes backwards. No wonder that in this ridiculous posture it loses its balance and, having made the inevitable grimaces, collapses with curious capers" (*ibid.*, p. 124). Each party, in other words, attempts to push a more advanced party out of the way, while simultaneously protecting itself against even more retrograde political factions. Parliamentary cretinism is the result, and Bonaparte is able to take power.

Yet the revolution of 1848 with its Bonapartist dénouement is not historically meaningless. Although Bonaparte is an unprincipled adventurer who is motivated only by personal passion and material self-interest, he is not the master of his own destiny. An Hegelian hero *manqué* and *malgré lui*, he draws his vocation "from a concealed fount . . . from that inner Spirit, still hidden beneath the surface, which, impinging on the outer world as on a shell, bursts it in pieces . . ." (Hegel, 1956, p. 30). Bonaparte's exercise of executive power strips "the halo from the entire state machinery, profanes it and makes it at once loathsome and ridiculous" (Marx, 1852, p. 197). Hence what appears to be an historical movement in a circle is actually a process of social transformation:

The revolution is thorough. . . . First it perfected parliamentary power, in order to be able to overthrow it. Now that it has attained this, it perfects *executive power*, reduces it to its purest expression, isolates it, sets it up against itself as the sole target, in order to concentrate all of its forces of destruction against it. And when it has done this second half of its preliminary work, Europe will leap from its seat and exultantly exclaim, "Well burrowed, old mole!" (*ibid.*, p. 185).

The bourgeoisie discredits parliamentary power, Bonaparte discredits executive power, and the stage is set for the demise of state power altogether. The second French revolution, for all its farcical appearance, is just as world-historical as the first.

Here, then, we have a clash of world views. Marx interprets the second French revolution as the birth throes of socialism. Hegel was wrong. The reconstitution of the state renders the earlier constitution null and void. But Hegel, not intimidated by Marx's twisting of the historical dialectic, might well rejoin that the second French revolution did in fact ratify the first. The monarchy, which rose from its grave during the post-Napoleonic period, was conclusively laid to rest in 1851. The modern state, twice born, was now securely of this world.

There is yet another possibility. One might contend that the second Napoleon completed the work begun by the first—that between them they constructed the prototype of modern absolutism.

3.

If *The Eighteenth Brumaire* contained only a radicalized Hegelian interpretation of the state and revolution, it would not occupy its present position in our inquiry. But it is a twice-told tale, and the second telling is quite different from the first.

"Men make their own history," Marx states in the second paragraph of the text, "but they do not make it just as they please; they do not make it under circumstances chosen by themselves, but under circumstances directly encountered, given and transmitted by the past" (*ibid.*, p. 103). On the one hand, this proposition establishes limits and constraints upon subjectivity and free will. Neither individuals nor collectivities are unconstrained in their choices of action, bourgeois notions of individual autonomy to the contrary notwithstanding. On the other, it is not History or the *Weltgeist* that makes history, but human beings themselves.

In other words, history cannot be adequately interpreted from an epistemological position of either free will or mechanical determinism. It is rather to be understood as an interplay between freedom and necessity, a process in which individuals and collectivities engage and seek to transform the circumstances that have formed them.

We might also say that social circumstances constitute a resistance to the realization of both interests and desires. This resistance, Marx contends, is subjective as well as objective. The mode of production into which human individuals are born and which constitutes their field of action has an ideological as well as a political economic dimension:

> [The] tradition of all the dead generations weighs like a nightmare on the brain of the living. And just when . . . [people] seem engaged in revolutionising themselves and things, in creating something that has never yet existed, precisely in such periods of revolutionary crisis they anxiously conjure up the spirits of the past to their service and borrow from them names, battle-cries and costumes in order to present the new scene of world history in this time-honoured disguise and this borrowed language. (*ibid.*, p. 104)

Concretely, Marx is referring to the borrowings from Roman history during the first French revolution and the borrowings from both Rome and the first revolution during the revolution of 1848. But he is making two more general points. First, the present tends to be seen through the optic of the past; habits of thought linger on even as their material foundation erodes. Second, people "anxiously conjure up the spirits of the past" when they are engaged in revolutionary action. They disguise the historically unknown in the robes of the historically familiar and thereby shield themselves from the anxiety that accompanies their actions.

The second point might be generalized even further: Uncertainty generates anxiety; anxiety activates defensive tendencies. Because political action in general and revolutionary action in particular involve high levels of uncertainty, they generate or threaten to generate correspondingly high levels of anxiety. Hence there is built into political life a tendency for people to defend against rather than to engage situational realities, a tendency that is accentuated precisely in the instance of radically transformational action.

In Marx's view, the line of argument developed in the second paragraph of *The Eighteenth Brumaire* continues the one initiated in the first. There is a dialectical logic to historical processes, but historical processes consist of human activity. Conscious activity mediates the laws of historical development. From our perspective, however, the imputation of a dialectical logic to history is extremely questionable, especially when it is attached to notions of ontological necessity and epistemological certainty—to the idea that one can know the Truth and interpret history in the light of it. To be sure, there is an intelligibility to historical processes. History is not chaotic. It consists of definite structures and patterns of development; and even its breaks, ruptures, and reversals may lead to the formation of new modalities of social interaction, sometimes even to ones in which human freedom is more adequately realized. But we refuse to make the leap from contingency to necessity, or from the piecemeal analysis of historical events to grand schemata of dialectical unification. In so doing we take our stand precisely on the grounds laid out in the second paragraph of *The Eighteenth Brumaire*. And from this position the line of reasoning initiated in the first paragraph seems to be a defense against anxiety. Marx's Hegelianism is the spirit of his philosophical past, here conjured up to defend him from the uncertainty and anxiety inherent in his choices of revolutionary action.

4.

First intermission. Marx believed that he possessed a knowledge of historical processes that was scientifically generated and demonstrably true. Forms of consciousness could be evaluated by the truth-standard of this scientific knowledge. When they deviated from or fell short of it, they were ipso facto false. In a broad sense, false consciousness could include deviations and inadequacies resulting from error or ignorance. But simple error and ignorance, which are correctable through education and experience, must be differentiated from systematic falsity, that is, forms of thought that are structured against or function to disguise the truth. At the level of political life these forms of consciousness are characterized as ideological. Revolutionary theory, which is based on scientific knowledge, thus could be differentiated from bourgeois ideology, and one then could proceed to the scientific investigation of the origins of ideology and the practical tasks of revolutionary transformation.

Because this model of historical and political knowledge did not live up to its billing, the charges of ideology that it leveled against the bourgoisie were in turn delivered against it. Eventually the very idea of a truth about human affairs and, correspondingly, the distinction between true and false consciousness, were called into question. Plato's divided line, which had been dialectically transmuted by Hegel and materialized by Marx, finally crumbled. Like Nietzsche's madman, we seemingly found ourselves in a world with neither gods nor absolutes. We became the variable measure of all things; or rather, we became the the lack of a measure for any thing. The age of the hollow men—unrestrained relativism—had arrived.

Unrestrained relativism is, however, no more satisfactory than epistemological absolutism. It begs the question of truth and falsity, and is itself a begged question. Unrestrained relativism maintains that there is no truth-claim that is valid at all times and in all places. But maintaining such a position is itself an absolute truth-claim and so self-contradictory. Hence we seem trapped between a Scylla of absolutism and a Charybdis of relativism.

The issue also might be posed this way. If all human action involves uncertainty and anxiety, all consciousness is more or less defensively distorted. Where are we then to find an undistorted consciousness, in the light of which to judge the degree of distortion? But again, if we say that all consciousness is distorted by anxiety, this statement is likewise distorted. If we are not playing the game of Epimenides the Cretan, we are once more wandering blindly through an epistemological night in which all cows are black.

Let's shift the focus. If we fall victim to false consciousness when we absolutize our claims to political knowledge, we paralyze our political will when we beg the question of distinguishing between true and false political knowledge. We throw up our hands and retreat from the political battlefield to the relative comfort of merely discursive interactions. In the former instance we defend ourselves against anxiety through the denial of uncertainty; in the latter instance we defend ourselves against anxiety by the avoidance of engaged activity.

This shift of focus implies, if not a standard of truth and falsity, at least a position from which to address the issue. The truth is to be demonstrated in practice. It cannot be known in advance, and no proof is absolutely conclusive. To establish the truth we must be able to learn from our errors, and to learn from our errors we must be able to tolerate the anxiety that accompanies uncertainty. We must be able to maintain an experimental attitude, even when there are lives in the balance.

5.

As indicated above, Marx portrays the events of 1848–1851 as a line of descent or political regression. Less advanced political positions follow more advanced ones, until we have finally returned to a caricature of Napoleon I and the Napoleonic Empire. "To the rear, march!" is the political order of the day. Further, each political position is based in the interests and way of life of a social class. Thus the socialists, who come to the fore in the initial phase of the revolution, represent the interests of the working class. The republicans represent the "people," meaning the antimonarchical bourgeoisie. The social democrats represent the petty bourgeoisie. The Party of Order, with its Legitimist (Bourbon) and Orleanist wings, represents landed property and capital, respectively. And Bonaparte, finally, represents the peasantry.

These social classes, through the agency of their political representatives and in the ideological forms appropriate to each of them, wage
political warfare on a variably defined constitutional battlefield, that is,
a battlefield where constitutional enactments and revisions are available
stratagems. For all the variation, however, the battlefield contains three
stable topographical features: parliament, the presidency, and the people.
    With the actors in their places and the stage set, we may continue.

6.

The proletariat, in Marx's account, was active only in the opening
moments of the drama. Because it played a leading role in the overthrow
of Louis Philippe in February 1848, it "impressed its stamp upon . . . [the
new régime] and proclaimed it to be a *social republic*," a political order in
which freedom must be actualized socioeconomically as well as politically (*ibid.*, p. 109). When it realized its interests were being betrayed and
its dream was slipping away, it rebelled (the June insurrection). The
uprising was brutally suppressed and the proletariat "recede[d] into the
background of the revolutionary stage" (*ibid.*, p. 110).
    It is easy enough to see in Marx's narrative of the insurrection a
version of the life and death struggle for independence and recognition,
here carried out within the relationship of lordship and bondage rather
than in a state of nature. However, we might ask: Does the proletariat,
in the course of the battle, develop a mind of its own? Thus we come to
Marx's interpretation of proletarian class consciousness.
    Marx had a double attitude toward the proletariat. On the one hand,
he viewed it as the embodiment of the project of human emancipation;
on the other, he recognized that its members were not born into the world
with an understanding of social reality and their historical destiny. He
did not believe that actual proletarian consciousness began as revolutionary class consciousness. This equation, or relationship of self-recognition,
had rather to be brought into existence. The proletariat needed to become
actually what it only was potentially. He, and other revolutionary intellectuals, had a two-fold role to play in this regard. They were to be both
teachers and organizers. They were to open the book of social reality so
that the proletariat could see itself and its situation theoretically; and they
were to facilitate political organization and aid the proletariat in developing a political form commensurate with its social interests.
    Yet Marx did not overestimate his own role in the process. History
itself was the great teacher, he believed, and the proletariat was objectively situated in such a way that it would learn its lessons—painfully,
and a bit at a time (*ibid.*, pp. 106-107):

[P]roletarian revolutions . . . criticise themselves constantly, interrupt themselves continually in their own course, come back to the apparently accomplished in order to begin again afresh, deride with unmerciful thoroughness the inadequacies, weaknesses and paltrinesses of their first attempts, seem to throw down their adversary only in order that he may draw new strength from the earth and rise again, more gigantic, before them, and recoil again and again from the indefinite prodigiousness of their own aims, until a situation has been created which makes all turning back impossible, and the conditions themselves cry out:

> Hic Rhodus, Hic Salta!
> Hier ist die Rose, hier tanze!

This is an articulation of the idea of the self-activity of the proletariat, its union of theory and practice, the process of critical self-reflection through which it comes-to-be. It is Marx's solution to the problem of recognition, here conjoined to the issue of true and false consciousness.

The solution doesn't work, and for at least three reasons. First, Marx treats a possible convergence between subject and object, consciousness and situational reality, as necessary and complete rather than contingent and partial. It may well be the case, in given instances, that oppressed people will find themselves drawn toward revolutionary action by the interplay of their interests and the manifold of events. But there is no historical instance of consciousness and circumstance coming so neatly into line with each other. And even if, when, and to the extent that such a convergence occurs, it cannot be prophesied but only projected. The transformation of contingency into inevitability is Marx's way of placing his rose on the cross of the present.

Our first criticism repeats, at a more concrete level, our objection to Marx's Hegelian determinism. Just so, it leads on to the second criticism. Although Marx acknowledges that the proletariat may not see its political way clearly in the short run, he rules out in advance the possibility that it might lose its political way in the long run. He desires, to put it another way, to grant the proletariat, and only the proletariat, an exemption from false consciousness.

There are two ways in which such an exemption might be secured. It could be argued that proletarian class interests are directly reflected into proletarian class consciousness. As society polarizes objectively, the proletariat becomes increasingly revolutionary. But why would the proletariat, alone among social classes, have such an unmediated relationship between interests and consciousness? For all other classes there is a middle term, to wit, social and psychological factors that lead to distortions of consciousness. Why not also for the proletariat? Alternatively, if we limit the source of false consciousness to anxiety—that is, if we take the combination of uncertainty and anxiety to be the predominant source of false consciousness—then it could be argued that the proletariat has no cause for alarm. Its victory and the fall of the bourgeoisie are equally inevitable. But for one thing, this presumed inevitability is the product of a residual Hegelianism. And for another, the necessity is itself hypothetical, contingent, or retrospective: If the proletariat arrives at true class consciousness and if it is politically successful, then bourgeois domination will come to an end and the socialist era will begin. The issue will no longer be in doubt and there will no longer be an occasion for political anxiety. Until then, however, contingency and uncertainty remain. Indeed, the level of uncertainty for the proletariat is uniquely high. The proletariat, and only the proletariat, must leap into the unknown, create a social order that has never yet existed, if it is to realize its interests. Hence by Marx's own argument one would conclude that the proletariat would be peculiarly prone to false consciousness—that it would be driven away from Rhodes with at least as much force as it would be driven toward it.

Third, Marx endows the proletarian movement with a kind of personal subjectivity, and a highly intellectual one at that. He does not confront the complex synchronic and diachronic relationship—the fissures as well as fusions—that constitute a mass movement.[2] He treats the movement as if it were an individual who was attempting to learn from experience, instead of a collectivity consisting of contingently connected individuals. Moreover, this composite individual is a stranger to emotional distress. It is a collective embodiment of critical or dialectical reason, more active but almost as intellectualized as Habermas' emancipatory self-reflection. It is, in short, an idealized self-projection, Marx himself writ large and emotionally unscarred.

There is a more general way of reaching the same conclusion. Marx's conception of scientific inquiry was strongly realist. Social as well as natural science discovered the truth about its object and could reflect that truth as in a mirror. Like Hegelian philosophy, it left no gap or disjunction between subject and object. Hence Marx could identify his theory of history with history itself. This was *his* act of self-recognition. The theory, in turn, prescribed a determinate role for the proletariat. As Marx stated it in *The Holy Family*, it "is not a question of what this or that proletarian, or even the proletariat as a whole, at the moment considers as its aim. It is a question of *what the proletariat is*, and what, in accordance with its *being*, it will be historically compelled to do" (Marx & Engels, 1845a, p. 37). Because eventually consciousness reflects social being, in time the proletariat will find itself in a situation of self-recognition: Proletarian class consciousness = (historical reality = Marx's theory). In good Hegelian fashion the real is the rational and the rational is the real. Only Marx takes Hegel one step further: The rational is realized in practice and the situation is accordingly transformed.

We, by contrast, recognize in Marx's trinity formula of proletarian class consciousness, historical reality, and revolutionary theory a double occlusion of subjectivity and contingency. First, social or cultural science involves a play of subjectivities. It cannot meet the criteria of certitude characteristic of the natural sciences, and even the natural sciences involve elements of subjectivity and contingency. Hence one cannot identify the theory with the reality it interprets. Second, and as argued above, even if Marx hadn't breached an important epistemological barrier, his own interpretation of false consciousness implicates the proletariat, imposes upon it a condition of struggle. Of all classes the proletariat will have to labor the hardest to have a mind of its own. There can be no guarantee that its efforts will be rewarded with success.

Thus Marx's solution to the problem of recogniton (revolutionary self-consciousness) fails. But if we accept the epistemological limits of emancipatory praxis and combine the "psychoanalytic" dimension of his theory with the programmatic one, we can reformulate the problem: How do we build a mass movement that is (1) oriented toward the realization of its interests; (2) equipped to manage the uncertainty and anxiety that accompany emancipatory praxis; and (3) capable of learning from its political experience?

7.

With the proletariat forcibly removed from the stage, we come next to the bourgeoisie and the petty bourgeoisie.

The class interests of the bourgoisie may be stated positively and negatively. Positively, the bourgeoisie aims at self-enrichment. The realization of this interest requires that politics be a means to monetary ends, that is, that the state function so as to facilitate the accumulation of capital. Hence its interests are narrow, mercenary, in a word, venal. This venality is covered over by claims of revolutionary grandeur. Negatively, the aim of the bourgeoisie is to secure its rule against and dominion over any other class, and especially to establish and protect its right to the unlimited exploitation of the labor-power of the working class. Hence its interests are particularistic. But just as its ideology serves to cover its venality in a cloak of heroic glory, so appeals to patriotic and universalistic political values disguise the particularity of its interests.

The petty bourgeoisie, Marx observes, is a *"transition class"* in which the opposed interests of the bourgeoisie and proletariat are blunted

(Marx, 1852, p. 133). Its democratic representative "imagines himself elevated above class antagonisms generally." He acknowledges that there is a privileged class, in opposition to which he claims to be the people's tribune, the spokesman for its rights and interests. But he aims at the moderation rather than the elimination of privilege and, withal, at harmonizing rather than superseding the antithesis of capital and wage labor (*ibid.*, p. 130). In practice this means that the petty bourgeoisie does not have a will of its own, no matter how much it proclaims its commitment to freedom. Bound as it is to the preservation of the bourgeois order, its democratic or even social democratic proclamations are functional components of bourgeois ideology.

Like so much of Marx's class analysis, these characterizations of class interest and ideology have retained their validity with the passage of time. This very fact, however, amounts to a critique of Marx's historical vision. Marx wanted to believe that the bourgeoisie is pushed into false consciousness not only by venality and particularity but also by the historically transitory nature of its class interests. Foresensing its doom, it anxiously blinds itself to the reality of its historical situation. Yet despite the Malthusian (and other) nightmares of its ideologists, the bourgeoisie has displayed a pronounced confidence in its ability to survive the ravages of time. This confidence might have proved unwarranted if society had polarized sharply into the rich and the poor. But new middling strata have replaced the old, and these new versions of the petty bourgoisie have quite successfully carried out the mission of mediating the socioeconomic extremes.

Leaving aside for a moment purely economic arguments, one might say that Marx left out of his account one of the structural features of lordship and bondage: house slaves.

8.

Marx may have been incorrect in foreseeing an end to the game of politics in France, but he had an acute understanding of its rules.

The first rule was that the game was played by manipulating the rules. Throughout the period under consideration, Bonaparte and the parliamentary representatives of the bourgeoisie continually attempted to reshape the constitution in their own interests. For Bonaparte this meant the abrogation of Article 45, which limited his presidency of the Republic to one term. For parliament this involved using all the means at its disposal to limit the power of the executive and to ensure that Bonaparte left office on schedule.

Bonparte won the game, parliament lost it. Indeed, parliament self-destructed. Divided by faction, it was not able to engage in the struggle with the same singleness of purpose as its presidential rival. In the end its members fell victim to *"parliamentary cretinism,* which holds all those infected by it fast in an imaginary world and robs them of all sense, all memory, all understanding of the rude external world" (*ibid.*, p. 161). Lost in their dream world, cut off from the people and even from the rest of the bourgeoisie (which was only too willing to sever its ties with its impotent and disputatious representatives), they were unable to defend thmselves against presidential attacks upon their constitutional prerogatives. They fought with Bonaparte only over secondary points, over displacements from the real issues. Then they vented their "repressed rage;" but then, too, its intensity appeared absurd (*ibid.*, p. 155). By the time Bonaparte was ready for his *coup d'état*, they had already given themselves a *coup mortel*.

Here we have an unusually good specimen of politics conducted in the paranoid–schizoid position. Bonaparte is parliament's persecutory object or Other, whose presence induces both anxiety and rage. Unable to engage this object and these feelings, parliament withdraws, becomes self-encapsulated and lost in fantasy. Having split itself off from the external object that is the source of its fears, it splits internally as well. The parliamentary house without windows is also a body without organs.

From another angle one might see parliament as a flight–fight group. The appearance of legislative work overlays its operative basic assumption, which is to flee in panic from the ghost of Napoleon I.

But Marx was not staging a psychodrama. The psychopathology of parliamentary politics reflected the contradictory conditions of bourgeois dominance. Because bourgeois social interests were defined against those of the people while its political power was derived from them, it "was compelled by its class position to annihilate, on the one hand, the vital conditions of all parliamentary power, and therefore, likewise, its own, and to render irresistible, on the other hand, the executive power hostile to it" (*ibid.*, p. 139). Bonaparte—Bonapartism—was needed to save the bourgeoisie from itself.

Not for the first time, and not for the last.

9.

If Article 45 tipped the constitutional balance in parliament's favor, the electoral laws tipped it decisively in Bonaparte's. Parliament was elected by districts, the president by direct national suffrage. Parliament exhibited "in its individual representatives the manifold aspects of the national spirit, but in the President this national spirit . . . found its incarnation" (*ibid.*, p. 117). In other words, parliament had a mediated, while the president had an unmediated, relationship with the nation, the people as a whole. An inverse version of the Hegelian sovereign, who was to be the ultimate mediator, here the president functioned as the antithesis of the process of mediation. He was the One who spoke directly for the Many and who, by so doing, silenced the parliamentary multitude.

10.

The bourgeoisie in parliament has now gone the way of the proletariat in the streets. The stage is empty save for Bonaparte.

By the time we reach the Bonapartist moment in *The Eighteenth Brumaire* we are in no danger of falling under its spell. Bonaparte himself has been reduced to decidedly human proportions and, given the parliamentary cretinism of the bourgeoisie, his successful *coup* does not seem at all miraculous or mysterious. Moreover, by providing a class analysis of Bonaparte's triumph, Marx establishes a method for criticizing so-called "great man" theories of history more generally. The appearance of greatness, which fascinates historians the way the Bonapartes of the world fascinate their followers, is an artifact of a covert process of abstraction: One first removes the structural determinants of events from the picture, so that only the individual leader remains; one then pronounces the leader to be the cause of which the event is the effect. The great man, to put it another way, is a conceptual fetish, a part endowed with the power of the whole, a politicized phallus. Marx's critical method demonstrates that he is merely an appendage of the body politic.

11.

Bonaparte's triumph represents the inability of the bourgeoisie to rule itself, on the one hand, and the political empowerment of the lumpenproletariat by the peasantry, on the other.

Marx contends that Bonaparte's immediate entourage, sometimes organizationally embodied in the Society of December 10, was drawn from the disintegrated residue of bourgeois society, the mass of "vagabonds, discharged soldiers, discharged jailbirds, escaped galley slaves, rogues, mountebanks, *lazzaroni*, pickpockets, tricksters, gamblers, *maquereaus*, brothel keepers, porters, *literati*, organ-grinders, rag-pickers, knife grinders, tinkers, beggars" that the French term *la bohème* (*ibid.*, p. 149). These unseemly minions were also infiltrated into the enormous

French bureaucracy, which thus became a Bonapartist vehicle. *L'état,
c'est ça!*

Hegel argued consistently that an unmediated relationship is a contradiction in terms. We see that he was correct. Although Bonaparte's
relationship to the French people was not electorally particularized, the
bureaucracy created a material link between president and populace.

Bonaparte and his lumpen proletarian cohort were at one end of this
great electoral and bureaucratic chain of being. The small-holding peasantry—a class at the end of its historical rope—was at the other. The
members of this class were the beneficiaries of the land reforms of
Napoleon I. By 1850, however, the freedom he gave them had become
the conditions that enslaved them. Two generations had sufficed to demonstrate the economic irrationality of small-scale peasant agriculture. Yet
historical tradition "gave rise to the belief of the French peasants in a
miracle that a man named Napoleon would bring glory back to them"
(*ibid.*, p. 188). Hence they were Bonapartist. Moreover the peasants, even
more than the bourgeoisie, were "incapable of enforcing their class
interests in their own name." Although they constituted a class insofar
as their "economic conditions of existence" separated their "mode of life,
their interests, and their culture from those of other classes," they cannot act as a political class because "their mode of production isolates them
from one another instead of bringing them into mutual intercourse." They
cannot represent themselves and, consequently, "their representative
must at the same time appear as their master" (*ibid.*, p. 187). And
because the peasantry was the largest class in France, their pseudo-
Napoleonic master became the master of society in general.

We have no trouble recognizing in Marx's depiction of Bonaparte's
success a prototype of the totalitarian régimes of our own century. The
peasantry, as it turned out, was not the only social class incapable of
becoming a political class, that was more a mass of disjoined individuals
than a self-organizing collectivity. Nor was Bonaparte's fusion of bureaucracy and elements of the lumpen proletariat historically unique—witness the rise of the Third Reich. But Marx's explanation is incomplete.
Bonaparte's appeal was not limited to the peasantry, much less the conservative peasantry; and by Marx's own acount there is an ideological,
hence also a psychological, dimension to the phenomenon. Anxiety and
illusion have yet a part to play.

12.

Second intermission. Marx employs two principal sets of metaphors
in *The Eighteenth Brumaire*. The first is the Hegelian satire, the presentation of the second revolution and the second Napoleon as farce or satyr

play. The second involves the presentation of French politics as lunacy
or insanity. We have seen various instances of the latter usage, and we
have taken them seriously; that is, we have assigned to them or assumed
for them a conceptual meaning. But we have yet to give them the textual
place they deserve. For if the second coming of Napoleon is a farce, its
author is a madman:

> The nation feels like that mad Englishman in Bedlam who fancies that
> he lives in the times of the ancient Pharoahs and daily bemoans the
> hard labour that he must perform in the Ethiopian mines as a gold
> digger, immured in this subterranean prison, a dimly burning lamp
> fastened to his head, the overseer of slaves behind him with a long
> whip, and at the exits a confused welter of barbarian mercenaries, who
> understand neither the forced labourers in the mines nor one another,
> since they speak no common language. "And all this is expected of
> me," sighs the mad Englishman, "of me, a freeborn Briton, in order to
> make gold for the old Pharoahs." "In order to pay the debts of the
> Bonaparte family," sighs the French nation. (*ibid.*, p. 105)

The French nation is mentally enslaved by Bonapartism. Historically
disoriented and deluded, it labors to line the pockets of a fantasmal
Napoleon.

Taken together, these two sets of metaphors have attracted postmodernist or deconstructionist attention. Most notably there is an essay
by Jeffrey Mehlman, who finds a "certain Freudian problematic insis-
tent within" Marx's text (1977, p. 7). A certain problematic—also "a certain exteriority," "a certain collapse," "a certain intertextual stratum," "a
certain Freud," "a certain form of laughter," "a certain parasitism,"
"a certain proliferating energy"—in a word, a certain would-be Lacanian
moment, an opening for interpretation in the mode of Derrida and
Bataille. Mehlman treats the profusion of invictive and ridicule that Marx
heaps upon Bonaparte as signifying "a break with the notion of class
representation" (*ibid.*, p. 14) and as a marker of the place where "Marx
vents his hilarity" as "History skids off course" and "dialectic is ruin-
ously squandered" (*ibid.*, p. 28). Bonapartism is the historical uncanny
or—as Terry Eagleton restates Mehlman's point—"the non-representa-
tive joker in the dialectical pack" (1981, p. 162).

As a theory of textual interpretation, deconstruction challenges the
notion of representation—that there is a signified somehow represented
by a signifier, a reality beneath the play of language. Mehlman extends
this line of criticism to politics. Bonapartism is nonrepresentational; it
involves a deconstruction of the logic of class interests.

Mehlman, it is clear, runs roughshod over the text and its author.
He is a Bonapartist critic rather than a critic of Bonapartism. He is try-

ing to break in upon and break down Marxist discourse the way he says Bonapartism breaks into Marx's class analysis. He arbitrarily disregards the argument Marx intends to make in favor of the one he himself proposes and, what is worse, fails to differentiate between his interpretation and the object being interpreted. He is perversely Hegelian. He reduces the object of criticism to the subjectivity of the critic. Thus Eagleton is entirely justified when he attempts to bring Mehlman back to his senses by pointing out that Marx's aim, and one quite successfully carried out, is to demonstrate that Bonapartism signified "a contradictory condensation of class forces—the space of a continual struggle"—and one with ominous historical implications (*ibid.*).

Let's restore the text. The two sets of metaphors are, I believe, intended to give an aesthetic dimension to an underlying conceptual structure. History involves repetitions. These repetitions are not random occurrences. They are dialectically meaningful. The second occurrence is the mediation, middle term, or negative moment in the dialectical process. It is the plunge toward nothingness, the ceasing-to-be, through which something new comes-to-be. It is the revealed irrationality of the existing social reality and, as such, the fire from which the phoenix of the future will arise. Hence it may *appear* to be ridiculous and crazy when Bonaparte claims to be the first Napoleon risen from his grave and the people believe in this laughable apparition. But history is crazy like a fox, and—to revert to the level of metaphor—it has a wicked sense of humor. When the play is done, a new world will have been won. S/he who laughs last, laughs best.

13.

Last act. There is more to Bonapartism than is to be found in Marx's interpretation of it. Marx's metaphors have a conceptual meaning he did not intend to give them. Bonapartism does disrupt the logic of class interests and the dialectical rationality of history. If it is dialectical at all, it is the negative moment without restraint, cut loose from its triadic moorings, an historical irrationality that can be rationalized but not made rational. Bonapartism is the nightmare Marxism didn't choose, the mirror in which its meanings are inverted, the perversion of its aims, and the disease to which, in the form of Stalinism, it falls victim.

In the chapter on anthropology we differentiated between dialectical and defensive processes. In dialectical processes the negative moment mediates a course of healthy development, in defensive ones the negative moment predominates. The ends/means relationship is inverted.

Insanity is the extreme form of this inversion: self-destruction over self-preservation, hatred over love, the death-drive over the life-drive. It is the product of anxiety pushed to the point of terror; and terror is the product of the collapse of psychic structure. Thus insanity is a self-perpetuating, vicious circle.

Marx's metaphor of the madhouse must be taken literally. Bonapartism is political insanity. But it is not indeterminate. It is an instance of bureaucratization and group-emotion mediating and cutting across the lines of class struggle. It is precisely a totalization, or an attempted totalization, of social reality. Just as neurosis and psychosis are extreme versions of trends that can be found in healthy psyches, so Bonapartism is an extreme version of the modern political disease. It is the dis-integrating as well as the dis-integration of the modern state. And it, too, is a vicious circle, a turning in a widening gyre and a center that cannot hold.

Just here there is a lesson to be learned from the clinical practice of psychoanalysis. As we observed in the case of Mr. I, clinical treatment has a dis-integrating effect upon the personality of the patient. It cracks open reified and self-defeating characterological structures, gives transferential life to the ghosts of the past, brings to the surface the craziness from which the patient fled and of which s/he lives in fear. But it provides a work structure and an emotional relationship within which the regression can be (hopefully, partially) contained. Hence the expression, "regression in the service of the ego"—the descent into a kind of madness is necessary for the ascent into a higher level of sanity.

When Bonapartist tendencies escape from the relative rationality of class struggle, they resemble a massive transference neurosis or psychosis. But politics lacks the structural features that make the psychoanalytic dialectic possible. Unlike patient and analyst, who have a common interest, political classes have antagonistic ones. Unlike the therapeutic dyad, which operates within a framework of personal identity, politics operates through collectivities and multiplicities. Consequently political regression is likely to be just that, namely, a profoundly destructive falling back into unrestrained group-emotional processes.

We have saved the worst part for last: *the dis-integration of existing social structures is not only the occasion for political regression; it is a necessary condition for political progression.* Like pleasure and pain, the potential for political progression and the potential for political regression are generated by the same circumstances. When social structures shatter, it is possible to see the irrationalities they contained and concealed. Thus there does arise a possibility of enlightenment, which a revolutionary movement must do its best to realize. But group fantasies are released at the same time, as defenses against uncertainty and anxiety. If they are bureaucratically mobilized and mediated by instrumental rationality, the result is the horror we have come to know only too well.

We have finally arrived at the terms of our own dilemma.

C. Toward Political Sanity/On Our Own

1.

"Emancipate yourselves from mental slavery
None but ourselves can free our minds."[3]

2.

In the last part of *Anti-Oedipus*, Deleuze and Guattari offer us a way out of our dilemma, an escape, an anti-identity for our time. They invite us to become nomads. The critical principle of disengagement and displacement is here articulated as a plan of action. Anarchists who run away live to write another day.

Here, as so often, the problem is proposed as the solution. Our society, which is strikingly different from the one Marx criticized and Freud analyzed, tends to make nomads of us all. It dislocates and terrifies us, sends us into anxious retreat from a reality we seem unable to change. What then? Deleuze and Guattari recommend that we follow the example of Hegelian self-consciousness, which is "at home with itself in its other-being as such" (Marx, 1844b, p. 118).

We will have to look for another way.

3.

We began the inquiry with skeptical doubts about the continued relevancy of the psychoanalytic-marxist project. Partially these were self-doubts, partially they were objections from a postmodernist position. Now, having settled our accounts with Hegel and with the Hegelian tendency in Marxist praxis, it seems only fair to settle our accounts with postmodernism as well. Perhaps by so doing we will discover whether or not our own doubts can be put to rest.

It would not be realistic, however, to expect a last minute revelation, much less redemption. There is no conclusion to the inquiry, only a self-consciousness about the process that leads to our present stopping point. If, looking back, we recognize ourselves and our situation in the criticisms, concepts, constructions, and configurations of which the inquiry consists, then the present version of psychoanalytic-marxism has a heuristic value. If we do not see ourselves in it, or see only our past, then—like other such fantasies—it may be chased back into the philosophical and/or historical night.

4.

It is important to distinguish between a possible postmoder*nity* and postmodern*ism*, as well as between the various postmodernist tendencies. Postmodernity is or would be a new mode of social production, postmodernisms are styles of thinking and theorizing.

As to postmodernisms, a line might be drawn between deconstruction as an orientation toward and technique of cultural criticism (especially as a way of reading texts) and postmodernist social theories, which often depart notably from deconstruction in both object and method. There is, to be sure, a notable blurring of this line. Deconstructionist techniques and linguistic modalities have been wildly applied to social practices, so that every interpretation becomes a reading and every object a text.

A fairytale: Once upon a time there was a style of criticism in which Freudian concepts were placed under a law of displacement, so that movement away from any point of engagement became the first principle of any and all critical activity. Displacement, which for Freud is a neuroticizing defense against psychic pain, was honored rather than analyzed. Moreover, the critic's desire to flee from the scene became an interpretive crime: Her/his failure of psychoanalytic will was attributed to the text or its author.

The law of displacement was a more or less manifest aspect of this style. There was a less obvious aspect as well, namely, the motive for the flight.

For example: Suppose we place Freud or a Freudian text in the role of primal father, the incarnation or possessor of the phallus, conceived within a patriarchal order as the aegis of power. Suppose also that the hypnotic or charismatic power of the phallus derives in part from a concealed source: from the mother's body, her breasts, vagina and uterus, her powers of life and death. Hence there is a double presence, although in a form that denies or represses the better part of the content.

Next there are the children of this father/mother, who are envious and covetous of a power they do not possess. Manifestly they acquiesce to it, or argue among themselves about it. Under the surface they indulge in fantasies of appropriating it. Because these fantasies originate in the relationship to the mother, they are alimentary—fantasies of ingestion. And because they are fueled by envy, the eating of the primal flesh is angry and destructive. The phallus/vagina/breast is chewed into little pieces, digested in bile, and excreted. The result is fecalized Freud. But on the surface the fecalization of Freud is replaced by fancy words and rhetorical flourishes. This is a flight away from the fantasized engagement, schizoid retreat from a paranoid interaction. But one never gets far from the fantasies one attempts to leave behind. The repressed always shows through the forms repressing it.

The world is my text; I shall fear no evil. . . .

5.

A similar movement away from social reality is found in the work of Jean Baudrillard and other abstract postmodernists, who shift social criticism from the level of production to that of consumption, or deny the relevance of this distinction along with any distinction between reality and appearance. Masks, mirrors, signifiers without signifieds, all gyrate around each other recursively and without top or bottom. Concepts and metaphors are melted into each other or are just plain melted down. Social theory models itself upon a media event rather than locating itself in relation to such events and seeing what they represent.

Wild deconstruction and abstract postmodernism are fun and games, not to be taken seriously. Oddly, most of the players of these games, who make not taking things seriously a part of the game, take themselves very seriously indeed—or not so oddly.

6.

Of greater consequence is the position staked out by Foucault and his followers, which we have taken into account at various points along our way. In part this tendency may be interpreted as a critique of modernity, or even of capitalism, a ruthless criticism of everything existing and very much in a Marxist and psychoanalytic tradition. But one aspect of the position is the contention that Marxism and psychoanalysis have outlived their usefulness, if they ever had any. Here we have a serious and concrete postmodernism.

We might frame the issue this way.

Somewhere along the Western historical line, scientific reason was liberated from metaphysics and joined to commercial activity and politics. By the nineteenth century a distinctive social reality had emerged, consisting of industrial or industrializing capitalism and the modern state, along with a Right and Left opposition. Marxism emerged as the leading praxis or perhaps ideology of the Left, various forms of romanticism and reactionary nationalism as the ideologies of the Right.

The Marxist Left had a critical relationship to capitalism but presupposed its accomplishments. It identified itself with scientific reason and progressivist views of economic production. It meant to preserve these features of capitalism while going beyond them.

Cut to 1968 and yet another attempt to change, not merely understand, the world. In the emancipatory movements of that time the so-called Old Left played a mixed part—an especially unhelpful part where it was organized into communist party bureaucracies. These bureaucracies were scarcely distinguishable from those of the capitalist state, or those of Eastern Europe and the Soviet Union. It was not just a flight of fancy to see oneself as struggling against an international power structure, totalizing if not yet totalized, one-dimensionalizing if not yet one-dimensionalized. And it is understandable that one might fear to become what one was fighting against, thus to demonstrate once more the universal applicability of Michels' iron law of oligarchy. Better to multiply than to unify the radical entities.

In this context the question was raised: Are the theories and practices we have used to understand, criticize, and attempt to transform the world still relevant? Has the world changed fundamentally while we weren't watching? Are we trapped in a time warp that renders us irrelevant or even reactionary? Have our own theories and practices, which we have viewed as part of the solution, become part of the problem? Hasn't the time come to radically rethink the problematics of our situation?

7.

Cut to 1990. The breakdown of so-called Marxist régimes in Eastern Europe was widely hailed as the start of a new age.

No doubt the disintegration of the Soviet system is world-historical, but in what way?

If we dispassionately analyze the Soviet experience, we begin by noting the disparity between the aspirations of the revolution of 1917 and the backwardness of the Russian nation. In such a situation communism was out of the question. The attempt to impose it could only result in a bureaucratization of society and the utilization of Marxism as an ideology of economic development. An ideology, not a theory: In the process of modernization, the interests of the many must necessarily be sacrified to the interests of the few—and just as necessarily this must be denied. Which is to say, it is precisely Marxist theory that provides the standpoint from which to analyze the impossibility of Marxist practice in the Soviet situation.

After 70 or so years Soviet rulers reach the same conclusion: Communism is not possible in the Soviet Union. But then, in a peculiarly Hegelian fashion, they attempt to turn back the clock. Lenin, Stalin, and their heirs are unceremoniously swept into the dustbin of history and we are returned to the chaos of 1917. Searching through the rubble the would-be Great Russians come eventually to the graves of the tsars and of their aspiring bourgeois ministers. Stolypin and Witte walk again. The ancient religious and ethnic prejudices, buried during the last decades, rise from their graves and sweep through the land. A second coming indeed!

Here we have an inverse historical repetition, an antidialectical negation of the negation, an attempt to undo the past and start over again. The second Russian revolution is neither a confirmation nor a parody of the first. It is an attempt to deny the reality of the first, and of the conditions from which it developed. The communist revolution was intended as a cure for a disease. In the Russian context it was the wrong prescription. But this doesn't mean that there wasn't a disease.

To which it might be rejoined, "Soviet Marxism was not merely a failed attempt at a political cure. It, too, was a disease."

Quite right. Hence we shed no tears at its grave and we do not desire its resurrection.

"But," the argument continues, "there is more than one body in the tomb. Marx claimed that socialist revolution 'cannot draw its poetry from the past, but only from the future' (1852, p. 106). His poetry of the future has become the poetry of the past. The time has come to surrender the idea that philosophy finds its material weapons in the proletariat while the proletariat finds its intellectual weapons in philosophy. Don't misunderstand me. I, too, recognize the pathologies of capitalism; and I share your proclaimed interest in human freedom. Indeed, the revolutions of 1990-1991 are testimonies to the enduring human desire for self-determination. But proletarian praxis is dead, and one should let the dead bury their dead."

This argument cannot be dismissed out of hand. There is a tradition of political struggle, of class struggle, extending from the revolutions of 1789 and 1848 to our own time. The Soviet Union, no matter how crookedly, held up the Marxist banner in that struggle. The existence of Soviet

Marxism, that is, created a bipolar international situation and consequently a space within which it was possible to wage the battle against specifically capitalist domination. The fall of Soviet Marxism closed that space. Does it close all such spaces? Does it signify the end of class struggle and Marxist praxis? Must we now build new roads to human liberation? And is this what, practically speaking, postmodernism means, namely, post-Marxism?

8.

Let's start again.

Modernity is a complex and discursively meaningful notion. But it also involves a shift of meaning and perhaps a glissade. Not so long ago we would have used the term capitalism, and we would have viewed a term like modernity as euphemistic. Maybe some of us still do.

We wish to speak to one another, so we must also be prepared to listen—an accommodation: modernism = capitalism.

Put this way, it seems clear that we have not cast off the old Adam. Modernist or capitalist problems remain, unsolved. When some postmodernists claim that they are no longer relevant, that an entirely new set of problems has superseded them, then they are engaged in a denial of social reality. Economic exploitation, social injustice, and political oppression are just as real as ever they were. So, too, are the objective possibilities of bringing these perversions of human mutuality to an end. Neither the problems nor the prospects go away because a scattering of intellectuals choose not to look at them.

We might, however, take postmodernity in a more inclusive sense. It could be argued that our present situation has definable characteristics that differentiate it qualitatively from any and all earlier ones. It need not be denied that old problems remain. Instead, the claim would be that their meaning has been radically altered, that they are parts of a new whole.

There are three empirical features of our world that might incline us to view it as postmodern:

• We have clearly reached the ecological limits of capitalism, at least a capitalism based on fossil fuels and the one-way utilization of natural resources. We have placed the ecological viability of the human species in doubt. Further, if human society does not end with an ecological whimper, it might end with a thermonuclear bang. In both regards and in a complete break with historical precedent, we have developed the capability of terminating human existence. We have not developed a corresponding capability for countering this threat.

• Nineteenth-century and earlier distinctions between social systems are decreasingly applicable to our situation. The interpenetration of economic production and politics, along with the nearly universal mediation of human experience by bureaucratic practices, are the order of day. These enormous bureaucratic systems are, moreover, internationally linked. There is both a world market and an international power structure. Politically and economically the situation is oligopolistic—not monolithic, not monopolistic, but also not pluralistic.

• For better or worse the accumulation of scientific knowledge has continued, at an ever more dizzying pace. Especially important in this regard is the qualitative transformation of our capacity to store and communicate information. Where once there was a rather sharp dichotomoy between a world of knowledge shut up in books and a world of social practices outside these literary boundaries, now the extremes fall within a vast ebb and flow of information. It is almost as if consciousness and social being have lost their distinctiveness. More modestly, it is fair to say that the globalization of economic relations has produced and been mediated by globalized communication.

As Marx argued, capitalism has proved to be both world-historical and self-transforming; not self-transforming, however, in the way he predicted or, as we would now say, in the way he wished and imagined. Instead of socialism we have . . . postmodern capitalism.

9.

In the preface I stated that my aim was to hew a psychoanalytic-marxist path between Hegelianism and postmodernism. I can now restate this position in more concrete terms. In order to situate ourselves politically we must avoid thinking that nothing has changed or that everything has changed. Capitalism is not dead, but neither does it much resemble its nineteenth century incarnation. We do live in novel circumstances—call them postmodern, if you will. But the evils with which we struggle have exceedingly ancient roots.

Diagnostically, then, we might see the totalizations of Hegelian ideality as anticipations of the hypertotalizations of late capitalism reality. But as psychoanalytic-marxists we add the claim that these universalizations disguise quite concrete and specific relationships of domination. Correspondingly we might see the postmodernist insistence on multiplicity as a protest against a bad totality—difference not as description but as defiance and defense of freedom. But we question the efficacy of dispersal, displacement, and flight from the center as emancipatory strategies.

We could put it another way. As critics of *postmodern* capitalism we focus on an historically specific form of capitalist domination, in which an increasingly consolidated (monopolated, the invisible man might say) power structure maintains itself with apparent ease against an increasingly fragmented opposition. As critics of postmodern *capitalism* we focus our attention on class, gender, and race as interpenetrating structural modalities of domination. And following each line of criticism to its phenomenological end, we come upon the disruption of the metabolic processes linking the human species to its nonhuman environment. Thus when we reverse perspective and view our situation from the bottom up, we see a dialectical relationship—an extremely malignant one—in which the immediacy or premise is the violation of sensuous existence, the particularity consists of specifc forms of domination, and the generality is precisely the instrumentally rational totalization of these destructive processes.

Recall the anthropological abstractions developed in Chapter 6, specifically the configuration of sensuous interaction, work/desire, and conscious interaction. As anthropology this configuration is a potential for historical development. Here—in the preceding paragraphs, and in the preceding chapters—we have the present realization of that potential. Judged against a standard of human flourishing, it is a perverse realization.

When it comes to social pathologies, we are all physicians. We must find ways of healing ourselves.

10.

The problematic of postmodern capitalism gives rise to an historically specific project of human emancipation. It might be articulated in the following seven principles.

• Transform systems of alienated labor into communities within which individuals work freely and creatively.

• Make individual and collective interests mutually inclusive rather than mutually exclusive.

• Remove the barriers and impediments to emotional growth and well-being.

• Do not follow desire beyond the limits of possible human experience.

• At all levels of interaction and along all lines of difference—sexual, racial, generational, territorial—aim at the achievement of mutual recognition.

• Replace hierarchical social organizations with participatory ones.

• Preserve and restore the natural/environmental conditions for human well-being.

The first two principles are classically Marxist. The next two signify the lessons of psychoanalysis. The fifth summarizes and amplifies the first four from the standpoint of recognition. All five principles could, I think, be summarized in the familiar Marxist terms: the creation of communities in which the free development of each individual is a condition for the free development of all.

The sixth principle is simultaneously ancient, modern, and postmodern. Long ago Aristotle argued that political freedom requires that citizens be capable of ruling and being ruled in turn. Marxist notions of participatory democracy echo this Aristotelian position. But the postmodern bureaucratization and centralization of social production makes meaningful political participation ever more difficult and ever more vital. If we are to retain and extend our individual and collective autonomy, we must resist the power of the capitalist desiring-machines. Flight will not do. Rather, we must find ways of using and sharing social power—without, as Foucault rightly warns, becoming enamored of it.

The last principle, which mirrors our uniquely precarious historical situation, is oriented toward ecological sanity or rationality. It aims at a restoration of the sensuous metabolism that unites us with each other and the nonhuman world, and it requires a greening of critical theory. As such, it carries us beyond classical Marxism but not beyond psychoanalytic-marxism. Classical Marxism is anthropocentric. It preserves uncritically the species-level narcissism characteristic of the Enlightenment. Vital for the emancipation of humanity from premodern limitations on human flourishing, this practical and psychological self-aggrandizement has become—by dialectical inversion—a grave threat to human survival. It must be surrendered—without, however, foresaking the project of human emancipation that has been its historical companion.

Psychoanalysis, by contrast, has a more complex relationship to the progressivism of the Enlightenment. Although Freud identified it with the scientific *Weltanschauung*, he was profoundly skeptical of the idea that we could progress against or by dominating nature. Hence Marcuse was following Freud's lead when he found in psychoanalysis a protest against the performance principle and a psychological footing for the project of pacifying our relationship to nature. Moreover, as Fred Alford points out, the Kleinian variant of psychoanalytic theory helps to identify a possible state of mind—associated by the Kleinians with the depressive position—in which we cease to treat our environment merely as a means to our own ends (Alford, 1989, pp. 157–159). Most of all, when psychoanalytic theory is joined to feminism, it leads us to recognize that conquering nature also means damaging it.

In other words, a psychoanalysis freed from the strictures of bourgeois ideology inclines toward an ecological extension of the problematics of both recognition and reparation; likewise a Marxism freed from the excesses of instrumental rationality. Hence if there were to be a psychoanalytic-marxist banner, it would have inscribed upon it: *Save the Earth/ Free the People.*

11.

The world is not unrecognizable from a psychoanalytic-marxist standpoint nor is the psychoanalytic-marxist project outdated. Yet the old battle cry, "workers of the world, unite," rings hollowly in our ears. The truth, Marx said, must be realized in practice. But who is to be the practitioner?

No, that puts it the wrong way. When we stand back and speculate on possible agents of transformational action, we are disempowering ourselves. We are being merely philosophical. We only begin to think politically when we recognize that we ourselves are agents of transformational action, and when we seek to join our theories to emancipatory practices.

Thus the question becomes: How do we build movements of human liberation and ecological restoration? Or to recur to an earlier formulation, how do we build mass movements that are: (1) oriented toward the realization of their interests; (2) equipped to manage the uncertainty and anxiety that accompany emancipatory praxis; and (3) capable of learning from their political experience?

Without trying to be exhaustive (as if such a thing were possible), our investigations suggest the following points:

• Political action must be grounded in the lived experience of the individuals involved. There are no privileged positions from which our experience can be interpreted; rather, collective effort is required to uncover the deeper determinants of everyday living.

• Learning from experience is difficult. For oppressed peoples the culturally dominant modes of thought stand in their way. Moreover, engagement with problematical realities induces anxiety and therefore a tendency toward magical thinking. Thus the need for phenomenological, critical, and self-critical methodologies.

• For all of us interests and desires interpenetrate in a complex and anxiety-inducing fashion. Consequently we tend to split off the one from the other, to think only in terms of interests or only in terms of desires. When we can tolerate the anxiety generated by this interpenetration of opposites, however, we place ourselves in a position to grasp social reality more firmly—with both hands, as it were.

• Although late capitalism has a variety of homogenizing effects, it does not unify its victims into an undifferentiated mass. There are rather discrete collectivities of oppressed people—far more differentiated than even our tripartite analysis of class, gender, and race suggests. These local struggles must be waged in their own terms. Otherwise there is once again the imposition of the One upon the Many. But this does not mean that no interaction between local movements is possible or desirable. To the contrary, capitalism tends to fragment and atomize oppositional movements. It is a real perversity to celebrate rather than to combat this fragmentation and multiplication of depoliticized entities. Hence there is a need to link oppositional movements to each other while simultaneously resisting the temptation to establish a first among equals.

• Linking oppositional movements involves confrontation between their often conflicting immediate interests. Although there is a general interest in human emancipation and planetary restoration, there are various cleavages and differential realizations of interest within the existing situation. We must recognize these differences and work with them. But we must also struggle against the tendency to form ourselves into flight–fight groups around them.

• The more successful a specific political movement, the more it becomes subject to bureaucratic distortion and the entrenchment of elites. There is no theoretical remedy for this tendency, only the necessity of waging an on-going struggle against it. Again, Foucault's admonishment is relevant. We must beware of fetishizing organizational power and of losing ourselves in the performance of political roles.

• In this last regard there is something to be learned from clinical psychoanalysis. The analyst must learn to be dispassionate amidst storms of passion, and to differentiate transferential fantasies from interactional realities. No political actor can be quite so dispassionate, for s/he always has an axe to grind. But restraint of passion is a precondition for rational and responsible choices of action.

None of these principles is particularly original, but they are psychoanalytic-marxist. This does not mean that psychoanalytic-marxism itself is or should be an emancipatory movement. It is rather a heuristic device, that is, a set of concepts in which the problematics of emancipatory movements are reflected and, perhaps, clarified.

12.

Although we do not find it possible to share Marx's comforting belief that the socialist revolution is the immanent negation of capitalism, we have not abandoned dialectical reason. But we center dialectical reason in ourselves and not in our circumstances. Politically speaking, dialectics is a *logic of transformational action*. We aim at the negation of a negation.

Our situation amounts to a set of constraints and negations—constraints that determine the possibilities for transformational action, negations that determine the desirability of transformational action. Taken together, constraints and negations define a field of possible choices and commitments, a field that must itself be defined through practical engagement and theoretical reflection. Indeed, our investigations have been, within the modality of theory, just such an attempt at definition.

The transformational project that arises through this process denotes, as Habermas argued, a hope or set of hopes. It also engenders fear. We fear the disappointment we suffer when hopes are unrealized; and if we are not naive, if we have studied the conditions under which transformational action becomes necessary and possible, we also have a fear of making things worse instead of better.

What then? We find ourselves in a situation in which psychoanalytic-marxist values are not realized; we can envision and hope for one in which they are. Hence the project, which determines our relationship to the situation. We make choices and take action aimed at the transformation of the situation and the realization of the project—not shots in the dark, and not logical derivations. If we succeed, negations are negated; if not, then not. So it goes.

13.

This much is also dialectical. The rationality of the existing mode of production has become profoundly irrational, that is, a threat to human survival and so a kind of insanity. The question is, can we bear the uncertainty and anxiety that must necessarily attend the struggle to give up our fetishisms and addictions, to transform the structures of selfhood and the social practices that dominate us and tend toward our mutual destruction?

*   *   *   *   *

If the game is lost then we're all the same
No one left to place or take the blame.
We will leave this place an empty stone,
Or that shining ball of blue we can call our home.

Ashes, ashes, all fall down.[4]

Notes

CHAPTER 1

1. I use the lowercase "m" in psychoanalytic-marxism to signify the difference between my theoretical position and more orthodox versions of Marxist theory. The uppercase "M" is used in all other instances.

2. We will employ this combined method later on, especially in Chapter 8.

3. Later on we will discuss reflexivity—that is, the role of self-consciousness —in emancipatory praxis.

4. But also see the comments on the complexity involved in its use in Chapter 5.

5. My thanks to Blake Ferris for the idea of a "sameness which is no sameness."

6. This method is close to the progressive–regressive method outlined by Sartre in *Search for a Method* (1968).

CHAPTER 2

1. I have constructed the debate around a synopsis of the two theories. Although this involves the retelling of often-told tales, it seems better to err in the direction of repetition than of ellipsis.

I might add that, quite apart from the controversial relationship of Marx and Freud, there is a rich history of controversy about the interpretation of the two theories. Those readers who are familiar with these debates will recognize in what follows the interpretive choices I have made. In any case, I hope these choices won't be mistaken for interpretive last words.

The argument in this chapter might be compared to those put forward by Lichtman (1982, Chapters 1–2).

2. In the 1840s in Europe there were property qualifications for political participation. By definition a member of the proletariat is not an owner of private property.

3. Or as Marx puts it later on in *Capital, 1*, "It is not the worker who employs the conditions of his work, but rather the reverse, the conditions of work employ the worker" (1867, p. 548).

4. In Chapter 7 we will modify this model, in part by incorporating the elements of social structure Marx adumbrates in *The German Ideology* (Marx & Engels, 1845b). The present version, however, brings out more clearly the differences between Marx and Freud.

5. Both sets of ideological meanings can be found in Locke's classic articulation of liberalism. In his *Two Treatises of Government* (Laslett, 1960), he begins from a state of nature, in which God's law and human reason coincide, all individuals are free and equal, and private property is acquired and legitimated by labor. Government, which arises as a response to the inconveniences of the state of nature, rests upon contract and consent. We will return to this point in Chapter 10.

6. It must be remembered that Freud was very far from being a Marx scholar. What he knew of Marxism came primarily through diamat (Second and Third International) interpretations of the theory. He was responding to dogmas, not problematics.

7. Freud empties Marx's view of history of all content in order the better to criticize it for its abstract quality. In the process of rejecting dialectics he mentions a variety of "material" factors (such as the development of weapons) that he considers to be among the real determinants of historical change. He conveniently ignores the fact that Marx and Marxists have exhaustively analyzed such factors. The main point for the moment, however, is Freud's rejection of historical dialectics.

8. I personally take a position in these debates. Like a number of others I place psychoanalysis outside the purview of the positive sciences; unlike a number of others I do not view it as a hermeneutic enterprise but rather as an emancipatory praxis (Wolfenstein, 1990b). I shall return to this question in Chapter 5.

9. Perhaps this is a good time to remind ourselves that, as in the exposition of Marxism, our present aim is to bring into focus the simple conceptual elements, the thinnest of the abstractions, from which the theory is constructed. In reality and in the more concrete forms of the theories things aren't nearly so simple.

10. The name as well as the content of Freud's "metapsychology" reflects his Aristotelian heritage, as well as his desire to replace metaphysics with modern physics, that is, the epistemology of the natural sciences.

11. I am using "desire" to mean something more mental than a drive and more persevering than a wish. The usage will be further clarified in Chapter 4.

CHAPTER 3

1. Whether it is meaningful to oppose the One to the All is historically variable. When, for example, individual rights exist but are trampled upon, the concept of the individual versus society is meaningful. Where such rights don't

exist or there are no major intrasocial conflicts of interest, it isn't. But Reich (apparently unconsciously) universalizes the self-interested individual who fears for her/his rights—the very individual he wishes to treat as the pathological byproduct of patriarchal and private property social relations.

2. It might seem that the relationship is reversible, that analysis could begin at either end of Reich's continuum—that Reich could argue from the history of production to the individual psyche—but this is not the case. Because the relationship between society and the individual is external, history ≠ human nature, and human nature must necessarily be granted ontological priority: "It" must always be there beneath or as the substratum of all historical transformations.

3. See also the discussion of Rubin (1975) in Chapter 4.

4. Reich continues: "However, a certain analyst did once jokingly admit that while it was true that an airplane was a penis symbol, all the same it got you from Berlin to Vienna" (Reich, 1929, p. 43).

5. Although Fromm accurately cites "Dialectical Materialism and Psychoanalysis" in his critique, Reich had grounds for complaining that Fromm attended only to the letter and not the spirit of his argument (in Baxandall, 1972, p. 65 ff.). The tone of Fromm's remarks is, however, respectful and appreciative; Reich responds with characteristic stridence and acerbity

6. Although not more trouble, and probably less, than most psycho-historians: His use of questionnaire research methods to explore the social character of the Weimar working class was a pioneering attempt to operationalize psychoanalytic concepts (Fromm, 1984). One might also compare his work to that of Adorno and others in *The Authoritarian Personality* (1950). For the classical criticisms of this kind of research, see Christie and Jahoda (1954).

7. Fromm, who viewed relativism as pathology, would probably object to such an approach to his text. Yet as his own references indicate, in his historical analysis he is responding almost as much to *The Protestant Ethic and the Spirit of Capitalism* (Weber, 1905) as he is to Marx and the orthodox Marxists. He accepts from Weber the significance of religion for interpreting history, but he treats it in Marxist fashion as ideology and in psychoanalytic fashion as psychic defense. It is not going too far afield, then, to extend this Weberian trend from theory to method.

8. Interestingly, Fromm analogizes posthypnotic suggestion to the falsi-fication of free will, thought, and feeling. Later we will find that the relationship is not just analogical.

9. Fromm's approach resembles that of object relations psychoanalysts like Harry Guntrip. It also resembles, although less closely, that of Margaret Mahler and her coworkers, given their tendency to focus primarily upon problems of separation and individuation.

10. While we are on the subject of contradictions: There are reams of criticism of Marcuse's work, while there are relatively few serious criticisms of the work of Reich and Fromm. This difference is not proportional to the value of their respective efforts. To a considerable extent it is a product of Marcuse's active role in New Left politics, which gave his individual work a collective meaning. That meaning, however, was in part a media creation. Odd though it may seem, Marcuse, his philosophy, and his New Left political involvement were media

events. Yet Marcuse was a determined critic of the culture industry and the media-mediated manipulation of consciousness. Hence the irony and, if irony is a contradiction, the contradiction.

For a thorough and sympathetic treatment of Marcuse's work, see Kellner (1984).

11. But not in psychoanalytic practice: "While psychoanalytic theory recognized that the sickness of the individual is ultimately caused and sustained by the sickness of his civilization, psychoanalytic therapy aims at curing the individual so that he can continue to function as part of a sick civilization without surrendering to it altogether" (Marcuse, 1962, p. 224). The theory is critical, the practice is not.

When we come to Habermas we will find that another view is possible.

12. The term "surplus repression" is clearly meant as a complement or analogy to Marx's surplus labor and surplus value. It is, for just that reason, misleading. The analogy is between alienation and repression, on the one hand, and labor-power and libido, on the other. Marx's point is that alienation produces a surplus labor value which accrues to the capitalist. Marcuse's point ought to be that repression produces a surplus libidinal value which accrues to the production process. When there is historically excessive repression, then a super-surplus of alienated libido is produced.

CHAPTER 4

1. The categories "women" and "Third World people" are theoretical reflections of actual social movements. They also reflect the ideological tensions in these movements. See below, page 136.

2. Our discussion of Habermas is limited to *Knowledge and Human Interests*. Related arguments are developed in his *On the Logic of the Social Sciences* (1988), but they do not call for a separate discussion. On the other hand, Habermas played a significant part in the debate about modernity and postmodernity. I have had his *The Philosophical Discourse of Modernity* (1987) in mind at various points along the way.

For a critical appraisal of Habermas and the question of modernity see the essays in Bernstein (1985) and in *Praxis, 8,* 1989, especially the thoughtful one by Fred Dallmayr.

3. Readers too often ignore the chapter in *The Wretched of the Earth* on "colonial war and mental disorders" and consequently interpret Fanon as writing in praise of violence, when in fact he views it only as a necessary evil. Here, again, we have a kind of misrecognition, and one that fits only too well with white racist stereotypes.

4. This section is based on Wolfenstein (1990b).

5. For an exceptionally clear exposition and critique of major themes in *Anti-Oedipus*, see Robert D'Amico (1978).

6. So far as the last commandment is concerned, I am tempted to add: Practice what you preach.

7. This formulation of the relationship is explicated in the feminist section of this chapter.

8. Their criticism applies to Schneider as well, as becomes evident when comparing this diagram with the one on page 113.

9. Compare, for example, Marx's historical analysis in *The German Ideology* or *Capital, 1*, with the one in Part 3 of *Anti-Oedipus*. The two treatments are, in both method and content, incompatible. The former, indeed, qualifies as history; the latter does not.

10. A far more vivid articulation of the creation of a body without organs can be found in Deleuze and Guattari (1987, pp. 149–166).

11. In this regard *Anti-Oedipus* might well be compared to the work of James Glass (1985, 1989) and Peter Sedgwick (1982), where insanity is treated both seriously and compassionately. One might also consult Gabel (1975), who suggestively links clinical schizophrenia to false consciousness.

12. Deleuze and Guattari separate schizophrenia and paranoia, making the former a free flow of desire occurring at molecular levels of experience, the latter a despotic containment of desire at molar levels of experience. Such a separation is, however, simply a case of wishful thinking.

13. This is not to say that Kleinians have been insensitive to social issues or unwilling to use Klein's concepts for social analysis. But it is difficult, from a Kleinian position, to give the objectivity of social forces their due.

14 . I attempt to take some account of the complex relationship between race, gender, and class in Chapters 7 and 8.

15. For a more detailed review of socialist feminism through the early 1980s, see Alison Jagger's *Feminist Politics and Human Nature* (1983).

16. For Campioni and Grosz, adding psychoanalysis to Marxism doesn't help: "What remains problematic about any 'union' of Marxism and psychoanalysis is the presumption of masculinity as the norm of subjectivity. It is significant that what remains ignored by both Marxism and psychoanalysis is precisely the specificity of the *female* body and the consequent difference in psychical functioning between the sexes" (*ibid.*, p. 387).

17. Jane Gallop's *The Daughter's Seduction* (1982), subtitled "Feminism and Psychoanalysis," begins with Mitchell and goes on to provide a sophisticated and accessible account of Lacan and the Lacanian feminists. Throughout she raises the question: Who is seducing whom?

For an analysis which, in my judgment, puts Lacan in his proper and considerably smaller place, see Flax (1990, pp. 89–107).

18. I do not wish to reduce the engagement of psychoanalysis and feminism to this one line of development. Of special importance is the alternative approach based on object relations versions of psychoanalysis.

19. Later on we shall have to refine the distinction. See Chapter 8, Section B, "Sexual Parts and Part-Objects."

20. Rubin also argues against the use of the term "patriarchy" as the general signifier of male dominant sex/gender systems: "Patriarchy is a specific form of male dominance, and the use of the term ought to be confined to the Old Testament-type pastoral nomads from whom the term comes, or groups like them" (Rubin, 1975, p. 168). If by patriarchy one means sex/gender relationships that fall under the rule of the father, then the use cannot be so narrowly confined. To be sure, it does obscure important historical differences to use the term

indifferently, for example, for the Roman family and the modern one. If we keep the historical variations in mind, however, there is something to be said for retaining the term as a way of designating the objective or institutional side of male dominance. It is concise, and it focuses our attention on the role of the father.

21. But see Hartsock's critique, below.

22. See the discussion of this point in Elisabeth H. Hazard's (1987) *Women on the Right: Fighting for a New Social Contract.*

23. The same duality is characteristic of racial discourse. On the one hand, it is claimed that black and white are fundamentally the same—a claim that is criticized as a reflection of white hegemony: Blacks are to integrate into white society, where at best they would have the status of imitation whites. On the other hand, it is claimed that black and white are fundamentally opposed. Black people must define themselves for themselves and against the white world. This black nationalist or separatist position, however, leaves no room for biracial or multiracial solutions to problems of oppression.

We will return to this point when we come to racial issues in Chapter 8.

24. A related critique of "mother-monopolized child rearing" is developed by Isaac Balbus (1982), who also links the problematics of feminism to a neo-Hegelian, post-Marxist critique of political domination and repressive technology.

25. If we compare Hartsock's position to Chodorow's, a characteristic difference in feminist perspectives emerges. Stated in extreme terms: Is women's mothering the problem or the solution? Is it disempowering or empowering?

26. For clarity's sake I should add that my objection is to the truth-claims Hartsock attaches to standpoint epistemology, and not to the idea that such standpoints exist. The practical and theoretical vectors of race, gender, and class provide three such emancipatory standpoints, none of which is reducible to the other and all of which are in opposition to social practices and ideologies of domination.

For a later development of Hartsock's position, see her "Postmodernism and Political Change: Issues for Feminist Theory" (1989–1990).

27. For other examples of the feminist engagement with critical theory, see Benhabib and Cornell (1987).

28. Three points of reference:

• The issues raised by *The Production of Desire* are elucidated in my review of the book and Lichtman's response thereto (Wolfenstein, 1984; Lichtman, 1984). The broader context of Kovel's work can be seen in the essays collected as *The Radical Spririt* (1988).

• My *The Victims of Democracy* (1990c), originally published in 1981, belongs to the same historical period as the two works here being considered. It is also an attempt at the paradigmatic engagement of Marxism and psychoanalysis. Because its main arguments are constitutive of my interpretive perspective, it seemed both pedantic and redundant to include it at this point.

• In order to limit the length of the exposition, I am bypassing certain other works that might have been considered here. On the one hand, there are specific inquiries that use and comment upon both psychoanalytic and Marxist categories without, however, aiming at the construction of a psychoanalytic-marxist theory (Jacoby, 1975; Lasch, 1979). On the other, there are more paradigmatic works

(Brown, 1973; Meynell, 1981) which either do not fit within or do not force a redefinition of the present project.

29. Credit where credit is due: Although Sartre is most responsible for the linkage of project and praxis, it is also fundamental for Marcuse. See especially his use of the concepts in *One-Dimensional Man*.

30. Ecological concerns have not been ignored in the discourses we have been reviewing. They are especially prominent in feminist writings. But the "greening" of critical theory needs to be taken considerably further.

CHAPTER 5

1. At this point I am bypassing a complicated methodological discussion. Marx is part of a tradition of thinkers who distinguish between two phases of theorization, but the name and nature of the two phases vary. Thus: analysis/ synthesis, regression/progression, critique/construction, phenomenological reduction/logical reconstruction, or even discovery/demonstration and hypothesis formation/hypothesis testing. Working through these relationships, although vital in certain instances, does not seem central to our present aims and interests.

2. See also Chapter 1, pages 12–13.

3. Lorraine Code provides a sensitive critique of epistemic privilege in *What Can She Know?* (1991, Chapter 8).

4. I am leaving aside the obvious point that the reduction of knowledge to power is itself a truth-claim and that, as such, it involves a standard of validation.

5. In the present discussion I aim at elucidating a few important features of theoretical knowledge, and nothing more.

6. For a dialectical approach to feminism and epistemology, and one which has certain affinities with my own, see Jennifer Ring, *Modern Political Theory and Contemporary Feminism: A Dialectical Analysis* (1991).

7. There is a prior question. The reduction of ceasing-to-be and coming-to-be to Being and Nothing is problematical. But for one thing, Hegel is aware of the problem, and for another, working it through would take us further afield metaphysically than we need to go.

8. One could also argue that Hegel's beginning is not a beginning—not just because it is a product of phenomenological inquiry, but because it contains an unacknowledged problem of recursion or infinite regression. Being vanishes into Nothing, Nothing vanishes into Being: What is the meaning of this "vanishing"? Hegel attaches the idea of immediacy to it, but it is clearly a ceasing-to-be/coming-to-be. Hence each of the two passages can be analytically reduced to Being and Nothing, thence to ceasing-to-be/coming-to-be, and so on to infinity.

Note, however, that a Kantian solution to this problem is not available. It is built into the concepts themselves, not into their objective or ontological employment.

CHAPTER 6

1. What follows is a very condensed version of the actual process by which I arrived at the present set of concepts.

2. "Activity" in this formulation is simply a shorthand for "interaction."

3. It is hard to know exactly when human experience begins, meaning by "experience" events that leave some kind of memory traces. If, however, one believes that the first two or three months of neonatal life have developmental significance, I don't see how one can exclude birth and the period immediately preceding it.

4. I am going to assume the mother as primary nurturer. After all, we are mammals; by nature, nursing is a maternal activity. This does not mean that men cannot do it; but for them to do it, an historically developed technical intervention (the bottle and nipple) is required.

5. Recognition at this level is portrayed with great sensitivity and sophistication by Benjamin in *The Bond of Love: Psychoanalysis, Feminism, and the Problem of Domination* (1988).

6. One might test the adequacy of the exposition by comparing it with the perspective of D. W. Winnicott, say as synoptically presented in his *Human Nature* (1988). If one could develop Winnicott's more concrete psychoanalytic notions within the anthropology being developed here—especially, but not only, within the framework for analyzing psychic pain—then it would pass the test. If it precludes the development of these more concrete psychoanalytic notions, then it fails.

7. Conflating dialectical development and defense in the realm of emotional life is parallel to conflating working-qua-objectification and alienated labor in the realm of economic life. In each instance so doing confuses the perversion of the process with the process itself.

8. I do not mean to deny that a little girl can have a castration-like emotional experience. She might fear the loss of her clitoris. But her fears of violation and lasceration are not limited to this anxiety.

9. The term "life-activity" parallels the idea of a life-world. It means simply the actions ordinarily involved in living.

CHAPTER 7

1. See the discussion of Marx's model in Chapter 2.

2. For the moment we are ignoring political activity and its relationship to both culture and social production. But see Section D below.

3. I do not mean to suggest that no other class divisions exist in advanced capitalist societies, and I most certainly don't insist upon this specific usage of class and stratum. But I do think we require a way of talking about the linked realities of structural polarization and the variable ways of life that mediate the polarity.

4. Reich's *The Mass Psychology of Fascism* might seem to be a counter-example, but in fact, as in Fromm's *Escape from Freedom*, the psychological dimension of the analysis concerns the distribution and aggregation of character types.

I should also note that, because we have not discussed it previously, in this chapter we will treat the concept of a psychological or emotional group in moderate detail.

5. Freud offers a rather more complex diagram of a group just after articulating its definition (*ibid.*, p. 116).

6. The same points apply to assessment in the psychoanalytic clinical situation.

7. One could also say that it is rational to choose means that will realize interests and irrational to choose means that won't realize them. But a tendency formulation of ends and means, although looser, is more realistic.

8. A distinction should be drawn between rational action and rational choices of action. In the former instance an observer assesses the rationality of an action; in the latter, the actor makes the assessment. The present contention is that in either instance the assessment depends upon the realizability of the interest and the rationality of the group function.

9. This is no longer a deficiency, if indeed it ever was, in purely Marxist theorizing. By contrast, it is an even more notable deficiency in psychopolitical studies, which tend to be either narrowly focused on leadership (as befits theorists who are wedded to psychological individualism) or watered down into studies of attitudes and personality profiles.

CHAPTER 8

1. Fowkes translates *Gerberei* as a "tanning." It also means, more colloquially, a thrashing. Marx probably intended both meanings. I prefer the one making possible a bit of word play.

2. What follows might also be compared to Irigaray (1985b, pp. 170–197).

3. Marriage is not the only contractual relationship through which male domination is secured. Prostitution is an obvious example. More generally, as Carole Pateman persuasively argues in *The Sexual Contract*, in the Western contractarian tradition, "only one sex has the right to enjoy civil freedom" (1988, p. 225). Contracts are made about women but not by them, except in those instances where the contracts are disguised forms of male domination.

4. For a variation on this theme see Hartsock (1985, p. 234).

5. Flax (1990) develops a parallel argument concerning gender in postmodernism (pp. 210–216).

6. See also Hartsock (1985, p. 157).

7. Some people prefer to designate what I am calling racist attitudes as prejudice, and to employ the term "racism" only when a relationship of domination is involved.

8. The title of a book by Julius Lester (1968).

9. For class analyses of African-Americans in the United States, see Glasgow (1981), Hacker (1992), Hutchinson (1990), Jaynes and Williams (1989), Landry (1987), and Newman (1978).

CHAPTER 9

1. Kovel's *The Age of Desire* is particularly relevant in this regard. See especially his treatment of mental health bureaucracies. For a shrewd assessment of the psychoanalytic profession in the United States, see Kirsner (1990).

2. We should also be wary of mystifying clinical experience as we attempt to demystify it. After all, many of the same communicative problems are involved when we attempt to share via publication the reality of any experience whatsoever. For a more thorough discussion of the difficulties involved in psychoanalytic publication, see the "commentary" section of W. R. Bion's *Second Thoughts* (1967).

CHAPTER 10

1. Psychoanalytic patients do not live solely in psychoanalytic consulting rooms. They experience the conflicts of interest and relationships of domination characteristic of their societies. It is the task of both patient and analyst to recognize these for what they are. But the distinctive feature of psychoanalytic work is the exploration of the subterranean world of desire, in the interest of which objective social reality is placed in the background.

2. Once Marx leaves the high plane of historical generality and descends into the particularity of actual events, a much more complex picture of the proletariat emerges. Thus the double structure of the opening paragraphs anticipates a recurrent tension in the text.

3. B. Marley, "Redemption Song," Bob Marley Music Inc. (1980).

4. R. Weir and J. Barlow, "Throwing Stones," Ice Nine Publishing Co. (1989).

Bibliography

Adams, D. (1980). *The Restaurant at the End of the Universe*. New York: Pocket Books.

Adorno, T. W. (Ed.). (1950). *The Authoritarian Personality*. New York: Harper & Brothers.

Adorno, T. W. (1973). *Negative Dialectics*. New York: Seabury Press.

Alexander, R. (1981). On the Analyst's "Sleep" during the Psychoanalytic Session. In J. Grotstein (Ed.), *Do I Dare Disturb the Universe?* (pp. 45–57). Beverly Hills, CA: Caesura Press.

Alford, C. F. (1989). *Melanie Klein and Critical Social Theory*. New Haven, CT: Yale University Press.

Althusser, L. (1970). *For Marx*. New York: Vintage Books.

Althusser, L. (1971). *Lenin and Philosophy*. New York: Monthly Review Press.

Amott, T., & Matthaei, J. (1991). *Race, Gender, and Work: A Multicultural Economic History of Women in the United States*. Boston: South End Press.

Arato, A., & Gebhardt, E. (Eds.). (1982). *The Essential Frankfurt School Reader*. New York: Continuum.

Avineri, S. (1972). *Hegel's Theory of the Modern State*. London: Cambridge University Press.

Balbus, I. (1982). *Marxism and Domination: A Neo-Hegelian, Feminist, Psychoanalytic Theory of Sexual, Political, and Technological Liberation*. Princeton, NJ: Princeton University Press.

Barker, E. (Ed.). (1958). *The Politics of Aristotle*. New York: Oxford University Press.

Barrett, M. (1988). *Women's Oppression Today: The Marxist/Feminist Encounter*. London: Verso.

Bataille, G. (1977). *Death and Sensuality*. New York: Arno Press.

Baxandall, L. (Ed.). (1972). *Sex-Pol*. New York: Vintage Books.

Benhabib, S. (1984). Obligation, Contract, and Exchange: On the Significance of Hegel's Abstract Right. In Z. A. Pelczynski (Ed.), *The State and Civil Society* (pp. 159–177). New York: Cambridge University Press.

Benhabib, S., & Cornell, D. (Eds.). (1987). *Feminism as Critique*. Minneapolis: University of Minnesota Press.

Benjamin, J. (1977). The End of Internalization: Adorno's Social Psychology. *Telos, 32*, 42–64.

Benjamin, J. (1980). The Bonds of Love: Rational Violence and Erotic Domination. *Feminist Studies, 6*, 144–174.

Benjamin, J. (1988). *The Bonds of Love: Psychoanalysis, Feminism, and the Problem of Domination*. New York: Pantheon Books.

Bernstein, J. M. (1984). From Self-Consciousness to Community: Act and Recognition in the Master–Slave Relationship. In Z. A. Pelczynski (Ed.), *The State and Civil Society* (pp. 14–39). New York: Cambridge University Press.

Bernstein, R. J. (Ed.). (1985). *Habermas and Modernity*. Cambridge, MA: MIT Press.

Bion, W. R. (1959). *Experiences in Groups*. New York: Basic Books.

Bion, W. R. (1967). *Second Thoughts*. New York: Jason Aronson.

Bion, W.R. (1970). Attention and Interpretation. In *Seven Servants*. New York: Jason Aronson, 1977.

Bion, W. R. (1977). *Seven Servants*. New York: Jason Aronson.

Bornemann, E. (Ed.). (1976). *The Psychoanalysis of Money*. New York: Urizen Books.

Breger, L. (1981). *Freud's Unfinished Journey*. London: Routledge & Kegan Paul.

Breitman, G. (Ed.). (1965). *Malcolm X Speaks*. New York: Grove Press.

Brennan, T. (Ed.). (1989). *Between Feminism and Psychoanalysis*. London: Routledge.

Breuer, J., & Freud, S. (1895). Studies in Hysteria. In J. Strachey (Ed. & Trans.), *The Standard Edition of the Complete Psychological Works of Sigmund Freud* (Vol. 2). London: Hogarth Press.

Brown, B. (1973). *Marx, Freud, and the Critique of Everyday Life*. New York: Monthly Review Press.

Brown, D. G. (1977). Drowsiness in the Countertransference, *International Review of Psycho-Analysis, 4*, 481–492.

Brown, N. O. (1959). *Life against Death*. New York: Vintage Books.

Burnet, J. (1930). *Early Greek Philosophy*. London: A. & C. Black.

Campioni, M., & Grosz, E. (1991). Love's Labours Lost: Marxism and Feminism. In S. Gunew (Ed.), *A Reader In Feminist Knowledge* (pp. 366–397). London: Routledge.

Camus, A. (1956). *The Rebel*. New York: Vintage Books.

Chodorow, N. (1978). *The Reproduction of Mothering*. Berkeley: University of California Press.

Chodorow, N. (1989). *Feminism and Psychoanalytic Theory*. New Haven, CT: Yale University Press.

Christie, R., & Jahoda, M. (Eds.). (1954). *Studies in the Scope and Method of "The Authoritarian Personality."* Glencoe, IL: Free Press.

Code, L. (1991). *What Can She Know? Feminist Theory and the Problem of Knowledge*. Ithaca, NY: Cornell University Press.

Conrad, J. (1902). Heart of Darkness. In M. D. Zabel (Ed.), *The Portable Conrad* (pp. 490–603). London: Penguin Books, 1976.

Dahmer, H. (1977). Psychoanalysis as Social Theory. *Telos, 32*, 27–41.

Dahmer, H. (1978). Sexual Economy Today. *Telos, 36*, 111–126.

Dallmayr, F. (1989). The Discourse of Modernity: Hegel, Nietzsche, Heidegger (and Habermas). *Praxis, 8,* 377–406.

D'Amico, R. (1978). Desire and the Commodity Form. *Telos, 35,* 88–124.

De Beauvoir, S. (1949). *The Second Sex.* New York: Alfred A. Knopf, 1968.

Deleuze, G. (1988). *Foucault.* Minneapolis: University of Minnesota Press.

Deleuze, G., & Guattari, F. (1972). *Anti-Oedipus: Capitalism and Schizophrenia.* Minneapolis: University of Minnesota Press, 1983.

Deleuze, G., & Guattari, F. (1987). *A Thousand Plateaus.* Minneapolis: University of Minnesota Press.

De Sade, M. (1795). Philosophy in the Bedroom. In *The Marquis de Sade.* New York: Grove Press, 1965.

Dickes, R. (1965). The Defensive Function of an Altered State of Consciousness: A Hypnoid State. *Journal of the American Psychoanalytic Association, 13,* 356–403.

Dinnerstein, D. (1976). *The Mermaid and The Minotaur.* New York: Harper & Row.

Dostoevsky, F. (1864). *Notes from Underground.* New York: Bantam Books, 1974.

Dubois, W. E. B. (1903). *The Souls of Black Folks.* New York: Library of America, 1990.

Eagleton, T. (1981). *Walter Benjamin or Towards a Revolutionary Criticism.* New York: Schocken Books.

Eisenstein, Z. R. (Ed.). (1979). *Capitalist Patriarchy and the Case for Socialist Feminism.* New York: Monthly Review Press.

Eliot, T. S. (1934). *The Complete Poems and Plays.* New York: Harcourt, Brace, & World.

Ellison, R. (1947). *The Invisible Man.* New York: Vintage Books, 1989.

Engels, F. (1884). The Origin of the Family, Private Property, and the State. In K. Marx & F. Engels, *Selected Works* (Vol. 2, pp. 170–327). Moscow: Foreign Languages Publishing House, 1962.

Epps, A. (Ed.). (1968). *The Speeches of Malcolm X at Harvard.* New York: William Morrow & Co.

Fairbairn, W. R. (1954). *An Object-Relations Theory of the Personality.* New York: Basic Books.

Fanon, F. (1952). *Black Skins, White Masks.* New York: Grove Press, 1967.

Fanon, F. (1961). *The Wretched of the Earth.* New York: Grove Press, 1966.

Fichte, J. G. (1794). *The Science of Knowledge* (P. Heath & J. Lachs, Eds.). London: Cambridge University Press, 1982.

Flax, J. (1990). *Thinking Fragments.* Berkeley: University of California Press.

Foucault, M. (1977). *Discipline and Punish.* New York: Pantheon Books.

Foucault, M. (1980). *Power/Knowledge.* New York: Pantheon Books.

Foucault, M. (1987). *Mental Illness and Psychology.* Berkeley: University of California Press.

Freeman, K. (1978). *Ancilla to the Pre-Socratic Philosophers.* Cambridge, MA: Harvard University Press.

Freud, S. (1912). The Dynamics of Transference. *Standard Edition* (Vol. 12, pp. 97–108).

Freud, S. (1913). Totem and Taboo. *Standard Edition* (Vol. 13, pp. 1–162).

Freud, S. (1915). Instincts and Their Viscissitudes. *Standard Edition* (Vol. 14, pp. 111–140).

Freud, S. (1919). Lines of Advance in Psycho-Analytic Therapy. *Standard Edition* (Vol. 17, pp. 159–168).

Freud, S. (1920). Beyond the Pleasure Principle. *Standard Edition* (Vol. 18, pp. 3–64).

Freud, S. (1921). Group Psychology and the Analysis of the Ego. *Standard Edition* (Vol.18, pp. 67–143).

Freud, S. (1923). The Ego and the Id. *Standard Edition* (Vol. 19, pp. 12–66).

Freud, S. (1927a). The Future of an Illusion. *Standard Edition* (Vol. 21, pp. 3–56).

Freud, S. (1927b). Fetishism. *Standard Edition* (Vol. 21, pp. 149–157).

Freud, S. (1930). Civilization and Its Discontents. *Standard Edition* (Vol. 21, pp. 59–145).

Freud, S. (1933a). New Introductory Lectures on Psycho-Analysis. *Standard Edition* (Vol. 22, pp. 3–182).

Freud, S. (1933b). Why War? *Standard Edition* (Vol. 22, pp. 197–215).

Freud, S. (1940). Splitting of the Ego in the Process of Defense. *Standard Edition* (Vol. 23, pp. 273–278).

Fromm, E. (1932a). The Method and Function of an Analytic Social Psychology. In *The Crisis of Psychoanalysis* (pp. 138–162). Greenwich, CT: Fawcett Publications, 1970.

Fromm, E. (1932b). Psychoanalytic Characterology and Its Relevance for Social Psychology. In *The Crisis of Psychoanalysis* (pp. 164–187). Greenwich, CT: Fawcett Publications, 1970.

Fromm, E. (1941). *Escape from Freedom.* New York: Holt, Rinehart & Winston.

Fromm, E. (1970). *The Crisis of Psychoanalysis.* Greenwich, CT: Fawcett Publications.

Fromm, E. (1973). *The Anatomy of Destructiveness.* New York: Holt, Rinehart & Winston.

Fromm, E. (1984). *The Working Class in Weimar Germany.* Cambridge, MA: Harvard University Press.

Frosh, S. (1987). *The Politics of Psychoanalysis.* London: Macmillan Education.

Gabel, J. (1975). *False Consciousness.* New York: Harper & Row

Gabriel, T. (1983). *Freud and Society.* London: Routledge & Kegan Paul.

Gallop, J. (1982). *The Daughter's Seduction.* Ithaca, NY: Cornell University Press.

Gerth, H. H., & Mills, C. W. (Eds.). (1958). *From Max Weber.* New York: Oxford University Press.

Giddings, P. (1984). *When and Where I Enter.* New York: Bantam Books.

Glasgow, D. (1981). *The Black Underclass.* New York: Vintage Books.

Glass, J. (1985). *Delusions: Internal Dimensions of Political Life.* Chicago: University of Chicago Press.

Glass, J. (1989). *Private Terror/Public Life: Psychosis and the Politics of Community.* Ithaca, NY: Cornell University Press.

Goethe, J. W. (1832). *Faust.* New York: Bobbs-Merrill Co., 1965.

Gouldner, A. W. (1980). *The Two Marxisms.* New York: Oxford University Press.

Griffin, S. (1981). *Pornography and Silence.* New York: Harper & Row.

Grotstein, J. (Ed.). (1981). *Do I Dare Disturb the Universe?* Beverly Hills, CA: Caesura Press.

Gunew, S. (Ed.). (1991). *A Reader in Feminist Knowledge.* London: Routledge.

Guntrip, H. (1971). *Psychoanalytic Theory, Therapy, and the Self.* New York: Basic Books.

Habermas, J. (1971). *Knowledge and Human Interests.* Boston: Beacon Press.

Habermas, J. (1987). *The Philosophical Discourse of Modernity.* Cambridge, MA: MIT Press.

Habermas, J. (1988). *On the Logic of the Social Sciences.* Cambridge, MA: MIT Press.

Hacker, A. (1992). *Two Nations.* New York: Charles Scribner's Sons.

Hartmann, H. (1950). Comments on the Psychoanalytic Theory of the Ego. *Psychoanalytic Study of the Child, 5,* 74–96.

Hartsock, N. C. M. (1979). Feminist Theory and the Development of Revolutionary Strategy. In Z. R. Eisenstein (Ed.), *Capitalist Patriarchy and the Case for Socialist Feminism* (pp. 55–77). New York: Monthly Review Press.

Hartsock, N. C. M. (1985). *Money, Sex, and Power.* Boston: Northeastern University Press.

Hartsock, N. C. M. (1989–1990). Postmodernism and Political Change: Issues for Feminist Theory. *Cultural Critique, 14,* 15–83.

Hazard, E. H. (1987). *Women on the Right: Fighting for a New Social Contract.* Unpublished Ph.D. Dissertation, University of California, Los Angeles.

Hegel, G. W. F. (1802/1804). *System of Ethical Life and First Philosophy of Spirit* (H. S. Harris & T. M. Knox, Eds.). Albany: State University of New York Press, 1979.

Hegel, G. W. F. (1807). *The Phenomenology of Spirit.* New York: Oxford University Press, 1977.

Hegel, G. W. F. (1812). *The Science of Logic.* New York: Humanities Press, 1969.

Hegel, G. W. F. (1821). *The Philosophy of Right.* New York: Oxford University Press, 1967.

Hegel, G. W. F. (1830). *The Philosophy of Mind.* London: Oxford University Press, 1971.

Hegel. G. W. F. (1892). *Lectures on the History of Philosophy* (Vols. 1–3). London: Kegan Paul, Trench, Trubner, & Co.

Hegel, G. W. F. (1956). *The Philosophy of History.* New York: Dover Publications.

hooks, bell. (1981). *Ain't I a Woman: Black Women and Feminism.* Boston: South End Press.

Horkheimer, M. (1974). *Critique of Instrumental Reason.* New York: Seabury Press.

Horkheimer, M. (1987). *Eclipse of Reason.* New York: Seabury Press.

Horkheimer, M., & Adorno, T. W. (1972). *Dialectic of Enlightenment.* New York: Seabury Press.

Horney, K. (1933). The Denial of the Vagina. In *Feminine Psychology* (pp. 147–161). New York: W. W. Norton, 1967.

Horney, K. (1967). *Feminine Psychology.* New York: W. W. Norton.

Hoy, D. C. (Ed.). (1986). *Foucault: A Critical Reader.* New York: Basil Blackwell.

Hutchinson, E. (1990). *The Mugging of Black America.* Chicago: African American Images.

Hyppolite, J. (1974). *Genesis and Structure of Hegel's Phenomenology of Spirit.* Evanston, IL: Northwestern University Press.

Ilting, K.-H. (1984). Hegel's Concept of the State and Marx's Early Critique. In Z. A. Pelczynski (Ed.), *The State and Civil Society* (pp. 93–113). New York: Cambridge University Press.

Inwood, M. J. (1984). Hegel, Plato and Greek *Sittlichkeit.* In Z. A. Pelczynski (Ed.), *The State and Civil Society* (pp. 40–54). New York: Cambridge University Press.

Irigaray, L. (1985a). *Speculum of the Other Woman.* Ithaca, NY: Cornell University Press.

Irigaray, L. (1985b). *This Sex Which Is Not One.* Ithaca, NY: Cornell University Press.

Jacobson, E. (1964). *The Self and the Object World.* New York: International Universities Press.

Jacoby, R. (1975). *Social Amnesia.* Boston: Beacon Press.

Jacoby, R. (1983). *The Repression of Psychoanalysis: Otto Fenichel and the Political Freudians.* New York: Basic Books.

Jagger, A. M. (1983). *Feminist Politics and Human Nature.* Totowa, NJ: Rowman & Allanheld.

Jay, M. (1973). *The Dialectical Imagination.* Boston: Little, Brown & Co.

Jaynes, G., & Williams, R. (Eds.). (1989). *A Common Destiny: Blacks and American Society.* Washington, DC: National Academy Press.

Jordan, W. (1969). *White over Black.* Baltimore: Penguin Books.

Kant, I. (1781). *Critique of Pure Reason.* New York: St. Martin's Press, 1965.

Kant, I. (1788). *Critique of Practical Reason.* Indianapolis, IN: Bobbs-Merrill Co., 1956.

Kant, I. (1790). *Critique of Judgment.* New York: Hafner Press, 1951.

Kaufmann, W. (Ed.). (1954). *The Portable Nietzsche.* New York: Viking Press.

Kellner, D. (1984). *Herbert Marcuse and the Crisis of Marxism.* Berkeley, CA: University of California Press.

Kelly, G. A. (1972). Notes on Hegel's Lordship and Bondage. In A. MacIntyre (Ed.), *Hegel: A Collection of Critical Essays* (pp. 189–218). Garden City, NY: Doubleday.

Kipling, R. (1956). *Just So Stories.* Garden City, NY: Doubleday.

Kirsner, D. (1990). Mystics and Professionals in the Culture of American Psychoanalysis. *Free Associations, 20,* 85–103.

Klein, M. (1946). Notes on Some Schizoid Mechanisms. In *Envy and Gratitude* (pp. 1–24). New York: Dell Publishing, 1975.

Klein, M. (1952). Some Theoretical Conclusions Regarding the Emotional Life of the Infant. *Envy and Gratitude* (pp. 61–93). New York: Dell Publishing, 1975.

Klein, M. (1975). *Envy and Gratitude.* New York: Dell Publishing.

Kohut, H. (1977). *The Restoration of the Self.* New York: International Universities Press.

Kojève, A. (1969). *Introduction to the Reading of Hegel.* Ithaca, NY: Cornell University Press, 1980.

Kortian, G. (1984). Subjectivity and Civil Society. In Z. A. Pelczynski (Ed.), *The State and Civil Society* (pp. 197–210). New York: Cambridge University Press.

Kovel, J. (1971). *White Racism*. New York: Random House.

Kovel, J. (1981). *The Age of Desire*. New York: Pantheon Books.

Kovel, J. (1988). *The Radical Spirit*. London: Free Association Books.

Lacan, J. (1977). *Écrits*. New York: W. W. Norton.

Lacan, J. (1981). *The Four Fundamental Concepts of Psycho-Analysis*. New York: W. W. Norton.

Laclau, E. (1987). Psychoanalysis and Marxism. *Critical Inquiry, 13*, 330–333.

Laing, R. D. (1967a). *The Divided Self*. New York: Ballantine Books.

Laing, R. D. (1967b). *The Politics of Experience*. New York: Ballantine Books.

Landry, B. (1987). *The New Black Middle Class*. Berkeley: University of California Press.

Laplanche, J., & Pontalis. J.-B. (1973). *The Language of Psycho-Analysis*. New York: W. W. Norton.

Lasch, C. (1979). *The Culture of Narcissism*. New York: Warner Books.

Lasch, C. (1981). The Freudian Left and the Cultural Revolution. *New Left Review, 129*, 23–34.

Laslett, P. (Ed.). (1960). *John Locke: Two Treatises of Government*. New York: New American Library.

Lauer, Q. (1976). *A Reading of Hegel's Phenomenology of Spirit*. New York: Fordham University Press.

Lessing, D. (1963). *The Golden Notebook*. New York: McGraw-Hill.

Lewis, H. B. (1976). *Psychic War in Men and Women*. New York: New York University Press.

Lester, J. (1968). *Look Out, Whitey! Black Power's Gon' Get Your Mama*. New York: Grove Press.

Lichtman, R. (1982). *The Production of Desire*. New York: The Free Press.

Lichtman, R. (1984). Response to Professor Wolfenstein's Review of *The Production of Desire*.*Canadian Journal of Political and Social Theory, 8*, 124–128.

Lukács, G. (1971). *History and Class Consciousness*. Cambridge, MA: MIT Press.

Lyotard, J.-F. (1984). *The Postmodern Condition*. Minneapolis: University of Minnesota Press.

Macalpine, I., & Hunter, R. (Eds.). (1955). *Daniel Paul Schreber: Memoirs of My Nervous Illness*. London: Wm. Dawson & Sons.

MacIntyre, A. (1970). *Herbert Marcuse*. New York: Viking Press.

MacIntyre, A. (Ed). (1972). *Hegel: A Collection of Critical Essays*. Garden City, NY: Doubleday & Co.

Malcolm X (1966). *The Autobiography of Malcolm X*. New York: Grove Press.

Mannheim, K. (1936). *Ideology and Utopia*. New York: Harcourt, Brace, and World.

Marcuse, H. (1960). *Reason and Revolution*. Boston: Beacon Press.

Marcuse, H. (1962). *Eros and Civilization*. New York: Vintage Books.

Marcuse, H. (1964). *One-Dimensional Man*. Boston: Beacon Press.

Marcuse, H. (1968). *Negations*. Boston: Beacon Press.

Marcuse, H. (1969). *An Essay on Liberation*. Boston: Beacon Press.

Marcuse, H. (1970). *Five Lectures*. Boston: Beacon Press.

Marcuse, H. (1972). *Counter-Revolution and Revolt*. Boston: Beacon Press.

Martineau, A. (1986). *Herbert Marcuse's Utopia*. Montreal: Harvest House.

Marx, K. (1843a). Contribution to the Critique of Hegel's Philosophy of Law. In K. Marx & F. Engels, *Collected Works* (Vol. 3, pp. 5–129). New York: International Publishers, 1975.

Marx, K. (1843b). On the Jewish Question. In R. Tucker (Ed.), *The Marx–Engels Reader* (pp. 26–52). New York: W. W. Norton, 1978.

Marx, K. (1844a). Contribution to the Critique of Hegel's *Philosophy of Right*: Introduction. In R. Tucker (Ed.), *The Marx–Engels Reader* (pp. 53–65). New York: W. W. Norton, 1978.

Marx, K. (1844b). Economic and Philosophic Manuscripts of 1844. In R. Tucker (Ed.), *The Marx–Engels Reader* (pp. 66–142). New York: W. W. Norton, 1978.

Marx, K. (1845). Theses on Feuerbach. In R. Tucker (Ed.), *The Marx–Engels Reader* (pp. 143–145). New York: W. W. Norton, 1978.

Marx, K. (1850). The Class Struggles in France. In *Collected Works* (Vol. 10, pp. 47–145). New York: International Publishers, 1978.

Marx, K. (1852). The Eighteenth Brumaire of Louis Bonaparte. In *Collected Works* (Vol. 11, pp. 103 197). New York: International Publishers, 1979.

Marx, K. (1857). *Grundrisse*. Middlesex: Penguin Books, 1973.

Marx, K. (1859). Preface to A Contribution to the Critique of Political Economy. In R. Tucker (Ed.), *The Marx-Engels Reader* (pp. 3–6). New York: W. W. Norton, 1978.

Marx, K. (1867). *Capital* (Vol. 1). New York: Vintage Books, 1977.

Marx, K., & Engels, F. (1845a). The Holy Family. In K. Marx & F. Engels, *Collected Works* (Vol. 4, pp. 7–211). New York: International Publishers, 1975.

Marx, K. & Engels, F. (1845b). The German Ideology. In R. Tucker (Ed.), *The Marx–Engels Reader* (pp. 146–200). New York: W. W. Norton, 1978.

Marx, K., & Engels, F. (1848). The Communist Manifesto. In R. Tucker (Ed.), *The Marx–Engels Reader* (pp. 469–500). New York: W. W. Norton, 1978.

Marx, K., & Engels, F. (1962). *Selected Works* (Vol. 2). Moscow: Foreign Languages Publishing House.

Marx, K., & Engels, F. (1975a). *Collected Works* (Vol. 3). New York: International Publishers.

Marx, K., & Engels, F. (1975b). *Collected Works* (Vol. 4). New York: International Publishers.

Marx, K., & Engels, F. (1975c). *Selected Correspondence*. Moscow: Progress Publishers.

Marx, K., & Engels, F. (1978). *Collected Works* (Vol. 10). New York: International Publishers.

Marx, K., & Engels, F. (1979). *Collected Works* (Vol. 11). New York: International Publishers.

McLaughlin, J. T. (1975). The Sleepy Analyst: Some Observations on States of Consciousness in the Analyst at Work. *Journal of the American Psychoanalytic Association, 23,* 363–382.

Mehlman, J. (1977). *Revolution and Repetition*. Berkeley: University of California Press.

Meynell, H. (1981). *Freud, Marx and Morals*. Totowa, NJ: Barnes & Noble Books.

Miliband, R. (1977). *Marxism and Politics*. Oxford: Oxford University Press.

Millett, K. (1970). *Sexual Politics*. Garden City, NY: Doubleday.

Mitchell, J. (1975). *Psychoanalysis and Feminism*. New York: Random House.

Navickas, J. L. (1976). *Consciousness and Reality: Hegel's Philosophy of Subjectivity*. The Hague, The Netherlands: Martinus Nijhoff.

Nederman, C. (1987). Sovereignty, War, and the Corporation: Hegel on the Medieval Foundations of the Modern State. *Journal of Politics, 49*, 481–499.

Nelson, C., & Grossberg, L. (Eds.). (1988). *Marxism and the Interpretation of Culture*. Chicago: University of Illinois Press.

Newman, D. (1978). *Protest, Politics, and Prosperity*. New York: Pantheon Books.

Nietzsche, F. (1883–1885). Thus Spoke Zarathustra. In W. Kauffmann (Ed.), *The Portable Nietzsche* (pp. 103–439). New York: Viking Press, 1954.

Nietzsche, F. (1887). *On the Genealogy of Morals*. New York: Vintage Books, 1967.

Nietzsche, F. (1888). *Ecce Homo*. New York: Vintage Books, 1967.

Norman, R. (1976). *Hegel's Phenomenology: A Philosophical Introduction*. London: Sussex University Press.

O'Brien, M. (1981). *The Politics of Reproduction*. London: Routledge & Kegan Paul.

Ollman, B. (1970). The Marxism of Wilhelm Reich: The Social Function of Sexual Repression. In *Social and Sexual Revolution* (pp. 176–203). Boston: South End Press, 1979.

Orwell, G. (1949) Nineteen Eighty-Four. In *The Complete Penguin Novels of George Orwell*. New York: Penguin Books.

Pateman, C. (1988). *The Sexual Contract*. Stanford, CA: Stanford University Press.

Pelczynski, Z. A. (Ed.). (1971). *Hegel's Political Philosophy: Problems and Perspectives*. London: Cambridge University Press.

Pelczynski, Z. A. (Ed.). (1984a). *The State and Civil Society*. New York: Cambridge University Press.

Pelczynski, Z. A. (1984b). Political Community and Individual Freedom in Hegel's Philosophy of the State. In Z. A. Pelczynski (Ed.), *The State and Civil Society* (pp. 55–76). New York: Cambridge University Press.

Plant, R. (1980). Economic and Social Integration in Hegel's Political Philosophy. In D. Verene (Ed.), *Hegel's Social and Political Thought* (pp. 59–90). Atlantic Highlands, NJ: Humanities Press.

Plant, R. (1983). *Hegel: An Interpretation*. London: Basil Blackwell.

Plant, R. (1984). Hegel on Identity and Legitimacy. In Z. A. Pelczynski (Ed.), *The State and Civil Society* (pp. 227–243). New York: Cambridge University Press, 1984.

Pontalis, J.-B. (1981). *Frontiers in Psychoanalysis*. New York: International Universities Press.

Poster, M. (Ed.). (1988). *Jean Baudrillard*. Stanford, CA: Stanford University Press.

Preuss, P. (1982). Selfhood and the Battle: The Second Beginning of the *Phenomenology*. In M. Westphal (Ed.), *Method and Speculation in Hegel's Phenomenology* (pp. 71–83). Atlantic Highlands, NJ: Humanities Press.

Rabinow, P. (Ed.). (1984). *The Foucault Reader*. Middlesex: Penguin Books.

Racker, H. (1968). *Transference and Counter-Transference*. New York: International Universities Press.

Rauch, L. (1983). *Hegel and the Human Spirit*. Detroit: Wayne State University Press.

Reich, I. O. (1969). *Wilhelm Reich: A Personal Biography*. New York: St. Martin's Press.

Reich, W. (1929). Dialectical Materialism and Psychoanalysis. In L. Baxandall (Ed.), *Sex-Pol* (pp. 3–74). New York: Vintage Books, 1972.

Reich, W. (1932). The Imposition of Sexual Morality. In L. Baxandall (Ed.), *Sex-Pol* (pp. 91–249). New York: Vintage Books, 1972.

Reich, W. (1933). *The Mass Psychology of Fascism*. New York: Farrar, Straus, & Giroux, 1970.

Reich, W. (1934). What Is Class Consciousness? In L. Baxandall (Ed.), *Sex-Pol* (pp. 277–358). New York: Vintage Books, 1972.

Reich, W. (1942). *The Function of the Orgasm*. New York: Orgone Institute Press.

Reiter, R. (Ed.). (1975). *Toward an Anthropology of Women*. New York: Monthly Review Press.

Ricoeur, P. (1970). *Freud and Philosophy*. New Haven, CT: Yale University Press.

Riedel, M. (1984). *Between Tradition and Revolution*. London: Cambridge University Press.

Ring, J. (1991). *Modern Political Theory and Contemporary Feminism: A Dialectical Analysis*. Albany: State University of New York Press.

Rouse, W. H. D. (Ed.). (1956). *Great Dialogues of Plato*. New York: New American Library.

Rowbotham, S. (1973). *Woman's Consciousness, Man's World*. Middlesex: Penguin Books.

Rowbotham, S. (1974). *Women, Resistance and Revolution*. New York: Vintage Books.

Rubin, G. (1975). The Traffic in Women: Notes on the "Political Economy" of Sex. In R. Reiter (Ed.), *Toward an Anthropology of Women* (pp. 157–210). New York: Monthly Review Press.

Said, E. (1983). *The World, the Text, and the Critic*. Cambridge, MA: Harvard University Press.

Saffioti, H. (1978). *Women in Class Society*. New York: Monthly Review Press.

Sartre, J.-P. (1968). *Search for a Method*. New York: Vintage Books.

Sartre, J.-P. (1976). *Critique of Dialectical Reason*. London: NLB.

Schmidt, J. (1981). A Paideia for the "Burger Als Bourgeois": The Concept of "Civil Society" in Hegel's Political Thought. *History of Political Thought, 2*, 469–493.

Schneider, M. (1975). *Neurosis and Civilization*. New York: Seabury Press.

Schroyer, T. (1973). *The Critique of Domination*. Boston: Beacon Press.

Sedgwick, P. (1982). *Psycho Politics*. New York: Harper & Row.

Shakespeare, W. (1605). Macbeth. In *William Shakespeare: The Complete Plays* (pp. 969–996). New York: Harper & Brothers, 1953.

Siebert, R. J. (1980). Hegel's Concept of Marriage and Family: The Origin of Subjective Freedom. In D. Verene (Ed.), *Hegel's Social and Political Thought* (pp. 177–214). Atlantic Highlands, NJ: Humanities Press.

Smith, A. (1776). *The Wealth of Nations.* Chicago: University of Chicago Press, 1976.

Smith, J., & Kerrigan, W. (Eds.). (1983). *Interpreting Lacan.* New Haven, CT: Yale University Press.

Sraffa, P. (1975). *Production of Commodities by Means of Commodities.* Cambridge: Cambridge University Press.

Stern, D. N. (1985). *The Interpersonal World of the Infant.* New York: Basic Books.

Stoller, R. (1975). *Perversions.* New York: Pantheon Press.

Stoller, R. (1979). *Sexual Excitement: The Dynamics of Erotic Life.* New York: Pantheon Books.

Taylor, C. (1975). *Hegel.* London: Cambridge University Press.

Tennyson, A. (1898). *The Poetic and Dramatic Works of Alfred Lord Tennyson.* Boston: Houghton Mifflin Co.

Tucker, R. (Ed.). (1978). *The Marx-Engels Reader.* New York: W. W. Norton.

Verene, D. (1980). *Hegel's Social and Political Thought.* Atlantic Highlands, NJ: Humanities Press.

Wallace, W. (1904). *The Logic of Hegel.* London: Oxford University Press.

Weber, M. (1905). *The Protestant Ethic and the Spirit of Capitalism.* New York: Charles Scribner's Sons, 1958.

Westphal, M. (1979). *History and Truth in Hegel's Phenomenology.* Atlantic Highlands, NJ: Humanities Press.

Westphal, M. (Ed.). (1982). *Method and Speculation in Hegel's Phenomenology.* Atlantic Highlands, NJ: Humanities Press.

Westphal, M. (1984). Hegel's Radical Idealism: Family and State as Ethical Communities. In Z. A. Pelczynski (Ed.), *The State and Civil Society* (pp. 77–92). New York: Cambridge University Press.

Whitebook, J. (1988). Perversion and Utopia: A Study in Psychoanalysis and Social Theory. *Psychoanalysis and Contemporary Thought, 11,* 415–446.

Winnicott, D. W. (1960). Ego Distortion in Terms of True and False Self. In *The Maturational Processes and the Facilitating Environment* (pp. 140–152). New York: International Universities Press, 1965.

Winnicott, D. W. (1965). *The Maturational Processes and the Facilitating Environment.* New York: International Universities Press.

Winnicott, D. W. (1988). *Human Nature.* London: Free Association Books.

Wolfenstein, E. V. (1984). Marxist Despondency. *Canadian Journal of Political and Social Theory, 8,* 115–122.

Wolfenstein, E. V. (1985). Three Principles of Mental Functioning in Psychoanalytic Theory and Practice. *International Journal of Psycho-Analysis, 66,* 77–94.

Wolfenstein, E. V. (1989). He Who Loses His Self Shall Find It: Self-Certainty and Freedom in Hegel's *Phenomenology of Spirit* and Psychoanalytic Practice. *Discours Social/Social Discourse, 2,* 279–309.

Wolfenstein, E. V. (1990a). Group Phantasies and the Individual: A Critical Analysis of Psychoanalytic Group Psychology. *Free Associations, 20,* 150–180.

Wolfenstein, E. V. (1990b). A Man Knows Not Where to Have It: Habermas,

Grünbaum, and the Epistemological Status of Psychoanalysis. *International Review of Psycho-Analysis, 17,* 23–45.

Wolfenstein, E. V. (1990c). *The Victims of Democracy: Malcolm X and the Black Revolution.* London: Free Associations.

Wolfenstein, M. (1969). Loss, Rage, and Repetition, *Psychoanalytic Study of the Child, 24,* 432–460.

Yeats, W. B. (1921). The Second Coming. In *The Collected Poems of W. B. Yeats* (pp. 184–185). New York: Macmillan.

Index

Critical analysis, 6, 7, 11
  transformational, 7, 20–22
Critical theory, 107
  Alford on, 128, 129, 132, 133
  Benjamin on, 152
  Frankfurt school of, 173
  on gender and race, 169
  Marcuse on, 86–88, 93
Critique of Pure Reason (Kant), 107, 182,
    187
Cultivation, agricultural, 60
Cultural production, 266
Culture, 266
  in capitalism, 329
  Freud on, 34, 35, 43
  and race, 332
  and social production, 259, 260

De-Stalinization and de-colonization, 95,
    97–103, 169
Death-drive, 34, 35, 42, 94, 125
  and flight response, 240, 242
  and hate, 238
  Marcuse on, 79–81, 83, 90
  Reich on, 56
  and sensuous interactions, 223–227
  in work and play, 234
Deconstructionism, 99, 414, 418, 419
Defenses, 7, 241–244, 248
  compared to dialectics, 415
  of groups, 273, 274
  Kovel on, 164
  Lichtman on, 158
Deleuze, G., 95, 114–128, 417
  on desiring-production, 115–120, 123,
    126, 127, 292
Denial process, 361
Dependency in groups, 273, 274
Depressive position, 129–133, 244, 273,
    353
Desires, 115–120, 237, 238, 245, 430
  of collective formations, 268, 269, 275
  Deleuze and Guattari on, 115–120
  as economic force, 264
  Hegel on, 199, 203
  and interests, 9, 10, 426
  Kovel on, 160–166
  and passions, 169
  in psychoanalytic theory, 5, 9, 10, 213,
    214, 354, 356
  Reich on, 56

and work, 213–217, 233
  in capitalism, 255
  in childhood, 214, 237, 238
  and recognition, 228–250
  relationship between, 232, 247, 265
Desiring-machines, 121, 123, 227
Desiring-production, 168
  Deleuze and Guattari on, 115–120, 123,
    126, 127, 292
Destructiveness, 292
  Fromm on, 68, 69, 73, 74, 126
  Marcuse on, 79, 85
Determinate Being, 189, 190
Development process, 65, 66
  dialectics of, 239, 241, 242, 244, 248,
    254
  domination in, 249, 250
Diachronic perspective, 67, 210, 258,
    285
"Dialectical Materialism and Psychoanaly-
    sis" (Reich), 54, 55
Dialectics, 8, 11, 12, 168, 186–197
  and approach of Freud, 46
  of Being and Nothing, 189, 190
  and defensive processes, 415
  of development, 239, 241, 242, 244, 248,
    254
  of Fromm, 67
  of Hegel, 117, 187–197
  inversion in, 5, 415, 416
  of Kovel, 161, 162
  of Marcuse, 77, 83, 84, 89
  of Marx, 8, 11, 12, 45, 46, 50
  of recognition, 117, 151, 228, 230–
    232
  of Reich, 54–56, 90
  representation of, 188, 207
  restraint in use of, 13, 14
  speculative, 187
  of subjects and objects, 192, 193
  of theory and practice, 207
  and transformational action, 428
Dickes, R., 359, 361, 372
Differences and sameness, 12, 13, 135, 197
  in classes, 135
  in identity, 12, 108
  in sexes, 135, 136, 142–144, 152, 212, 317–
    320
Dinnerstein, D., 137, 144, 148, 154, 155
Diremption, 188
Disavowal process, 361
Displacement, Freud on, 418

458

Index

Hypnoid state, defensive use of, 359, 361,
363, 364, 370–372

Id, 41, 249, 352, 353, 373
Identification
introjective, 377
projective, 352, 359, 376, 377
reciprocal, 358
Identity, 12, 13
differences in, 12, 108
gender, 310, 311
political, 284
racial, 100–102
I = I, 108, 198–200, 202, 203, 290, 317
Imagination, 228, 235, 245, 251
"Imposition of Sexual Morality" (Reich),
58, 62
Incest taboo, 142
Indeterminate Being, 190
Individuals, 212, 213, 278
Fromm on, 64, 65, 71
Marcuse on, 83–85
psychology of, 76
Reich on, 55, 56
in social production, 259, 260, 267, 268,
277, 278
social roles of, 278
in society, 277, 278
Individuation, Fromm on, 64, 65
Infants. See Children and infants
Insanity. See Sanity
Instincts
Freud on, 34, 44, 79, 80
Fromm on, 63, 64, 66
Kovel on, 162
Marcuse on, 79–81, 83–85
Reich on, 56–58
Institutions
groups in, 275
political, 282, 284
Instrumental reason, 132, 133
Integral quiescence, 79, 220
Integration, racial
in schools, 331, 332
and separatism, 339, 340, 343
Interests, 5, 9, 10
of bourgeoisie, 409, 410
collective, 268–271, 275–277, 282
and desires, 9, 10, 426
political, 282
and rationality, 59–61, 268, 276

of ruling class, 270, 341
social, 60, 61, 282
Internalization, 57, 58, 64, 249
Intrauterine experience, 219–221, 245,
248, 321, 322
memory of, 255, 256
Invisible Man (Ellison), 334–336, 345–
349
Irrationality. See Rationality
Isolation and aloneness, Fromm on, 64,
66–69, 127, 292

Job decision, clinical psychoanalysis of,
382–385
Judgment, Kant on, 107, 108

Kant, I., 75, 76, 87, 105–108, 182, 187
Kinship systems. See Family
Klein, M., 94, 126, 273, 305
Alford on, 128–132
Kleinian psychoanalysis, 128–132, 380
Knowledge, 13, 177–183
absolute, 187, 195
and communication, 180, 183
and epistemological privilege, 149, 150,
178
historical, 404
Kant on, 107, 187
political, 388, 404, 405
and power, 96, 179
psychoanalytic, 388
scientific, 179, 180, 183
social, 178
transformational, 180, 183
valid, 180, 185
Knowledge and Human Interests (Habermas),
95, 104, 111, 173
Kohut, H., 374, 375, 380
Kojève, A., 116, 117
Kovel, J., 96, 155, 156, 160–167, 180

Labor. See Work
Labor-power, 27
buying and selling of, 298–300, 304, 305,
307, 308, 316
Lacan, J., 95, 117, 140
Laing, R. D., 113, 121
Language, 248, 249
and consciousness, 213, 251, 252

Work (*continued*)
  value of, 26, 27
  of women, 138, 264, 265, 311, 318
Work group, 273, 274, 275
Workers, 23, 24
  alienation of, 23–26, 48, 236

as commodity, 23
objectification of, 23, 25
as property of capitalist, 23, 24
Working day, length of, 300, 301
Wretched of the Earth (Fanon), 97, 102, 103,
  432